Title Page

MostUsedWords.com

Italian English Frequency Dictionary

Essential Vocabulary

2.500 most used words & 421 most common verbs

+ 5000 useful example sentences to help you become fluent fast.

+ Contains International Phonetic Alphabet entries for easy pronunciation.

Covers 90% of all spoken Italian & 85% of all written Italian

First Printing, 2016

Jolie Laide LTD
12/F, 67 Percival Street, Hong Kong

www.MostUsedWords.com

Contents

1. Why this dictionary was created

This dictionary was created because I needed a word list of the most frequent used words & verbs in Spanish, to help me understand Spanish in the shortest amount of time possible.

I started passing it around to friends and got great feedback on it, so I decided to turn it into a book.

Because it was such handy tool, I repeated the process for several other languages. Currently available frequency dictionaries are Spanish, Dutch, German, Portuguese, Russian and French. Visit www.mostusedwords.com to keep up with new releases and updates.

Why study by frequency?

If you´re not familiar with the importance of frequency word lists when it comes to language learning, here is a short summary:

Language learning is fun, but can be overwhelming. Almost every language as hundreds of thousands different words, but most of them you will rarely use. That's why it makes sense to study only the words you actually need to know to have conversations and read in your desired language.

Frequency dictionaries are usually either text based, or based on speech. The unique advantage of using subtitles as a method of frequency sorting is that it covers both speaking and reading (73% and 83% respectively). The overlap ensures you have all the vocabulary you need.

By only studying the words you will actually use, it is possible to gain a good grasp of a language in a short amount of time. By knowing 2500 words, you can express yourself in everyday situations and be fluent enough have conversations with locals.

On average, you only use 1000 different words in any language on a daily spoken basis. This translates to roughly 95% of all words you use daily speech. When it comes to reading, 2500 words will get you to understand around 85% of all words used in written text. This is usually enough to learn new words you don't know from context.

Tim Ferris quoted these statistics when learning Spanish. Since Italian and Spanish are quite similar and share a common origin, it's safe to assume they are applicable to Italian as well.

- 95% fluency Spanish: 2.500 most common words
- 98% fluency Spanish: 100.000 most common words.

So, in order to reach 95% fluency in both reading and speaking, you would need to know about 2.500 words. To add a 3% increase to your useful vocabulary, you would need to learn another 97.500 words! Talk about diminish returns.

This is idea is based on the Pareto Principle.

You might have heard about it. Pareto was an Italian economist who discovered that 80% of the output comes from only 20% of the input (or material, or effort).

On language learning, this principle is on steroids. Here´s why:

The corpus examined consisted of nearly 1 million Italian words. First we needed to define words. We filtered out a lot of entries. Amongst other things, we left out proper nouns (names of objects and people), and took the root verb whenever we encountered a verb conjugation.

2. Study tips

While you are free to do study any way you want with this dictionary, I would like to give you some pointers. **By learning just 28 new words a day, you can build up your vocabulary to fluency in three months**. If you dedicate yourself and learn 43 new words daily, two months is possible. Here are a couple of tips to build up your vocabulary fast, and to keep remembering what you previously learned.

Spaced repetition

Hack your brains ability to store and recall information. The most efficient way of studying is by incorporating the system of spaced repetition. This way you can store information faster, and for a longer amount of time. Paul Pimsleur published a paper in 1968 on spaced repetition. He came up with the following intervals: 5 seconds, 25 seconds, 2 minutes, 10 minutes, 1 hour, 5 hours, 1 day, 5 days, 25 days, 4 months, and 2 years.

You do not need to time yourself with a stopwatch, as there are upper and lower bounds to the intervals. Just revisited the words you have previously learned from time to time, with above guidelines in mind.

(Interactive language learning software and audio courses are based on this principle, and they **can** work really well. To see which ones are great investments, and which ones are terrible, read our reviews of different 3rd party language learning methods, audio courses, software and apps on www.mostusedwords.com/reviews)

Example sentences

Read the example sentences and their translations. The sentences are structured in a way that the most used words, appear most often. This helps you discover new words through context, naturally get a sense of grammar, and discover common idioms and expressions. Due to the principle of spaced repetition, learning this way helps you internalize words faster too.

Mnemonics

By creating a little story with a word, it's easier to remember. The more visual it is, the easier it is to remember. My favorite is the Spanish "caber". Caber means to fit. Now picture in your mind a bear and a cab. The bear wants to get in the cab, but it's having difficulties. After all, it's really hard *to fit a bear in a cab*. By creating little visual stories like these, it's much easier to remember vocabulary.

Read

Reading and speaking the words out loud greatly helps with building your vocabulary and developing a sense of grammar, pronouncuation and listening skills. Reading helps solidify your vocabulary, because you are using the method of spaced repetition while reading. When you read, and don´t know a word, you can usually discover it by the context. For some reason, words discovered through context are more easily remembered than when you study them from a list.

Anyway, you can get bilingual books from either a (specialized) bookstore or from www.mostusedwords.com/parallel-texts. Our selection is ever expanding, so check for updates regularly. It currently spans the range from English to Italian, Italian, Italian, Italian Dutch and French etc.

Listen

Turn on the Italian (internet) radio, download songs in Italian, and watch Italian series. Conversing along with your favorite soap opera is a great way of getting around a new language.

Immerse

Change your phone and/or computer into Italian. Nothing helps you acquire a new language as much as necessity.

Of course, total immersion is the best way of learning a new language fast. But you don't have to move to a different country to learn a new language.

Cognates

Italian and English share **about 30% of their vocabulary in cognates**. Instant vocabulary doesn't get any better than this. Cognates are words that share a common etymological origin.

Use these 5 cognate rules to find cognates between English and Italian.

–ction	=	–zione	action	=	azione
–tion	=	–zione	attention	=	attenzione
–ist	=	–ista	artist	=	artista
–ty	=	–tà	community	=	comunità
–ce	=	–za	importance	=	importanza
				=	
mid-word				=	
–ct–	=	tt	actor	=	attore

Verbs

Below is a short overview of (regular) verb conjugations in the present tense.

	amare	**credere**	**dormire**	**finire**
Io	*amo*	*credo*	*dormo*	*finisco*
Tu	*ami*	*credi*	*dormi*	*finisci*
lui/lei/Lei	*ama*	*crede*	*dorme*	*finisce*
Noi	*amiamo*	*crediamo*	*dormiamo*	*finiamo*
Voi	*amate*	*credete*	*dormite*	*finite*
loro/Loro	*amano*	*credono*	*dormono*	*finiscono*

Important verbs	**essere**	**Avere**	**andare**	**stare**	**dare**	**fare**
Io	*sono*	*ho*	*vado*	*sto*	*do*	*faccio*
Tu	*sei*	*hai*	*vai*	*stai*	*dai*	*fai*
lui/lei/Lei	*è*	*ha*	*va*	*sta*	*dà*	*fa*
Noi	*siamo*	*abbiamo*	*andiamo*	*stiamo*	*diamo*	*facciamo*
Voi	*siete*	*avete*	*andate*	*state*	*date*	*fate*
loro/Loro	*sono*	*hanno*	*vanno*	*stanno*	*danno*	*fanno*

3. How to use this dictionary

Part of Speech		***Abbrevations***
Adjective	=	*adj*
Adverb	=	*adv*
Article	=	*art*
Conjunction	=	*conj*
Interjection	=	*interj*
Feminine	=	*f*
Masculine	=	*m*
Neuter	=	*n*
Noun, common	=	*nc*
Noun, feminine	=	*nf*
Noun, masculine	=	*nm*
Noun, masculine and feminine	=	*nm/f*
Numeral	=	*num*
Plural	=	*Pl*
Singular	=	*sg*
Collequial	=	*coll*
Formal	=	*form*
Preposition	=	*prep*
Pronoun	=	*pron*
Subject	=	*subj*
Object	=	*obj*
Direct object	=	*dir-obj*
Indirect object	=	*indir-obj*
Verb	=	*verb*

On Part of Speech definitions

We made the decision to give the most common use of a word as the part of speech. It does however, not mean that this is the only part of speech the word can be used for. Certain verbs (or conjugations thereof) can be used as adjectives, and certain words can be verbs as well as nouns. Some words can be adverbs, adjectives and pronouns, etc.

When there is not a dominant use of a word, we have given both part of speech options.

International Phonetic Alphabet (IPA)

In the beginning, pronouncution can be tricky. The IPA entries for each term can help you, by telling you how to pronounce a word the right way. For more information, visit www.internationalphoneticalphabet.org.

4. Italian-English Frequency Dictionary

Rank	Italian - *Part of Speech* IPA	**English Translation** Italian Example Sentence *English Example Sentence*
1	**non** - *adv* non	**not, non** Naturalmente, la gente comune non vuole la guerra; né in Russia, né in Inghilterra, né in America, né del resto in Germania. Questo è comprensibile. *Naturally, the common people don't want war; neither in Russia nor in England nor in America, nor for that matter in Germany. This is understandable.*
2	**che** - *conj; pron; adj* ke	**that; which, who; what** Lui che cosa vede? *What does he see?*
3	**e, ed** - *conj* e, ed	**and** L'Unione contribuisce alla salvaguardia e allo sviluppo di questi valori comuni. *The Union contributes to the preservation and to the development of these common values.*
4	**il, lo, l', la, i, gli, le*** - *art* il, lo, l', la, i, ʎi, le*	**the** Ieri ho trascorso una serata fantastica con i miei fratelli e i miei amici, anche il barbecue era ottimo. *Yesterday we had a good evening with my brothers and friends, and a very nice barbecue.*
5	**un, uno, una** - *art; pron* un, uno, una	**a, an; one** Io sono un venditore, e come venditore so di non avere mai avuto davvero il controllo. Il tuo marchio è ciò che la gente dice su di te quando non sei presente nella stanza, come recita il detto. *I'm a marketer, and as a marketer, I know that I've never really been in control. Your brand is what other people say about you when you're not in the room, the saying goes.*
6	**a** **al, allo, all', alla, ai, agli, alla* - *prep*	**to, in, at**

	a	Ma se io non sono disposto a farlo, le dirò io o chiunque altro che, purtroppo, sono a corto di tempo, non ho il tempo. *But if I'm not willing to do it, I'll tell myself or anyone else that unfortunately I'm short of time, I don't have the time.*
7	**essere** - *verb*	**to be**
	ˈɛssere	È vero che il comportamento non può essere legiferato, e la legislazione non può fare in modo che mi amiate, però la legislazione può frenarvi dal mio linciaggio, e penso che sia abbastanza importante. *It is true that behavior cannot be legislated, and legislation cannot make you love me, but legislation can restrain you from lynching me, and I think that is kind of important.*
8	**per** - *prep*	**for, to, by, in**
	per	Non ha molto senso per me che io debba pagare più tasse di te anche se tu fai più soldi di me. *It doesn't make much sense to me that I have to pay more income tax than you even though you make more money than I do.*
9	**in** **nel, nello, nell', nella, nei, negli, nelle - prep*	**in, into**
	in	Lui è un ragazzo tenace che riesce sempre a uscire in cima. È il tipo di ragazzo che riesce a volgere ogni situazione a suo vantaggio. *He's a tenacious guy who always manages to come out on top. He's the kind of guy who can turn any situation to his advantage.*
10	**sì** - *int*	**yes, yeah**
	sˈi	"Conosci Brian?" "Sì, lo conosco bene." "Davvero? Da quanto tempo lo conosci?" "Da sei anni." *"Do you know Brian?" "Yes, I know him well." "Really? Since when do you know him?" "I've known him for six years."*
11	**mi** - *pron*	**me**
	mi	La capacità inesauribile dell'uomo di credere a ciò che preferisce essere vero piuttosto che ciò che l'evidenza dimostra di essere probabile e possibile mi ha sempre stupito. *Man's unfailing capacity to believe what he prefers to be true rather than what the evidence shows to be likely and possible has always astounded me.*

12 **avere** - *verb*
avere

to have

La situazione economica prevista ed il conseguente calo dei consumi potrà avere degli effetti negativi sui ricavi nel mercato dell'Editoria

The economic forecasts and the consequent fall in consumer spending could have a negative impact on the revenues in the publishing sector

13 **si** - *pron*
si

one-, its-, thems-, him-, her-, yourself

Quello che è importante non è a quale università ci si è laureati, ma quello che si ha imparato mentre la si frequentava.

What's important isn't which university you've graduated from, but what you learned while you were there.

14 **ma** - *conj*
ma

but

Ma, dopo tutto, è il leader del paese che determina la politica ed è sempre una cosa facile trascinarvi le persone, se si tratta di una democrazia o una dittatura fascista o di un Parlamento o di una dittatura comunista.

But, after all, it is the leaders of the country who determine the policy and it is always a simple matter to drag the people along, whether it is a democracy or a fascist dictatorship or a Parliament or a Communist dictatorship.

15 **ti** - *pron*
ti

you

Questo corso ti offre l'opportunità di studiare questi settori strettamente connessi in un ambiente stimolante e dinamico.

This course offers you the opportunity to study these closely related fields in an exciting and dynamic environment.

16 **cosa** - *pron; nf*
k'ɔza

what; thing

Cosa può fare?

What can it do?

17 **con** - *prep*
kon

with, by

State qui con lei.

Stay here with her.

18 **no** - *adv*
n'ɔ

no, not

Non sono sicuro se dovrei andare a studiare o no all'estero in Australia o in Canada.

I'm not sure whether I should go study abroad in Australia or Canada.

19 **da** **from**
dal, dallo, dall', dalla, dai, dagli, dalle

da

I rifiuti prodotti dall'attività, costituiti da residui degli imballaggi, sono smaltiti in conformità alle disposizioni di Legge.
The waste produced by our activities, constituted by leftover packaging, is disposed of in compliance with the dispositions of the Law

20 **se** - *conj* **if**

se

If Jesus Christ was the being which those mythologists tell us he was, and that he came into this world to suffer, which is a word they sometimes use instead of 'to die,' the only real suffering he could have endured would have been 'to live.'

Se Gesù Cristo è l'essere che i mitologi ci dicono che era e che è venuto in questo mondo per soffrire, che è una parola che a volte usano invece di 'morire', l'unica vera sofferenza avrebbe potuto sopportare sarebbe stato 'vivere'.

21 **come** - *pron* **as, how**

kome

Come l'hai trovato?
How did you find it?

22 **io** - *pron* **I**

ˈio

Io ritengo che la politica del Mediterraneo dev'essere rilanciata per gli aspetti politici, culturali ed economici.

I feel that a boost needs to be given to the political, cultural and economic aspects of the Mediterranean policy.

23 **ci** - *pron* **ourselves, us**

tʃi

Noi ci siamo seduti.
We sat down.

24 **questo** - *adj; pron* **this; such, this one**

kwesto

È la prima volta che fai questo tipo di lavoro: dovresti seguire esattamente il manuale finché non prendi più esperienza.
It's your first time doing this kind of work. You should follow the manual exactly until you get more experience.

25 **qui** - *adv; conj* **here; where**

kwi

Voglio che tu scopra se Tom sta progettando di venire qui da solo o meno.

I want you to find out if Tom is planning to come here by himself.

26 **bene** - *adj; adv; nm* — **very; well, good; good, asset**

bˈɛne

Qualcosa ovviamente non va bene.

Something's obviously wrong.

27 **tu** - *pron* — **you**

tu

Tu mi sembri il tipo di uomo che non fa mai quello che non vuole.

You strike me as the kind of man who never does anything he doesn't want to do.

28 **di** *del, dello, dell', della, dei, degli, delle -prep* — **of, to; than, and**

di

Penso di essere innamorata di te.

I think I'm in love with you.

29 **me (stesso)** - *pron* — **me (myself)**

me (stesso)

Il cuore dell'uomo è il luogo dove vive il diavolo; sento a volte un inferno dentro di me.

The heart of man is the place the devil dwells in; I feel sometimes a hell within myself.

30 **mio** - *pron* — **my**

mˈio

Il mio invito al pubblico è di entrare in contatto con la loro creatività e spontaneità interiore per massimizzare il potenziale di questo incontro durate il convegno.

My invitation to the audience is to get in contact with inner creativity and spontaneity to maximize the potential of encounters during the Conference.

31 **solo** - *adj* — **only**

solo

uesta vittoria da sola non è il cambiamento che cerchiamo. È solo la possibilità per noi di procedere al cambiamento.

This victory alone is not the change we seek. It is only the chance for us to make that change. And that cannot happen if we go back to the way things were.

32 **tutto** - *adv; nm* — **all**

tutto

Tutto a un tratto vidi una forma umana in lontananza, e, con mia sorpresa, ben presto riconobbi che il viaggiatore era una donna.

All at once I saw a human form in the distance, and, to my surprise, soon recognized that the traveler was a woman.

33 **te** - *pron*
te

you
A me non piace il teatro, ma ci vado comunque perché piace a te.
I don't like the theater, but I go nevertheless because you like it.

34 **più** - *adj; adv*
pju

more, most
Per me non c'è niente di più tenero di una coppia di anziani che va per strada mano nella mano.
Nothing seems so tender to me as an old couple walking down the street holding hands.

35 **lei** - *pron*
lˈɛi

she, her
A causa di aver bevuto un po' di caffè forte, lei non è stata in grado di dormire per tutta la notte.
On account of having drunk some strong coffee, she wasn't able to sleep all night long.

36 **ne** - *adj; pron*
ne

any; of it, of them
Tom mi ha offerto una birra, però gli ho detto che io non ne volevo.
Tom offered me a beer, but I told him I didn't want one.

37 **fare** - *verb*
fare

to do
Questo modulo vuole offrire preziosi consigli su cosa fare prima, durante e dopo un colloquio telefonico.
This module provides valuable hints on what to do before, during and after a telephone interview.

38 **quando** - *adv; conj*
kwando

when
Negli Stati Uniti si ha la scelta, quando si entra in un ristorante, di sedersi nella sezione per fumatori o nella sezione per non fumatori.
In the U.S., you have the option, when you enter a restaurant, to sit in the smoking or non-smoking section.

39 **fatto** - *nm; adj*
fatto

fact, event; made, done
Il fatto che ciò non si verifichi è un fatto negativo specie per le realtà inserite a Firenze e a Roma
The fact that this opportunity should be thwarted is a negative one

40 **perché** - *conj; adv*
perkˈe

because, why; why
Gli esperti dicono che i prezzi del caffè stanno salendo principalmente perché la gente è disposta a pagare di più.
Experts say coffee prices are rising mainly because people are willing to pay more.

41 **sapere** - *verb*
sapere

to know
Senza sapere che cosa sia la forma, non si può accertare se essa sia distintiva, né se sia comune o funzionale.

Without knowing what the shape is, it cannot be ascertained whether it will be distinctive, nor can it be ascertained whether it is common or functional.

42 **ora** - *adv; conj; nf*
ora

now; now; now, time, hour
Quando ho visto Tom per la prima volta, ho saputo che era diverso da tutti gli altri uomini che avevo incontrato fino ad ora.
When I first laid eyes on Tom, I knew he was different from any other man I'd ever met.

43 **o** - *conj*
'ɔ

or
Come gli scenziati continuano a ripetere, non c'è necessariamente qualcosa di buono o di cattivo in ogni scoperta scientifica.
As scientists keep insisting, there is neither good nor bad in any scientific discovery.

44 **andare** - *verb*
andare

to go, move, proceed, run
Penso che dovreste andare adesso.
I think you should go now.

45 **mai** - *adv*
mai

never
Tu dirai e farai delle cose che i tuoi genitori hanno detto e fatto, anche se avevi giurato di non farlo mai.
You will say and do things your parents said and did, even if you swore you would never do them.

46 **chi** - *pron*
ki

who
Chi è il tuo avvocato?
Who is your lawyer?

47 **dire** - *verb*
dire

to say
Io non potevo proprio dire di no.
I just couldn't say no.

48 **così** - *adv; conj*
koz'i

so, thus; that
Solo così supereremo ogni sorta di afflizioni, di ingiustizie e di terrorismo.
Only then shall we overcome all manner of afflictions, injustices, and terrorism.

49 **quello** - *pron*

one

kwello

Il pilaf con carne costa otto yuan. Il pilaf vegetariano costa solo quattro yuan.

The pilaf with meat is eight yuan. The vegetarian pilaf is only four yuan.

50 **oh** - *int*

o

oh

Oh no! Non stavo prestando attenzione e ho lasciato il mio cellulare al ristorante!

Oh no! I wasn't paying attention and left my cell phone in the restaurant!

51 **anche** - *adv; nf*

aŋke

also, even; anchor

Anche tu puoi facilmente diventare un miliardario... se sei un milionario.

You too can easily become a millionaire... if you are a billionaire.

52 **molto** - *adv; adj*

molto

very, much

La tua vita andrà molto più liscia se solo rinunci e accetti la verità.

Your life will go much smoother if you just give up and accept that truth.

53 **lui** - *pron*

lˈui

him, he

Tra i pasti, di solito lui riesce a mettere da parte un'abbondante riserva di dolci, gelati, popcorn e frutta.

Between meals, he usually manages to stow away a generous supply of candy, ice cream, popcorn and fruit.

54 **volere** - *verb*

volere

to want

Un vecchio uomo con una cuffia da notte aprì la finestra e guardò fuori. Rimproverò con rabbia: "Che cosa volete a quest'ora della notte?"

An old man in a nightcap opened the window and looked out. He called down angrily: "What do you want at this hour of night?"

55 **niente** - *pron; nm*

njˈɛnte

nothing, anything, none

Dopo una pedalata non c'è niente di meglio che una confortevole pausa in questo centro benessere.

After a bicycle ride there is nothing better than a relaxing break at this wellness centre.

56 **grazie** - *int*

grattsje

thank you

Grazie per il cioccolato! Spero che le frittelle ti siano piaciute, e spero che abbia passato una bella giornata pure tu.

Thanks for the chocolate! I hope you enjoyed the pancakes, and I hope you had a great day as well.

57 **dove** - *adv*
dove

where
Ne Medio Oriente, abbiamo esposto il mio lavoro in posti dove ci sono pochi musei.

In the Middle East, I experienced my work in places without [many] museums.

58 **tuo** - *adj*
t'uo

your
Non vedo l'ora di vederti con il tuo cappello e il tuo vestito.
I'm looking forward to seeing you in your cap and gown.

59 **allora** - *adv*
allora

then
Se i soldi non fanno la felicità, allora li dia a me. Io sarò felice.
If the money doesn't make you happy, then give it to me. I will be happy.

60 **stare** - *verb*
stare

to stay
Fuori fa così caldo che voglio stare tutto il giorno in casa con l'aria condizionata.

It's so hot outside that I want to spend all day in my air conditioned house.

61 **potere** - *verb; nm*
potere

to be able; power
Mi ha sempre stupito constatare, nell'animo umano, la coesistenza tra il potere di governare e quello di perdonare.

It has always astonished me to see in the human soul the co-existence of the power to rule and the potential to forgive.

62 **prima** - *adv; art*
prima

first, before; before
Prima di alzarmi dal letto, passo un po' di tempo a pensare a cosa farò per il resto della giornata.

Before I get out of bed, I spend a little time thinking about what I'll be doing the rest of the day.

63 **noi** - *pron*
noi

we
I nostri clienti possono aspettarsi da noi anche tutto questo, al pari di una produzione accompagnata passo a passo.

Our customers can also expect all those from us! Also comprehensive accompanied manufacturing.

64 **primo** - *num; adj*
primo

first
La linea è il primo passo verso avanti della linea di masse della politica dell'avanguardia.

The Line is the first step forward for the mass line of the politics of the vanguard.

65 **suo (- a)** - *pron*
s'uo (

his (her)

Il più grande problema dell'immigrazione è il suo carattere multiculturale. Il problema non è che i lavoratori migrano quando è necessario, ma il gap culturale insormontabile che li separa dalle società ospitanti. Senza andare oltre, l'immigrazione musulmana in Europa è un buon esempio.

The biggest problem of immigration is its multicultural character. The trouble is not that workers migrate when necessary, but the insurmountable cultural gap that separates them from the host societies. Without going any further, Muslim immigration in Europe is a good example.

66 **due** - *adj; num*
d'ue

two

Ha dato due lezioni durante questa sessione con un approccio pratico

he gave two lectures during this session with a practical approach

67 **ancora** - *adv; conj*
aŋkora

yet, still, more; more

Il vento soffia ancora forte.

The wind still blows hard.

68 **casa** - *nf*
kaza

house, home

In questa situazione di incertezza e di rischio la Casa Editrice ha continuato ad investire per migliorare quantità e qualità

In this situation of uncertainly and risk, the publishing house continued to invest in improving the quality and quality

69 **fa** - *adv*
fa

ago

Quattro giorni fa sono stato testimone e parte di un avvenimento davvero straordinario.

Four days ago I witnessed and participated in a truly extraordinary event.

70 **qualcosa** - *nf*
kwalk'ɔza

something, anything

Quando parli, tu stai solo ripetendo quello che sai già. Ma se tu ascolti, puoi imparare qualcosa di nuovo.

When you talk, you are only repeating what you already know. But if you listen, you may learn something new.

71 **vero** - *nm*

true

vero | È un altare dedicato non al Dio Uno e Trino, ed a Suo Figlio Gesù Cristo, Nostro Redentore, ma è rivolto ad un "Dio" che ha ben 72 nomi e che si nasconde sotto i simboli di tutti questi Nomi perché il suo vero nome è Lucifero!

It is an altar dedicated not to the God One and Trine, and to His Son Jesus Christ, Our Redeemer, but it is dedicated to a "God" who has 72 names and who is hiding under the symbols of all of these Names because his real name is Lucifer!

72 **su** **sul, sullo, sulll', sulla, sui, sugli, sulle - adv; prep* — **on,up; on, about**

su *sul, sullo, sulll', sulla, sˈui, suʎʎi, sulle

Chiederò in giro e vedrò se riesco a scoprire se qualcuno ha idee su come risolvere il problema.

I'll ask around and see if I can find out if anyone has ideas on how to solve the problem.

73 **saio** - *nm* — **habit**

sajo

Parrà strano, ma possiamo indossare il saio, molto simile al vestito degli sceicchi.

It seems strange that we are allowed to wear the habit, which is very similar to that of the sheiks.

74 **sempre** - *adv* — **always**

sˈɛmpre

Inoltre, ci sono sempre ingorghi sulle strade di Reggio Emilia, per cui si spreca un sacco di tempo mentre si è bloccati in un ingorgo.

Furthermore, there are always traffic jams on Reggio Emilia's roads, so you'll waste lots of time while stuck in a traffic jam.

75 **loro** - *pron* — **their**

loro

Dopo di che me ne sono andato ma poi mi sono accorto di aver lasciato la mia borsa a casa loro.

After that, I left, but then I realized that I forgot my backpack at their house.

76 **vi** - *pron; adv* — **you; there**

vi

Vi è un numero crescente di persone che preferiscono una vita virtuale online che una vera vita offline.

There is a growing number of people who prefer a virtual life online than a real life offline.

77 **ehi** - *int* — **Hey**

	ei	Ehi! La vostra palla ha appena rotto la mia finestra! *Hey! Your ball just broke my window!*
78	**dovere** - *verb; nm* dovere	**to have to, muste, should; duty, obligation** La preghiera è in se stessa un particolare dovere per un Vescovo *Prayer is itself a particular duty for a Bishop*
79	**signore** - *nm/f* siɲɲore	**Mr. / Mrs.** Questo è il libro più recente del signor Miller, e noi speriamo che non sia l'ultimo. *This is Mr Miller's latest book, and we hope it will not be his last.*
80	**tempo** - *nm* tˈɛmpo	**time, weather** Il vostro tempo è limitato, per cui non lo sprecate vivendo la vita di qualcun altro. Non fatevi intrappolare dai dogmi, che vuol dire vivere seguendo i risultati del pensiero di altre persone. *Your time is limited, so don't waste it living someone else's life. Don't be trapped by dogma - which is living with the results of other people's thinking.*
81	**certo** - *adj; adv* tʃˈɛrto	**certain; of course;** Ho trovato che la voce fosse vera fino a un certo punto. *I found the rumor to be true to a certain extent.*
82	**voi** - *pron* voi	**you** Aspettate qui con gli asini per un po'. Io e il bambino andremo a pregare e torneremo da voi immediatamente.' *You wait here with the donkeys for a while. I and the child will go to pray and we will come again immediately to you.'*
83	**vita** - *nf* vita	**life, waist** Non aver nessuna paura di fronte alla vita. Credi che la vita sia degna di essere vissuta e che il tuo credere contribuisca a che sia così. *Be not afraid of life. Believe that life is worth living, and your belief will help create the fact.*
84	**forse** - *adv* forse	**perhaps** Forse stasera non ci vedremo ma in ogni caso ci sentiamo per telefono, d'accordo? *Maybe tonight we won't see each other but, in any case, one of us will ring the other, is that ok?*
85	**adesso** - *adv* adˈɛsso	**now** La porta adesso è chiusa.

The door is now closed.

86 **fuori** - *adv* | **out, outside**
fw'ɔri
Se vuoi sapere che cosa sono gli Stati Uniti, vai fuori nella natura, dove si trova la bellezza.
If you want to know what beauty is, go out into the wild; there you will find beauty.

87 **li** - *pron* | **them**
li
Ciò dimostra che la gestione dei soggiorni degli immigrati non è solo una questione giuridica o di ordine pubblico ma anche di normale convivenza tra i nuovi venuti e le strutture della società che li accoglie.
This shows that the management of immigrants' stays is not only a matter of law or public order but also a matter of normal coexistence between the newcomers and the structures of society that receive them.

88 **davvero** - *adv* | **really**
davvero
Salve a tutti, sono davvero felice di annunciare la prossima straordinaria novità in arrivo per SingStar nell'aggiornamento di giugno.
Hi everyone, I'm really pleased to be able to let you know about a great new gameplay feature coming soon to SingStar in the June update.

89 **anno** - *nm* | **year**
anno
Il padre di Roger Miller è morto quando aveva solamente un anno e sua madre si è ammalata appena dopo, quindi è stato mandato a vivere con suo zio a Erick, Oklahoma.
Roger Miller's father died when he was only one year old and his mother became sick soon after, so he was sent to live with his uncle in Erick, Oklahoma.

90 **poi** - *adv* | **then**
p'ɔi
Il tizio sta rovistando in un cassetto, poi alza lo sguardo, sorride in modo sinistro.
The guy is fiddling with a drawer, then he looks at me, smiles in a sinister fashion.

91 **altro** - *adj; pron* | **other, another, more**
altro
Ho ricevuto la sua lettera l'altro giorno.
I received her letter the other day.

92 **dio** - *nm* | **God**

	d'io	Chi ha l'amore è in Dio e Dio è in lui, poiché Dio è amore. *He who has love, is in God, and God is in him, for God is love.*
93	**via** - *prep; adv; nf* v'ia	**via, by; away; street, way** Se dovessi perdere la tua via, questa è la tua bussola, la tua guida per ritornare al percorso che seguirai. *Should you lose your way, this is your compass, your guide back to the path you will follow.*
94	**vedere** - *verb* vedere	**to see** Come è possibile credere senza vedere? È che il vero non è forse quello che si vede. *How is it possible to believe without seeing? Perhaps the real is not what one sees.*
95	**proprio** - *adj; nm; pron; adv* pr'ɔprjo	**one's own; own; its; just, exactly** Chi ascolta per la prima volta la propria voce registrata ha l'impressione di ascoltare un estraneo. *One who listens to their recorded voice has the sensation of listening to a stranger.*
96	**parte** - *nf* parte	**part** Gli piaceva attribuire la maggior parte dei suoi errori e delle sfortune della sua vita a un padre tirannico. *He liked to blame most of his faults and misfortunes of his life on a tyrannical father.*
97	**ok** - *int* ok'ɛi	**ok** "Io voglio che il mio elfo scuro sia blu." "OK... Quello è viola. Sarai viola per questa settimana." *"I want my dark elf to be blue." "OK... That one's purple. You'll be purple for this week."*
98	**beh, be** - *int* b'ɛ, be	**well!** Funziona allo stesso modo in tutti i paesi. Beh, quasi. *It works the same way in every country. Well, almost.*
99	**credo** - *nm* kredo	**creed, credo** È evidente come il credo aziendale sia ormai orientato alla lavorazione del tubo di medio/grandi dimensioni *It is evident how the corporate belief has turned to processing medium/large tubes*
100	**ciao** - *int* tʃao	**hello, bye** È inutile che tu mi dica "Ciao, come stai?" se poi non hai altro da dirmi.

There's no point telling me "Hi, how are you?" if you have nothing else to say.

101 **volta** - *nf*
vˈɔlta

time, turn, vault

La probabilità di questa catena di eventi che accadono tutti in una volta è uno ogni due milioni di voli - circa una volta ogni due mesi ai livelli attuali di traffico aereo.

The probability of this chain of events all happening at once is one in 2 million flights - about once every two months at current levels of air traffic.

102 **quanto** - *adv; conj*
kwanto

as, how much; than

Le ho solo chiesto quanto ha pagato per quel vestito dall'aspetto banale e lei si infuriò con me.

I only asked her what she paid for that dull-looking dress and she flew off the handle at me.

103 **uomo** - *nm*
wˈɔmo

man

Tom conosceva un uomo il cui padre era un pilota di elicotteri durante la guerra del Vietnam.

Tom knew a man whose father was a helicopter pilot during the Vietnam War.

104 **nessuno** - *adj; pron*
nessuno

no; nobody, no one, none, anyone

Nessuno deve preoccuparsi delle proprie opinioni, anche religiose, a patto che la loro espressione non turbi l'ordine pubblico stabilito dalla legge.

No one may be questioned about his opinions, and the same for religious opinions, provided that their manifestation does not trouble the public order established by the law.

105 **padre** - *nm*
padre

father

Tom fece l'impossibile per cercare di convincere sua madre a trasferisrsi in una casa più piccola dopo la la morte del padre.

Tom did his darndest to try and convince his mother to downsize into a smaller house after his father died.

106 **dopo** - *prep; adv*
dopo

after

Tom è venuto a Boston dopo aver preso il diploma di scuola superiore.

Tom came to Boston after graduating from high school.

107 **amico** - *nm/f*

friend

amiko | A me serve un amico.
I need a friend.

108 **porre** - *verb* | **to put, place**
porre | La legge ha lo scopo di porre rimedio a decenni di discriminazione nei confronti delle minoranze etniche del paese.
The law is meant to redress decades of discrimination against the country's ethnic minorities.

109 **lavoro** - *nm* | **work, job**
lavoro | Fortuna e duro lavoro sono necessari se vuoi avere successo nella vita.
Luck and hard work are necessary if you want to advance in life.

110 **qualcuno (- a)** - *pron* | **someone**
kwalkuno (| Ho bisogno di qualcuno che mi stringa tra le sue braccia e mi dica che andrà tutto bene.
I need someone to hold me and tell me everything will be alright.

111 **già** - *adv* | **already**
dʒˈa | Per i restanti ordini le negoziazioni sono in corso e molte raccomandazioni
per l'acquisto sono gia' state inoltrate al Cliente.
For the residual orders negotiations are in progress and many recommendations for
purchasing have been already sent to Client.

112 **meglio** - *adv* | **better, best**
mˈɛʎʎo | Meglio essere odiati per quello che si è che essere amati per quello che non si è.
Better to be hated for who you are than loved for who you're not.

113 **giorno** - *nm* | **day**
dʒorno | Lei beve della birra analcolica quasi ogni giorno perché la birra è la sua bevanda preferita, però non vuole bere alcol ogni giorno.
She drinks non-alcoholic beer almost every day because beer is her favorite drink, but she doesn't want to drink alcohol every day.

114 **cazzo** - *nm; int* | **dick; fuck**
kattso | Che piacere vedere un ragazzino della sua età che sa cosa cazzo è la vera musica.

		What a pleasure to see a kid his age who knows what the fuck real music is.
115	**cui** - *pron* kˈui	**which** Il venerdì è il giorno in cui sono meno occupata. *Friday is when I am least busy.*
116	**bisogno** - *nm* bizoɲɲo	**need** Cosa siamo diventati come società quando abbiamo bisogno dell'alcol per divertirci. È diventato un pretesto per il comportamento bizzarro e la cara vecchia dissolutezza. *What have we become as a society when we need alcohol to enjoy ourselves. It has become a pretext for outlandish behaviour and just plain old debauchery.*
117	**ogni** - *adj* oɲɲi	**every** Better don't venture here. I'm serious, any of you would regret. Better close the topic and forget everything written here. *È meglio non introdursi qui. Sul serio, ogni di voi si pentirà. È meglio terminare questo colloquio e dimenticare ogni cosa che è stata discussa.*
118	**venire** - *verb* venire	**to come** Domani non voglio venire con te a vedere la partita di calcio, voglio andare con Paolo a vedere un film. *Tomorrow I don't want to come with you to see the soccer game, I want to go with Paolo to see a movie.*
119	**ecco** - *adv* ˈɛkko	**here** Ecco la buona notizia: si lavora. Ed ecco la cattiva notizia: si lavora sempre più spesso in nero. *Here's the good news: there's work. And here comes the bad news: there's work, but it's ever more often under the table.*
120	**senza** - *conj* sˈɛntsa	**without** La mia esperienza del mondo sarebbe molto più superficiale senza la capacità di comunicare in molte lingue. *My experience of the world would be much shallower without the ability to communicate in lots of languages.*
121	**ce** - *pron* tʃe	**us** Non ho molti soldi, ma in un modo o nell'altro, ce la farò. *I don't have a lot of money, but I get along somehow.*
122	**male** - *adv; nm*	**bad, evil**

male | Se non volete entrare in un pasticcio, non dite nulla di male su Tom e Mary.

If you don't want to get into a mess, don't say anything bad about Tom and Mary.

123 **troppo** - *adv*
trˈɔppo

too much

Il rapporto tra la Chiesa cattolica e gli ebrei non è sempre stato, nella storia, felice o facile. Troppo spesso è stato scritto in mezzo alle lacrime.

The history of the relationship between the Catholic Church and the Jews was not always a happy or an easy one. Too often it was written in tears.

124 **qualche** - *adj; pron*
kwalke

some, few, any; a few

"A che ora ritorna tua sorella dal lavoro?" "Non lo so, ma penso che lei arrivi a casa qualche minuto prima di me."

"When does your sister come back from work?" "I don't know, but I think she'll arrive at home a few minutes before me."

125 **mamma** - *nf*
mamma

mom

Avevo nove anni quando ho chiesto a mia mamma se Babbo Natale esisteva davvero.

I was nine years old when I asked my mom if Santa Claus really existed.

126 **tanto** - *adv*
tanto

much, so

Nell'era della posta elettronica sono tanto felice quando un amico mi spedisce una vera lettera.

In the era of email, I'm so happy when a friend sends me a real letter.

127 **prego** - *int*
prˈɛgo

please, you're welcome

Ti prego, per l'amore degli uomini, impara la tua lingua!

Please, for the love of mankind, learn your language.

128 **modo** - *nm*
mˈɔdo

way, manner

A Singapore, un modo di punire i criminali è di frustarli o di colpirli più volte con un bastone sulla schiena.

In Singapore, one method to punish criminals is to whip or beat them multiple times on their back with a cane.

129 **grande** - *adj*
grande

great, great

La discrepanza tra le storie delle due parti coinvolte nell'incidente era così grande che le autorità hanno fatto fatica a decidere chi dicesse la verità.

The discrepancy between the stories of the two parties involved in the accident was so great that the authorities had a hard time deciding which side was telling the truth.

130 **tra** - *prep*
tra

between, among

Spesso la differenza tra quello che si è e quello che si vuole essere causa malumori e insicurezza.

Often, the difference between what you are and what you want to be causes bad mood and insecurity.

131 **guardare** - *verb*
gwardare

to look, watch

Il conducente non deve guardare il monitor mentre è alla guida.

The driver must not watch the monitor while driving.

132 **favore** - *nm*
favore

favor

Potresti chiudere la finestra, per favore?

Could you close the window, please?

133 **quindi** - *adv*
kwindi

then

Non ho dormito granché la notte scorsa quindi ho avuto la testa ciondolante dal sonno durante tutta la giornata lavorativa.

I didn't get much sleep last night so I was nodding off all day at work.

134 **sembrare** - *verb*
sembrare

to seem, look, appear, sound

A me non piace sembrare pessimista, però John è un caso totalmente disperato. Non è neppure disperato. Ha perso la testa!

I don't like seeming pessimistic, but John's a total basket case. He's not just useless either. He's lost his mind!

135 **soldo** - *nm*
soldo

money

Se avessi ricevuto un soldo per ogni volta che una donna mi ha respinto, sarei un uomo ricco!

If I had a nickel for everytime a woman has turned me down, I'd be a rich man!

136 **parlare** - *verb*
parlare

to speak, talk

Mi ha detto che non gli dirà cosa mi è successo il giorno che mi ha visto parlare della storia della ragazza che è stata uccisa.

He told me that she will not tell him what happened to me on the day he saw me talking about the story about the girl who got killed.

137 **dispiacere** - *verb*

to displeasure, dislike, be sorry

dispjatʃere

Mi dispiace di non essere stato in grado di darti informazioni sui contatti di mio cugino.

I'm sorry I haven't been able to give you my cousin's contact info.

138 **gente** - *nm*
dʒˈɛnte

people

In Inghilterra, i parchi che scelgono razze rare di animali come loro tema stanno diventando sempre più popolari tra la gente.

In England, parks taking rare breeds of animals as their theme are becoming increasingly popular with people.

139 **tre** - *adj; num*
tre

three

Se ci sono due persone in una stanza e tre escono, uno deve entrare, in modo che nessuno si trovi nella stanza.

If there are two in a room and three go out, one must go in, so that none is in the room.

140 **madre** - *nf*
madre

mother

Quando si scrive in una lingua diversa dalla nostra lingua madre, è molto facile da produrre frasi che suonano strane.

When we write in a language other than our mother tongue, it is very easy to produce sentences that sound strange.

141 **momento** - *nm*
momento

moment

Non c'è nulla di più fastidioso di un gruppo di giovani ragazze che provano a parlare tutte nello stesso momento.

There's nothing more annoying than a group of young girls all trying to talk at the same time.

142 **aspettare** - *verb*
aspettare

to wait

In altri tempi, la gente non avrebbe esitato ad accendersi una sigaretta nelle stazioni, nei ristoranti o nelle sale d'aspetto degli ospedali.

At one time, people would not have hesitated to light up a cigarette in stations, restaurants, or hospital waiting rooms.

143 **nuovo** - *adj*
nwˈɔvo

new

Il problema di molti insegnanti di lingua è che sottovalutano le nuove tecnologie nei loro metodi di insegnamento.

The problem of many language teachers is that they underrate new technologies in their teaching methods.

144 **successo** - *nm*
suttʃˈɛsso

success

L'unica colpa di Pinocchio era che aveva troppi amici. Tra questi c'erano molti mascalzoni ben noti, che non si curavano di un accidente per lo studio o per il successo.

Pinocchio's only fault was that he had too many friends. Among these were many well-known rascals, who cared not a jot for study or for success.

145 **mondo** - *nm*
mondo

world
L'obesità è considerata di gran lunga il problema di salute più grave che deve affrontare il mondo sviluppato.

Obesity is considered by far the most serious health issue facing the developed world.

146 **piacere** - *verb*
pjatʃere

to pleasure; like
Nella cittadina di Tolmezzo, invece, si scopre il piacere di passeggiare sotto i portici del centro storico tra i negozi

In the town of Tolmezzo, on the other hand, you will discover the pleasure of walking under the arcades of the old town.

147 **nostro** - *pron*
nˈɔstro

our
Sono rimasta sorpresa quando Tom ha detto che stava facendo domanda per un posto di lavoro presso la nostra azienda.

I was surprised when Tom said he was applying for a job at our company.

148 **forza** - *nf*
fˈɔrtsa

power
Le tue belle parole sono una fonte di forza per me durante questo brutto periodo.

Your kind words are a source of strength for me at this difficult time.

149 **oggi** - *adv; nm*
ˈɔddʒi

today
La nostra cena di oggi sarà molto semplice: pane, formaggio di capra, fichi e vino.

Our dinner today will be very simple: bread, goat cheese, figs and wine.

150 **ah** - *int*
a

ha
Ah! Se fossi ricca, mi comprerei una casa in Spagna.

Ah! If I were rich, I'd buy myself a house in Spain.

151 **figlio** - *nm*
fiʎʎo

son
La data di effetto per il figlio neonato di un assicurato corrisponde al giorno della nascita.

The effective date for a newborn child of an insured person is the day of birth.

152 **dentro** - *prep*
dentro

in, inside
Questa pasta è molto salutare, dentro ci si possono trovare molte verdure!

This pasta is very healthy, in it you can find lots of vegetables!

153 **ragazzo** - *nm/f*
ragattso
boy, boyfriend / girl. girlfriend
Tom era sempre geloso del fratello più giovane perché sapeva che Jack era il ragazzo dagli occhi azzurri della madre.
Tom was always jealous of his younger brother because he knew Jack was their mother's blue-eyed boy.

154 **pensare** - *verb*
pensare
to think
Soltanto le persone poco informate pensano che una lingua serva unicamente a comunicare. Una lingua costituisce anche un modo di pensare, una maniera di vedere il mondo, una cultura.
Only uninformed people think that language is used only to communicate. Language is also a way of thinking, a way of seeing the world, a culture.

155 **accordo** - *nm*
akkˈɔrdo
agreement, deal
Che tu sia d'accordo o no non importa, io lo faccio comunque.
Whether you agree or not, I'm going to do it.

156 **fossa** - *nf*
fossa
pit, dich, gravel
L'acqua di raffreddamento viene scaricata in una fossa di gocciolamento.
Cooling water is discharged into a seepage ditch.

157 **donna** - *nf*
dˈɔnna
woman
La traduzione è come una donna. Se è bella non sarà fedele; se è fedele non sarà certamente bella.
Translation is like a woman. If it is beautiful, it is not faithful. If it is faithful, it is most certainly not beautiful.

158 **giusto** - *adj; adv*
dʒusto
right, just, fair; correctly
Vedrai due edifici giusto di fronte al museo, e il ristorante è nel più alto fra i due.
You'll see two buildings right opposite the museum, and the restaurant is in the taller of the two.

159 **nome** - *nm*
nome
name
Almeno in inglese, il nome di tutti i continenti finisce con la stessa lettera con cui comincia.
In English at least, the name of all the continents end with the same letter that they start with.

160 **avanti** - *adv*
forward, ahead, on

avanti | Il coraggioso cavaliere fa un passo in avanti e bacia la dama sulla mano.

The brave knight steps forward and kisses the lady on the hand.

161 **eh** - *int* | **huh**
ˈɛ | "Dormire in un cassonetto, eh?", chiese Al-Sayib. "Deve essere stata una esperienza puzzolente."

"Sleeping in a dumpster, huh?" Al-Sayib asked. "That must have been a smelly experience."

162 **subito** - *adv* | **immediately, at once**
subito | Siccome ne ho abbastanza di questo inverno, vorrei che arrivasse subito la primavera!

I'm fed up with this winter, I want spring right now!

163 **signora** - *nf* | **lady, Mrs.**
siɲɲora | La signora Brown mise in guardia Beth sul fatto che, se non avesse mangiato correttamente, sarebbe rimasta sempre grassa.

Mrs. Brown warned Beth that if she didn't eat properly she would be permanently overweight.

164 **bastare** - *verb* | **to suffice**
bastare | I soldi che ho ora non bastano per i miei bisogni.

The money I have now falls short of what I need.

165 **notte** - *nm* | **night**
nˈɔtte | In ogni caso, è la verità che in questa notte di neve una vecchia donna sola era seduto sul lato della strada.

Anyhow, it's the truth that on this snowy night a lone old woman was sitting on the side of the road.

166 **bello (bel)** - *adj; nm/f* | **nice,beautiful; handsome, hunk/ beautiful woman**
bˈɛllo (bˈɛl) | Infine da non perdere l'enorme e magnifico luogo di Spagna, il posto più bello a Siviglia.

Finally do not miss the huge and magnificent Place of Spain, the most beautiful place in Seville.

167 **lì** - *adv* | **there**
lˈi | Per fortuna, mia madre era ancora lì, a parlare con un genitore di un altro bambino, quindi è venuta da me e mi ha portato a casa.

Fortunately, my mother was still there, talking with a parent of another kid, so she came to me and took me home.

168 **portare** - *verb* | **to bring**

	portare	La cosa migliore è portare un cappellino in testa durante i freddi inverni di Mosca. *It's best to wear a cap on your head during the cold Moscow winters.*
169	**sicuro** - *adj* sikuro	**sure, safe, secure** Mi dispiace, e sono sicuro che ho abbastanza ferito i tuoi sentimenti. Vorrei scusarmi per questo. *I am sorry, and I'm sure I hurt your feelings quite a bit. I would like to apologize for this.*
170	**testa** - *nf* tˈɛsta	**head** In Medicina Classica Cinese l'insonnia rappresenta uno squilibrio energetico concentrato nella testa e causato da diversi fattori quali l'eccesso di preoccupazione, lo stress, l'età, traumatismi fisici e psicologici etc. *In Classical Chinese Medicine, insomnia is an imbalance of energy concentrated in the head, which is caused by different factors such as anxiety, stress, age, physical and psychological traumas, etc*
171	**faccia** - *nf* fattʃa	**face** Per ciascuna superficie selezionata, inverte la direzione del vettore normale , e scambia il ruolo delle facce. *For each selected surface, it inverts the normal vector's direction.*
172	**sentire** - *verb* sentire	**to feel, hear** I bambini hanno bisogno di uno spazio adeguato in cui vivere, di luoghi in cui giocare e di quartieri in cui potersi sentire al sicuro. *Children need a decent place to live, places to play and neighbourhoods in which they can feel safe.*
173	**persona** - *nf* persona	**person** Non ci si sposa con qualcuno con cui si può vivere - ci si sposa con la persona senza di cui non si può vivere. *You don't marry someone you can live with — you marry the person whom you cannot live without.*
174	**appena** - *adv* appena	**just, (as) soon (as)** Sto ascoltando un audiolibro di Harry Potter con il Walkman che ho appena comprato. *I'm listening to a Harry Potter audio book with the Walkman I just bought.*
175	**sotto** - *adv; prep*	**under, below; under**

sotto

Vivere non vuol dire aspettare che passi la tempesta, vuol dire imparare a danzare sotto la pioggia.

Life isn't about waiting for the storm to pass, it's about learning to dance in the rain.

176 **prendere** - *verb*
prˈɛndere

to take

Tom pensava di avere un sacco di tempo per prendere il suo aereo, però ce l'ha fatta solo per il rotto della cuffia.

Tom thought he had plenty of time to catch his plane, but he only just made it by the skin of his teeth.

177 **merda** - *nf*
mˈɛrda

shit

Ah, merda. Ho fatto cadere il mio aggeggio nel lavello.

Ah, crap. I dropped my doohickey into the sink.

178 **tipo** - *nm*
tipo

type, kind

Che tipo di comportamento considerate in generale come tipicamente maschile?

What kind of behavior would you generally consider as typically male?

179 **morto** - *adj*
mˈɔrto

dead, died

Un uomo scendeva da Gerusalemme a Gerico e incappò nei briganti che lo spogliarono, lo percossero e poi se ne andarono, lasciandolo mezzo morto.

A certain man was going down from Jerusalem to Jericho, and he fell among robbers, who both stripped him and beat him, and departed, leaving him half dead.

180 **paura** - *nf*
paura

fear

Quello di cui aveva più paura Tom era il pensiero di potere non essere in grado di camminare di nuovo.

What scared Tom the most was the thought that he might not be able to walk again.

181 **pronto** - *adj; adv*
pronto

ready

Il professore mi chiese se ero pronto e aggiunse che tutti mi attendevano al portone della scuola.

The teacher asked me if I was ready, adding that everybody was waiting for me at the school gate.

182 **buono** - *adj; nm*
bwˈɔno

good; voucher, coupon

Sono buono con voi questa mattina.

I'm being good to you this morning.

183 **presto** - *adv* pr'ɛsto

soon, early

Anche se vengono pubblicati molti libri, la cosa che sarà presto di valore è proprio poco.

Though many books are published, hardly a few of them are of value.

184 **moglie** - *nf* moʎʎe

wife

Se alcuno viene a me, e non odia suo padre, e sua madre, e la moglie, e i figliuoli, e i fratelli, e le sorelle, anzi ancora la sua propria vita, non può esser mio discepolo.

If any man come to me, and hate not his father, and mother, and wife, and children, and brethren, and sisters, yea, and his own life also, he cannot be my disciple.

185 **ideare** - *verb* ideare

to design

Ogni scuola potrà ideare un progetto simile scegliendo le ricette della tradizione dei bambini coinvolti.

Every school could design a similar project, choosing recipes from the traditions of the participating children.

186 **capire** - *verb* kapire

to understand

Conoscere e capire il mondo e le persone che hanno creato l'età moderna è un viaggio alla scoperta di sé stessi.

To know and understand the world and the people who created the modern age is a trip at the discovery of themselve.

187 **stesso** - *adj; pron* stesso

same; itself

Tom non si fida di nessuno: né degli amici, né della moglie, né dei figli, e perfino neanche di se stesso.

Tom doesn't trust anyone: neither his friends, nor his wife, nor his children, nor even himself.

188 **problema** - *nf* probl'ɛma

problem

Ci sono stati molti colpi di scena nella storia, ma finalmente abbiamo risolto il problema.

There were a lot of twists and turns to the story, but we finally solved the problem.

189 **amore** - *nm* amore

(my) love

Mettimi come un sigillo sul tuo cuore, come un sigillo sul tuo braccio; perché l'amore è forte come la morte.

Set me as a seal upon thine heart, as a seal upon thine arm: for love is strong as death.

190 **insieme** - *adv; nm*
insjˈɛme

together; set, whole

Non è solo andare al cinema a vedere i film. Piuttosto, si va al cinema per ridere e piangere insieme a duecento persone.

You don't just go to the cinema to watch films. Rather, you go to the cinema in order to laugh and cry together with two hundred people.

191 **papà** - *nm*
papˈa

dad, daddy

Il papà di Tom è morto di stress per troppo lavoro 5 anni fa.

Tom's father died from karoshi five years ago.

192 **succedere** - *verb*
suttʃedere

to happen, occur, succeed

Non importa cosa succede, tenete la porta chiusa a chiave e non venite fuori.

No matter what happens, keep the door locked and don't come outside.

193 **volgere** - *verb*
voldʒere

to turn

I lavori di costruzione stanno volgendo al termine..

The construction work is coming to an end.

194 **domani** - *adv; nm*
domani

tomorrow

Io ne ho bisogno entro domani.

I need it by tomorrow.

195 **tesoro** - *nm*
tezˈɔro

treasure

Il tesoro supremo è la conoscenza, il tesoro centrale sono i bambini e il tesoro più basso è la ricchezza materiale.

The supreme treasure is knowledge, the middle treasure is children, and the lowest treasure is material wealth.

196 **caso** - *nm*
kazo

case

L'Espositore si impegna a indennizzare, su richiesta, e tenere indenne l'Organizzatore nel caso di eventuali reclami, responsabilità, perdite, cause, procedimenti legali, danni, sentenze, spese, costi (incluse spese legali) e oneri di qualsiasi tipo.

The Exhibitor agrees to attend a pre-registration inspection prior to the commencement of the Exhibition, where requested by the Organiser and in accordance with the Organiser's instructions from time to time. 16.4 The Exhibitor agrees to on demand indemnify and keep indemnified the Organiser against all claims, liabilities, losses, suits, proceedings, damages, judgments, expenses, costs (including legal fees) and charges of any kind.

197 **ragione** - *nm*
radʒone

reason

Per una qualche ragione, il microfono non ha funzionato prima.

For some reason the microphone didn't work earlier.

198 **storia** - *nf*
stˈɔrja

history, story

L'audacia di Cesare fu l'inizio di una carriera militare e politica molto distinta. Con il tempo, come Alessandro Magno e Napoleone Bonaparte, divenne una delle figure più famose nella storia del mondo.

Caesar's audacity was the beginning of a very distinguished military and political career. In time, like Alexander the Great and Napoleon Bonapart, he became one of the most famous figures in world history.

199 **okay** - *int*
okˈɛi

okay

Doveva venir fuori qualcosa di particolare", racconta Claus Staniek, architetto del 54F, "altrimenti i Beni culturali non avrebbero dato l'okay.

We had to come up with a very special design, otherwise the office for the preservation of historical monuments wouldn't have given its approval," says 54F architect Claus Staniek.

200 **qua** - *adv*
kwa

here

Qua sotto puoi leggere le istruzioni che ti saranno date durante l'esame finale.

Below, you can read the instructions you will be given during the final exam.

201 **fino** - *prep; adv; adj*
fino

till; even; fine, subtle

Tutta la gente lodò l'abito dell'imperatore senza vederlo per non sembrare stupida, fino a quando un bambino disse: "Ma il re è nudo!"

The people all praised the emperor's clothes without telling him the truth so as not to seem stupid, until a little boy said, "The emperor is naked!"

202 **nulla** - *nf; pron* nulla
nothing; nothing, anything
Io sono abbastanza sicura che Tom non farà nulla di folle.
I'm pretty sure Tom won't do anything crazy.

203 **trovare** - *verb* trovare
to find
Al fine di far emergere il tuo talento al massimo hai bisogno di una professione più adatto a te, di trovare un nuovo posto di lavoro.
In order to bring out your talents to the full you need to a profession more suited to you, to find a new work place.

204 **dare** - *verb* dare
to give
Tom potrebbe prendere in considerazione di dare a Mary il prestito ha chiesto.
Tom might want to consider giving Mary the loan she asked for.

205 **mano** - *nm* mano
hand
Meno dell'uno per cento della popolazione è veramente ambidestra, ossia, non hanno una mano dominante.
Less than one percent of the population is truly ambidextrous, that is, they have no dominant hand.

206 **servire** - *verb* servire
to serve
S'accorse che le cose che aveva studiato a scuola non servivano nel mondo degli affari.
He found that the things he had studied in school were not useful in the business world.

207 **famiglia** - *nf* famiʎʎa
family
La nostra famiglia ha una tradizione centenaria di produzione di questi dolci ad Amara, il luogo in cui sono nato, tra i fiumi Tigri ed Eufrate: la biblica Babele.
Our family has a long tradition of hundreds of years of making these sweets in my birthplace in Amara, between the rivers Tigris and Euphrates in Iraq, the biblical Babel.

208 **terra** - *nf* tˈɛrra
land, earth
La foresta amazzonica è la più grande foresta tropicale sulla Terra.
The Amazonian forest is the largest tropical forest on Earth.

209 **fratello** - *nm* fratˈɛllo
brother
Ma suo fratello, quello più agile e più mobile, escogitò un tipo di abitazione più adattabile, meno rigido - la tenda pieghevole... Era l'Avventuriero.

But his brother, more agile and mobile, thought up a more adaptable, less rigid habitation - the folding tent ...he was the Adventurer.

210 **leggere** - *verb*
leddʒere

to read
Per me, leggere a casa è preferibile a leggere seduti accanto a gente sconosciuta in una biblioteca.
Read the list we sent you and check that all the sentences sound natural to you.

211 **scusare** - *verb*
skuzare

to excuse
Tom pensa che Mary dovrebbe scusarsi con John per non aver fatto quello che diceva avrebbe fatto.
Tom thinks Mary should apologize to John for not doing what she said she'd do.

212 **fine** - *nm; nf; adj*
fine

purpose; end; fine
All'inizio hanno cercato di ignorarti, poi hanno cominciato a ridere di te, e dopo a lottare con te. Alla fine vinci tu.
At first they try to ignore you, then they start to laugh at you, then they fight you. In the end you win.

213 **secondo** - *prep; nm; adv; adj*
sekondo

according to; second
Il Rio delle Amazzoni è il secondo fiume più lungo del mondo dopo il Nilo.
The Amazon is the second longest river in the world after the Nile.

214 **ciò** - *pron*
tʃˈɔ

that, it
Nessuno sembrava aver fatto attenzione a ciò che aveva detto.
Nobody seems to have paid attention to what he said.

215 **aiuto** - *nm*
ajuto

help
Con l'aiuto della più moderna tecnica di ricerca vengono trovate, nell'estesa banca dati, aziende produttrici adeguate.
With the assistance of most modern search technology, the suitable production companies and their appropriate contact information.

216 **polizia** - *nf*
politts'ia

police
Tra altri vent'anni, gli Stati Uniti non saranno più in grado di essere la polizia per il mondo.
In another twenty years, the United States will no longer be able to be the police for the world.

217	**piano** - *nm; adj*	**plan, floor, piano; plane, flat**
	pjano	Dopo aver chiesto la mia chiave alla reception, ho preso l'ascensore per andare al mio piano.
		After asking for my key at the front desk, I took the elevator to my floor.
218	**diavolo** - *nm*	**Devil**
	djavolo	Gli angeli hanno due ali, il Diavolo ha una coda.
		Angels have two wings, the Devil has a tail.
219	**meno** - *adv; adj; prep; conj*	**less; less; unless; no so (much as)**
	meno	Accetto di cuore la massima: "Il governo migliore è quello che governa di meno".
		I heartily accept the motto, "That government is best which governs least".
220	**morire** - *verb*	**to die**
	morire	Morire non è il contrario di vivere: si passa la propria vita a vivere, ma non si passa la propria morte a morire.
		Dying is not the opposite of living: we spend our life living while we don't spend our death dying.
221	**neanche** - *adv; conj*	**not even, neither; not even**
	neaŋke	Tom non mi darebbe neanche la possibilità di spiegare perché ho fatto quello che ho fatto.
		Tom wouldn't even give me a chance to explain why I did what I did.
222	**quale** - *adj; pron; conj*	**what, which; which; as**
	kwale	Che la donna sia per natura destinata ad obbedire è dimostrato dal fatto che ogni donna posta nella posizione innaturale di assoluta indipendenza contemporaneamente si attacchi a un qualche tipo di uomo, dal quale è controllata e dominata.
		That woman is by nature intended to obey is shown by the fact that every woman who is placed in the unnatural position of absolute independence at once attaches herself to some kind of man, by which she is controlled and governed.
223	**vostro** - *pron*	**your (pl)**
	vˈɔstro	Ancora una volta vi ringrazio molto per il vostro aiuto e servizio rapido!
		Again thank you very much for all your help and prompt service!
224	**là** - *adv*	**there**

l'a — I miei capelli sono scompigliati stamani. Almeno passami uno specchietto - dovrebbe essere in quel cassetto là.

My hair's messed up this morning. At least lend me a hand mirror - it should be shut in the drawer there.

225 **strada** - *nf*
strada
(large) street, road
Gli pneumatici si sono deteriorati a causa dell'attrito tra la gomma e la superficie della strada.
Tires wear down because of friction between the rubber and the road surface.

226 **occhio** - *nm*
ˈɔkkjo
eye
Gli occhi di Virginia si riempirono di lacrime e lei si nascose il viso con le mani.
Virginia's eyes grew dim with tears, and she hid her face in her hands.

227 **giro** - *nm*
dʒiro
tour
Durante il suo giro in Italia, visitò diverse città famose per la loro bellezza scenica, per esempio Napoli e Firenze.
During his tour of Italy, he visited several cities which are famous for their scenic beauty, for instance, Naples and Florence.

228 **quasi** - *adv*
kwazi
almost, nearly
Non subiscono quasi mai violenze fisiche.
They are almost never physically abused.

229 **salvo** - *prep; adj*
salvo
save, but; safe
Sono solito alzarmi alle sette e andare a letto alle undici, salvo la domenica.
I usually get up at seven and go to bed at eleven except on Sundays.

230 **credere** - *verb*
krˈedere
to believe
Non credi che dovresti aiutare Tom?
Don't you think you should help Tom?

231 **mentre** - *conj*
mentre
while, as, whereas
E mentre lei non è più con noi, so che mia nonna sta osservando, insieme alla famiglia che mi ha reso quello che sono.
And while she's no longer with us, I know my grandmother's watching, along with the family that made me who I am.

232 **bambino** - *nm/f*
bambino
child, baby, boy/girl
Lei era una bambina, però non aveva paura.
She was a child, but she wasn't afraid.

233 **sera** - *nf*
sera

evening
Ieri sera non avevo voglia di uscire e sono rimasto a casa a guardare un film.
Last night I did not feel like going out and I stayed home watching a movie.

234 **film** - *nm*
film

movie
Il problema di questo film è che le scene violente e le scene divertenti sono mescolate assieme.
The problem with this movie is that the violent scenes and the funny scenes are mixed together.

235 **uccidere** - *verb*
uttʃˈidere

to kill
I patrioti dicono sempre di morire per il loro paese e mai di uccidere per il loro paese.
Patriots always talk of dying for their country, and never of killing for their country.

236 **indietro** - *adv*
indjˈɛtro

back
Il mio orologio va indietro di tre minuti al giorno.
My watch loses three minutes a day.

237 **contro** - *adv; prep*
kontro

against, counter; against, versus
Tom era alla guida della macchina che si è schiantata contro il supermercato a Park Street.
Tom was the driver of the car that crashed into the supermarket on Park Street.

238 **tornare** - *verb*
tornare

to return
Per tornare alla mappa normale, toccare l'icona del traffico, quindi toccare Mappa normale.
To return to the normal map, tap the traffic icon, and then tap Show Normal Map.

239 **acqua** - *nf*
akkwa

water
I rimedi omeopatici non contengono altro che acqua, in quanto la sostanza originale è stata diluita al punto che non ne rimane alcuna molecola.
Homeopathic remedies contain nothing but water since the original substance has been diluted to the point where not a single molecule remains.

240 **nessun** - *adj*
nessun

no
Questi diritti e queste libertà non possono in nessun caso essere esercitati in contrasto con i fini e i principi delle Nazioni Unite.

These rights and freedoms may in no case be exercised contrary to the purposes and principles of the United Nations.

241 **abbastanza** - *adv*
abbastantsa
enough
La mia fidanzata ha perso l'ultimo treno per la fine del mondo, e ciò è abbastanza problematico.
My girlfriend missed the last train to the world's end, and that's enough of a problem.

242 **minuto** - *adj; nm*
minuto
minute
In termini di tempi medi si è registrato un aumento di circa un minuto per la riconsegna del primo bagaglio e di circa due minuti per l'ultimo rispetto alle prestazioni erogate nel 2008.
On average, an increase of one minute in baggage reclaim times was registered for the first bag and approximately two minutes for the last bag compared with the service provided in 2008.

243 **finito** - *adj*
finito
finished, over
Io non ho mai finito di leggere i libri che non mi piacciono.
I've never finished reading the books that I don't like.

244 **cercare** - *verb*
tʃerkare
to search
Oltre a Macchine per imballaggio a vuoto è possibile cercare anche altri prodotti e servizi.
You can also search here with Vacuum packaging machines for further products and services.

245 **tardi** - *adv*
tardi
late
Probabilmente farà tardi quindi faresti meglio a dirgli un'altra volta che l'incontro è alle sette per sicurezza.
He's likely to be late so you'd better tell him again that the meeting time is seven to make double sure.

246 **veramente** - *adv*
veramente
really
Penso che sia un metodo che non posso veramente consigliare, a meno che voi non siate pronti ad incorrere in un fallimento.
I think this not a method that I can really recommend unless you are willing to risk failure.

247 **chiamare** - *verb*
kjamare
to call
Utilizzare i tasti NUMERO per inserire il numero di telefono che si desidera chiamare.
Use the NUMBER keys to enter the telephone number you want to call.

248 **guerra** - *nf* gw'ɛrra

war

C'è una regola che funziona in ogni calamità. Che si tratti di peste, guerra, o carestia, i ricchi diventano più ricchi e i poveri sempre più poveri. I poveri aiutano persino ad organizzarla.

There is one rule that works in every calamity. Be it pestilence, war, or famine, the rich get richer and poor get poorer. The poor even help arrange it.

249 **piccolo** - *adj* pikkolo

little, small

C'era un piccolo numero di stranieri fra i visitatori del museo.

There was a sprinkling of foreigners among the visitors in the museum.

250 **cuore** - *nm* kw'ɔre

heart, core

È quello che si ottiene a dare il proprio cuore a qualcuno che non lo meritava.

That's what you get for giving your heart to someone who never deserved it.

251 **nemmeno** - *adv; conj* nemmeno

not even, neither

Rincresce rilevare che fra i tanti musei della provincia nessuno, nemmeno quelli che si occupano del mare prenda in considerazione il fenomeno che negli ultimi due secoli ha maggiormente segnato la storia.

Sad to say, none of the museums in the territory - not even those most concerned with the sea have taken into consideration the event which during the last two centuries has had the greatest impact on the history.

252 **forte** - *adj; nm; adv* f'ɔrte

strong; forte; loudly

Il cielo diventava sempre più scuro e il vento soffiava sempre più forte.

The sky grew darker and darker, and the wind blew harder and harder.

253 **bravo** - *adj; nm* bravo

good, fine, clever; bravo

È vero che Wendy è cresciuta in una località di mare, però non è una brava nuotatrice.

It is true Wendy grew up at the seaside, but she isn't a good swimmer.

254 **giù** - *adv*

down

dʒu | Sono successe tante cose. È come se il mondo intero si sia capovolto a testa in giù.

So much has happened. It's as if the whole world is flipped upside down.

255 **stasera** - *nf* — **tonight, this evening**
stazera
I miei genitori vanno spesso al cinema con i loro amici, ma stasera stanno guardando un film in televisione.
My parents often go to the cinema with their friends, but this evening they're watching a film on TV.

256 **comunque** - *adv; conj* — **anyway; though**
komuŋkwe
Comunque tu la veda, le probabilità sono contro di noi.
No matter how you look at it, the odds are stacked against us.

257 **numero** - *nm* — **number**
numero
Il numero di studenti che erano in ritardo per la scuola era molto più piccolo di quanto mi aspettassi.
The number of students who were late for school was much smaller than I had expected.

258 **punto** - *nm* — **point**
punto
È incline a guardare tutto dal punto di vista della sua praticità e non è né avaro né stravagante.
He is inclined to look at everything from the standpoint of its practicality and is neither stingy nor extravagant.

259 **roba** - *nf* — **stuff, things**
rˈɔba
Non riesci a chiudere la valigia per quanta roba ci hai infilato.
You can't get the suitcase closed because you've stuffed too much into it.

260 **scuola** - *nf* — **school**
skwˈɔla
Non voleva fare il compito oggi, quindi ha fatto finta di star male e non è andato a scuola
He didn't want to take today's test, so he made believe that he was sick, and didn't go to school.

261 **felice** - *adj* — **happy**
felitʃe
Per di più, il sorriso del nostro personale dell 'hotel sarà felice di aiutarvi con qualsiasi richiesta.
On top of that, the friendly staff of the hotel will be happy to help you with any enquiry.

262 **vecchio** - *adj; nm/f* — **old; old (wo)man**

v'ɛkkjo — Se non è possibile smaltire correttamente il vecchio apparecchio, rivolgersi a Vega per l'eventuale restituzione e il riciclaggio.
If you have no way to dispose of the old instrument properly, please contact us concerning return and disposal.

263 **perdere** - *verb* — **to lose**
p'ɛrdere — Se le leggi sono i loro nemici, essi saranno i nemici delle leggi; e coloro che hanno molto da sperare e nulla da perdere saranno sempre pericolosi.

If laws are their enemies, they will be enemies to laws; and those who have much to hope and nothing to lose, will always be dangerous.

264 **uscire** - *verb* — **to go out, leave**
uʃʃire — È possibile scegliere il volume d'aria che si desidera far uscire dalla parte superiore e dalla parte posteriore della stufa in maniera indipendente, regolando la potenza di ventilazione direttamente con il telecomando.

The air volume that you wish to exit from the upper and rear parts of the stove can be set separately by adjusting the ventilation power directly with the remote control.

265 **città** - *nf* — **city**
tʃitt'a — Tom è nato in una piccola città non troppo lontana da Boston.
Tom was born in a small town not too far from Boston.

266 **importare** - *verb* — **to import**
importare — Questo messaggio viene visualizzato se si tenta di importare un file stereo quando tutte le tracce stereo sono già registrate
This message appears if you try to import a stereo file when all the stereo tracks in the song already have recordings

267 **dietro** - *prep; nm; adj; adv* — **behind; back, rear; after; after**

dj'ɛtro — Per un momento ha avuto sul viso uno strano sorriso. Che cosa pensi, che cosa si nasconde dietro quel sorriso?
That person has had an odd grin on his face for a while. What do you suppose is behind it?

268 **invece** - *adv* — **instead**
invetʃe — Adesso che sei giovane dovresti viaggiare invece di passare il tempo davanti al computer.

You should travel while you're young instead of spending time in front of the computer.

269 **lasciare** - *verb*
laʃʃare

to leave

Ogni individuo ha diritto di lasciare qualsiasi paese, incluso il proprio, e di ritornare nel proprio paese.

Everyone has the right to leave any country, including his own, and to return to his country.

270 **importante** - *adj*
importante

important

Ciò che è importante non è l'università in cui ci si è laureati, ma ciò che si ha imparato all'università.

What is important is not which university you've graduated from but what you've learned in the university.

271 **figlia** - *nf*
fiʎʎa

daughter

Sbarzaglia ha deciso di investire di pieni poteri la giovanissima figlia Simona, a cui ha ceduto in toto la gestione dell'impresa.

Gianni Sbarzaglia decided to invest his young daughter Simona with full powers and entrusted her with the company management.

272 **sperare** - *verb*
sperare

to hope

Prendo lezioni di danza da quando ho tre anni e spero di diventare una ballerina.

I have been taking ballet lessons since I was three and hope to be a ballerina.

273 **chiedere** - *verb*
kjˈɛdere

to ask (for), enquire

Mi chiedevo, vorresti venire al cinema con me stasera?

I was wondering, would you like to go to a movie with me tonight?

274 **poco** - *adj; adv; nm*
pˈɔko

little; a litte, not much; bit

Non voglio rinunciare alle mie idee, anche se alcune di queste sono un poco estreme.

I don't want to lose my ideas, even though some of them are a bit extreme.

275 **verso** - *prep; nm*
vˈɛrso

to, towards; direction, way

Compio serenamente il mio primo passo verso l'eternità, lascio la vita per entrare nella storia.

Serenely I take my first step towards eternity and leave life to enter history.

276 **marito** - *nm*

husband

marito | Una donna ha portato al fotografo una foto del suo defunto marito che indossa un cappello.

A woman brought an old picture of her dead husband, wearing a hat, to the photographer.

277 **migliore** - *adj* | **best**
miʎʎore | E io non sarei qui questa sera senza il sostegno continuo della mia migliore amica degli ultimi 16 anni, la roccia della nostra famiglia, l'amore della mia vita, la prossima first lady della nazione, Michelle Obama.

And I would not be standing here tonight without the unyielding support of my best friend for the last 16 years, the rock of our family, the love of my life, the nation's next first lady, Michelle Obama.

278 **quattro** - *adj; num* | **four**
kwattro | Ci sono molti tipi strani in palestra alle quattro di mattina. E con fierezza io sono uno di essi.

There are a lot of weirdos at the gym at 4 in the morning. And proudly, I'm one of them.

279 **puttana** - *nf* | **whore**
puttana | Io mi chiedo se mia madre mi sta nascondendo qualcosa. Mi ha chiamato "figlio di puttana" oggi.

I wonder if my mother is hiding something from me. She called me a "son of a bitch" today.

280 **cinque** - *adj; num* | **five**
tʃiŋkwe | Ho cinque figli. Due di loro sono ingegneri, un altro è un insegnante e gli altri sono studenti.

TI have five sons. Two of them are engineers, another is a teacher and the others are students.

281 **almeno** - *adv* | **at least**
almeno | Tom crede che sia assolutamente necessario bere almeno un litro d'acqua ogni giorno.

Tom believes it's absolutely necessary to drink at least a liter of water every day.

282 **ricordo** - *nm* | **memory**
rikˈɔrdo | Hanno aperto il loro album fotografico del matrimonio e hanno fatto una passeggiatina lungo il viale dei ricordi.

They opened up their wedding album and had a little stroll down memory lane.

283 **però** - *conj; adv* | **but, yet; however**

per'ɔ — Stabilità, rigore e completamento del mercato non sono però sufficienti se non riparte una strategia di investimenti

Stability, rigour and completion of the single market are however not sufficient if we don't adopt a new strategy of investment.

284 **sangue** - *nm* — **blood**

saŋgwe

Il dottore ha analizzato il campione di sangue per verificare la presenza di anemia.

The doctor analyzed the blood sample for anemia.

285 **settimana** - *nf* — **week**

settimana

Sono convinto che qualche settimana in un centro estivo ben organizzato possa essere più educativo di un intero anno di scuola.

I have the conviction that a few weeks in a well-organized summer camp may be of more value educationally than a whole year of formal school work.

286 **entrare** - *verb* — **to enter**

entrare

Avevo addosso le mie cuffie, così non ho sentito Tom entrare nella stanza.

I had my headphones on so I didn't hear Tom enter the room.

287 **fata** - *nf* — **fairy, femme fatale**

fata

Fortunatamente, la fata getta su di lui un sortilegio: sarà afflitto da un terribile attacco di bulimia il giorno delle nozze.

Fortunately, the fairy casts a spell on him: he will fall victim to a terrible bout of bulimia on the day of his wedding.

288 **colpa** - *nf* — **fault, guilt; blame**

kolpa

Non sarà colpa tua se tuo figlio fa qualcosa che non va: ha venticinque ora, non è vero?

It won't be your fault if your son does anything wrong: he is twenty-five now, isn't he?

289 **dottore** - *nm* — **doctor, Dr.**

dottore

Biancaneve era così pallida che il dottore le consigliò di uscire a prendere il sole.

Snow White was so pale that the doctor suggested she go out in the sunshine.

290 **possibile** - *adj* — **possible**

possibile

Ho corso il più velocemente possibile, ma non sono riuscito a prendere l'ultimo treno.

I ran as fast as possible, but I was not in time for the last train.

291 **piede** - *nm* pjˈɛde

foot

Durante le vacanze io e mia sorella siamo stati in un piccolo paese ai piedi del Monte Fuji.

During the vacation my sister and I stayed at a small village at the foot of Mt. Fuji.

292 **vicino** - *adj; adv* vitʃino

close, near

Se si registrano delle immagini vicino a trasmettitori radio o linee ad alta tensione, immagini e/o suoni potrebbero risultare disturbati.

If you record near radio transmitters or high-voltage lines, the recorded pictures and/or sound may be adversely affected.

293 **amo** - *nm* amo

hook, bait

Noi dobbiamo ancora cercare l'amo.

We still have to look for the hook.

294 **passare** - *verb* passare

to pass, spend, switch

Il mio interesse è riguardo al futuro perché è là che passerò il resto della mia vita.

My interest is in the future because I'm going to spend the rest of my life there.

295 **media** - *nf* medja

media, average

Anche se tutti i paesi del mondo e tutti i media riconoscono la legittimità di quel regime razzista, rimarrà sempre razzista sul piano morale.

Even if all countries of the world and all the news media were to recognize the legitimacy of this racist regime, on the moral level it would always remain racist.

296 **capitare** - *verb* kapitare

to happen, occur

Tu sei la cosa migliore che mi sia mai capitata.

You're the best thing that's ever happened to me.

297 **ultimo** - *adj* ˈultimo

last, latest

La mia ragazza ha perso l'ultimo treno per la fine del mondo, e ciò è abbastanza problematico.

My girlfriend missed the last train to the world's end, and that's quite a problem.

298 **qual** - *adv; pron* kwal

everytime, whenever; what, which

Chi sono io? Da dove vengo? C'è vita dopo la morte? Qual è il significato della vita sulla terra?

Who am I? Where do I come from? Is there life after death? What is the meaning of life on earth?

299 **andata** - *nf*
andata

going

Tranne che nei casi di "forza maggiore" (3), il rimborso delle spese di viaggio e di soggiorno è strettamente limitato ad un viaggio di andata e ritorno per riunione, a partire dal luogo di origine e per le date concordate nella lettera di nomina.

Except in the case of "force majeure" (3), the reimbursement of travel and subsistence expenses will be strictly limited to one return travel per meeting from the point of origin and for the dates agreed in the appointment letter.

300 **vivere** - *verb*
vivere

to live

È l'ansia del possesso che, più di ogni altra cosa, impedisce alle persone di vivere con libertà e nobiltà.

It is preoccupation with possession, more than anything else, that prevents men from living freely and nobly.

301 **riuscire** - *verb*
rjuʃʃire

to succeed, able

È bastato un attimo della mia vita per riuscire a conoscerti e amarti, ma non basterebbe tutta la mia vita per riuscire a dimenticarti.

Only one moment of my life was enough to manage to know and love you, but my entire life would not be enough to manage to forget you.

302 **pure** - *adv*
pure

also

Le donne più felici, come pure le nazioni più felici, non hanno una storia.

The happiest women, like the happiest nations, have no history.

303 **stanza** - *nf*
stantsa

room

Quell'uomo in piedi accanto alla porta e quella donna vicino alla finestra dall'altro lato della stanza hanno memoria fotografica.

That man standing near the door and that woman on the opposite side of the room next to the window have photographic memories.

304 **telefono** - *nm*
tel'ɛfono

phone, telephone

Durante la vita di mia nonna, sia i telefoni che che i computer sono diventati all'ordine del giorno.

In my grandmother's lifetime, both telephones and computers have become commonplace.

305 **ascoltare** - *verb*
askoltare

to listen
Non credo che ci sia alcuna giustificazione per il suo comportamento. Allo stesso tempo, dobbiamo ascoltare quello che ha da dire.
I don't think there is any excuse for his behavior. At the same time, we should listen to what he has to say.

306 **buongiorno** - *int*
bwondʒorno

good morning
Buongiorno. Mi chiamo John Reindle. Lavoro all'ambasciata americana a Praga.
Hello. My name is John Reindle. I work at the American Embassy in Prague.

307 **conoscere** - *verb*
konoʃʃere

to know
Grazie ad Apollo, è possibile conoscere con certezza le entrate e pianificare con facilità qualsiasi investimento a breve e medio termine.
Thanks to Apollo, it is possible to predict the revenue with certainty and easily plan all short and medium term investments.

308 **significare** - *verb*
siɲɲifikare

to mean
Collaborazione scuola-museo significa, o dovrebbe significare, lavorare sulla base di un progetto educativo.
Collaboration means, or should mean, work on the basis of an educational project.

309 **musica** - *nf*
muzika

music
Questo video interesserà a chiunque piaccia la musica classica, specialmente a coloro i quali piace il violoncello.
This video will interest everyone who likes classical music, especially those who like the cello.

310 **conto** - *nm*
konto

bill
I passeggeri non meritano un trattamento simile, poiché saranno loro alla fine a pagare il conto.
Passengers do not deserve that - as it is they that will ultimately foot the bill.

311 **corpo** - *nm*
kˈɔrpo

body
La usi come crema per il corpo quando esce dalla doccia.
Use it as a body cream when you get out of the shower.

312 **culo** - *nm*
kulo

ass
Mi hai detto di avere un bel culo. Lo hai fatto per ingannarmi, o cosa?

You told me you had a nice ass. Was that a misleading statement then?

313 **serio** - *adj* s'ɛrjo

serious

Le banche e i gestori patrimoniali di tutto il mondo sono obbligati a prendere sul serio il trasferimento di ricchezza dall'Occidente all'Asia.

The world's banks and investment managers are forced to take the wealth transfer from the western world to Asia seriously.

314 **mezzo** - *nm; adj* m'ɛddzo

half, middle, means; half, middle

Era nel mezzo di una storia divertente quando si è interrotto per rispondere al telefono.

He was in the middle of a funny story when he stopped to answer the telephone.

315 **visitare** - *verb* vizitare

to visit, see

Lei è una ragazza inglese di origine indiana che va a visitare l'India.

She's an English girl of Indian origin who goes to visit India.

316 **difficile** - *adj* diff'itʃile

difficult

Posso tradurre dal tedesco all'inglese abbastanza bene, ma nell'altra direzione è più difficile.

I can translate from German to English pretty well, but the other way around is more difficult.

317 **sopra** - *adv; prep* sopra

above, on

Le dinamiche macroeconomiche e finanziarie sopra descritte non sono governabili dal management, che ha individuato alcuni fattori di rischio che potrebbero avere impatti sullo scenario di base.

The macroeconomic and financial trends described above cannot be controlled by management, which has identified certain risk factors that could affect the base scenario.

318 **mangiare** - *verb* mandʒare

to eat

Tom ha perso la lista della spesa che sua madre gli aveva dato e ha comprato solo cose che voleva mangiare.

Tom lost the shopping list his mother had given him and just bought things he wanted to eat.

319 **provare** - *verb* provare

to try

Preferirei non perdere tempo a provare a imparare una lingua che non ho bisogno di sapere.

I'd rather not waste my time trying to learn a language that I don't need to know.

320 **ieri** - *adv; nm*
j'ɛri
yesterday
Quando ho finito di lavorare ieri sera ho notato che uno dei miei colleghi aveva lasciato dati di vendite e marketing nella sala riunioni.
When I left work last night, I noticed that one of my colleagues had left marketing and sales data in a conference room.

321 **genere** - *nm*
dʒ'ɛnere
gender, kind, genre
Tale funzione consente di impostare il sintonizzatore sulla ricerca automatica delle stazioni che stanno trasmettendo il tipo di programma (genere) che si desidera ascoltare.

This function lets you set the tuner to automatically search for stations which are currently broadcasting the type of program (genre) you want to listen to.

322 **fuoco** - *nm*
fw'ɔko
fire
Ha perso la ragione quando ha visto la sua casa distrutta dal fuoco.
He lost his reason when he saw his house burn down.

323 **strano** - *adj*
strano
strange
Noi ci aspettavamo che Takahashi si ubriacasse e dicesse alcune cose strane, ma ha finito per non bere troppo, quindi non era interessante.
We expected Takahashi to get drunk and say some weird stuff, but he ended up not drinking too much, so it wasn't interesting.

324 **paese** - *nm*
paeze
country, village
Le imposte sul reddito (correnti e differite) sono determinate in ciascun Paese in cui il Gruppo opera secondo una prudente interpretazione delle normative fiscali vigenti.

Income taxes (both current and deferred) are calculated in each country where the Group operates and are based on prudent interpretations of current fiscal laws.

325 **signorina** - *nf*
siɲɲorina
young lady
Essendo stata in America per molti anni, la signorina Tanaka è un'ottima oratrice della lingua inglese.

Having been in America for many years, Miss Tanaka is a very good speaker of English.

326 **parola** - *nf*
word

par'ɔla | Lui non sa dire una parola di francese, però in compenso parla l'inglese come un nativo.
He can't say one word of French, but then again he speaks English like a native

327 **magari** - *adv* | **maybe, perhaps, even**
magari | Magari non ti piace leggere certe cose.
Maybe you don't like reading certain things.

328 **fortuna** - *nf* | **luck**
fortuna | Tutto ciò che io ho realizzato deriva da un duro lavoro. Tutte le brutte cose che mi accadono sono dovute alla cattiva sorte. Tutto ciò che tu hai realizzato deriva dalla buona fortuna. Tutte le brutte cose che ti succedono sono dovute alla tua mancanza di etica del lavoro.
Everything I accomplished came from hard work. All bad things that happen to me are due to bad luck. All things you accomplish come from good luck. All bad things that happen to you are due to your lack of work ethic.

329 **mese** - *nm* | **month**
meze | Quello che è cominciato 21 mesi fa nel cuore dell'inverno non può finire in questa notte autunnale.
What began 21 months ago in the depths of winter cannot end on this autumn night.

330 **gioco** - *nm* | **game**
dʒ'ɔko | Spiegazione del gioco: ogni gruppo tira il dado gigante e si dirige nella casella corrispondente, dove troverà una relativa domanda a cui dovrà rispondere.
Explanation of the game: each group throws the giant die and moves to the corresponding square, where they will find a question they must answer.

331 **qualsiasi** - *adv* | **any**
kwals'iazi | Alcune persone non hanno un insieme coerente di principi, ma adottano qualsiasi principio sia loro di utilità immediata.
Some people do not have a consistent set of principles; they just adopt whatever principles benefit them at the moment.

332 **resto** - *nm* | **rest**
r'ɛsto | Eseguire il resto dei passi seguendo le istruzioni visualizzate sullo schermo del computer.
Perform the rest of the steps in accordance with the instructions displayed on the computer screen.

333 **sorella** - *nf* | **sister**

sor'ɛlla La visita ha dato slancio e vigore agli sforzi di collaboratori e volontari, per dare rapidamente una nuova casa alla nostra sorella africana.
The visit gave momentum and vigour to the efforts of colleagues and volunteers to quickly create a new home for our African sister.

334 **davanti** - *adj; adv; prep* **front; in front**
davanti Ha preso la mia bicicletta davanti ai miei occhi; non me l'ha nemmeno chiesta!
She took my bicycle before my eyes; she didn't even ask me for it!

335 **re** - *nm* **king**
re Una repubblica è una nazione il cui capo non è un re o una regina, ma un presidente.
A republic is a nation whose head is not a king or queen, but a president.

336 **foto** - *nm* **photo**
f'ɔto Lei mi ha fatto vedere una foto di sua madre quando era studentessa.
She showed me a picture of her mother as a schoolgirl.

337 **domanda** - *nf* **demand, question**
domanda Tom ha chiesto a diverse persone la stessa domanda.
Tom asked several people the same question.

338 **parere** - *verb; nm* **to think, seem; opinion**
parere La moglie di Tom era palesemente assente dalla sua festa di compleanno, quindi pare che le voci del loro allontanamento siano probabilmente vere.
Tom's wife was notably absent from his birthday party, so it seems rumors of their estrangement are likely true.

339 **pace** - *nm* **peace**
patʃe Ogni persona che cerca di controllare il suo destino non troverà mai la pace.
He who seeks to control fate shall never find peace.

340 **tenere** - *verb* **to hold, keep**
tenere Tu sei la donna più bella che io abbia mai tenuto tra le mie braccia.
You're the most beautiful woman I've ever held in my arms.

341 **mente** - *nm* **mind**

mente | Guardare o leggere della fantascienza è un'esperienza liberatoria e di espansione per la mente.

Watching or reading sci-fi is a liberating and expanding experience for the mind.

342 **sacco** - *nm; adv* | **bag, sack; a lot**
sakko | Fece un sacco di soldi a New York e tornò alla piccola città dove nacque.

He made a lot of money in New York and went back to the small town where he was born.

343 **auto** - *nm* | **car**
auto | Molte persone pensano che le auto d'epoca abbiano un prezzo superiore al loro valore effettivo.

Many people think that antique cars are overpriced.

344 **finire** - *verb* | **to end, finish**
finire | Ho seguito lezioni di project management e sto per finire un corso di laurea in risorse umane, che è quello di cui mi voglio occupare nella vita.

I have taken courses in project management and am now on my way to finishing a degree in human resources, which is what I want to do for a living.

345 **verità** - *nf* | **truth**
verit'a | Quel che fa più male è che tu non hai sentito di potermi dire la verità.

What hurts the most is that you didn't feel you could tell me the truth.

346 **paio** - *nm* | **pair**
pajo | Tom ha comprato una macchina fotografica un paio di giorni fa, però l'ha già persa.

Tom bought a camera just a couple of days ago, but he's already lost it.

347 **cane** - *nm* | **dog**
kane | Il dog trekking consiste in un'escursione a piedi con un cane assicurato alla persona mediante un'imbragatura.

Dog trekking consists of an excursion on foot with a dog attached to the person with a harness.

348 **attimo** - *nm* | **moment, instant**
'attimo | Io ho pensato per un attimo che noi avessimo un problema.

I thought for a minute we had a problem.

349 **senso** - *nm* | **direction, sense, meaning**

s'ɛnso

Ogni pistola che è prodotta, ogni nave da guerra varata, ogni razzo sparato significa, nel senso finale, un furto ai danni di coloro che hanno fame e non sono nutriti, quelli che hanno freddo e non sono vestiti.

Every gun that is made, every warship launched, every rocket fired signifies, in the final sense, a theft from those who hunger and are not fed, those who are cold and not clothed.

350 **lavorare** - *verb*
lavorare

to work

Vai a lavorare, manda i tuoi figli a scuola. Segui la moda, agisci normalmentee, cammina sui marciapiedi, guarda la TV. Tieniti bene per la vecchiaia. Obbedisci alla legge. Ripeti con me: io sono libero.

Go to work, send your kids to school. Follow fashion, act normal, walk on the pavements, watch TV. Save for your old age. Obey the law. Repeat with me: I am free.

351 **vivo** - *adj*
vivo

alive, live

In questo modo, è stata garantita la presenza dell'Unione europea, che è viva, nonostante la crisi che stiamo attraversando.

This has ensured the presence of the European Union, which is alive, despite the crisis we are experiencing .

352 **andato** - *adj*
andato

gone

Sono andato a riaccompagnarla alla stazione.

I have been to the station to see him off.

353 **attenzione** - *nm*
attentsjone

caution

Ho letto con attenzione la tua lettera, e la tua situazione mi è parsa molto tipica e prevedibile in una relazione di coppia.

I have read your letter closely, and your situation seems very typical and foreseeable in a relationship.

354 **fra** - *prep*
fra

between, among

Una correlazione fra la personalità e il gruppo sanguigno non è mai stata scientificamente provata.

A connection between personality and blood type has not been scientifically proven.

355 **pistola** - *nf*
pist'ɔla

gun

Voglio sapere cos'è successo alla pistola che hai ricevuto da Tom.

I want to know what happened to the gun you received from Tom.

356 **festa** - *nf*
f'ɛsta

party

Mary pensava che Tom non fosse alla festa di Halloween, però in realtà lui la stava osservando da dietro la sua maschera da lupo mannaro.

Mary thought that Tom wasn't at the Halloween party, but in fact he was secretly observing her from behind his werewolf mask.

357 **presidente** - *nm*
prezidˈɛnte

president

Ho passato tanti anni in qualità di presidente che sento che è giunto il momento di dimettermi.

I've spent so many years as chairman that I feel it's time I stepped down.

358 **unico** - *adj*
ˈuniko

alone, single, unique

Perché qualche poveraccio in una fattoria vuole rischiare la sua vita in una guerra quando il meglio che può uscirne è tornare alla sua fattoria in un unico pezzo.

Why would some poor slob on a farm want to risk his life in a war when the best that he can get out of it is to come back to his farm in one piece.

359 **bere** - *nm*
bere

drinking

I cammelli possono percorrere centinaia di chilometri, durante diversi giorni, senza bere una goccia d'acqua.

Camels can travel over hundreds of kilometers during several days without drinking a drop of water.

360 **fantastico** - *adj*
fantastiko

fantastic

Sei la persona più fantastica della mia vita.

You're the most fantastic person of my life.

361 **affare** - *nm*
affare

deal, bargain, business, affair

Si trasferì a Madrid per prendere le redini degli affari di suo padre.

He moved to Madrid to take the reins of his father's business.

362 **cielo** - *nm*
tʃˈɛlo

sky

Visto lo stato del cielo, domani a quest'ora il tifone si sarà scatenato completamente.

From the look of the sky, the typhoon will probably be raging in all its fury about this time tomorrow.

363 **coraggio** - *nm*
koraddʒo

courage

Dubito che Tom abbia il coraggio di lottare per quello in cui crede.

I doubt that Tom has the courage to stand up for what he believes in.

364 **spiacere** - *verb* spjatʃere
to be sorry
Ci spiace, ma la persona che stai cercando di contattare non è disponibile.
We are sorry, the person you are trying to contact is not available.

365 **ufficio** - *nm* uffitʃo
office
Il sostegno operativo può essere esteso anche agli Stati membri, con l'invio dell'ufficio mobile di Europol, unitamente ad analisti ed esperti dedicati [...] in grado di fornire assistenza in loco.
Operational support can also be extended to Member States by sending the Europol mobile office, with dedicated analysts and experts, to provide on-the-spot assistance in the Member States.

366 **caro** - *adj; nm* karo
dear, expensive; dear
Il mio caro amico Tom mi ha convinto ad andare a Boston.
My good friend, Tom, convinced me to go to Boston.

367 **agire** - *verb* adʒire
to act
Questo balsamo agirà come una pellicola protettiva sopra l'ustione.
This salve will act as a protective film over the burn.

368 **smettere** - *verb* smettere
to stop
Gli è stato detto dal medico di smettere di fumare, ma non sembra riuscire a rinunciare.
He has been told by the doctor to give up smoking, but he cannot seem to give it up.

369 **dormire** - *verb* dormire
to sleep
Per una qualche ragione, non riusciva a dormire.
For some reason, she couldn't sleep.

370 **facile** - *adj* fˈatʃile
easy
Tutti sono capaci di imparare una lingua straniera, però è tutto più facile per coloro che hanno talento.
Everyone is capable of learning a foreign language, but it's all much easier for those with talent.

371 **giovane** - *adj* dʒˈovane
young
Giovanni, che è il più giovane in una famiglia di sette, è il pupillo dei suoi genitori.
John, who is the youngest in a family of seven, is the apple of his parents' eyes.

372 **divertente** - *adj*
divertente

funny, humorous
Tom raccontò una battuta a Mary, però lei non pensava che fosse divertente.
Tom told Mary a joke, but she didn't think it was funny.

373 **generale** - *adj; nm*
dʒenerale

general
Il generale americano Custer fu sconfitto nella battaglia di Little Bighorn dai nativi americani il 25 giugno 1876.
The U.S. General Custer was defeated at the Battle of the Little Bighorn by Native Americans on June 25, 1876.

374 **controllo** - *nm*
kontrˈɔllo

control
Rischiamo di perdere il controllo della situazione se non agiamo in fretta.
We risk losing control of the situation if we don't act quickly.

375 **voce** - *nm*
votʃe

entry, voice, item
Lei gli parla sempre ad alta voce, poiché lui è duro di orecchie.
She always speaks to him in a loud voice because he's hard of hearing.

376 **lungo** - *prep; adj; nm*
luŋgo

long; along; length
Anche se i suoi genitori le avevano detto di no per lungo tempo, l'hanno finalmente lasciata andare in Europa da sola.
Although her parents had said no for a long time, they finally let her go to Europe alone.

377 **gran** - *adj*
gran

great
Nel senso stretto del termine, una vera democrazia non è mai esistita e mai esisterà. È contro l'ordine naturale che il gran numero dovrebbe governare e che i pochi debbano essere governati.
In the strict sense of the term, a true democracy has never existed, and never will exist. It is against natural order that the great number should govern and that the few should be governed.

378 **esatto** - *adj*
ezatto

exact
"Aspetta, non eravamo in questo posto un momento fa?" "Esatto. Siamo tornati indietro. Che strano."
" Wait, isn't this the place we were at a moment ago? " " That's right. We came back. That's strange."

379 **probabilmente** - *adv*
probabilmente

probably
Probabilmente intendeva che la gente va alle dimostrazioni solo per farsi vedere invece di protestare per davvero.

He probably meant that people go to demonstrations just to show up instead of actually protesting.

380 **cenare** - *verb* tʃenare

to have dinner

Non ho bisogno di cenare. Dopo la riunione ho intenzione di andare a bere qualcosa.

I don't need dinner. After the meeting I'm going out for drinks.

381 **libro** - *nm* libro

book

Quando si sta leggendo un libro in inglese, non è una grande idea cercare ogni parola che non si conosce.

When you're reading an English book, it isn't a great idea to look up every word you don't know.

382 **arrivare** - *verb* arrivare

to arrive

Devo andarmene prima che arrivi Tom.

I need to leave before Tom arrives.

383 **squadra** - *nf* skwadra

team

La squadra di calcio di tuo fratello ha vinto la partita e sta festeggiando la vittoria.

Your brother's soccer team won the game and is celebrating right now.

384 **scritto** - *adj* skritto

written

La lettera che avete scritto deve essere corretta e ricopiata anche se l'avete già rifatta più volte.

The letter you wrote must be corrected and transcribed, even if you already rewrote it many times.

385 **cristo** - *nm* kristo

Christ

La messa è una cerimonia cattolica per ricordare Gesù Cristo mangiando e bevendo.

Mass is a Catholic ceremony of remembering Jesus Christ by eating and drinking.

386 **cerca** - *nf* tʃerka

search

Ci sono molte opzioni che è possibile usufruire quando siete in cerca di trasporto, ma questo è un aspetto che molte persone non hanno capito.

There are many options that you can avail when you are seeking transportation but this is an aspect that many people have not realized.

387 **attento** - *adj*

careful

att'ɛnto

Si dovrebbe essere più attenti rispetto a come si parla con quelle persone.

You should be more careful with respect to how you talk to those people.

388 **voglia** - *nf*
v'ɔʎʎa

desire

Per quanto io abbia molta voglia di sapere il suo nome, sono troppo timido per andare a domandarglielo.

Even though I really want to know his name, I don't have enough courage, and I'm afraid to go ask.

389 **esattamente** - *adv*
ezattamente

exactly

Tom e Mary hanno dato esattamente le stesse risposte all'esame, il che ha fatto insospettire l'insegnante.

Tom and Mary gave exactly the same answers on the test which made the teacher suspicious.

390 **cura** - *nf*
kura

care

La madre di Lucy le dice di prendersi cura della sua sorella più giovane.

Lucy's mother told her to take care of her younger sister.

391 **chiaro** - *adj*
kjaro

clear; light

Questo libro vi darà una chiara idea dello stile di vita americano.

This book will give you a clear idea of the American way of life.

392 **lontano** - *adj*
lontano

far

Tom vive in una fattoria con sua moglie, Mary, non troppo lontano da Boston.

Tom lives on a farm with his wife, Mary, not too far from Boston.

393 **tratta** - *nf*
tratta

section, trade, bill, draft

Nessun individuo potrà essere tenuto in schiavitù o in servitù; la schiavitù e la tratta degli schiavi saranno proibite sotto qualsiasi forma.

No one shall be held in slavery or servitude; slavery and the slave trade shall be prohibited in all their forms.

394 **pazzo** - *adj*
pattso

crazy

L'unica differenza tra me e un pazzo è che io non sono pazzo.

The only difference between me and a madman is that I'm not mad.

395 **stronzo** - *nm*

shit, asshole

	strontso	Con tutto il dovuto rispetto, signor Presidente, lei è uno stronzo! *With all due respect, Mr. President, you are an asshole!*
396	**ordine** - *nm* ˈordine	**order** Ha messo in ordine la sua stanza prima che i suoi ospiti arrivassero. *She put her room in order before her guests arrived.*
397	**perfetto** - *adj* perfˈɛtto	**perfect** Tom era in prigione quella sera, quindi ha l'alibi perfetto. *Tom was in jail that night so he has the perfect alibi.*
398	**sbagliato** - *adj* zbaʎʎato	**mistaken, incorrect, wrong** Mio fratello è un buon cittadino. Era solo nel posto sbagliato al momento sbagliato. *My brother is a well doer. He was just at the wrong place at the wrong time.*
399	**dieci** - *adj; num* djˈɛtʃi	**ten** Mi ci sono voluti dieci minuti per andare a piedi fino alla stazione della metro. *It took me ten minutes to walk to the metro station.*
400	**restare** - *verb* restare	**to stay, remain, maintain** Restare zitta, ridotta al silenzio durante l'infanzia del Bambino Gesù, Maria si immerge in un nuovo silenzio ed in silenzio si trasforma seguendo l'esempio del Verbo fatto carne, che è suo figlio, il suo Dio, il suo unico amore. *She remains silent, reduced to silence during the childhood of the Infant Jesus, Mary immerses herself in a new silence and she transforms herself into silence, following the example of the Word made flesh, which is her Son, her God, her only love.*
401	**stupido** - *adj* stˈupido	**stupid** No, ho l'impressione che quel tipo sia più uno stupido che un ingenuo. *No, I feel like he's not "pure", but rather "dull"*
402	**aria** - *nf* arja	**air** Quando ti trovi in un gruppo indeciso, proponi, con aria sicura, qualcosa che nessuno accetterebbe. *When you are with an indecisive group, confidently propose something that no one would agree to.*
403	**passo** - *nm*	**passage, step, pace, stride**

passo — È stato un passo per nulla rapido e semplice, che ha richiesto la creazione di nuovi centri di ricerca e sviluppo

This step has been neither fast nor simple. It has required the creation of new Research and Development centers

404 **motivo** - *nm* — **reason**
motivo — Il motivo di questo risultato è essenzialmente dovuto al fatto che il protocollo ha consentito di ridurre i livelli di perdite sia attraverso la regolazione della pressione, ma soprattutto con l'individuazione di 246 perdite.

The reason of this result is essentially caused by the fact that the protocol has allowed to reduce the losses levels both through the pressure regulation and especially with the individualization of 246 hidden losses.

405 **prossimo** - *adj* — **next**
prˈɔssimo — A quest'ora il prossimo anno, avrai visitato quasi tutte le località importanti del Giappone.

By this time next year, you will have visited almost all the famous places in Japan.

406 **alcuni** - *pron; adj* — **some, several; few, any**
alkuni — Alcuni dottori dicono qualcosa per far piacere ai propri pazienti.
Some doctors say something to please their patients.

407 **fermo** - *adj; nm* — **still, firm; stop, arrest**
fermo — Da quando sto provando a fare delle foto a quel bambino che non mi sta fermo un attimo.

The baby never kept still while I was taking his picture.

408 **viaggio** - *nm* — **travel, trip, journey**
vjaddʒo — Se nella domanda viene incluso il viaggio internazionale, il club o distretto ospite dovrà confermare che ha provveduto ad estendere l'invito a recarsi sul posto, sostiene e approva in pieno i viaggiatori e verifica che il viaggio è necessario per attuare il progetto.
If international travel is included in the application, the host club or district must confirm that it has extended a travel invitation, fully supports and approves Rotarian travelers, and verifies that international travel to the club or district is needed to implement the project.

409 **finché** - *conj* — **until, till**
fiŋkˈe — Finché non provi non saprai mai se sei in grado di farlo o meno.

You'll never know whether or not you can do it until you try.

410 **mettere** - *verb* m'ettere | **to put**
"Lo metterai su Kongregate?" "Sì, c'è un periodo di due settimane in cui il gioco sarà disponibile soltanto su Armor Games, visto che lo sponsorizzano, ma subito dopo lo caricherò su Kongregate".
"Are you going to put this on Kongregate?" "Yes, there is a two-week period where the game will only be available on Armor Games since they're sponsoring it, but I will upload it to Kongregate after that."

411 **aspetto** - *nm* asp'ɛtto | **appearance, look, aspect**
In alcune situazioni, non riceveremmo mai critiche sul nostro aspetto, come l'abbigliamento o l'acconciatura dei capelli.
In some situations, we would never receive criticism about our appearance, such as clothing or hair.

412 **campo** - *nm* kampo | **field**
La casa di campagna era completa, con una piscina, una griglia, un campo da calcio e un tavolo da biliardo.
The country house was complete, with a swimming pool, a barbecue, a soccer field and a pool table.

413 **papa** - *nm* papa | **Pope**
Anche le persone che non credono nella Chiesa cattolica venerano il papa come leader simbolico.
Even people who don't believe in the Catholic church venerate the Pope as a symbolic leader.

414 **arrivo** - *nm* arrivo | **arrival**
Quello che viviamo non è un punto di arrivo, ma un punto di partenza.
This is not the end of our journey but rather a beginning.

415 **camera** - *nf* k'amera | **room**
Nella mia nuova casa il salotto è al pianterreno e la camera da letto al primo piano.
In my new house, the living room is on the ground floor and the bedroom is on the first floor.

416 **benissimo** - *adv* benissimo | **very well, fine**
Puoi lasciare benissimo questa decisione a tua figlia.
You may as well leave such a decision to your daughter.

417 **milione** - *adj; num* | **million**

	miljone	Il carbone, il metano e il petrolio sono i resti di piante e animali vissuti milioni di anni fa. *Coal, natural gas and oil are the remains of plants and animals that lived millions of years ago.*
418	**diventare** - *verb* diventare	**to become** Io penso che Tom non diventerà mai famoso. *I think Tom will never become famous.*
419	**ospedale** - *nm* ospedale	**hospital** test campione di sangue del soggetto in un centro medico o in ospedale. *Test the subject's blood sample at a medical center or hospital.*
420	**zio** - *nm* dz'io	**uncle** Ci sono voluti solamente circa cinque minuti per arrivare a casa di mio zio dalla stazione in auto. *It took only about five minutes to get to my uncle's house from the station by car.*
421	**soltanto** - *adv* soltanto	**only, solely** L'integrazione dell'economo ella dinamica del Consiglio Generale non è stata soltanto una strategia di lavoro, ma una visione della vita consacrata. *The integration of the treasurer into the workings of the General Council was not just a work strategy, but a vision of consecrated life.*
422	**bocca** - *nf* bokka	**mouth** Sadako voleva dire di più, ma bocca e lingua non volevano saperne di muoversi. *Sadako wanted to say more, but her mouth and tongue wouldn't move.*
423	**né** - *conj* n'e	**neither, nor** Né lui, né lei volevano lavare i piatti e così loro due hanno deciso di mangiar fuori. *Neither he nor she wants to do the dishes, and so the two of them decided to eat out.*
424	**zitto** - *adj* dzitto	**silent, quiet** Il fatto che lui sia rimasto zitto l'ha fatta imbestialire. *He said nothing, which made her angry.*
425	**continuare** - *verb*	**to continue**

kontinware | Se continui a bere così tanto potresti ritrovarti facilmente a diventare un alcolizzato.

If you go on drinking so much, you may well end up an alcoholic.

426 **bagno** - *nm* | **bathroom**

baɲɲo | Ci sono tre camere da letto, una cucina, una sala da pranzo, un salotto e un bagno.

There are three bedrooms, a kitchen, a dining room, a living room, and a bathroom.

427 **durante** - *prep; adv* | **during, in, over; while**

durante | Quando ero giovane, ero un po' trasandato e ci sono stati momenti in cui non mi sono fatto il bagno per due settimane durante l'estate.

When I was young, I was a bit scruffy and there were times when I didn't take a bath for up to two weeks during the summer.

428 **ricevere** - *verb* | **to receive**

ritʃevere | Non c'è bisogno di andare a un'università della Ivy League per ricevere una buona istruzione.

You don't have to go to an Ivy League college to get a good education.

429 **idiota** - *adj; nmf* | **idiotic, stupid; idiot**

idjˈɔta | Dobbiamo imparare a vivere insieme come dei fratelli, altrimenti moriremo tutti insieme come degli idioti.

We must learn to live together as brothers or perish together as fools.

430 **colpo** - *nm* | **hit**

kolpo | Un esame più attento rivelò che il teschio era stato schiacciato da qualche duro colpo.

Closer examination revealed that the skull had been crushed by some heavy blow.

431 **fretta** - *nf* | **hurry**

fretta | Alla fine di una giornata di lavoro, tutti hanno fretta di tornare a casa.

At the end of a working day, everybody is in a hurry to get home

432 **causa** - *nf* | **cause**

kˈauza | Fino a quando non si indagherà sulle reali cause del bullismo, questo probabilmente non finirà mai.

If we don't thoroughly examine the cause of bullying, bullying will probably never go away.

433 **iniziare** - *verb*
inittsjare

to start
Per iniziare, rivolgetevi alla persona che meglio conosce la vostra area di responsabilità: il vostro supervisore.

You should begin by consulting the person who best understands your area of responsibility: your supervisor.

434 **giocare** - *verb*
dʒokare

to play
La cosa che non capisco è perché in una giornata così bella non venga permesso ai bambini di giocare fuori.

What I don't understand is why the children aren't being allowed to play outside on such a nice day.

435 **permettere** - *verb*
permettere

to allow
Un passaporto vi identifica come cittadini di un Paese e vi permette di viaggiare all'estero.

A passport identifies you as a citizen of a country and allows you to travel to foreign countries.

436 **arma** - *nf*
arma

weapon
Pensavo che avesse un'arma e allora gli ho sparato.

I thought that guy had a weapon, so I shot him.

437 **bastardo** - *nm*
bastardo

bastard
Perdona il tuo nemico, ma ricordati il nome di quel bastardo.
Forgive your enemy, but remember the name of that bastard.

438 **gruppo** - *nm*
gruppo

group, band
Il gruppo continuerà a monitorare la normativa del settore delle energie rinnovabili, con particolare riferimento alla politica di incentivazione, soprattutto in Italia.

The Group will continue to monitor regulations in the renewables sector, with particular focus on incentives policies, aboveall in Italy.

439 **genitore** - *nm*
dʒenitore

parent
Entrambi i miei genitori erano disoccupati, ma non lasciò che ciò impedisse loro di accudire adeguatamente me e i miei ventitré fratelli e sorelle.

Both of my parents were unemployed, but they didn't let that stop them from properly looking after me and my 23 brothers and sisters.

440 **situazione** - *nm*
sitwattsjone

situation
La situazione degli abitanti del villaggio è meglio di dieci anni fa in molti modi.

The situation of the villagers is better than ten years ago in many ways.

441 **denaro** - *nm* denaro

money

Tom non aveva abbastanza denaro per comprare tutto quello di cui aveva bisogno.

Tom didn't have enough money to buy everything he needed.

442 **alto** - *adj* alto

high, tall

Il consumo di alcol è più alto nell'Europa dell'est che nell'Europa dell'ovest.

Alcohol consumption is higher in Eastern Europe than in Western Europe.

443 **preoccupare** - *verb* preokkupare

to worry

Verso la fine della sua vita, ha iniziato a preoccuparsi molto su quale sarebbe la sua eredità.

Near the end of his life, he started to worry a lot about what his legacy would be.

444 **onore** - *nm* onore

honor

Alla cerimonia di inaugurazione fu scoperta una targa in onore del fondatore.

At the inauguration ceremony a plaque was unveiled in honor of the founder.

445 **sogno** - *nm* soɲɲo

dream

Il musicista sente la matematica, il matematico pensa alla musica: la musica il sogno, la matematica la vita lavorativa.

The musician feels mathematics, the mathematician thinks music: music the dream, mathematics the working life.

446 **giornata** - *nf* dʒornata

day

In nessun paese diverso dall'Inghilterra, è stato detto, si può fare un'esperienza di quattro stagioni nel corso di una sola giornata.

In no country other than England, it has been said, can one experience four seasons in the course of a single day.

447 **deciso** - *adj* detʃizo

decided

Non importa quali sarebbero state le difficoltà, ero deciso a fare di questa donna una attrice.

No matter what the difficulties, I was resolved to make an actress out of this woman.

448 **capello** - *nm*

hair

kapello | Qualcuno mi ha detto di recente che lo spray per capelli va bene per uccidere i ragni.

Someone told me recently that hairspray is good for killing spiders.

449 **pezzo** - *nm*
p'ɛttso
piece
Un enorme pezzo di ghiaccio è scivolato giù dal tetto e ha colpito il terreno con un tonfo.

A large piece of ice slid from the roof and hit the ground with a loud thud.

450 **addio** - *nm*
add'io
goodbye, farewell
Il discorso di addio di Jane ci ha reso molto tristi.

Jane's farewell speech made us very sad.

451 **fondo** - *nm; adj*
fondo
background, bottom, fund; deep
La musica che non trasmette sentimenti, immagini, pensieri, ricordi, è unicamente rumore di fondo.

Music that doesn't transmit feelings, images, thoughts, or memories is just background noise.

452 **traduzione** - *nm*
traduttsjone
translation
Una traduzione è come una donna. Se è bella, non è fedele. Se è fedele, quasi certamente non è bella.

Translation is like a woman. If it is beautiful, it is not faithful. If it is faithful, it is most certainly not beautiful.

453 **mandare** - *verb*
mandare
to send
A me piacerebbe mandare una cartolina di congratulazioni a Madonna per la nascita di sua figlia.

I'd like to send a congratulations card to Madonna for the birth of her baby girl.

454 **ormai** - *adv*
ormai
by now, almost, by then
Non serve a nulla strillare adesso, ormai è troppo tardi. La festa è finita.

Yelling about it won't help now. You should have done that when it counted.

455 **piuttosto** - *adv*
pjutt'ɔsto
rather, quite, pretty
Preferirei rimanere a casa piuttosto che uscire in una giornata così fredda.

I would rather stay at home than go out on such a cold day.

456 **oltre** - *adv; prep*
oltre
over; over, more than, beyond
L'ultima volta che ho fumato è stata ben oltre un anno fa.

The last time I smoked was well over a year ago.

457 **matrimonio** - *nm*
matrimˈɔnjo

marriage, wedding

Il terzo matrimonio di Tom era infelice, e stava considerando di divorziare un'altra volta ancora.

Tom's third marriage was unhappy and he was considering yet another divorce.

458 **circa** - *adv; prep*
tʃirka

about

La popolazione della sua città è circa cinque volte maggiore di quella della mia.

The population of your city is about five times as large as that of my town.

459 **qualunque** - *adj*
kwaluŋkwe

any

Il libro è pieno di teorie tirate per i capelli prive di qualunque fondamento scientifico.

The book is full of far-flung theories without any basis in scientific fact.

460 **futuro** - *adj*
futuro

future

La mia opinione su questo governo è che abbia bisogno di una politica economica più forte, altrimenti in futuro si andrà incontro a grossi problemi.

My impression of this government is that they need a more forceful economic policy, otherwise they'll encounter large problems in the future.

461 **sicurezza** - *nf*
sikurettsa

safety, security

I tre fattori fondamentali per la felicità sono: la sicurezza economica, percepire uno scopo nella propria vita, e buone relazioni personali.

The three fundamental factors for happiness are: financial security, a sense of purpose in one's life, and good personal relationships.

462 **scelta** - *nf*
ʃelta

choice

Le persone più ragionevoli avrebbero capito che il governo non aveva altra scelta che prendere la decisione che ha preso.

Most reasonable people would understand that the government had no choice but to make the decision that it did.

463 **odio** - *nm*
ˈɔdjo

hatred

Loro sono unanimi nel loro odio per me - e io accolgo con favore il loro odio.

They are unanimous in their hate for me—and I welcome their hatred.

464 **cibo** - *nm*
tʃibo

food

Il cibo è da sempre un protagonista del nostro cinema e sono molti i registi italiani che hanno fatto proprio del cibo un attore indiscusso dei loro film, raccontando attraverso la tavola anche le nostre tradizioni enogastronomiche.

Food has always played a leading role in our cinema, and many Italian directors have made food one of the stars of their films, in classic scenes that speak volumes about our food and wine traditions.

465 **fame** - *nm*
fame

hunger

Tom non aveva mangiato nulla in tutta la giornata e aveva molta fame.

Tom hadn't eaten anything the whole day and was very hungry.

466 **prigione** - *nm*
pridʒone

prison

L'uomo chiese clemenza, ma fu condannato a venti anni di prigione per il suo crimine.

The man pleaded for mercy, but he was sentenced to twenty years in prison for his crime.

467 **guaio** - *nm*
gwajo

trouble

Ed il guaio peggiore è che il potere sfidato finisce per convincersene diventando la prima vittima della sua stessa propaganda.

And the worst trouble is that the challenged power finishes up by convincing itself, thus becoming the first victim of its own propaganda.

468 **mattina** - *nf*
mattina

morning

All'alba del mattino vi era la povera piccina, con le guance pallide e la bocca sorridente, appoggiata al muro. Era stata congelata a morte l'ultima sera dell'anno; e il sole di Capodanno salì e brillo su di un piccolo cadavere!

In the dawn of morning there lay the poor little one, with pale cheeks and smiling mouth, leaning against the wall. She had been frozen to death on the last evening of the year; and the New Year's sun rose and shone upon a little corpse!

469 **semplice** - *adj*
sˈemplitʃe

simple

Anche se non è facile mettersi a studiare il cinese, però è più semplice di quello che pensi.

Although it seems very difficult to study Chinese, it's not as hard as you think.

470 **chiunque** - *pron*
kjuŋkwe

anyone

Ma se io non sono disposto a farlo, vi dirò io o chiunque altro che, purtroppo, sono a corto di tempo, non ho il tempo.

But if I'm not willing to do it, I'll tell myself or anyone else that unfortunately I'm short of time, I don't have the time.

471 **brutto** - *adj; nm*
brutto

ugly, bad, nasty; bad, ugliness

Abbiamo sentito che il tempo era brutto, quindi abbiamo deciso di annullare il viaggio.

We heard it was bad weather, so we decided to cancel the trip.

472 **usare** - *verb*
uzare

to use

Esistono due modi per specificare quali sono lingua, nazione e locale da usare per l'installazione e sul sistema installato.

There are two ways to specify the language, country and locale to use for the installation and the installed system.

473 **speciale** - *adj*
spetʃale

special

La maternità e l'infanzia hanno diritto a speciale protezione ed assistenza. Tutti i bambini nati nel matrimonio o fuori di esso, devono godere della stessa protezione sociale.

Motherhood and childhood are entitled to special care and assistance. All children, whether born in or out of wedlock, shall enjoy the same social protection.

474 **cambiare** - *verb*
kambjare

to change

Il prezzo dell'oro cambia da giorno a giorno.

The price of gold varies from day to day.

475 **funzionare** - *verb*
funtsjonare

to function

Tom non starà qui abbastanza a lungo per imparare davvero come funzionano le cose.

Tom won't be here long enough to really learn how things work.

476 **sistema** - *nf*
sistˈɛma

system

Il sistema di scrittura giapponese è molto complicato, ha tre alfabeti con più di duemila caratteri.

The Japanese writing system is very complicated, it has three alphabets with more than two thousand characters.

477 **natale** - *nf*
natale

Christmas

"Me ne sono andato alle sei ieri." "Per prendere il treno?" "No, per comprare alcuni regali di Natale."

"I left at six yesterday." "To take the train?" "No, to buy some Christmas presents."

478 **messaggio** - *nm* messaddʒo

message

Tom e Mary si scambiano più di 200 messaggi di testo ogni giorno.

Tom and Mary exchange more than 200 text messages every day.

479 **incidente** - *nm; adj* intʃidˈɛnte

accident, incident; incident

Sono stupita di sentire che il mio migliore amico è morto la notte scorsa in un incidente d'auto.

I'm flabbergasted to hear that my best friend died last night in a car accident.

480 **radio** - *adj; nm* radjo

radio

Roger Miller ha iniziato a scrivere canzoni perché amava la musica che sentiva alla radio.

Roger Miller began writing songs because he loved the music he heard on the radio.

481 **aereo** - *adj; nm* aˈɛreo

air, aerial; plane, airplane

Si dice che la maggior parte degli incidenti aerei avviene nelle fasi di atterraggio o di decollo.

They say most airplane accidents occur at landing or takeoff stages.

482 **buonanotte** - *int* bwonanˈɔtte

good night

Diede a sua madre il bacio della buonanotte.

She kissed her mother good night.

483 **finalmente** - *adv* finalmente

finally

Anche se i suoi genitori le avevano detto di no per lungo tempo, l'hanno finalmente lasciata andare in Europa da sola.

Although her parents had said no for a long time, they finally let her go to Europe alone.

484 **assolutamente** - *adv* assolutamente

absolutely

Non abbiamo molti soldi, ma ne abbiamo abbastanza per comprare quello di cui abbiamo assolutamente bisogno.

We don't have to have a lot money, but we have enough to buy what we absolutely need.

485 **ottimo** - *adj* ˈɔttimo

excellent

Il nuovo nastro è versatile, a parte l’efficacia della pulizia ha un ottimo livello di resistenza all’idrolisi ed ha un colore contrastante.

The new, versatile belt type stands apart for its good cleaning capabilities, high level of resistance to hydrolysis and contrasting blue colour.

486	**solito** - *adj; nm* s'ɔlito	**usual** è necessario uno sforzo che vada ben oltre il solito bilancio europeo. *A budget effort is required that is far removed from the usual European budget.*
487	**avvocato** - *nm* avvokato	**lawyer** Lo stipendio di un insegnante è minore di quello di un avvocato. *The salary of a teacher is lower than that of a lawyer.*
488	**compagnia** - *nf* kompaɲɲ'ia	**company** Gli studenti spesso studiano con la musica in sottofondo e la gente al lavoro per casa di solito accende la televisione o la radio per tenersi compagnia. *Students often study with music playing in the background, and people working around the house will usually turn on the television or radio to keep them company.*
489	**ve** - *pron* ve	**you** Io ve l'avevo detto che noi avevamo molto in comune. *I told you we had a lot in common.*
490	**nave** - *nm* nave	**ship** I passeggeri dormivano nelle loro cabine quando la nave ha colpito un iceberg enorme. *The passengers were asleep in their cabins when the ship hit a huge iceberg.*
491	**gentile** - *adj* dʒentile	**kind, gentle** Le persone di questa città, in generale, sono gentili con i visitatori. *The people in this town, generally speaking, are kind to visitors.*
492	**peccare** - *verb* pekkare	**to sin** Una persona che non ha commesso un peccato semplicemente perché non ne è tentato non può essere accusata di peccare. *A person who did not commit a sin simply because he or she was not tempted to do so cannot be accused of sinning.*
493	**servizio** - *nm*	**service, report**

servittsjo

Colui che ha reso un servizio deve tacere; tocca a chi l'ha ricevuto di parlare.

The one who has rendered a service should hold his tongue; it is up to the one who has received it to speak.

494 **scena** - *nf*
ʃˈɛna

scene

La bellezza della scena andava al di là di ogni possibilità di descrizione.

The beauty of the scene was beyond description.

495 **incredibile** - *adj*
iŋkredibile

unbelievable

Fare delle immersioni alle Filippine è stato incredibile, però sono emozionata di tornare a Sydney adesso!

Diving in the Philippines was incredible, but I'm excited to be heading back to Sydney now!

496 **tv** - *nm*
tivvˈu

TV

Non c'è niente da fare; tanto vale che guardi la TV.

There's nothing to do, so I may as well watch television.

497 **specie** - *nf*
spˈɛtʃe

species, kind

Tom voleva dare qualcosa di speciale a Mary per il suo compleanno.

Tom wanted to give Mary something special for her birthday.

498 **spesso** - *adv; adj*
spesso

often; thick

Vivo vicino al mare, quindi ho spesso l'occasione di andare in spiaggia.

I live near the sea so I often get to go to the beach.

499 **entrambi** - *adj*
entrambi

both, either

Un'organizzazione ed i suoi fornitori sono interdipendenti ed un rapporto di reciproco beneficio migliora la capacità di entrambi di creare valore.

An organization and its suppliers are interdependent and a mutually beneficial relationship enhances the ability of both to create value.

500 **veloce** - *adj*
velotʃe

fast, quick

Il motto di Twitter è "Il modo più semplice e veloce per avere a portata di mano tutto ciò che ti interessa."

The motto of Twitter is "The best way to discover what's new in your world".

501 **intorno** - *adv*
intorno

around, round

Se mi comporto in modo strano intorno a voi, vuole dire che mi sento a mio agio con voi.

If I act weird around you, it means I'm comfortable with you.

502 **addossare** - *verb* addossare

to lean

Non puoi addossare a me tutta la colpa!

You cannot put the entire blame on me!

503 **parto** - *nm* parto

birth, childbirth

Nella stanza d'ospedale, l'infermiera che indossava abiti bianchi e l'ostetrica si stavano preparando per il parto.

In the hospital room, the nurse wearing white clothes and the midwife were preparing for the delivery.

504 **provato** - *adj* provato

tried

Ho provato ogni dieta che sia stata pubblicata e ancora non ho perso peso.

I have tried every diet that has ever been published and I still haven't lost weight.

505 **pagare** - *verb* pagare

to pay

Bilancio: La Fondazione e il partner strategico devono pagare tutti i costi associati con la formazione.

Budget: The Foundation and the strategic partner pay all costs associated with the training.

506 **calma** - *nf* kalma

calm

Non ho bisogno della tua risposta ora, pensaci con calma e rispondi tra qualche giorno.

I don't need your answer now, you can sleep on it and come back in a few days.

507 **tizio** - *nm* tittsjo

someone, person, guy, chap

Anna non era poi così male, e capiva bene perché il tizio che la affiancava fosse cotto di lei.

Anna wasn't bad at all, and he could well understand why the guy working with her had a crush on her.

508 **sette** - *adj; num* sˈɛtte

seven

Le coste del Golfo e quelle atlantiche sono le principali produttrici di frutti di mare e sede di sette porti importanti.

The Gulf and Atlantic coasts are major producers of seafood and home to seven major ports.

509 **segreto** - *nm* segreto

secret

Aveva un sorriso imbarazzato sul suo volto quando lei gli disse che aveva scoperto il suo segreto.

He had a sheepish grin on his face when she told him that she had found out his secret.

510 **pieno** - *adj*
pjˈɛno

full

Venuta la sera, dato che era un po' stanco, volle sedersi di fronte a una nuova caffetteria situata all'angolo di un nuovo boulevard, ancora pieno di ghiaia e già mostrante i suoi splendori incompiuti.

Evening come, since you were slightly tired, you wished to sit in front of a new Café located on the corner of a new boulevard, still full of gravel and already showing its unfinished splendors.

511 **cariare** - *verb*
karjare

to rot

Esistono diversi tipi di disturbo: la tosse, il mal di gola, il raffreddore, il dente cariato, i disturbi dell'attenzione e dell'iperattività.

There are different kinds of illnesses and disorders: a cough, a sore throat, a cold, tooth decay, attention disorders and hyperactivity.

512 **arrivederci** - *int*
arrivedertʃi

goodbye

Io non ho mai avuto l'occasione di dire arrivederci a Tom.

I never got a chance to say goodbye to Tom.

513 **ritardo** - *nm*
ritardo

delay, retardation

Mi rammarico per il ritardo nella scrittura a lei per ringraziarla per la sua ospitalità durante la mia visita nel suo paese.

I regret the delay in writing to you to thank you for your hospitality on my visit to your country.

514 **grosso** - *adj*
grˈɔsso

big, thick

Quando lo incontrai, mi ricordai improvvisamente che gli avevo prestato una grossa somma di denaro il mese prima.

When I met him, I suddenly remembered lending him a large sum of money the previous month.

515 **esercito** - *nm*
ezˈɛrtʃito

army

Tom ha abbandonato sua moglie e si è arruolato nell'esercito.

Tom abandoned his wife and joined the army.

516 **freddo** - *adj*
freddo

cold

Ogni pistola che è prodotta, ogni nave da guerra varata, ogni razzo sparato significa, nel senso finale, un furto ai danni di coloro che hanno fame e non sono nutriti, quelli che hanno freddo e non sono vestiti. Questo mondo di armi non sta spendendo solo i soldi. Sta spendendo il sudore dei suoi operai, il genio dei suoi scienziati, le speranze dei suoi figli.

Every gun that is made, every warship launched, every rocket fired signifies, in the final sense, a theft from those who hunger and are not fed, those who are cold and not clothed. This world in arms is not spending money alone. It is spending the sweat of its laborers, the genius of its scientists, the hopes of its children.

517 **vestito** - *nm*
vestito
dress, dressed
Prendere i medicinali sempre subito dopo essermi vestito: questo rituale è importante per me, per non dimenticare nulla.
Always take the medication immediately after getting dressed: This ritual is important for me so I do not forget anything.

518 **santo** - *adj; nm/f*
santo
holy; saint
Questa fortezza spagnola è stata trasformata in un bel tempio santo.
This Spanish fortress was converted into a beautiful holy shrine.

519 **libero** - *adj*
l'ibero
free
Ogni individuo ha doveri verso la comunità, nella quale soltanto è possibile il libero e pieno sviluppo della sua personalità.
Everyone has duties to the community in which alone the free and full development of his personality is possible.

520 **centro** - *nm*
tʃ'ɛntro
center
Tom vive in un appartamento di tre camere al centro di Boston.
Tom lives in a three-bedroom apartment in downtown Boston.

521 **dimenticare** - *verb*
dimentikare
to forget
Non dimenticare di fare una prova preliminare su una piccola superficie in modo da verificare che non si provochino deteriorazioni del supporto.

Do not forget to carry out a preliminary test in a small inconspicuous area to check that the substrate does not deteriorate.

522 **lettera** - *nf*
l'ettera
letter
Io sono il Prodigioso Spaghetto Volante. Non devi avere altri mostri prima di Me. (Dopo va bene, semplicemente usa le protezioni.) Il solo Mostro che merita la lettera maiuscola sono Io!

I am the Flying Spaghetti Monster. Thou shalt have no other monsters before Me. (Afterwards is OK; just use protection.) The only Monster who a capitalized letter is Me!

523 **cavallo** - *nm*
kavallo

horse

È passato un po' di tempo dall'ultima volta che sono andata a cavallo.
It's been a while since I rode a horse.

524 **grado** - *nm*
grado

degree

Gli astronomi stimano la temperatura interna di Giove a 20.000 gradi Celsius, circa tre volte superiore alla temperatura del nucleo terrestre.

Astronomers estimate Jupiter's core temperature at 20,000 degrees Celsius, approximately three times greater than the temperature of the Earth's core.

525 **chiave** - *nf*
kjave

key

Non importa cosa succede, tenga la porta chiusa a chiave e non venga fuori.

No matter what happens, keep the door locked and don't come outside.

526 **fallo** - *nm*
fallo

foul

Lui commette un fallo tattico, e dovrebbe essere felice che riceve solo un cartellino giallo.

He makes a tactical foul, and should be happy he receives only a yellow card.

527 **mare** - *nm*
mare

sea, seaside

L'azzurro è il colore del cielo, e di conseguenza anche del mare, dei laghi e dei fiumi.

Light blue is the color of the sky and, consequently, is also the color of the sea, lakes, and rivers.

528 **treno** - *nm*
trˈɛno

train

Pertanto è necessario se si sta spostando dall'aeroporto alla città con il treno di ricambio circa 30 minuti.

Therefore you would need to spare about 30 minutes if you are moving from the airport to the city by train.

529 **sinistro** - *adj*
sinistro

left

Tom si fece male al ginocchio sinistro durante l'allenamento, così John dovette giocare al posto suo.

Tom hurt his left knee during practice, so John had to play the game in his place.

530 **completamente** - *adv* kompletamente

completely

Grazie a Facebook, lo stalking non è più il bastione di pochi appassionati devoti, ma un compito altamente automatizzato abbastanza comodo anche per la casalinga impegnata.

Thanks to Facebook, stalking is no longer the bastion of a few devoted enthusiasts, but a highly automated task convenient enough even for the busy housewife.

531 **scoperto** - *adj; nm* skop'ɛrto

uncovered, open, bare; overdraft

I fisici hanno scoperto che gli atomi sono costituiti da vortici di energia che si avvitano su se stessi e vibrano costantemente.

Physicists discovered that atoms are made up of vortices of energy that are constantly spinning and vibrating.

532 **caffè** - *nm* kaff'ɛ

coffee, café

Lui non le ha regalato un ramo di rose però l'ha invitata a prendere un caffè e ha parlato con lei.

He didn't give her a bucket of roses, but he took her out for a coffee and talked to her.

533 **rumore** - *nm* rumore

noise

Ci sono state molte lamentele negli ultimi giorni circa la quantità di rumore proveniente dal tuo appartamento.

There have been a lot of complaints in the last few days about the amount of noise coming from your apartment.

534 **sesso** - *nm* s'ɛsso

sex

Se io voglio fare sesso nella mia settantina, ho il diritto all'esistenza di un luogo che mi fornisca quel piacere.

If I want to have sex in my seventies, I have the right that a place exists to provide me that pleasure.

535 **silenziare** - *verb* silentsjare

to mute

Per silenziare o riattivare i microfoni della videocamera durante una chiamata, premere il pulsante del telecomando.

To mute or unmute the camera microphones during a call, press the mute button on the LifeSize remote control.

536 **uh** - *int* u

uh

Uh... Come funziona questo?

Uh... How's that working?

537 **intenzione** - *nf*

intention

	intentsjone	Mia cara, se il cibo non è pronto alle sette, ho intenzione di andare al ristorante. *My love, if the food isn't ready by seven o'clock, I'm going to go to the restaurant.*
538	**laggiù** - *adv* laddʒu	**over there, down there** Quella donna in piedi laggiù è la donna più bella che abbia mai visto. *That woman standing over there is the most beautiful woman I've ever seen.*
539	**rapporto** - *nm* rappˈɔrto	**relationship** I rapporti fondati sul denaro terminano quando il denaro non c'è più. *Relationships built on money will end when the money runs out.*
540	**ricordare** - *verb* rikordare	**to remember** Lui ricorderebbe ancora una volta alla gente che questa non era solo la sua decisione personale, ma molte decisioni altrui. *He would remind people again that it was decided not only by him but by many others.*
541	**maestro** - *nm* maˈɛstro	**master, teacher, meastro** Il mio maestro di inglese mi ha raccomandato di leggere questi libri. *My English teacher recommended that I read these books.*
542	**terribile** - *adj* terribile	**terrible** Il vento e la pioggia si sono combinati per formare una terribile tempesta. *The wind and rain combined to make a terrible storm.*
543	**fronte** - *nf* fronte	**front, forehead** Il professore mi ha chiesto di leggere il mio compito di fronte a tutta la classe. *The teacher asked me to read my paper in front of the class.*
544	**otto** - *adj; num* ˈɔtto	**eight** Niente agisce come antidoto migliore per il romanticismo che giovani uomini e giovani donne che fanno geometria insieme alle otto ogni mattina. *Nothing acts as a better antidote for romance than young men and women doing geometry together at eight o'clock every morning.*
545	**pubblico** - *adj*	**public**

	p'ubbliko	Ho bisogno di fare una chiamata urgente. C'è un telefono pubblico qui vicino? *I need to make an urgent call. Is there a public phone near here?*
546	**cervello** - *nm* tʃerv'ɛllo	**brain** Ci sono dei giorni in cui sento che il mio cervello vuole abbandonarmi. *There are days where I feel like my brain wants to abandon me.*
547	**interessare** - *verb* interessare	**to affect** Solo perché un certo libro non interessa ai lettori, non vuol dire che la colpa sia del libro. *Just because a certain book does not interest readers does not mean that the fault lies in the book.*
548	**tranquillo** - *adj* traŋkwillo	**quiet** Io penso che sia ora di un fine settimana tranquillo. *I think it's time for a quiet weekend.*
549	**rispetto** - *nm* risp'ɛtto	**respect** La ragione per cui molti studenti di lingue non diventano fluenti è che pensano in quantità maggiore rispetto all'agire. *The reason why many language learners never become fluent is that they talk the walk more than they walk the talk.*
550	**destro** - *adj* destro	**right** Tom è ambidestro e può usare la mano destra ugualmente come la sua sinistra. *Tom is ambidextrous and can use his right hand equally as well as his left.*
551	**aiutare** - *verb* ajutare	**to help** Loro ci hanno aiutati. *They helped us.*
552	**nero** - *adj* nero	**black** Il passaporto del presidente degli Stati Uniti è nero, non blu come quello di un cittadino comune. *The U.S. president's passport is black, not blue like an average citizen's.*
553	**mille** - *adj* mille	**one thousand** L'asteroide ha ferito più di mille persone e ha rotto molte finestre

The asteroid injured over a thousand people and broke many windows.

554 **diritto** - *nm; adj; adv*
diritto
right, law; straight; straight
Tutti hanno il diritto di essere di cattivo umore una volta ogni tanto.
Everyone is entitled to be moody once in a while.

555 **accidente** - *nf*
attʃidˈɛnte
accident, fit, incident, damn
Non m'importa un accidente di quel che la gente pensa di me.
I don't care a damn what people think of me.

556 **peggio** - *adj*
pˈɛddʒo
worse
Da ieri sera ho un mal di testa palpitante, mi sento male e ora è anche peggio.
I've been having a terrible headache since last night, I feel horrible, it's the worst feeling.

557 **realtà** - *nf*
realtˈa
reality
L'amore è l'unica realtà e non è un semplice sentimento. È la verità ultima che sta alla base della creazione.
Love is the only reality and it is not a mere sentiment. It is the ultimate truth that lies at the heart of creation.

558 **consiglio** - *nm*
konsiʎʎo
advice, council, board
Io non posso dare consigli a Tom. Lui non mi ascolta mai.
I cannot advise Tom. He never listens to me.

559 **stanotte** - *adv*
stanotte
tonight
Sarà un piacere per noi tornare a distruggere stanotte uno dei nostri posti preferiti di tutto il mondo.
It will be a pleasure for us to destroy one of our favorite places in the whole world again tonight.

560 **diverso** - *adj*
divˈɛrso
different
Io ho diversi amici che parlano il francese discretamente bene.
I have several friends who speak French fairly well.

561 **dolore** - *nm*
dolore
ache, pain
Perdonami per il dolore che ho causato a te e alla tua famiglia.
I'm sorry for the pain I caused you and your family.

562 **impossibile** - *adj*
impossibile
impossible
Che Tom in anno abbia risparmiato una cifra da poter comprarsi quasi una casa, è impossibile.

There's no way Tom can save up enough money in one year to buy a house.

563 **anima** - *nf* ˈanima

soul

Sul mio letto, durante la notte, ho cercato colui che l'anima mia ama.

In my bed by night I sought him whom my soul loveth.

564 **prova** - *nf* prˈɔva

test

Spesso la gente è abbastanza scettica riguardo alle cose finché non viene fornita una prova credibile.

People are often quite skeptical about things unless given believable proof.

565 **omicidio** - *nm* omitʃidjo

murder

Tom ha dichiarato che non aveva niente a che fare con l'omicidio di Mary.

Tom claimed he had nothing to do with Mary's murder.

566 **alcune** - *pron* alkune

several, some

Ci sono alcune regole che si devono tenere in mente quando si scrive un file di preconfigurazione.

There are a few rules to keep in mind when writing a preconfiguration file.

567 **vestire** - *verb* vestire

to dress

Dopo che Marco si è riposato un po', si alza, si lava, si veste e si prepara per uscire.

After Mark has had a bit of a rest he gets up, has a wash, gets dressed and gets ready to go out.

568 **rispondere** - *verb* rispondere

to answer

The great question that has never been answered, and which I have not yet been able to answer, despite my thirty years of research into the feminine soul, is "What does a woman want?"

La grande domanda che non ha mai avuto risposta, e alla quale non sono ancora stato in grado di rispondere, malgrado i miei trent'anni di ricerca sull'anima femminile è: che cosa vuole una donna?

569 **sedere** - *verb* sedere

to sit down

Tom era seduto sulla veranda con un caffè e una sigaretta a guardare il mondo passare.

Tom sat on the porch having a coffee and a cigarette and watched the world go by.

570 **governo** - *nm; adj*

government; governmental

gov'ɛrno

Oggi è il 4 giugno — un giorno in cui il governo cinese ha ucciso centinaia di persone a una manifestazione pacifica in piazza Tienanmen.

Today is the 4th of June — a day when the Chinese government killed hundreds of people on a peaceful demonstration on the Tiananmen square.

571 **linea** - *nf*
l'inea

line, figure

L'equatore è una linea immaginaria che divide il globo terrestre in due parti uguali.

The equator is an imaginary line which divides the globe into two equal parts.

572 **normale** - *adj*
normale

normal, regular

L'apparecchio, usato in modo appropriato durante il normale funzionamento, non richiede una particolare manutenzione.
If the instrument is used properly, no special maintenance is required in normal operation.

573 **tenente** - *nm*
ten'ɛnte

lieutenant

Il tenente Dan Anderson non riusciva a collegare Linda al crimine.
Lieutenant Dan Anderson couldn't link Linda to the crime.

574 **sorpreso** - *adj*
sorprezo

surprised

Rettich non è sorpreso del fatto che Wenders abbia adottato il 3D, che finora era una prerogativa dei film mainstream.
Rettich is not surprised that Wenders has embraced 3D, which until now has been very much the preserve of mainstream movies.

575 **colonnello** - *nm*
kolonn'ɛllo

colonel

Ma quando il Colonnello Arnauld ritornò in Isvezia, l'arcivescovo di Uppsala gli ribadì ancora il contrario, pregandolo di ripassare da lui, dopo aver terminato quella sua nuova missione
But when Colonel Arnauld returned to Sweden, the Archbishop of Uppsala reiterated to him what he had said before, begging him to get back to him as soon as he completed his new mission

576 **partire** - *verb*
partire

to leave

Non restano che cinque minuti prima che il treno parta, e lei non si è ancora fatta vedere.

There are only five minutes left till the train leaves and she hasn't appeared.

577 **guardia** - *nf* gwardja
guard
Nell'antica Roma, le guardie del corpo che circondavano i ricchi e potenti, erano chiamate satelliti.
In ancient Rome, the bodyguards who surrounded the wealthy and powerful to protect them, were called satellites.

578 **chiuso** - *adj* kjuzo
closed
Proprio in quel momento la porta si aprì e una creatura con un lungo becco infilò la testa e disse. "Nessuno entri fino alla prossima settimana." E la porta si chiuse con un botto.
Just then the door opened a little way, and a creature with a long beak put its head out for a moment and said: "No admittance till the week after next!" and shut the door again with a bang.

579 **manco** - *adv* maŋko
even, not even (with negative verb form)
Alessandro, il solito divo, non si degna manco di guardarmi
Alessandro, the same star ever, doesn't even deign to gimme a look

580 **cavolo** - *nm* kˈavolo
cabbage, kale
Marinare il pane tostato con olio d'oliva, sale e pepe e distribuire anch'esso sul cavolo cappuccio.
Soak the cubes of white bread in a mixture of olive oil, salt and pepper and put them on top of the cabbage too.

581 **base** - *nf* baze
basis
Anche se l'astrologia non ha basi scientifiche, è molto popolare e sembra che molte persone ci credano.
Although astrology has no scientific basis, it's very popular and it seems that many people believe in it.

582 **san** - *adj* san
St., saint
I contemporanei di San Francesco riconobbero in lui il Vangelo realizzato pienamente, nel suo anelare di seguire il Cristo.
St. Francis' contemporaries recognized in him the Gospel fully restored, when he yearned to follow Christ

583 **valere** - *verb* valere
to be worth
Un libro che non vale la pena leggere, non vale neanche la pena di essere comprato.
A book not worth reading is not worth buying in the first place.

584 **duro** - *adj*
duro

hard
Un esame più attento rivelò che il teschio era stato schiacciato da qualche duro colpo.
Closer examination revealed that the skull had been crushed by some heavy blow.

585 **chiamata** - *nf*
kjamata

(telephone) call
Per avviare la conferenza quando sono in linea due o più chiamanti, premere e tenere premuto il pulsante Chiamata per 3 secondi.
Begin conferencing while two or more callers are on the line by pressing and holding the Call button for 3 seconds.

586 **ordinare** - *verb*
ordinare

to order
Tom è entrato nel pub e ha ordinato una pinta di birra.
Tom walked into the pub and ordered a pint of beer.

587 **riguardo** - *nm*
rigwardo

regard, respect
Essi hanno eguali diritti riguardo al matrimonio, durante il matrimonio e all'atto del suo scioglimento.
They are entitled to equal rights in the respect of marriage, during marriage and at its dissolution.

588 **luogo** - *nm*
lwogo

place
Le opere d'arte create da Irma Paulon contengono la percezione di meraviglia assoluta, di silenzi e suoni, di forme e luoghi che si traducono in forme e materiali diversi.
The art created by Irma Paulon contains the perception of absolute wonder, silences and sounds, forms and places that are translated into various shapes using various materials

589 **personale** - *adj*
personale

staff
Inoltre, il personale impiegato dalle imprese sociali rientra spesso nelle categorie svantaggiate dal mercato del lavoro
Moreover, people they employ are often disadvantaged by the labour market

590 **incontro** - *nm*
iŋkontro

meeting, encounter
Il Competence Center serve come luogo di incontro tra problemi e soluzioni.
The Competence Center serves as a meeting place of problems and solutions.

591 **vincere** - *verb*
vintʃere

to win
Se un giorno dovessi vincere un milione di euro, probabilmente mi trasferirei in un altro stato portando con me mia madre.

If I won a million euros, I'd probably move to another country with my mother.

592 **interessante** - *adj*
interessante

interesting
La posizione panoramica e I dintorni rendono il castello interessante da visitare anche solo esternamente.
The panoramic position and the surroundings make the visit to the castle interesting even from outside only.

593 **sergente** - *nm*
serdʒente

sergeant
Il sergente Okada era in fin di vita, per le ustioni su tutto il corpo, ma respirava ancora.
Sergeant Okada was on the brink of death, suffering burns all over his body, but still breathing.

594 **altrimenti** - *adv; conj*
altrimenti

otherwise
Dobbiamo lasciare l'hotel prima delle dieci, altrimenti perdiamo il treno per Miami.
We must leave the hotel before 10 a.m., otherwise we will miss the train for Miami.

595 **posizione** - *nf*
pozittsjone

position
Ho imparato la posizione del loto al corso di yoga.
I learned the lotus position in yoga class.

596 **caldo** - *adj; nm*
kaldo

hot; heat
I muscoli di Tom erano affaticati e lui voleva andare a casa ed immergersi in un bagno caldo per un po'.
Tom's muscles were tired and he wanted to get home and soak in a hot bath for a while.

597 **nonno** - *nm*
nonno

grandfather
Il nonno è andato in pensione perché sta diventando vecchio.
Grandfather has retired because he is getting old.

598 **immaginare** - *verb*
immadʒinare

to imagine
Da quello che hai scritto, la sua reazione non è giustificata in nessuna maniera e immagino che possa renderti la vita impossibile.
For what you have written, your reaction is not justified in any manner, and I imagine it can make your life impossible.

599 **inferno** - *nm*
inferno

hell
Pregate, pregate molto, e fate sacrifici per i peccatori; molte anime vanno all'inferno, perché non c'è chi si sacrifichi e preghi per loro.

Pray, pray very much, and make sacrifices for sinners; for many souls go to hell, because there are none to sacrifice themselves and to pray for them.

600 **nonna** - *nf* — nonna

grandmother

Compro dei fiori perché andrò a trovare mia nonna questa sera.

I buy the flowers because I will pay visit to my grandmother this evening.

601 **dolce** - *adj; nm* — doltʃe

sweet, fresh; sweet, dessert

Quando si tratta di dolci, non riesco proprio a controllarmi.

When it comes to sweets, I just can't control myself.

602 **notizia** - *nf* — notittsja

news

I genitori di John sembravano sollevati alla notizia che il suo aereo era in orario.

John's parents seemed relieved to hear that his plane was on time.

603 **lunare** - *adj* — lunare

lunar, moon

Questo permette la determinazione della fase lunare corrente in relazione a qualsiasi località nel mondo.

This permits the determination of the current moon phase in relation to any location in the world.

604 **semplicemente** - *adv* — semplitʃemente

simply

Tutti erano semplicemente stupiti che lei fosse stata in grado di rimanere incinta a 48 anni.

Everyone was just flabbergasted that she was able to get pregnant at 48.

605 **medico** - *adj* — mediko

(medical) doctor

Il mio desiderio di diventare un medico è nato dall'esigenza di badare al mio fratello malato.

My desire to become a doctor grew out of looking after my sickly brother.

606 **esistere** - *verb* — ezistere

to exist

Quando ero un ragazzino, pensavo che se io fossi morto il mondo sarebbe solo scomparso. Che delusione infantile! Semplicemente non potevo accettare che il mondo avrebbe potuto continuare ad esistere senza di me.

When I was a kid, I thought that if I died the world would just disappear. What a childish delusion! I just couldn't accept that the world could continue to exist without me.

607 **esempio** - *nm*

example

ezempjo

In questo paese c'è solo qualche esempio del fatto che l'ideologia e la religione sono utili nella formazione del carattere delle persone.

In this country there are only few examples that ideology and religion are helpful in character building for people.

608 **zona** - *nf*
dzona

area

La casa rappresenta una divisione tra due zone opposte di Londra.

The house represents a division between two opposite zones of London.

609 **proposito** - *nm*
propozito

purpose, intention

Si è dato il proposito di scrivere sul suo diario ogni giorno.

He made a resolution to write in his diary every day.

610 **unire** - *verb*
unire

to unite

Io e i miei amici andiamo fuori stasera. Ti vorresti unire a noi?

My friends and I are hanging out tonight. Would you like to join us?

611 **inglese** - *adj; nmf*
inʎʎeze

English; English(wo)man

La Summer School realizzata in lingua inglese in occasione del 50° Anniversario dei Trattati di Roma.

The Summer School organized in English on the occasion of the 50th Anniversary of the Treaties of Rome.

612 **errore** - *nm*
errore

error

Ho dovuto impedire a Tom di commettere l'errore più grande della sua vita.

I had to stop Tom from making the biggest mistake in his life.

613 **scappare** - *verb*
skappare

to escape

Un incendio si può propagare molto più velocemente di quanto uno possa scappare.

A fire can spread faster than you can run.

614 **attraverso** - *adv; prep*
attraverso

through, across

La psicologia, che studia la mente umana e il comportamento umano, costruisce la conoscenza attraverso l'osservazione e la sperimentazione

Psychology, which studies the human mind and human behavior, builds knowledge by observation and experiments.

615 **programma** - *nf*

program

	programma	Se si sviluppa un nuovo programma e lo si vuole rendere della maggiore utilità possibile per il pubblico, la cosa migliore da fare è rendere tale programma libero, cosicché ciascuno possa ridistribuirlo e modificarlo sotto questi termini. *If you develop a new program, and you want it to be of the greatest possible use to the public, the best way to achieve this is to make it free software which everyone can redistribute and change under these terms.*
616	**perciò** - *conj; adv* pertʃˈɔ	**therefore; accordingly** Questo quadriennio costituirà, perciò, un itinerario fatto di "memoria", di riflessione e di preghiera *This quadrennium will constitute, moreover, a journey of "memory," of reflection, and of prayer*
617	**chiudere** - *verb* kjudere	**to close** Non dimenticate di chiudere la cerniera della tenda una volta entrate. *Don't forget to close the fly of the tent after you enter.*
618	**gamba** - *nf* gamba	**leg** Riposiamoci qui per un po'. Le mie gambe sono stanche e non posso proseguire oltre. *Let's take a short rest here. My legs are tired and I can't walk any more.*
619	**salute** - *nf; int* salute	**health; cheers, bless you** Dal punto di vista della salute, Tokyo non è un posto così buono in cui vivere. *From the viewpoint of health, Tokyo is not such a good place to live.*
620	**birra** - *nf* birra	**beer** Ho bevuto circa 20 birre, ma il poliziotto non si è accorto che ero ubriaco e mi ha lasciato andare. *I drank about 20 beers but the cop couldn't tell I was drunk and let me go.*
621	**comandante** - *nm* komandante	**commander** Loro avevano qualche dubbio sul loro comandante. *They had some doubts about their commander.*
622	**assassino** - *nm/f* assassino	**killer, murderer** Tom trovò le prove di cui avevamo bisogno per imprigionare l'assassino di Mary. *Tom found the evidence we needed to convict Mary's killer.*

623 **simile** - *adj*
simile

similar, alike

Per quanto riguarda la scrittura moderna, è raramente gratificante tradurla, anche se potrebbe essere facile. La traduzione è molto simile al copiare i quadri.

As far as modern writing is concerned, it is rarely rewarding to translate it, although it might be easy. Translation is very much similar to copying paintings.

624 **possibilità** - *nf*
possibilit'a

possibility

Non vi è alcuna possibilità che quello che dice può avere alcuna verità in esso.

There is no possibility that what he says may have any truth in it.

625 **rimanere** - *verb*
rimanere

to stay

Sono venuto in Giappone quattro anni fa con l'intenzione di rimanere per un anno.

I came to Japan four years ago intending to stay for one year.

626 **cacciare** - *verb*
kattʃare

to hunt, throw out

I miei genitori mi hanno cacciata di casa quando avevo 16 anni.

My parents threw me out of the house when I was 16.

627 **poliziotto** - *nm*
polittsjotto

policeman

L'Inghilterra è un paese in cui i poliziotti non hanno armi.

England is a land where the policemen carry no revolvers.

628 **questione** - *nf*
kwestjone

question

È il luogo dove non c'è persona in questione, e non si deve dire di abuso.

It is the place where there is no person in question, and you shouldn't say abuse.

629 **carta** - *nf*
karta

paper, card, map

Tom non riusciva a capire quello che era scritto sul pezzo di carta.

Tom couldn't make out what was written on the piece of paper.

630 **controllare** - *verb*
kontrollare

to check

Non riesco a controllare la mia e-mail. Il server non funziona.

I can't check my mail. The server is down.

631 **spettacolo** - *nm*
spettakolo

show, spectacle, performance

Lo spettacolo era così noioso che io e Ann ci siamo addormentati.

The show was so boring that Ann and I fell asleep.

632 **naturalmente** - *adv* naturalmente | **naturally**
Il libro più importante per imparare una lingua è, naturalmente, un dizionario.
The most important book to learn a foreign language is, naturally, a dictionary.

633 **scrivere** - *verb* skrivere | **to write**
L'ascolto di una lingua parlata è molto diverso dal leggere o scrivere la stessa lingua.
Listening to a language being spoken is very different from reading or writing the same language.

634 **contento** - *adj* kontento | **happy**
Sono contento che ci siamo lasciati alle nostre spalle tutto questo.
I'm glad we put all that behind us.

635 **volare** - *verb* volare | **to fly**
Abbiamo imparato a volare come gli uccelli, a nuotare come i pesci, ma abbiamo dimenticato come vivere da esseri umani.
We learned to fly like birds and swim like fishes, but we forgot how to live like humans.

636 **promettere** - *verb* promettere | **to promise**
Tom mi ha fatto promettere che non l'avrei detto a Mary.
Tom made me promise not to tell Mary.

637 **insomma** - *adv* insomma | **in short**
Non ho mangiato niente in tutto il giorno, insomma ho una fame da lupi.
I didn't eat anything all day, in short, I'm starving.

638 **chiesa** - *nf* kjeza | **church**
Il rapporto tra la Chiesa cattolica e gli ebrei non è sempre stato, nella storia, felice o facile.
The history of the relationship between the Catholic Church and the Jews was not always a happy or an easy one.

639 **oppure** - *conj* oppure | **or, or else**
Potresti essere forzato a combattere, sia che tu lo voglia oppure no.
You may be forced to fight, whether you want to or not.

640 **carne** - *nf* karne | **meat**
Non mangio né carne, né pesce, niente frutti di mare, né brodo di origine animale.

I do not eat meat, fish, shellfish, poultry or broth.

641 **pranzo** - *nm* prantso — **lunch**

Io ho mangiato della pizza per pranzo, per cui non voglio della pizza per cena.

I had pizza for lunch, so I don't want pizza for dinner.

642 **studio** - *nm* studjo — **office, study**

Se ha bisogno di un po' più di pratica, il nostro studio ha bisogno di una bella ripulita!

If you need some more practice, our study needs a good clean out!

643 **entro** - *prep* entro — **within, by**

tali eventi saranno tempestivamente notificati per iscritto entro 7 giorni dall'inizio dell'evento stesso

the occurrence of the force majeure is to be promptly notified in writing within 7 days from the beginning of the force majeure

644 **appuntamento** - *nm* appuntamento — **appointment**

Mi fanno male i denti. Devo prendere un appuntamento col mio dentista.

My teeth ache. I need to make an appointment with my dentist.

645 **pena** - *nf* pena — **penalty**

In alcuni paesi, la pena per il tradimento può essere il carcere a vita.

In some countries, the punishment for treason can be life in prison.

646 **bianco** - *adj* bjaŋko — **white**

Quando le persone sono venute fuori dalla fabbrica alla sera le loro facce sembravano bianche e malate.

When people came out of the factory in the evening, their faces looked white and ill.

647 **missione** - *nf* missjone — **mission**

Tom è stato forzato ad abbandonare la missione.

Tom was forced to abandon the mission.

648 **uso** - *nf* uzo — **use, usage**

Il museo racconta la scienza e la tecnologia attraverso l'uso di impostazioni interattive.

The museum focuses on science and technology by using interactive settings.

649 **fermare** - *verb* — **to stop**

fermare — Loro hanno iniziato a bere della vodka. E non sono sicuro su quando si sono fermati.

They started drinking vodka. And I'm not sure when they stopped.

650 **calmare** - *verb* — **to calm**

kalmare — Validare i sentimenti di un cliente arrabbiato è un modo efficace di calmare la situazione.

Validating an angry client's feelings is an effective way of defusing the situation.

651 **forma** - *nf* — **form**

forma — La più alta forma di ignoranza è respingere qualcosa di cui non si sa nulla.

The highest form of ignorance is to reject something you know nothing about.

652 **compleanno** - *nm* — **birthday**

kompleanno — Tom comprò una macchina fotografica da dare a Mary per il suo compleanno.

Tom bought a camera to give to Mary on her birthday.

653 **palla** - *nf* — **ball**

palla — Quando il portiere ha toccato la palla, l'arbitro ha assegnato un calcio d'angolo all'altra squadra.

When the goalkeeper touched the ball, the referee awarded the other team a corner kick.

654 **barca** - *nf* — **boat**

barka — Io voglio una barca che mi porterà molto lontano da qui.

I want a boat that will take me far away from here.

655 **nord** - *nm* — **north**

nord — Il Regno Unito è composto da Inghilterra, Scozia, Galles e Irlanda del Nord.

The United Kingdom is comprised of England, Scotland, Wales, and Northern Ireland.

656 **leggero** - *adj* — **light**

leddʒero — Lui è un po' leggero per essere un lottatore di sumo.

He is a little light for a sumo wrestler.

657 **cioè** - *adv* — **i.e., that is, namely**

tʃoˈɛ — Incontrai tuo padre la settimana scorsa cioè l'ultima settimana di giugno.

I met your father last week, so in the last week of June.

658 **braccio** - *nm* — **arm**

	brattʃo	Il ragazzino si sentiva al sicuro tra le braccia di suo padre. *The little boy felt secure in his father's arms.*
659	**informazione** - *nf* informattsjone	**information** Quando si perde una lingua si perdono informazioni sulla cultura, società e storia. *When we lose a language we lose information about culture, society and history.*
660	**certamente** - *adv* tʃertamente	**of course** I computer stanno certamente giocando un ruolo importante nella nostra vita, che ci piaccia o no. *Computers are certainly playing an important role in our life, whether we like it or not.*
661	**direttore** - *nm* direttore	**director, (senior) manager** Qual è la marca e il colore dell'auto del direttore? *What brand and what color is the director's car?*
662	**canzone** - *nf* kantsone	**song** Continuo a sentire la canzone da quello spot più e più volte nella mia testa. *I keep hearing the song from that commercial over and over in my head.*
663	**maledizione** - *nf; int* maledittsjone	**curse; damn** La famiglia sembrava essere sotto l'effetto di una maledizione. *The family seemed to be under a curse.*
664	**scarpa** - *nf* skarpa	**shoe** Le scarpe erano fatte di un qualche materiale morbido che sembrava pelle. *The shoes were made of some soft stuff that looked like leather.*
665	**colpire** - *verb* kolpire	**to hit** La boxe è stata definita come l'arte di colpire senza essere colpiti. *Boxing has been defined as the art of hitting without being hit.*
666	**schifo** - *nm* skifo	**disgust** E poi, nel bel mezzo di un magnifico pasto, ha iniziato a ruttare! Che schifo! *And then, in the middle of a magnificent meal, he started belching! How disgusting!*
667	**necessario** - *adj*	**necessary**

	netʃessarjo	Perché non mi hai detto che c'era? Era necessario che io lo sapessi il prima possibile! *Why didn't you tell me he was here? I had to know as soon as possible!*
668	**umano** - *adj* umano	**human** Il senso dell'olfatto di un cane è molto più acuto di quello di un essere umano. *A dog's sense of smell is much keener than a human's.*
669	**rosso** - *adj* r'ɔsso	**red** A Tom non piaceva il vino rosso, però ora lo beve quasi ogni giorno. *Tom didn't use to like red wine, but now he drinks it almost every day.*
670	**soldato** - *nm* soldato	**soldier** La presidenza francese si è inoltre mobilitata per la lotta contro il dramma dei bambini soldato e della pena di morte *The French Presidency has also continued to mobilise efforts against the scourge of child soldiers and the death penalty.*
671	**don** - *nm* don	**Don (title of respect/religious title)** i galeotti liberati da don Chisciotte sono più forti di lui e lo malmenano brutalmente. *the galley-slaves freed by Don Quixote are stronger than him and beat him up mercilessly.*
672	**correre** - *verb* korrere	**to run** In estate mi piace andare a correre all'aperto in campagna. *In summer, I like to go out for a run in the countryside.*
673	**regalo** - *nm* regalo	**gift, present** Il tuo regalo è stato come la scoperta di un'oasi nel mezzo di un deserto. *Your gift was like discovery of an oasis in the midst of a desert.*
674	**rubato** - *adj* rubato	**stolen** È possibile utilizzare questo sistema per scattare l'allarme di un'auto rubata. *You can use this system to set off the alarm of a stolen car.*
675	**carino** - *adj* karino	**cute, nice, pretty** Tu non hai idea di quanto siano carine le ragazze da queste parti! *You have no idea how pretty the girls are around here!*
676	**dunque** - *adv*	**therefore**

duŋkwe — Tutte le cose dunque che voi volete che gli uomini vi facciano, fatele anche voi a loro.
So in everything, do to others what you would have them do to you.

677 **bar** - *nm* — **bar, caffé**
bar — Tom ha gestito un piccolo bar vicino a Boston per un po' di anni.
Tom managed a small bar near Boston for quite a few years

678 **figliolo** - *nm* — **son, boy (affectuos or patronizing)**
fiʎʎolo — Può ben essere fiero del suo brillante figliolo.
He may well be proud of his bright son.

679 **classe** - *nf* — **class, classroom**
klasse — Tom è l'unico studente della nostra classe che sa parlare in francese.
Tom is the only student in our class that can speak French.

680 **stronzata** - *nf* — **bullshit**
strontsata — Con tutto il rispetto, penso che sia una stronzata.
With all due respect, I think it's bullshit.

681 **scherzare** - *verb* — **to joke**
skertsare — La guardia pensò che stessero scherzando finché non vide le loro pistole.
The guard thought they were joking until he saw their guns.

682 **vaffanculo** - *int* — **fuck off**
vaffaŋkulo — Quando stavo quindi per sussurrare un vaffanculo vero e proprio mi sono bloccato, pentito della mia antipatica irritazione.
I held my tongue, regretting my disagreeable irritation.

683 **benvenuto** - *adj; int; nm* — **welcome**
benvenuto — Lui si è alzato dalla sedia per darmi il benvenuto.
He rose from his chair to welcome me.

684 **banca** - *nf* — **bank**
baŋka — Tu pensi che i tuoi soldi siano al sicuro in una banca?
Do you think your money is safe in a bank?

685 **negozio** - *nm* — **shop, store**
negottsjo — Tom non ha comprato nulla in quel negozio perché pensava che i prezzi fossero troppo alti.
Tom didn't buy anything at that store because he thought the prices were too high.

686 **sud** - *nm* — **south**

sud

Quegli uccelli costruiscono il loro nido d'estate e volano verso sud d'inverno.

Those birds build their nests in the summer and fly to the south in the winter.

687 **spalla** - *nf*
spalla

shoulder

Mary è molto perfida e volta le spalle a Tom per giorni dopo il minimo disaccordo tra di loro.

Mary is very spiteful and gives Tom the cold shoulder for days after the slightest disagreement between them.

688 **mostro** - *nm*
mostro

monster

Il nome Mozilla venne creato adattando il nome Godzilla, il mostro che scatenava disordini nei film horror giapponesi

The Mozilla name came from adapting the name Godzilla, the monster that caused mayhem in Japanese horror films

689 **intendere** - *verb*
intendere

to hear, mean, intend

Brian è infuriato perché è evidente che Chris non intende restituire il denaro.

Brian is mad because Chris obviously does not intend to return the money.

690 **triste** - *adj*
triste

sad

Mi sento triste quando penso a tutta la gente che muore nelle guerre.

I feel sad when I think about all the people who die in wars.

691 **buonasera** - *int*
bwonazera

good evening

Bene, buonasera, e gente, questa sera vedremo un grande spettacolo!

Well, good evening, and boy, are you folks in for a great night of top-class sporting entertainment!

692 **attacco** - *nm*
attakko

attack

Zelda, tutti sono sotto attacco da parte delle forze del male degli uccelli! Io vado a Gamelon per attaccare. Se non si hanno notizie da parte mia in un mese, manda Link.

Zelda, everyone is under attack by the evil forces of the birds! I'm going to Gamelon to attack. If you don't hear from me in a month, send Link.

693 **toccare** - *verb*
tokkare

to touch

Tom si è piegato in avanti e si è toccato le dita dei piedi.

Tom leaned forward and touched his toes.

694 **muovere** - *verb*

to move

mwovere | Londra è una città così grande che i visitatori devono usare bus e metropolitana per muoversi.

London is such a large city that visitors must use buses and the underground railway to get about.

695 **affatto** - *adv* — **at all, quite**
affatto
Tom non era affatto soddisfatto del modo in cui la sua casa era stata pitturata.

Tom wasn't at all satisfied with the way his house had been painted.

696 **salare** - *verb* — **to salt**
salare
Salare e pepare i filetti di merluzzo, quindi versare il succo 1 di limone.

Season the cod fillets with salt and pepper and drizzle with 1 lemon juice.

697 **comprare** - *verb* — **to buy**
komprare
Lui ha deciso di non comprare la casa, in primo luogo perché era troppo costosa, e in secondo luogo perché era troppo lontana dal suo ufficio.

He decided not to buy the house, because in the first place it was too expensive, and in the second place it was too far from his office.

698 **qualcun** - *pron* — **meter; tape measure**
kwalkun
Se i genitori non riescono a gestirlo, allora deve essere qualcun altro a farlo, purtroppo.

If the parents can not handle that, then it must be someone else to do, unfortunately.

699 **metro(politana)** - *nm; (nf)* — **meter; tape measure; (underground, metro)**

metropolitana)
Ci si aspetta che si abbatta uno tsunami fino a 10 metri di altezza.
It is expected that the tsunami surge will be ten meters or less.

700 **scegliere** - *verb* — **to choose**
ʃeʎʎere
È un compito difficile scegliere tra cos'è "bene" o "male", ma bisogna farlo.

It is a difficult task, choosing what is "right" or "wrong", but you have to do it.

701 **professore** - *nm* — **teacher, professor**
professore
Gli studenti hanno riso sotto i baffi quando hanno visto che il professore si era messo il maglione al contrario.

The students laughed under their breath when they saw that the teacher had put on his sweater backwards.

702 **sbrigare** - *verb* | **to hurry up**
zbrigare
Faresti meglio a sbrigarti se vuoi tornare a casa prima che faccia buio.
You'd better hurry up if you want to get home before dark.

703 **adorare** - *verb* | **to worship, adore, love**
adorare
Adoro la cucina cinese, soprattutto i ravioli e il riso.
I love Chinese food, especially pot stickers and rice.

704 **comando** - *nm* | **command**
komando
Quando bisogna trasmettere più comandi, aspettare prima la risposta al primo comando da quest'unità e poi mandare un comando successivo.
If multiple commands are transmitted, be sure to wait for the response for the first command to come from this unit before sending the next command.

705 **pericoloso** - *adj* | **dangerous**
perikolozo
Usare l'inglese per comunicare tra giapponesi e cinesi non è solo ridicolo e inefficace, ma può rivelarsi molto pericoloso.
Using English to communicate between Japanese and Chinese is not only ridiculous and ineffective but can prove very hazardous.

706 **dannazione** - *nf* | **damn**
dannattsjone
"Dannazione! Ho dimenticato l'ombrello sul treno." "Sbadato!"
"Damn it! I forget my umbrella on the train." "Scatterbrain!"

707 **scommettere** - *verb* | **to bet**
skommettere
Tom ha scommesso cinquanta dollari che riusciva a mangiare più hot dog di me.
Tom bet me fifty dollars that he could eat more hot dogs than I could.

708 **occasione** - *nf* | **opportunity**
okkazjone
Bevo quando ho un'occasione per farlo e qualche volta anche quando non ce l'ho.
I drink when I have an occasion, and sometimes when I have no occasion.

709 **metà** - *nf* | **half**
metˈa
Circa la metà delle distese di ghiaccio del Canada sono scomparse negli ultimi sei anni.

About half of Canada's ice shelves have disappeared in the last six years.

710 **spazio** - *nm*
spattsjo

space
Siamo fatti della materia di cui son fatti i sogni; e nello spazio e nel tempo d'un sogno è racchiusa la nostra breve vita.
We are such stuff as dreams are made on, and our little life is rounded with a sleep.

711 **regola** - *nf*
regola

rule
Mi sono messo la regola di studiare inglese per tre ore ogni giorno.
I make it a rule to study English for 3 hours every day.

712 **contatto** - *nm*
kontatto

contact
Si assicuri di mettersi in contatto con me, se c'è qualcosa che posso fare per lei.
Be sure to get in touch with me, if there is anything I can do for you.

713 **spirito** - *nm*
spirito

spirit
Non sono un artista. Non ho mai avuto lo spirito per queste cose.
I am not an artist. I never had the knack for it.

714 **povero** - *adj; nm*
povero

poor; the poor
La democrazia esiste laddove non c'è nessuno così ricco da comprare un altro e nessuno così povero da vendersi.
Democracy exists where there is nobody so rich to buy another and nobody so poor to be supplied.

715 **appartamento** - *nm*
appartamento

flat, apartment
Lui era molto in ritardo con il suo affitto. Come risultato, è stato sfrattato dal suo appartamento.
He was way behind on his rent. As a result, he was evicted from his apartment.

716 **pelle** - *nf*
pelle

skin
Kate ha la pelle chiara, a differenza degli altri membri della sua famiglia.
Kate has white skin, unlike the others in her family.

717 **cucina** - *nf*
kutʃina

kitchen
Tom è andato in cucina e si è versato una tazza di caffè.
Tom went into the kitchen and poured himself a cup of coffee.

718 **fottere** - *verb*

to fuck

	fottere	Ho intenzione di fumare e me ne fotto di quello che dici. *I will smoke and I don't give a fuck about what you say.*
719	**combattere** - *verb* kombattere	**to fight** Ogni persona deve dare un mano a combattere il problema della povertà. *Each person must give a hand to combat the problem of poverty.*
720	**pomeriggio** - *nm* pomeriddʒo	**afternoon** Il primo parte alle cinque e mezza del pomeriggio e arriva alle otto e venticinque di sera. *The first one leaves at 17.30 and arrives at 20.25.*
721	**pianeta** - *nf* pjaneta	**planet** Loro sono entrambi riusciti a trovare il problema più grave che abbia mai affrontato il nostro pianeta. *They have both failed to find the most serious problem that has ever faced our planet.*
722	**ehm** - *int* em	**hum** Bravi, col vostro ineccepibile comportamento avete meritato la Medaglia Salvagente, a forma di... ehm... Ciambella *Good, with your flawless behavior you deserve the Lifesaving Medal, shaped like a – well, like a Lifesaver.*
723	**sposare** - *verb* spozare	**to marry** Dopo molti anni di sforzi per trovare l'uomo dei suoi sogni, Barbara ha abbandonato ogni speranza ed ha deciso di sposare Luciano. *After many years trying to get the man of her dreams, Barbara decided to give up all hope and to accept marrying Lucian.*
724	**ovunque** - *adv* ovuŋkwe	**everywhere, whereever** Carol ha fiuto per trovare ovunque la migliore cucina Thailandese della zona. *Carol has a nose for the best Thai cooking anywhere in town.*
725	**amare** - *verb* amare	**to love** Non riesco a fare a meno di amare il mio paese. *I can't help loving my country.*
726	**rompere** - *verb* rompere	**to break** Tra i 2 alberi appeso un grande ramo quasi a terra e la creazione di tenda Sher difficile, soprattutto perché è stato molto burrascoso e che avevano paura che la succursale potrebbe rompere.

Between the 2 trees hung up a large branch nearly to the ground and setting up the tent sher difficult, especially since it was very stormy and we were afraid that the branch might break

727 **tale** - *adv; pron; art* **such; such; a, an**
tale
Come tale è il caso, mi dispiace di non potere accettare il suo gentile invito.
As such is the case, I am sorry I can't accept your kind invitation.

728 **fiume** - *nm* **river**
fjume
Bill si è tuffato nel fiume per salvare il bambino che stava annegando.
Bill dived into the river to save the drowning child.

729 **nemico** - *adj; nm* **enemy**
nemiko
La posizione occupata dal nemico è così importante che lotteranno fino alla fine per occuparla.
The position held by the enemy is so important they will fight to the bitter end to hold it.

730 **ovviamente** - *adv* **obviously**
ovvjamente
Ovviamente quando non riesco a dormire la sera, il ticchettio dell'orologio mi mette l'ansia.
It's only when I can't sleep at night that the ticking of the clock becomes loud enough to bother me.

731 **armare** - *verb* **to arm**
armare
Hanno chiesto il permesso di armare le loro barche.
They asked for permission to arm their ships.

732 **lingua** - *nf* **tongue, language**
liŋgwa
La Conferenza prende atto che la Svezia e la Finlandia si sono prefisse di preservare e sviluppare i mezzi di sussistenza, la lingua, la cultura e lo stile di vita della popolazione Sami.
The Conference notes that Sweden and Finland are committed to preserving and developing the means of livelihood, language, culture and way of life of the Sami people

733 **borsa** - *nf* **bag**
borsa
Hanno rubato la borsa a mia sorella mentre tornava a casa la scorsa notte.
My sister was robbed of her bag on her way home last night.

734 **vino** - *nm* **wine**

vino | Data l'importanza del vino in questa regione, l'amministrazione del Land ha alcuni anni fa deciso di supportare un coordinamento delle ben otto aree vinicole distinte nella regione, ed ha favorito la sua stretta collaborazione con la Società di promozione regionale di proprietà del Land, ove il coordinamento delle strade del vino è diventato l'ufficio di gestione e promozione dei prodotti enoturistici.
In view of the importance of wine in this region, the Land administration decided some years ago to offer its support to a consortium of no less than eight distinct wine-producing areas in the region, and it favoured its close collaboration with the regional promotion society owned by the Land, where coordination of the wine routes has become manifest in the management and promotion office for wine and tourist products.

735 **destino** - *nm* | **destiny**
destino | Io credo nel destino, ma so anche che il destino può essere cambiato.
I believe in fate, but I also know that fate can be changed.

736 **sicuramente** - *adv* | **certainly**
sikuramente | Sicuramente il lavoro del Sinodo avrà un'ampia scia nella vita delle Chiese locali.
The work of the Synod may definitely have an ample wake in the life of the local Churches.

737 **piangere** - *verb* | **to cry**
pjandʒere | Mi scusi, signora, mi vergogno di piangere così di fronte a lei, ma non riesco a trattenere le lacrime.
Pardon me, madam, I'm ashamed to be crying like this in front of you, but I can't hold my tears.

738 **reale** - *adj* | **real, actual**
reale | Io sembro più grande in televisione di quanto non sia nella vita reale.
I look bigger on television than I do in real life.

739 **ballare** - *verb* | **to dance**
ballare | Sono l'unico brasiliano a non sapere il portoghese e a non saper ballare la samba.
I'm the only Brazilian who can't speak Portuguese and dance samba.

740 **urlo** - *nm* | **yell, cry, shout**

	urlo	Ma con un urlo violento riuscì a sottrarsi all'incanto di quello sguardo e corse via in paese più veloce che poté. *But with a wild cry, he tore himself away from those enchanted eyes and raced back to Noville.*
741	**nascere** - *verb* naʃʃere	**to be born** Non è possibile sviluppare il senso dell'umorismo; bisogna nascerci per averlo. *It's not possible to develop a sense of humour; you've got to be born with one.*
742	**alzare** - *verb* altsare	**to raise** Queste tasse hanno fatto alzare i prezzi di tutti i beni. *These taxes raised the prices on all goods.*
743	**aperto** - *adj* aperto	**open** Il nostro negozio è aperto ventiquattr'ore su ventiquattro e sette giorni su sette. *Our store is open 24/7.*
744	**ritorno** - *nm* ritorno	**return** Ci vogliono otto ore per un volo da Zurigo a Boston, ma solo sei per il ritorno. *It takes eight hours to fly from Zurich to Boston, but only six for the return trip.*
745	**nove** - *adj; num* nˈɔve	**nine** Il mio treno è partito da Kyoto alle sei ed è arrivato a Tokyo alle nove. *My train left Kyoto at six, and arrived in Tokyo at nine.*
746	**salvare** - *verb* salvare	**to save** Non c'è niente che possiamo fare per salvare Tom a questo punto. Tutto ciò che possiamo fare è pregare. *There's nothing we can do to save Tom at this point. All we can do is pray.*
747	**principe** - *nm* printʃipe	**prince** Il Principe è il capo dello Stato, ed è dotato di ampi diritti . *The Head of State is the Prince, who has extensive rights.*
748	**lista** - *nf* lista	**list** Alla fine, la coscienziosa ragazza lasciò perdere i suoi compiti di inglese, e cominciò a ripassare la sua lista di parole in Ainu. *At the end, the conscientious girl gave up with her English homework, and started to revise her list of Ainu words.*
749	**intero** - *adj; nm*	**entire, full, whole; whole**

intero

Sono successe tante cose. È come se il mondo intero si sia capovolto a testa in giù.

So much has happened. It's as if the whole world is flipped upside down.

750 **popolo** - *nm*
popolo

people

Il popolo di Medjugorje (ormai 20 milioni di pellegrini) non vuole privilegi, ma vuole gli stessi diritti degli altri fedeli.

The people of Medjugorje (now 20 million pilgrims) do not want any privileges.

751 **passaggio** - *nm*
passaddʒo

passage

Non posso dare un passaggio a Taninna a scuola in macchina. La mia macchina è rotta.

I cannot drive Taninna to school. My car is broken down.

752 **finestra** - *nf*
finestra

window

Tom aprì la finestra anche se sua madre gli disse di non farlo.

Tom opened the window even though his mother told him not to.

753 **ricerca** - *nf*
ritʃerka

search, research

Più del 90 % delle visite ad una pagina web provengono da motori di ricerca.

More than 90 percent of visits to a web page are from search engines.

754 **differenza** - *nf*
differentsa

difference

Considero i testimoni di Geova che bussano sempre alla mia porta non essere differenti dai fanatici religiosi che provano a impormi le loro credenze.

I consider the Jehovah's witnesses who knock on my door all the time to be no different from religious zealots trying to force their beliefs on me.

755 **saltare** - *verb*
saltare

to skip, jump

Per tre anni ha frequentato la scuola superiore, senza saltare un giorno o arrivare in ritardo una volta.

He attended the high school for three years without missing a single day or being late.

756 **tornio** - *nm*
tornjo

lathe

Il pezzo viene caricato automaticamente sul mandrino del tornio utilizzando un nastro trasportatore in entrata, ed espulso dopo la lavorazione.

Using an inlet conveyor belt, the part is automatically loaded into the lathe chuck and ejected after machining.

757 **tavolo** - *nm* tavolo
table
La casa di campagna era completa, con una piscina, una griglia, un campo da calcio e un tavolo da biliardo.
The country house was complete, with a swimming pool, a barbecue, a soccer field and a pool table.

758 **ridere** - *verb* ridere
to laugh
Nonostante le barriere della lingua, riusciamo a comunicare e a ridere della vita – la vita è più forte della morte!
Despite language barriers, we manage to communicate and to laugh about life – life is stronger than death!

759 **codice** - *nm* koditʃe
code, codex
Se vuoi mettere il tuo banner sul mio sito, basta che mi mandi il codice.
If you want to put your banner on my site, just send me the code.

760 **vento** - *nm* vento
wind
Io gli sono grato per aver afferrato il mio cappello che ho perso per strada per un colpo di vento.
I'm grateful to him for catching my hat that I lost on the windy street.

761 **speranza** - *nf* sperantsa
hope
Tom ha contrattato con il venditore nella speranza di ottenere un prezzo più basso.
Tom bargained with the salesman hoping to get a lower price.

762 **posto** - *nm* posto
place, spot, location
L'elicottero è così utile che un giorno potrebbe prendere il posto delle automobili e dei treni.
The helicopter is so useful that someday it may take the place of cars and trains.

763 **ufficiale** - *adj; nm* uffitʃale
official
Certi creoli ottengono uno stato ufficiale, per esempio come in Malesia.
Certain creoles obtain an official status, for example like in Malaysia.

764 **fregare** - *verb* fregare
to rub, care
Io me ne frego di quello che fai del tuo denaro.
I don't care what you do with your money.

765 **sparare** - *verb*
sparare

to shoot

In molte parti del mondo è illegale sparare a della selvaggina come cervi, alci o fagiani.

In many parts of the world it is illegal to shoot wild game such as deer, moose or pheasant.

766 **animale** - *nm; adj*
animale

animal

La civiltà di un popolo si misura dal modo in cui tratta gli animali.

The greatness of a nation and its moral progress can be judged by the way its animals are treated.

767 **libertà** - *nf*
libertˈa

freedom

Ogni individuo ha diritto alla libertà di movimento e di residenza entro i confini di ogni Stato.

Everyone has the right to freedom of movement and residence within the borders of each State.

768 **incontrare** - *verb*
iŋkontrare

to meet

Le ragazze volevano incontrare ragazzi bianchi perché quelli asiatici stavano uscendo con ragazze bianche.

The girls wanted to meet white boys because the Asian ones were going out with white girls.

769 **pesce** - *nm*
peʃʃe

fish

Tom mangia più pesce in una settimana di quanto ne mangi io in un anno.

Tom eats more fish in a week than I eat in a year.

770 **serata** - *nf*
serata

evening

Nel corso della serata sono stati serviti prodotti dell'eccellenza enogastronomica italiana .

During the evening Italian food and wine excellences were served.

771 **società** - *nf*
sotʃetˈa

society

Vestire un completo a giacca non fa di te un membro responsabile e maturo della società.

Wearing a suit doesn't turn you into a mature, responsible member of society.

772 **francese** - *adj*
frantʃeze

French

Il francese è parlato in Francia e in qualche zona in Italia.

French is spoken in France and in some parts of Italy.

773 **temere** - *verb*
temere

to fear, be afraid

Tom voleva invitare Mary ad un appuntamento, ma temeva che lei gli dicesse di no.

Tom wanted to ask Mary out, but he was afraid she would say no.

774 **livello** - *nm*
livello

level
Il mio livello di conoscenza del giapponese è debole, quindi non so scrivere bene.
My level of Japanese is weak, so I can't write well.

775 **stazione** - *nf*
stattsjone

station
Questa pizzeria con terrazza soleggiata presso la stazione a valle Diavolezza è ideale per una tappa prima della prossima discesa.
The pizzeria with the sun terrace at the Diavolezza valley station is ideal for the in-between stop before the next downhill run.

776 **americano** - *adj; nm/f*
amerikano

American; American
Il sindaco di Napoli si è scusato con un turista americano picchiato da residenti locali appena dopo essere stato rapinato.
The mayor of Naples has apologised to a US tourist who was beaten up by local residents shortly after he was mugged.

777 **computer** - *nm*
komputer

computer
Io non ho la più pallida idea di come funzioni il mio computer.
I don't have the slightest idea how my computer works.

778 **drogare** - *verb*
drogare

to drug
È nostra responsabilità, in quanto medici, trovare le vere cause invece che drogare i bambini con psicofarmaci.
As doctors, we need to find the real problems instead of drugging children.

779 **detective** - *nmf*
detektive

detective
Il detective della polizia non ha creduto alla storia di Tom.
The police detective didn't believe Tom's story.

780 **lato** - *nm*
lato

side
Per caso un sacerdote scendeva per quella stessa strada, ma quando lo vide, passò oltre dal lato opposto.
By chance a certain priest was going down that way, but when he saw him, he passed by on the other side.

781 **hotel** - *nm*
otel

hotel
L'hotel è troppo lontano per andarci a piedi. È meglio prendere un taxi.

It is too far to go on foot from here to the hotel. It is better to take a taxi.

782 **sezione** - *nf*
settsjone

section, department
Potremmo avere un tavolo nella sezione per non fumatori?
Could we have a table in the non-smoking section?

783 **imparare** - *verb*
imparare

to learn
A sei anni aveva imparato a usare la macchina da scrivere e disse al maestro che non aveva bisogno di imparare a scrivere a mano.
At the age of six he had learned to use the typewriter and told the teacher that he did not need to learn to write by hand.

784 **regina** - *nf*
redʒina

queen
La Regina di Gran Bretagna è il apo del governo.
The head of the state is the Queen of the Great Britain.

785 **cominciare** - *verb*
komintʃare

to begin
Tom ha tolto il libro dallo zaino e ha cominciato a leggere.
Tom took a book out of his knapsack and started reading.

786 **scorso** - *adj*
skorso

last
Sono stupito di sentire che il mio migliore amico è morto la scorsa notte in un incidente d'auto.
I'm flabbergasted to hear that my best friend died last night in a car accident.

787 **riguardare** - *verb*
rigwardare

to concern
I Reclami sulla qualità di un prodotto possono riguardare le modifiche nell'aspetto di un prodotto.
Product Quality Complaints may include changes in product appearance.

788 **naso** - *nm*
nazo

nose
Questa è la prima volta in assoluto che mi è sanguinato il naso d'inverno.
This is the first time I've ever had a nosebleed in winter.

789 **padrone** - *nm/f*
padrone

boss, master, owner, host/mistress, hostess
Siamo rimasti scioccati quando il padrone di casa ci ha alzato l'affitto di 200,00 dollari al mese.
We were shocked when the landlord raised our rent by $200.00 a month.

790 **seguire** - *verb*
segwire

to follow
Lei mi seguì in cucina e prese un coltello. Iniziò poi a tagliare le verdure.

She followed me into the kitchen and picked up a knife. She then started cutting vegetables.

791 **aprire** - *verb*
aprire

to open

Come fai ad avere dei voti così alti a scuola? Non ti ho mai visto aprire un libro per studiare.

How do you always get such good marks in school? I never see you even crack a book.

792 **alcun** - *adj*
alkun

any

So leggere e scrivere in inglese senza alcun problema.

I can read and write English without any problems.

793 **fiore** - *nm*
fjore

flower

La rosa è un fiore e la colomba è un uccello.

The rose is a flower and the dove is a bird.

794 **inutile** - *adj*
inutile

useless, unnecessary

John dichiarò che il venditore disonesto lo aveva indotto con l'inganno a comprare un inutile pezzo di ferro.

John claimed that the dishonest salesman had tricked him into buying a useless piece of machinery.

795 **danno** - *nm*
danno

damage

Se volete fare delle feste in casa mia, pulite tutto dopo e non rompete nulla, oppure pagate i danni.

If you want to have parties in my house, clean up everything afterwards, and don't break anything, or else pay for the damage.

796 **casino (casinò)** - *nm*
kazino (kazinˈɔ)

mess (casino)

Dopo tre ore al casinò, lui è sotto di 2.000 dollari. Tom non aveva niente a che fare con quel casino.

After three hours in the casino, he's $2,000 in the hole. Tom had nothing to do with that mess.

797 **tornire** - *verb*
tornire

to throw

A dodici anni sembra sapesse gia' tornire il legno del clarinetto e lavorare tutte le sue chiavi.

To twelve years he seems already knew to tornire the wood of the clarinet and to work all its keys.

798 **natura** - *nf*
natura

nature

Ho sempre pensato che un infarto fosse il modo in cui la natura ti dicesse di morire.

I always thought that having a heart attack was the way nature told you to die.

799 **cliente** - *nm*
kljente

customer
Lavorando part-time, ho trovato che alcuni clienti erano educati, mentre altri non lo erano.

Working part-time, I found that some customers were polite, whereas others were not.

800 **rendere** - *verb*
rendere

to make
Quando ti sposerai e avrai bambini ti renderai conto che le azioni parlano più forte delle parole.

When you get married and have kids, you'll realize that actions speak louder than words.

801 **immediatamente** - *adv*
immedjatamente

immediately
Tom è entrato nella stanza vuota e ha notato immediatamente una sigaretta accesa nel posacenere.

Tom entered the empty room and immediately noticed a lit cigarette in the ashtray.

802 **guida** - *nf*
gwida

guide, driving
Tom è stato accusato di guida in stato di ebbrezza dopo essere stato coinvolto in un incidente stradale a Boston.

Tom was charged with drunken driving after he was involved in a car accident in Boston.

803 **biglietto** - *nm*
biʎʎetto

ticket
Se mio marito troverà i biglietti per il concerto ne comprerà due anche per voi.

If my husband will find tickets for the concert, he will buy two also for you.

804 **zia** - *nf*
dzja

race, breed, stingray
Ho chiesto a mia zia di raccontare le storie dei suoi viaggi.

I asked my aunt to tell the stories of her travels.

805 **razza** - *nf*
rattsa

race, breed, stingray
Se nessuno parlasse a meno che avesse qualcosa da dire, la razza umana perderebbe ben presto l'uso della parola.

If nobody spoke unless he had something to say, the human race would very soon lose the use of speech.

806 **stamattina** - *nf*
stamattina

this morning
Nonostante fossi tornato tardi dalla festa la scorsa notte, ero fresco come una rosa stamattina.

Although I came back late from the party last night, I was as fresh as a daisy in the morning.

807 **intelligente** - *adj* | **intelligent, clever, smart**
intellidʒente
Utilizzando le Regole per selezionare o ignorare alcuni file e cartelle in modo intelligente, è possibile limitare il tempo e i supporti richiesti per un'operazione.

Using Rules to intelligently select or ignore certain files and folders, you can limit the amount of time and media required for an operation.

808 **blu** - *adj* | **blue**
blu
Lo sapevi che se si mischia il rosso con il blu si ottiene il lilla?
Did you know that if you mixed red and blue paint you obtained purple?

809 **effetto** - *nm* | **effect**
effetto
Io preferisco non prendere medicine, perché ho paura degli effetti collaterali del farmaco.

I prefer not to take medicine, because I am afraid of drug side effect.

810 **cambio** - *nm* | **change**
kambjo
Le operazioni a termine in valuta non ancora regolate sono convertite in euro ai tassi di cambio a termine per il periodo residuo dalla data di fine esercizio alla scadenza.

Forward currency transactions not yet closed out are converted into the currency of the capital at the forward rate for the term still to run on the closing date of the balance sheet.

811 **taxi** - *nm* | **taxi**
taksi
Tom, quando va al bar la sera, mette nel calzino un po' di soldi per taxi per tornare a casa.

Tom keeps enough money for a taxi fare home tucked in his sock when he goes out drinking.

812 **fortunato** - *adj* | **lucky**
fortunato
Sono così fortunato ad avere qualcuno che tiene a me.
I'm so lucky to have someone who cares.

813 **corso** - *nm* | **course**
korso
Il comitato di pianificazione si è riunito sei volte nel corso di dieci mesi.

The planning committee met six times over the course of ten months.

814 **giudice** - *nm* | **judge**
dʒuditʃe
L'avvocato chiese al giudice di prendere in considerazione l'età dell'accusato.

The lawyer asked the judge to make allowance for the age of the accused.

815 **accanto** - *adv* akkanto

next

Dalla casa accanto viene un rumore come di persone che chiacchierano. Mi chiedo se c'è una festa.

The house next door is a bit loud. I wonder if they're throwing a party.

816 **villaggio** - *nm* villaddʒo

village

Se si insegna a un uomo, si educa una persona. Se si insegna a una donna, si educa un intero villaggio.

If you teach a man, you educate one person. If you teach a woman, you educate a whole village.

817 **cinema** - *nm* tʃinema

cinema, movie theater

I cinema stanno perdendo sempre più entrate per via della pirateria informatica.

Movie theaters are losing more and more revenue due to internet piracy.

818 **stanco** - *adj* staŋko

tired

Mi stanco di scammed e ricevendo poo prodotti di qualità da un certo sito asta ben noto.

I get tired of getting scammed and receiving poor quality products from a certain well known auction site.

819 **lezione** - *nf* lettsjone

lesson

Prende lezioni di canto e di danza, per non parlare di lezioni di nuoto e tennis.

She takes singing and dancing lessons, not to mention swimming and tennis lessons.

820 **decisione** - *nf* detʃizjone

decision

Ha preso la decisione di tenere un diario di ogni giorno.

He made up his mind to keep a diary every day.

821 **bordo** - *nm* bordo

edge

Tom ha quasi avuto un attacco di cuore quando ha visto Mary in piedi sul bordo del tetto.

Tom nearly had a heart attack when he saw Mary standing on the edge of the roof.

822 **segno** - *nm* seɲɲo

sign

Un segno di una celebrità è spesso che il suo nome vale più dei suoi servizi.

		A sign of a celebrity is often that his name is worth more than his services.
823	**ponte** - *nm* ponte	**bridge** A solo 15 minuti a piedi dal Ponte Carlo, questo hotel a 4 stelle sorge nel centro di Praga, in un palazzo neo-rinascimentale risalente al 1884, e offre spaziose camere con aria condizionata e connessione Wi-Fi gratuita. *Just a 15-minute walk from Charles Bridge, this 4-star hotel in the centre of Prague is located in a Neo-Renaissance palace dating from 1884. It offers spacious, air-conditioned rooms and free Wi-Fi.*
824	**club** - *nm* klub	**club** L'anno scorso mia sorella faceva parte del club di pallacanestro. *My sister belonged to the basketball club last year.*
825	**muro** - *nm* muro	**wall** Cosa dovremmo fare con questo elefante bianco che ci ha dato tua zia? È troppo brutto per appenderlo al muro. *What should we do with this white elephant your aunt gave us? It's way too ugly to go on the wall.*
826	**interno** - *adj; nm* interno	**internal; interior, inside** La polizia trovò delle scatole che contenevano marijuana e altre droghe all'interno del bagagliaio della vettura. *The police found boxes that contained marijuana and other drugs inside the trunk of the car.*
827	**energia** - *nf* enerdʒa	**energy** C'è una nuova energia da sfruttare, nuovi lavori da creare, nuove scuole da costruire, e nuove minacce da affrontare, alleanze da riparare. *There's new energy to harness, new jobs to be created, new schools to build, and threats to meet, alliances to repair.*
828	**spada** - *nf* spada	**sword** Se le azioni sono più forti delle parole, perché è più potente la penna della spada? *If actions are stronger than words, why is the pen mightier than the sword?*
829	**presentire** - *verb* prezentire	**to foresee** Il contesto in cui tali proposte verranno presentate non lascia presentire nulla di buono

The context in which these are to be tabled does not bode well.

830 **processo** - *nm* protʃesso
process
Il serial killer era freddo e distante durante il suo processo, ed è apparso non influenzato dal fatto che aveva ucciso così tante persone.
The serial killer was cold and distant during his trial, and appeared unaffected by the fact that he had murdered so many people.

831 **scoprire** - *verb* skoprire
to discover
Oltre 500 anni fa, il re di Spagna fece partire Cristoforo Colombo verso occidente per scoprire un nuovo itinerario verso l'Asia con il risultato che sappiamo.
More than 500 years ago, Spain's monarchs sent Christopher Columbus westwards to discover a new way to Asia – with the known result.

832 **segnale** - *nm* seɲɲale
signal, sign
Questa è una segreteria telefonica, dopo il segnale acustico lasciate un messaggio oppure inviate un fax, grazie.
This is an answering machine, after the beep leave a message or send a fax, thank you.

833 **ferire** - *verb* ferire
to hurt
Il peso della macchina può ferire una persona o causare gravi schiacciamenti!
The weight of the machine may injure a person and cause serious bruising!

834 **battaglia** - *nf* battaʎʎa
battle
Si possono vincere tutte le battaglie ma perdere comunque la guerra.
You can win all the battles yet lose the war.

835 **meraviglioso** - *adj* meraviʎʎozo
wonderful
Da quando sono guarito dalla mia grave malattia tutto della creazione è meraviglioso per me.
Since I recovered from my serious illness, all of creation is beautiful to me.

836 **pago** - *adj* pago
content, statisfied
Non pago di ciò, il relatore promuove anche la liberalizzazione dei servizi e dell'energia
Not satisfied with this, the rapporteur also promotes the liberalisation of services and energy

837 **porco** - *nm*
porko
pig
Prendi da bere, poi sgomiti verso il buffet e mangi come un porco!
You take a drink, then you elbow to the buffet and eat like a pig!

838 **ascolto** - *nm*
askolto
listening
Una ricerca limitata suggerisce che l'ascolto di musica può beneficiare le persone che hanno la malattia di Alzheimer in vari modi.
Limited research suggests that listening to music can benefit people who have Alzheimer's disease in various ways.

839 **ringraziare** - *verb*
riŋgrattsjare
to thank
Posso cominciare col ringraziare ognuno di voi per la vostra calorosa accoglienza?
May I begin by thanking every one for your warm welcome?

840 **prezzo** - *nm*
prettso
price
Io non riesco a credere che voi abbiate veramente venduto quella spazzatura a un prezzo così alto.
I can't believe that you really sold that junk for such a high price.

841 **grave** - *adj*
grave
serious, severe
In tutti i casi, la Banca non è responsabile per i danni di qualsiasi [...] natura causati all'interno dei rapporti di business con il Cliente, salvo in caso di sua grave colpa debitamente comprovata.
In all cases, the Bank is not liable for the damage of any kind [...] caused during the business relationship with the Client, except for the cases when its severe fault has been properly proven.

842 **infatti** - *adv*
infatti
indeed
Lui ha detto che sarebbe venuto e infatti è venuto.
He said he would come and he did come.

843 **eroe** - *nm*
eroe
hero
Forse non sapremo mai con certezza se Robin Hood era un vero eroe o un personaggio romanzesco, una cosa è certa – la sua leggenda è ancora viva!
Perhaps we will never know for sure whether Robin Hood was a real hero or a fictional character, but one thing is certain - his legend lives on!

844 **suonare** - *verb*
to play (music or instrument), sound, ring

swonare

Tom voleva scoprire chi era l'artista che stava suonando il violino in una tale maniera in una foresta dell'Arkansas.

Tom wanted to find out who was the artist who was playing violin in such a manner in an Arkansas forest.

845 **documento** - *nm*
dokumento

document

L'unico problema qui, è che non c'è nessuno che traduca questi documenti.

The only problem here is that there isn't anybody to translate these documents.

846 **comune** - *adj; nm*
komune

common; community, town

Gli sport più comuni del mondo sono: calcio, basket, football, rugby, baseball, cricket, hockey su ghiaccio, pallavolo, beach volley, ping-pong, golf, boxe, wrestling, badminton e bowling.

The most common sports games around the world are: Soccer, Basketball, Football, Rugby, Baseball, Cricket, Ice hockey, Volleyball, Beach volleyball, Tennis, Table tennis, Golf, Boxing, Wrestling, Badminton and Bowling.

847 **dente** - *nm*
d'ɛnte

tooth

Mi fanno male i denti. Devo prendere un appuntamento con il mio dentista.

My teeth ache. I need to make an appointment with my dentist.

848 **pensata** - *nf*
pensata

thought

La sua struttura, pensata per la creazione e la gestione di portafogli dinamici, lo rende un sistema ideale per l'acquisizione di dati da sistemi esterni.

Its structure, devised for the creation and management of dynamic portfolios, makes it an ideal system for the acquisition of data from external systems.

849 **memoria** - *nf*
memorja

storage

Guglielmo è lo studente migliore che io conosca. Impara immediatamente e ha una memoria fenomenale.

Guglielmo is the best student I know. He learns instantly and has a phenomenal memory.

850 **data** - *nf*
data

date

In che data è scoppiata la guerra dello Yom Kippur?

What date did the Yom Kippur War break out?

851 **terzo** - *adj; nm*

third

tertso — Così, il terzo motivo per cui ho voluto essere qui è strettamente legato al secondo.

So, the third reason that I wanted to be here relates closely to the second .

852 **massimo** - *adj; nm* — **maximum**
massimo — Quello studente in realtà ha ottenuto il massimo dei voti in inglese.
That student actually got full marks in English.

853 **miglior** - *adj* — **best**
miʎʎor — Se è infelice della sua vita privata, le suggerisco di registrarsi su Facebook. È il miglior modo per sbarazzarsene.

If you're unhappy with your private life, I suggest you register on Facebook. It's the best way to get rid of it.

854 **buio** - *adj; nm* — **dark; dark**
bwjo — La stanza era talmente buia che abbiamo dovuto trovare la porta a tastoni.

The room was so dark that we had to feel our way to the door.

855 **colore** - *nm* — **color**
kolore — In campagna, i colori del cielo e del fogliame sono completamente differenti da quelli visti in città.

In the country, the colors of the sky and of the foliage are entirely different from those seen in the city.

856 **matto** - *adj; nm* — **crazy; madman**
matto — Il buon giovane uomo, per evitare domande imbarazzanti, presentò la matta come sua sorella.

The nice young man, in order to avoid embarrassing questions, presented the crazy woman as his sister.

857 **cerchio** - *nm* — **circle; rim**
tʃerkjo — Un cerchio in cattivo stato o rotto deve essere cambiato in quanto può provocare delle perdite e può essere pericoloso per l'utilizzatore.

A rim in poor condition, i.e. broken or cracked, must be changed since it may cause leaks and place the user in danger.

858 **cellulare** - *adj* — **cell phone**
tʃellulare — Ho sempre detto che il tuo cellulare non ha mai funzionato bene.
I always said that your mobile never worked well.

859 **soprattutto** - *adv* — **mostly**

	soprattutto	Ascensore, parcheggio privato: un insieme di servizi particolarmente apprezzati dai nostri clienti per i quali le vacanze sono, sopratutto, sinonimo di sole e di tranquillitá. *Elevator, private parking: a range of services that are particularly appreciated by our customers for whom the holidays are, above all, synonymous with sunshine and peace.*
860	**difendere** - *verb* difendere	**to defend** Noi dobbiamo difendere la nostra libertà a tutti i costi. *We must defend our freedom at all cost.*
861	**corto** - *adj* korto	**short** Delle frasi corte sono più facili da leggere rispetto a delle frasi lunghe. *Short sentences are easier to read than long sentences.*
862	**supporre** - *verb* supporre	**to suppose** E l'influsso che esercita sull'agenda globale è più grande di quanto lasci supporre il suo impegno finanziario. *Its influence on the global agenda is greater than its financial commitment would let us assume.*
863	**maledetto** - *nm* maledetto	**accursed, damn** Non credo che queste dannate batterie siano in questo maledetto cassetto. *I don't think that those damn batteries are in this damn drawer.*
864	**opera** - *nf* ˈɔpera	**opera** Ritengo che realizzare un'opera del genere in questo particolare sia più un danno che un vantaggio! *I think that creating a work of this kind in this particular way will cause more harm than benefit!*
865	**partito** - *nm* partito	**party** La follia è qualcosa di raro fra gli individui, ma nei gruppi, nei partiti, nei popoli, nelle ere, è la norma. *Madness is something rare in individuals — but in groups, parties, peoples, ages it is the rule.*
866	**attentare** - *verb* attentare	**to attempt** In Miller nasce il sospetto che Rodolfo non sia sincero e voglia in realtà attentare all'onore di Luisa. *Miller begins to suspect that Rodolfo is not sincere and that he wishes in reality to dishonour Luisa.*
867	**persino** - *adv*	**even**

persino | Da classica città dormitorio che è, l'area pedonale è semideserta persino di giorno.

It's a classic commuter town, even during the day there are few people around.

868 **scendere** - *verb* — **to get off**
ʃendere
L'uomo sul quale vedrete lo Spirito scendere e fermarsi, è colui che battezzerà con lo Spirito Santo.
The man on whom you see the Spirit come down and remain is he who will baptize with the Holy Spirit.

869 **fede** - *nf* — **faith, wedding ring**
fede
Mentre Mary si lavava le mani, la fede nuziale le scivolò nello scarico del lavandino.
Mary's wedding ring was swept down the drain while she was washing her hands.

870 **esperienza** - *nf* — **experience**
esperjentsa
Visto che ora sei maggiorenne, quel tipo di esperienze non le devi fare per forza.
Now that you are 18 years old, you should not do such a thing.

871 **baciare** - *verb* — **to kiss**
batʃare
Baciare il proprio coniuge davanti a tutti è considerato un comportamento normale in alcuni paesi.
Kissing one's spouse in public is considered acceptable behavior in some countries.

872 **responsabile** - *adj; nm* — **responsible; person in charge**
responsabile
Sarà responsabile delle donne che lavorano in questa fabbrica.
You will be in charge of the women working in this factory.

873 **enorme** - *adj* — **huge**
enorme
Un piccolo fuoco nella foresta può diffondersi facilmente e diventare velocemente un enorme incendio.
A small forest fire can easily spread and quickly become a great conflagration.

874 **ex** - *adj; nmf* — **former; ex**
eks
Ho sentito dire che Tom è tornato con la sua ex.
I heard Tom is back with his ex.

875 **fiducia** - *nf* — **confidence**
fidutʃa
Il coraggio fa gli eroi, ma la fiducia costruisce l'amicizia.
Courage makes heroes, but trust builds friendship.

876 **ognuno** - *pron* — **each**

	oɲɲuno	In Francia al ristorante ognuno ha la sua tecnica per non pagare, in Cina è il contrario. *In France every restaurant has some method by which you don't have to pay, in China it is the opposite.*
877	**periodo** - *nm* perjodo	**period** Per quanto fosse occupato, nel periodo in cui visse fuori non dimenticò mai di scrivere a casa dei propri genitori tutte le settimane. *No matter how busy he was while living abroad, he never failed to write home to his parents at least once a week.*
878	**albero** - *nm* albero	**tree** Tom chiese a Mary di aiutare a decorare il suo albero di Natale. *Tom asked Mary to help decorate his Christmas tree.*
879	**verde** - *adj* verde	**green** Io ho sentito dire che in Inghilterra l'erba è verde anche d'inverno. *I hear the grass in England is green even in the winter.*
880	**azione** - *nf* attsjone	**action** La tua motivazione era ammirevole, ma la tua azione non lo era. *Your motive was admirable, but your action was not.*
881	**odore** - *nm* odore	**smell** I maiali hanno un cattivo odore, però hanno un senso dell'olfatto molto buono. *Pigs smell bad, but they have a very good sense of smell.*
882	**locale** - *adj; nm* lokale	**local; club** Tom non può prendere da bere in questo locale notturno perché è minorenne. *Tom can't get a drink in this club because he's underage.*
883	**latte** - *nm* latte	**milk** Mi stavo giusto chiedendo se forse ci fosse ancora un po' di latte nel frigorifero. *I was just wondering if maybe there was some more milk in the refrigerator.*
884	**bellezza** - *nf* bellettsa	**beauty** Non è necessario essere un artista al fine di sperimentare la bellezza ogni giorno *You don't need to be an artist in order to experience beauty every day.*

885 **vittima** - *nf*
vittima

victim
Si pensa che la vittima abbia ingerito una grande quantità di veleno per errore.
The victim is thought to have taken a large quantity of poison by mistake.

886 **congratulazione** - *nf*
koŋgratulattsjone

congratulation
Congratulazioni per essere stato accettato nella scuola in cui sei sempre voluto andare.
Congratulations on being accepted to the school you've always wanted to go to.

887 **tirare** - *verb*
tirare

to pull
Quando cerchiamo di scoprire il meglio degli altri, tiriamo fuori in qualche modo il meglio di noi stessi.
When we seek to discover the best in others, we somehow bring out the best in ourselves.

888 **colazione** - *nf*
kolattsjone

breakfast, lunch
Tom fa una breve corsetta intorno all'isolato ogni mattina prima di colazione.
Tom takes a quick jog around the block every morning before breakfast.

889 **isola** - *nf*
izola

island
L'isola vista dall'alto assomiglia a una pera come forma.
The island as seen from above resembles a pear in shape.

890 **filare** - *verb*
filare

to spin
Quando ero bambino, pensavo che lo zucchero filato e le nuvole fossero simili.
When I was a kid, I used to think that fairy floss and clouds were alike.

891 **contrario** - *nm*
kontrarjo

contrary
Io voglio studiare all'estero, anche se i miei genitori ne sono contrari.
I want to study abroad, even if my parents are against it.

892 **svegliare** - *verb*
zveʎʎare

to wake
Anche se ci troviamo qui stasera, sappiamo che ci sono americani coraggiosi che si svegliano nei deserti dell'Iraq e nelle montagne dell'Afghanistan per rischiare la vita per noi.
Even as we stand here tonight, we know there are brave Americans waking up in the deserts of Iraq and the mountains of Afghanistan, to risk their lives for us.

893 **legge** - *nf*

law

leddʒe | I sostenitori della salute hanno spinto per le leggi che limitano il fumo sul posto di lavoro.

Health advocates have pushed for laws restricting work-place smoking.

894 **chissà** - *int; adv* | **who knows!; perhaps**
kissˈa | Chissà perché quando sono presissimo il telefono non smette mai di suonare. Così quando mai finirò il mio lavoro?

Why does the phone have to ring all the time only when I'm busy? I can't get any work done because of it.

895 **dubbio** - *adj; nm* | **doubtful; doubt**
dubbjo | Nessuno ha mai messo in dubbio la mia lealtà in passato.
No one's ever questioned my loyalty before.

896 **camion** - *nm* | **truck**
kamjon | Ho evitato per un pelo di essere investito da un camion.
I narrowly escaped being run over by a truck.

897 **sissignore** - *int* | **Yes sir**
sissiɲɲore | Sissignore, e il suo paese è ora nell'Unione europea grazie alla forza dell'Europa!

Yes Sir, and your country is now in the European Union thanks to the strength of Europe!

898 **stella** - *nf* | **star**
stella | Le stelle cadenti riescono ad attraversare il cielo in meno di un secondo.

Shooting stars can fly across the sky in less than a second.

899 **malato** - *adj* | **ill, sick**
malato | Visto che sono stato malato per una settimana, sto facendo tutto il possibile per recuperare.

Since I was sick for a week, I am making every possible effort to catch up.

900 **nascondere** - *verb* | **to hide**
naskondere | Tom ha tenuto addosso il suo cappello per nascondere la sua calvizie.
Tom kept his hat on to hide his baldness.

901 **rischiare** - *verb* | **to risk**
riskjare | Se una donna non vuole rischiare non deve bere più di una unità alcolica prima di mettersi alla guida e un uomo non più di due.
In order not to run risks, a woman must not drink more than one alcohol unit before driving and a man no more than two.

902 **pressione** - *nf* | **pressure**

	pressjone	La stessa forza applicata ad una superficie più piccola produrrà una maggior pressione. *The same force spread over a smaller area will produce more pressure.*
903	**orribile** - *adj* orribile	**horrible** Vorrei solo che potessimo andar via da questo posto orribile. *I just wish we could leave this horrible place.*
904	**edificio** - *nm* edifitʃo	**building** Tom morì mentre provava a salvare un bambino da un edificio in fiamme. *Tom died trying to save a child from a burning building.*
905	**progetto** - *nm* prodʒetto	**project** I leader politici europei si riuniscono per cercare di salvare l'euro, e con esso lo stesso progetto di Unione europea. *The political leaders of Europe come together to try to save the euro, and with it the very project of European Union.*
906	**portato** - *adj* portato	**brought** La crisi dei missili di Cuba ha portato il mondo sull'orlo della guerra nucleare. *The Cuban Missile Crisis brought the world to the brink of nuclear war*
907	**età** - *nf* etˈa	**age** Un uomo che lavora dovrebbe essere pagato in base alle sue capacità, non alla sua età. *A working man should be paid in proportion to his skill, not his age.*
908	**divergere** - *verb* diverdʒere	**to diverge** Se si ordinano azionamenti che divergono da quelli standard, anche le condizioni menzionate possono divergere. *The conditions might be different when you order drives other than the standard.*
909	**camminare** - *verb* kamminare	**to walk** Camminava lentamente attraverso il parco per mostrare il suo nuovo taglio di capelli. *She walked slowly through the park to show off her new hairstyle.*
910	**capace** - *adj*	**capable, able**

kapatʃe — La salvezza di questo mondo umano risiede solo nel cuore umano, nell'umana capacità di riflettere, nella mitezza umana e nell'umana responsabilità.

This Salvation of this human world resides only in the heart of the human being, in the human capability to reflect, in humility and responsibility.

911 **calmo** - *adj*
kalmo

calm

I miei amici dicono sempre che io sono troppo calmo, però la mia famiglia dice sempre che sono troppo fastidioso.

My friends always say I'm too calm, but my family always says I'm too annoying.

912 **principessa** - *nf*
printʃipessa

princess

Loro hanno sventolato delle bandiere per dare il benvenuto alla principessa.

They waved flags to welcome the princess.

913 **sale** - *nm*
sale

salt

Mescolare fino a diventare schiuma il burro con i tuorli e l'uovo, lo zucchero a velo e le scorze di limone, il sale e la noce moscata.
Stir together the egg yolks and the egg, the icing sugar and the lemon zest, the salt and the nutmeg to make a frothy mix.

914 **scopo** - *nm*
skopo

purpose

Lei è andata a Los Angeles con lo scopo di studiare danza.

She went to Los Angeles for the purpose of studying dancing.

915 **dipendere** - *verb*
dipendere

to depend

La maggior parte delle grandi aziende giapponesi dipendono dalle esportazioni.

Most big Japanese companies depend on exports.

916 **gridare** - *verb*
gridare

to shout

Quando la BBC si degna di graziare i propri ascoltatori con un segnale di buona qualità, delle ben definite differenze nelle performance dei tre sintonizzatori si fanno sentire.

When the BBC choose to favour us with good quality signals definite identifiable performance differences emerge.

917 **stampa** - *nf*
stampa

press, printing

Come si vive in un paese dove non c'è libertà di stampa?

How does one live in a country where there is no freedom of the press?

918 **viso** - *nm*

face

	vizo	Purtroppo, molta gente crede a cose lette su una e-mail che troverebbe implausibili se dette viso a viso. *Sadly many people will believe things told to them via an email which they would find implausible face-to-face.*
919	**ottenere** - *verb* ottenere	**to get, obtain** È illegale negli Stati Uniti per le forze dell'ordine usare la tortura per ottenere informazioni. *It is illegal in the United States for law enforcement to use torture to get information.*
920	**rodere** - *verb* rodere	**to gnaw, fret, prey on** E così in quattro mesi trascorsi su di un letto d'ospedale, il tarlo aveva appena cominciato a rodere . *So with four months in a hospital bed the bug had just started to bite .*
921	**salire** - *verb* salire	**to go up, climb, rise** Salire su una delle barche in processione nella laguna regala un'esperienza di particolare suggestione. *Boarding on one of the boats in the procession on the lagoon is a highly evocative experience.*
922	**pensiero** - *nm* pensjero	**thought** Il solo pensiero di un serpente mi fa venire i brividi. *The mere thought of a snake makes me shiver.*
923	**dappertutto** - *adv* dappertutto	**everywhere** Gli ospiti erano molti, c'erano insegnanti e amici dappertutto. *There were many guests - most of them were our teacher's classmates and friends.*
924	**ristorante** - *nm* ristorante	**restaurant** Ho conosciuto un anziano che dice di non aver mai mangiato in un ristorante in tutta la sua vita. *I met an old man who says that he's never eaten at a restaurant in his whole life.*
925	**giornale** - *nm* dʒornale	**newspaper, journal** Quando il Signor Hilton voleva vendere la sua casa, l'ha fatta pubblicare sul giornale. *When Mr. Hilton wanted to sell his house, he advertised it in the newspaper.*
926	**test** - *nm* test	**test** Eseguire il test della conduttività in un'area priva di carburante o vapori infiammabili.

Always perform the conductivity test in an area free from flammable liquids or vapors.

927 **gatto** - *nm* gatto

cat

Io ho un gatto e un cane. Il gatto è nero e il cane è bianco.

I have a cat and a dog. The cat is black and the dog is white.

928 **giustizia** - *nf* dʒustittsja

justice

L'avvocato si è appellato al senso di giustizia della giuria.

The lawyer appealed to the jury's sense of justice.

929 **tranne** - *prep* tranne

except

A questo mondo, nulla può essere considerato come certo, tranne la morte e le tasse.

In this world nothing can be said to be certain, except death and taxes.

930 **albergo** - *nm* albergo

hotel

Io ho una collezione di asciugamani che ho rubato da molti alberghi diversi in cui ho soggiornato.

I have a collection of towels I've stolen from many different hotels I've stayed at.

931 **tiro** - *nm* tiro

shot, shooting, throw

Dal fischio dell'arbitro l'attaccante ha a disposizione 5 secondi per effettuare il tiro.

At the referee's whistle, the offensive player will have 5 seconds to take a shot on goal.

932 **relazione** - *nf* relattsjone

report

Ho letto con attenzione la sua lettera, e la sua situazione mi è parsa molto tipica e prevedibile in una relazione di coppia.

I have read your letter closely, and your situation seems very typical and foreseeable in a relationship.

933 **basso** - *adj; nm* basso

low, bottom, lower; bass

Lui ha due anni in più di me, però è più basso di me.

He's two years older than I am, but he's shorter than I am.

934 **compagno** - *nm/f* kompaɲɲo

companion, mate

Ho un compagno di classe che dice di sapere parlare il francese fluentemente.

I have a classmate who says he can speak French fluently.

935 **stavolta** - *adv* stavolta

this time

Tom è preparato meglio stavolta, quindi dovrebbe essere in grado di farcela.

Tom is better prepared this time, so he should be able to do it.

936 **crimine** - *nm* krimine

crime

A volte la povertà spinge la gente a commettere crimini.

Poverty sometimes drives people to commit crimes.

937 **angolo** - *nm* aŋgolo

angle, corner

Quando il portiere ha toccato la palla, l'arbitro ha assegnato un calcio d'angolo all'altra squadra.

When the goalkeeper touched the ball, the referee awarded the other team a corner kick.

938 **cappello** - *nm* kappello

hat

Io gli sono grato per aver afferrato il mio cappello che ho perso per strada per un colpo di vento.

I'm grateful to him for catching my hat that I lost on the windy street.

939 **operazione** - *nf* operattsjone

operation

Mi fa piacere sentire che tua sorella è fuori pericolo dopo l'operazione.

I'm glad to hear that your sister is out of danger after her operation.

940 **estate** - *nf* estate

summer

Ci sono persone a cui piace l'estate e persone a cui piace l'inverno.

There are people who like the summer and people who like the winter.

941 **desiderio** - *nm* deziderjo

desire

Vedrò se sarà possibile fare qualche cosa per soddisfare i suoi desideri.

I'll see if there's anything I can do to satisfy your desires.

942 **mercato** - *nm* merkato

market

Nel lungo periodo, l'aumento del livello del mare, eventi di ondate di tempesta estreme e alte maree interesseranno i servizi costieri e le infrastrutture da cui dipendono molti sistemi energetici, i mercati e i consumatori.

In the longer term, sea level rise, extreme storm surge events, and high tides will affect coastal facilities and infrastructure on which many energy systems, markets, and consumers depend.

943 **incinta** - *adj* intʃinta

pregnant

All'inizio del film, la ragazza scopre di essere incinta del suo fidanzato nero.

At the beginning of the film, the girl discovers that she's pregnant from her black boyfriend.

944 **rilassare** - *verb* rilassare | **to relax**
La capacità di lavorare duro è una caratteristica ammirevole, ma la capacità di rilassarsi non è meno importante.
The ability to work hard is an admirable quality, but the ability to relax is equally important.

945 **arte** - *nf* arte | **art**
La musica può essere definita come l'arte di produrre emozioni attraverso la combinazione di suoni.
Music can be defined as the art of producing emotion by the combination of sounds.

946 **coltello** - *nm* koltello | **knife**
Questa è la prima volta che mi sono tagliata un dito con un coltello.
This is the first time I've cut my finger with a knife.

947 **continuo** - *adj* kontinwo | **continuous**
Il risultato è una continua ricerca di cibo in un ambiente che cambia.
The result is a continual search for food in a changing environment.

948 **mosso** - *adj* mosso | **blurred, rough, wavy, moved**
Se la messa a fuoco della fotocamera non è impostata correttamente o la foto è un po' mossa, il risultato è un'immagine sfocata.
If the focus on the camera is not set perfectly, or the camera is moving when the picture is taken, the result is a blurred image.

949 **macchina** - *nf* makkina | **machine**
I miei amici erano così sbronzi, che non ho potuto far altro che accompagnarli a casa io in macchina.
My friends were so boozed up that I had to drive them home.

950 **preferire** - *verb* preferire | **to prefer**
Al mio amico piace vivere in città, ma sua moglie preferisce vivere nel loro piccolo cottage in campagna.
My friend likes to live in the city, but his wife prefers to live in their little cottage in the country.

951 **vite** - *nf* vite | **screw, grapevine, vine**
Per configurare il sistema, utilizzare lo strumento di sicurezza fornito per allentare la vite della porta di configurazione.

To begin system configuration, use the security tool provided to loosen the screw in the configuration door.

952 **buco** - *nm* buko

hole

Mi sono fatto un buco nei jeans quando sono caduto dalla bici.

I tore a hole in my jeans when I fell off my bike.

953 **centrale** - *adj; nf* tʃentrale

central; main office, (nuclear) power station

La paura dell'inquinamento ha scoraggiato la gente nel costruire case vicino alle centrali energetiche.

Fear of pollution discouraged people from building homes near power plants.

954 **lassù** - *adv* lassu

up there, above, yonder

„Ecco, uno scoiattolo!“ – „Cosa? Dove?“ – „Lassù sull'albero. Lo vedi?“ – „Sì, lo vedo!“

"There, a squirrel" "What? Where?" "Up there on the tree. Do you see it?" "Yes, I see it!"

955 **carriera** - *nf* karrjera

career

Quando era all'apice della sua carriera, uno scandalo ne provocò la caduta.

When he was at the height of his career, a scandal brought about his downfall.

956 **anello** - *nm* anello

ring

Lei ha un anello del valore di più di quanto possa immaginare.

She has a ring worth more than she can imagine.

957 **video** - *adj* video

video

Select predefined sound modes to suit your video or music.

Selezionare le varie modalità audio predefinite per personalizzare la riproduzione di video o musica.

958 **stile** - *nm* stile

style

Il termine 'tango stile milonguero' fu coniato nei primi anni '90 per descrivere il modo di ballare il tango che era prevalente nelle milonghe del centro di Buenos Aires negli anni '50.

The term 'milonguero style tango' was coined in the early 1990s to describe the style of dancing tango that was prevalent in the milongas of downtown Buenos Aires in the 1950s.

959 **contratto** - *nm* kontratto

contract

Invece di aspettare un contratto, possiamo gestire la cosa al telefono.

Instead of waiting for a contract, we can handle it over the phone.

960 **compito** - *nm*
kompito
task
L'altra notte, Mizuki era completamente ubriaca e stava camminando lungo il lago, quando è caduta nell'acqua.
Last night, Mizuki was completely drunk and she was walking along the lake, and then she fell in the water.

961 **paradiso** - *nm*
paradizo
paradise
Un piatto di pilaf con un po' di kebab è il paradiso in terra.
A plate of pilaf with some kebabs is heaven on earth.

962 **indirizzare** - *verb*
indiriddzare
to address
Il Consiglio di Amministrazione ha quindi adottato un Codice Etico che ha come obiettivo quello di indirizzare i comportamenti aziendali.
The Board of Directors thus adopted a Code of Ethics whose objective is to guide company behaviour

963 **domattina** - *adv*
domattina
tomorrow morning
Quando mi alzerò domattina, il sole brillerà e gli uccelli staranno cantando.
When I get up tomorrow morning, the sun will be shining and the birds will be singing.

964 **anzi** - *adv*
antsi
rather
"Io sono l'albero più bello del giardino", gridò il pesco, "anzi, di tutto il mondo."
"I am the most beautiful tree in the garden," exclaimed the peach tree, "or even in the whole world!"

965 **fingere** - *verb*
findʒere
to pretend
Puoi fingere di essere serio ma non puoi fingere di essere divertente.
You can pretend to be serious, but you can't pretend to be funny.

966 **riunione** - *nf*
rjunjone
meeting, reunion, assembly
Quella sera, l'università tenne una riunione per gli studenti stranieri e gli studenti cinesi che studiavano le lingue straniere.
That evening, the university held a meeting for foreign students and Chinese students studying foreign languages.

967 **torto** - *adj*
torto
injustice
La collettività si schiera con chi ha subíto il torto e per ciò stesso condanna l'offesa e l'offensore.

The Community take the side of the party who has suffered the wrong and that the Community therefore condemns the offence and the offender.

968 **troia** - *nf* troja | **slut**
È facile per una troia passare da ragazzo a un altro.
It's easy for a slut to go from guy to another.

969 **faccenda** - *nf* fattʃenda | **affair**
In ogni caso, la faccenda è ora approdata davanti al tribunale.
In any event, the case has now been taken up by the court.

970 **notare** - *verb* notare | **to note**
Credo di essere stata troppo impegnata per notare che Tom stava avendo dei problemi.
I guess I was too busy to notice that Tom was having problems.

971 **particolare** - *adj* partikolare | **particular**
Per il momento, non c'è niente di particolare che abbia bisogno di fare.
For the moment there's nothing in particular I need to be doing.

972 **inoltre** - *adv* inoltre | **also, besides**
Il suo cottage è ordinato e confortevole; inoltre, può contenere fino a dieci persone.
His cottage is neat and comfortable; moreover, it can accommodate as many as ten people.

973 **campione** - *nm; adj* kampjone | **sample, champion; champion**
Il dottore ha analizzato il campione di sangue per verificare la presenza di anemia.
The doctor analyzed the blood sample for anemia.

974 **agente** - *nm* adʒˈɛnte | **agent**
Gli agenti di polizia non sono autorizzati a bere alcolici mentre sono in servizio.
Policemen aren't permitted to drink on duty.

975 **politico** - *adj; nm* politiko | **political; politician**
Lui non ha mai dimenticato la sua ambizione di diventare un uomo politico di primo piano
He never forgot his ambition to become a leading politician.

976 **colpevole** - *adj* kolpevole | **guilty**
Tom si rifiutò di credere che Mary fosse colpevole.
Tom refused to believe that Mary was guilty.

977 **ghiaccio** - *nm*
gjattʃo

ice

La gente tende a dimenticare che l'acqua si ghiaccia effettivamente a zero gradi.

People tend to forget that water really freezes at zero degrees.

978 **fucile** - *nm*
futʃile

rifle, gun

Tom era impaurito dal fatto che Mary potesse sparargli con il fucile di suo padre.

Tom was scared Mary would shoot him with her father's rifle.

979 **utile** - *adj; nm*
utile

helpful, useful; profit

Il judo è un bene non solo per la salute dei giovani, ma è anche molto utile nella formazione della loro personalità.

Judo is not only good for young people's health but also very useful in forming their personalities.

980 **ispettore** - *nm*
ispettore

inspector

Un ispettore professionista si cala nel ruolo del cliente e redige rapporti secondo un set di criteri concordati.

A professional auditor plays the role of a customer and reports on an agreed set of criteria.

981 **autobus** - *nm*
autobus

bus

Potresti dirmi quale autobus o treno devo prendere per raggiungere il centro città?

Can you tell me which bus or train I can take to get to the town centre?

982 **dato** - *adj; nm*
dato

given; fact, datum

Questo si riferisce alla quantità di energia fornita in un dato momento.

This refers to the amount of electricity delivered at any given moment.

983 **ridicolo** - *adj*
ridikolo

ridiculous

Ma ricordate che anche il Salvatore fu tormentato, messo in ridicolo e alla fine, crocifisso perché non volle allontanarsi dalle proprie convinzioni.

But remember that the Savior himself was tormented, ridiculed, spat upon, and finally crucified because he would not waver in his conviction.

984 **altezza** - *nf*
altettsa

height

Il nuovo arrivato è stato all'altezza delle nostre aspettative.

The newcomer fell short of our expectation.

985 **guidare** - *verb*
gwidare

to lead
A dire il vero, io ho guidato la macchina di mio padre senza il suo permesso.
To tell the truth, I drove my father's car without his permission.

986 **decidere** - *verb*
detʃidere

to decide
Secondo te quante volte dovrò chiedere a Tom di pulire la sua stanza prima che si decida a farlo?
How many times do you think I'm going to have to ask Tom to clean his room before he cleans it?

987 **sottofondo** - *nm*
sottofondo

background
Gli studenti spesso studiano con la musica in sottofondo e la gente al lavoro per casa di solito accende la televisione o la radio per tenersi compagnia.
Students often study with music playing in the background, and people working around the house will usually turn on the television or radio to keep them company.

988 **valore** - *nm*
valore

value
Molte persone pensano che le automobili d'epoca abbiano un prezzo superiore al loro valore effettivo.
Many people think that antique cars are overpriced.

989 **campagna** - *nf*
kampaɲɲa

countryside, country
Le strade di campagna non sono affollate come le strade urbane.
Country roads aren't as crowded as city roads.

990 **tè** - *nm*
tˈɛ

tea
Adesso prendiamo una grossa porzione di spaghetti e una tazza di tè, miei cari signori e signore.
Now let's have a big portion of spaghetti and a cup of tea, my dear lords and ladies.

991 **vendere** - *verb*
vendere

to sell
Se mi ricordo correttamente, Tom ha venduto la sua macchina a Mary per appena 500 dollari.
If I remember correctly, Tom sold his car to Mary for just 500 dollars.

992 **cadere** - *verb*
kadere

to fall
Se il mio aereo non cade, e se non vengo rapito dai ladri di organi, ti scriverò due righe all'inizio della settimana.

If my plane doesn't crash, and if I do not get kidnapped by organ thieves, I will drop you a line at the beginning of the week.

993 **scatola** - *nf* skatola
box
Questa scatola è così grande che non è in grado di entrare nella mia borsa.
This box is so large that it cannot go into my bag.

994 **peso** - *nm* pezo
weight
Il ghiaccio sul lago s'è fatto troppo sottile e non può reggere il tuo peso.
The ice on the lake is too thin to bear your weight.

995 **magnifico** - *adj* maɲɲifiko
magnificent
Quel libro, che ho letto la settimana scorsa, è magnifico.
That book, which I read last week, is great.

996 **ragazzino** - *nm* ragattsino
little boy, sonny (condenscending)
Lui è venuto in Giappone quand'era un ragazzino di dieci anni.
He came to Japan when he was a boy of ten.

997 **ubriaco** - *adj* ubrjako
drunk
Tom voleva guidare, ma dal momento che era ubriaco Maria non glielo avrebbe lasciato fare.
Tom wanted to drive, but since he was drunk, Mary wouldn't let him.

998 **mentito** - *adj* mentito
false, deceptive
Nel corso degli anni mia madre mi ha mentito riguardo a così tante cose.
Over the years my mother lied to me about so many things.

999 **egli** - *pron* eʎʎi
he
Egli aprì la bocca come per parlare, ma non disse nulla.
He opened his mouth as if to speak, but didn't say anything.

1000 **sensazione** - *nf* sensattsjone
sensation
Tornare a provare di nuovo esattamente quella sensazione, quell'ispirazione di un momento unico, mentre nel 'qui ora' tutto cambia continuamente.
To go back and re-experience exactly that feeling, that inspiration, of one unique moment, while in the here and now, everything keeps changing.

1001 **principale** - *adj* printʃipale
main
Fino a un periodo recente, la funzione principale della donna era sposarsi e dare alla luce i bambini.

Until recently, the main function of women was to marry and give birth to children.

1002 **schiena** - *nf* skjena

back

Se il rivelatore di placca si libra in un angolo, non si ottiene la capacità ottimale di rilevazione, e visualizzare i pannelli che l'inclinazione ad angoli insoliti rendono difficile la lettura del display e mette pressione sul collo e sulla schiena.

If the detector plate hovers at an angle, you do not get the optimum detection capability, and view panels that tilt at odd angles make reading the display difficult and puts strain on your neck and back.

1003 **girare** - *verb* dʒirare

to turn

Ma di colpo gli incominciò a girare la testa e si risedette sulla sua vecchia sedia.

But he suddenly felt dizzy and he sat down again in his old chair.

1004 **orologio** - *nm* orolodʒo

clock, watch

Prima di impostare il timer, assicurarsi che l'orologio sia impostato correttamente.

Before setting the timer, ensure that the clock is set correctly.

1005 **insegnare** - *verb* inseɲɲare

to teach

Le scuole sono il luogo fondamentale in cui insegnare un consumismo alternativo.

Schools are the fundamental place in which to teach an alternative consumerism.

1006 **sbaglio** - *nm* zbaʎʎo

mistake

Un uomo che non fa mai sbagli è un uomo che non fa niente.

He who makes no mistakes makes nothing.

1007 **porgere** - *verb* pordʒere

to extend

Cogliamo l'occasione per porgere a tutti voi i nostri più sinceri auguri di Buon Natale e Felice Anno Nuovo.

May we take this opportunity of wishing you all our very best wishes for a Merry Christmas and a Happy New Year.

1008 **maestà** - *nf* maest'a

majesty

Maestà, vogliamo una stretta cooperazione col suo paese e lei è una delle poche personalità che hanno visitato il Parlamento europeo più di una volta.

Your Majesty, we want close cooperation with your country and you are one of the very few who have visited the European Parliament more than once.

1009 **contare** - *verb* kontare | **to count**

Se sei arrabbiato conta fino a dieci; se sei molto arrabbiato, conta fino a cento.

When angry, count ten; when very angry, a hundred.

1010 **cantare** - *verb* kantare | **to sing**

Tom ha scritto la canzone che ha cantato Mary la scorsa notte al pub.

Tom wrote the song that Mary sang last night at the pub.

1011 **angelo** - *nm* andʒelo | **angel**

Le sue parole erano come quelle di un angelo.

Her words were like those of an angel.

1012 **creare** - *verb* kreare | **to create**

Il preside della scuola vuole chiudere la mensa e creare una nuova sala ricreativa per gli studenti.

The director of the school wants to close the canteen and create a new recreation room for the students.

1013 **naturale** - *adj* naturale | **natural**

La famiglia è il nucleo naturale e fondamentale della società e ha diritto ad essere protetta dalla società e dallo Stato.

The family is the natural and fundamental group unit of society and is entitled to protection by society and the State.

1014 **importanza** - *nf* importantsa | **importance**

Questa è l'era dell'informazione e i computer hanno sempre maggiore importanza nella nostra vita quotidiana.

This is the age of information, and computers are having more and more importance in our everyday life.

1015 **baby** - *nmf* bab | **baby**

Io sono la baby sitter di Tom.

I'm Tom's nanny.

1016 **fumo** - *nm* fumo | **smoke**

Se il dispositivo non si avvia, se viene rilevato fumo oppure odori insoliti, o se non è possibile identificare i componenti danneggiati, rivolgersi alla Mr. Delli

If the device does not start, or if and smoke or unusual odors are detected, or if you cannot identify the damaged components, contact Mr. Delli

1017 **domenica** - *nf* domenika

Sunday

La mia famiglia è andata allo zoo a vedere i panda la scorsa domenica.

My family went to the zoo to see pandas last Sunday.

1018 **ucciso** - *nm/f* uttʃizo

victim, killed person

Le amiche di Sadako volevano costruire un monumento per lei e tutti i bambini che sono stati uccisi dalla bomba atomica.

Sadako's friends wanted to build a monument to her and all children who were killed by the atomic bomb.

1019 **cento** - *adj; num* tʃˈɛnto

hundred

Se si è pazienti in un attimo di rabbia, si fuggiranno cento giorni di dolore.

If you are patient in one moment of anger, you will escape a hundred days of sorrow.

1020 **rotta** - *nf* rotta

route

Si può prendere uno dei tanti autobus navetta che operano all'interno la rotta o meglio optare per i taxi.

You can take one of the many shuttle buses that operate within the route or rather opt for taxis.

1021 **nipote** - *nm* nipote

grandson, granddaughter, nephew, niece

Le immagini furono probabilmente collezionate dalla nipote di Elisabetta, l’arciduchessa Elisabetta Maria.

The pictures were probably collected by her granddaughter Elisabeth Marie.

1022 **teatro** - *nm* teatro

theater

Il teatro è destinato ad ospitare anche presentazioni di progetti di urbanistica ed architettura.

The theatre will also host presentations of urban and architectural, environmental and transportation projects.

1023 **militare** - *adj; nm* militare

military; soldier

I jihadisti sono in grado di decapitare i civili, uccidere i bambini e violentare le donne indifese, ma quando si tratta di combattere una forza militare non vogliono saperne a che fare e tornano qui nelle loro comode case con la coda fra le gambe.

Jihadis are capable of beheading civilians, murdering children and raping defenceless women, but when it comes to fighting a military force they don't want to know, and they come back here to their comfortable homes with their tails between their legs.

1024 **palazzo** - *nm* palattso

palace

"E cosa c'è nel palazzo sul lato opposto del cortile?" "Ci sono delle stalle al piano terra e dei fienili sopra di esse."

"And what's in the building on the other side of the yard?" "There are stables on the ground floor and haylofts above them."

1025 **convinto** - *adj* konvinto

convinced

Mary soffre di anoressia ed è convinta di essere grassa, ma la realtà è che lei è pericolosamente magra.

Mary suffers from anorexia and is convinced that she's fat but the reality is that she is dangerously thin.

1026 **innocente** - *nm; adj* innotʃente

innocent

Tutte le vostre accuse sono infondate. Lei è innocente, e noi lo proveremo.

All of your accusations are baseless. She is innocent, and we will prove that.

1027 **finale** - *adj; nm/f* finale

final; final, ending, finish/final (sports)

La partita è finita in pareggio, e il risultato finale è stato di due a due.

The game ended in a draw, and the final score was 2-2.

1028 **purtroppo** - *adv* purtroppo

unfortunately

Il fatto che sia stato provato concretamente che queste dichiarazioni sono senza fondamento purtroppo non impedisce che vengano ripetute.

The fact that these assertions have consistently proved to be without foundation unfortunately does not prevent their repetition.

1029 **innamorato** - *adj; nm* innamorato

in love; lover

"Da quanto tempo Tom è innamorato di te?" "Tom non è innamorato di me. È un mio amico."

"How long has Tom been in love with you?" "Tom is not in love with me. He's my friend."

1030 **breve** - *adj* breve

short

La componente dell'indebitamento a breve termine aumenta complessivamente di 9,5 milioni di euro in relazione all'incremento dei "debiti finanziari" di 8,6 milioni di euro derivante dalla citata riclassifica delle quote a breve dei debiti a medio/lungo termine.

The short-term debt component rose by 9.5 million euros overall, due to an increase of 8.6 million euros in borrowings deriving from the above-mentioned reclassification of short-term portions of medium- and long-term loans.

1031 **turno** - *nm*
turno

round, shift
I nostri genitori si sono presi cura di noi e ora è il nostro turno per prendersi cura di loro.
Our parents took care of us and now it's our turn to take care of them.

1032 **emergenza** - *nf*
emerdʒentsa

emergency
Mia madre mi ha sempre detto che dovrei mettere i soldi in banca ogni mese, così da avere abbastanza soldi in caso di emergenza.
My mother always told me that I should put money in the bank every month so I'd have enough money in case of an emergency.

1033 **improvviso** - *adj*
improvvizo

sudden
Non so quale sia il motivo del suo improvviso successo.
I don't know what the reason is for his sudden success.

1034 **fanculo** - *int*
faŋkulo

fuck
Fanculo vostra madre.
Fuck your mom.

1035 **tetto** - *nm*
tetto

roof
L'edificio di cui si riesce a vedere il tetto laggiù è la nostra chiesa.
The building whose roof you can see over there is our church.

1036 **montagna** - *nf*
montaɲɲa

mountain
Io e i miei colleghi abbiamo vissuto in una piccola cabina da due camere costruita sul bordo di una scogliera sulla montagna.
Me and my colleagues lived in a small 2 room cabin built on the edge of a cliff on the mountain.

1037 **bottiglia** - *nf*
bottiʎʎa

bottle
Tom ha comprato una bottiglia di vodka e un po' di profumo al duty-free.
Tom bought a bottle of vodka and some perfume at the duty-free shop.

1038 **pane** - *nm*

bread

pane

La prima colazione viene servita ogni mattina e comprende un
assortimento di frutta fresca, pane e salumi, mentre presso il ristorante dell'albergo potrete gustare specialità regionali e varie bevande.

Breakfast is served each morning and includes a variety of fresh fruits, breads and cold meats. Regional specialties, as well as a selection of drinks are available in the hotel's restaurant.

1039 **preoccupato** - *adj*
preokkupato

worried

Sono stato licenziato e poiché ho dei risparmi, per il momento, non sono preoccupato.

I got the sack but I've a little saved up, so for the time being I won't be troubled by living expenses.

1040 **ricco** - *adj*
rikko

rich

Una serie di seminari tematici ed un ricco e vario programma per il tempo libero consentiranno infine di approfondire la conoscenza ed avere esperienza diretta della realtà italiana.

A series of seminars and a rich and varied programme of free time will help you to deepen your knowledge and further your experience of the Italian reality.

1041 **discorso** - *nm*
diskorso

speech

Io ho davvero una brutta ansia da prestazione prima di dare un discorso.

I get really bad performance anxiety before I give a speech.

1042 **evitare** - *verb*
evitare

to avoid

Noi abbiamo imboccato una strada secondaria per evitare il traffico pesante.

We took a secondary road to avoid the heavy traffic.

1043 **accettare** - *verb*
attʃettare

to accept

Tom mi ha detto di non vedere il motivo per cui dovrebbe accettare l'offerta di Mary.

Tom told me that he could see no reason why he shouldn't accept Mary's offer.

1044 **immagine** - *nf*
immadʒine

image

Qualsiasi opera di un uomo, sia letteratura o musica o immagine o architettura o qualsiasi altra cosa, è sempre un ritratto di se stesso.

Every man's work, whether it be literature or music or a picture or architecture or anything else, is always a portrait of himself.

1045 **ministro** - *nm* ministro — **minister**

Il ministro ha nominato uno dei suoi amici intimi in una posizione chiave.

The minister appointed one of his cronies to a key position.

1046 **mantenere** - *verb* mantenere — **to keep, maintain**

La vita è come guidare una bicicletta. Per mantenere l'equilibrio si deve restare in movimento.

Life is like riding a bicycle. To keep your balance you must keep moving.

1047 **giardino** - *nm* dʒardino — **garden**

Tom voleva che Mary innaffiasse i fiori del suo giardino mentre lui era via.

Tom asked Mary to water the flowers in his garden while he was gone.

1048 **lottare** - *verb* lottare — **to fight**

All'inizio hanno cercato di ignorarti, poi hanno cominciato a ridere di te, e dopo a lottare con te. Alla fine vinci tu.

At first they try to ignore you, then they start to laugh at you, then they fight you, then you win.

1049 **distruggere** - *verb* distruddʒere — **to destroy**

Ai bambini non piacciono le persone che distruggono la natura.

Children don't like people who destroy nature.

1050 **po' (pò)** - *adv* po' (pˈɔ) — **bit**

Tom si sentì un po' a disagio mentre camminava lungo la strada deserta nel bel mezzo della notte.

Tom felt a little uneasy as he walked down the deserted street in the middle of the night.

1051 **retro** - *nm* retro — **back, rear**

Tom aprì la porta sul retro per far uscire il cane.

Tom opened the back door to let the dog out.

1052 **bicchiere** - *nm* bikkjere — **(drinking) glass**

Tom versò del vino in un bicchiere di plastica e lo porse a Mary.

Tom poured wine into a plastic cup and handed it to Mary.

1053 **pantalone** - *nm* — **trousers**

pantalone | Può trattarsi di un pantalone e di una camicia senza cuciture realizzata in un tessuto resistente, da abbinare con scarpe a mocassin.
It may consist of trousers and a seamless shirt made of a hard-wearing fabric, worn with moccasins.

1054 **tribunale** - *nm* | **court**
tribunale | I risultati del test della macchina della verità sono inammissibili in tribunale.
The results of a lie detector test are inadmissible in court.

1055 **gioia** - *nf* | **joy**
dʒoja | Pianse di gioia quando seppe che suo figlio era sopravvissuto all'incidente aereo.
She cried for joy when she heard that her son had survived the plane crash.

1056 **paziente** - *adj; nm&f* | **patient**
pattsjente | Il tessuto del polmone del paziente è stato danneggiato da anni di lavoro in una miniera di carbone.
The patient's lung tissue was damaged from years of working in a coal mine.

1057 **arrabbiare** - *verb* | **to get angry, get mad**
arrabbjare | Mi sono arrabbiato così tanto che non ero in grado di parlare.
I got so mad I wasn't able to speak.

1058 **genio** - *nm* | **genius**
dʒenjo | Il talento artistico e la creatività di Giorgio Moroder non sono limitati al suo genio musicale.
Giorgio Moroder's artistic talent and creative genius are not restricted to the field of music.

1059 **debole** - *adj* | **weak**
debole | Lei è stata malata per molto tempo ed è ancora troppo debole per muoversi.
She has been ill for a long time and she is still too weak to get about.

1060 **coppia** - *nf* | **couple**
koppja | La coppia si è seduta per un'affascinante cena all'aperto in giardino.
The couple sat down for a charming alfresco dinner in the garden.

1061 **arrestare** - *verb* | **to stop**

	arrestare	Tom non è stato in grado di fornire un alibi, quindi la polizia lo ha arrestato. *Tom wasn't able to provide an alibi so the police arrested him.*
1062	**allarme** - *nm* allarme	**alarm** Io stavo ascoltando il mio iPod, così non ho sentito l'allarme antincendio. *I was listening to my iPod, so I didn't hear the fire alarm.*
1063	**est** - *nm* est	**East** Ci sono molte spiagge nudiste nella Germania dell'Est. *There are many nudist beaches in East Germany.*
1064	**vissuto** - *adj* vissuto	**lived** Mia nonna era solita dire che sarebbe vissuta fino a cent'anni, ma morì quando ne aveva 85. *My grandmother used to say that she would live to be a hundred, but she died at the age of 85.*
1065	**condizione** - *nf* kondittsjone	**condition** Significa un enorme aumento dell'utilizzo dell'aria condizionata, che utilizza energia, costa soldi e crea inquinamento. *It means a huge increase in the use of air conditioning which uses energy, which costs money and creates pollution.*
1066	**cattivo** - *adj; nm/f* kattivo	**bad; baddie, bad person** Ecco la buona notizia: si lavora. Ed ecco la cattiva notizia: si lavora sempre più spesso in nero. *Here's the good news: there's work. And here comes the bad news: there's work, but it's ever more often under the table.*
1067	**cinese** - *adj; nmf* tʃineze	**Chinese** Siccome nei blog cinesi si usa spesso lo slang, frequentemente non li capisco del tutto, ma credo che questo esercizio abbia una buona influenza nei confronti del mio livello di cinese. *Because Chinese blogs use a lot of slang, I usually don't understand them that well, but I still think it's good for my Chinese.*
1068	**malattia** - *nf* malattja	**disease, illness** Se avessi saputo della tua malattia, ti sarei venuto a trovare in ospedale. *If I had known about your illness, I would have visited you in the hospital.*

1069 **dito** - *nm*
dito

finger
Questa è la prima volta che mi sono tagliato un dito con un coltello.
This is the first time I've cut my finger with a knife.

1070 **laboratorio** - *nm*
laboratorjo

laboratory
Io ho passato tre ore in laboratorio con Tom questo pomeriggio.
I spent three hours in the lab with Tom this afternoon.

1071 **preferito** - *adj*
preferito

favorite
Con mio rammarico, il mio programma televisivo preferito è andato fuori onda il mese scorso.
To my regret, my favorite TV show went off the air last month.

1072 **vittoria** - *nf*
vittorja

victory
Loro hanno detto le loro preghiere per la vittoria.
They said their prayers for victory.

1073 **dritto** - *adj; adv*
dritto

straight, upright; right
È difficile per un sacco vuoto stare dritto. Vai dritto e troverai la stazione.
It is hard for an empty sack to stand straight. Go straight, and you will find the station.

1074 **ferito** - *adj*
ferito

injured
Sua moglie è all'ospedale, è stata ferita in un incidente d'auto.
His wife is in the hospital because she was injured in a car crash.

1075 **unità** - *nf*
unitˈa

unit
L'Unità per la legge e l'ambiente fa avanzare la protezione ambientale dalle vie legislative e politiche.
The Unit for Law and the Environment advances environmental protection through legislation and policy avenues.

1076 **direzione** - *nf*
direttsjone

direction, management
Mentre quel'auto andava dove io stavo andando, capii che stavamo andando esattamente nella stessa direzione.
The car proved to be a slave, so I will not be a master.

1077 **sposato** - *adj*
spozato

married
Mentre era in Svezia, ha avuto una fidanzata svedese che gli ha insegnato lo svedese, poi l'ha sposata.

While in Sweden, he had a Swedish girlfriend who taught him Swedish, then he married her.

1078 **migliaio** - *adj; num*
miʎʎajo
thousand
Il criminale derubò il padrone di casa di un centinaio di migliaia di dollari e corse via.
The criminal robbed the landlord of a hundred thousand dollars and ran away.

1079 **occupare** - *verb*
okkupare
to occupy
Questa casa occupa una posizione conveniente, ma il guaio è che è troppo piccola per la mia famiglia numerosa.
This house is conveniently situated but the trouble is that it is too small for my large family.

1080 **sabato** - *nm*
sabato
Saturday
In realtà volevamo andare al cinema sabato, ma poi abbiamo cambiato idea e siamo rimasti a casa.
Actually we wanted to go to the movies on Saturday, but we changed our mind and stayed at home.

1081 **mattino, mattina** - *nm*
mattino, mattina
morning
È difficile credere che nessuno sia stato ricoperto dai detriti dell'edificio nel terremoto di questa mattina.
It's hard to believe that no one was covered by the building's debris in the earthquake this morning.

1082 **sentimento** - *nm*
sentimento
feeling
La rabbia, sentimento che esprime una volontà di opposizione e di reazione è, in generale, poco percepita e poco espressa dai bambini.
In general, anger (a feeling that expresses a will of reaction and opposition) is little perceived and little expressed by the children.

1083 **vuoto** - *adj*
vwoto
empty
La casa era vuota, tranne che per la presenza di un gatto.
The house was empty except for a cat.

1084 **spiaggia** - *nf*
spjaddʒa
beach
Il porto a nord della spiaggia adiacente, è durante il giorno ritrovo di un rivenditore di escatori locali e la sera con i suoi molti caffè e ristoranti che attrae turisti.
The Harbour to the North of the town's Beach adjacent, is during the day meeting place of local fishermen dealer and in the evening with its many cafes and restaurants attracting tourists.

1085 **testimone** - *nm*
testimone

witness
La nostra coscienza è il testimone dei nostri crimini più segreti.
Our conscience is the witness to our most secret crimes.

1086 **gas** - *nm*
gas

gas
Come tutti sanno, l'atmosfera è un miscuglio di molti gas.
As everyone knows, air is a mixture of gases.

1087 **dipartimento** - *nm*
dipartimento

department
Diventò la direttrice del dipartimento di cardiologia nell'ospedale della città.
She became the director of the cardiology department at the city hospital.

1088 **miglio** - *nm*
miʎʎo

mile
C'è un ponte due miglia più su lungo il corso del fiume.
There is a bridge two miles upstream.

1089 **smesso** - *adj*
smesso

stopped
Loro hanno aspettato sotto il portico fino a quando non ha smesso di piovere.
They waited on the porch until it stopped raining.

1090 **sedia** - *nf*
sedja

chair
Nella stanza di sinistra, in cui si trova un elegante camino, sono esposti un busto e un ritratto ottocenteschi del poeta e alcuni mobili, fra cui una sedia che gli appartenne.
In the room on the left, with its elegant chimneypiece, are a nineteenth century bust and portrait of the poet and some furniture, including a chair that belonged to him.

1091 **cadavere** - *nm*
kadavere

dead body
La polizia ha trovato un cadavere in una macchina abbandonata vicino al parco.
The police found a dead body in an abandoned car near the park.

1092 **obiettivo** - *nm*
objettivo

target, objective
L'obiettivo è quello di portare insieme le persone per rendere questo progetto un successo.
Their common aim was to make the project successful.

1093 **fianco** - *nm*
fjaŋko

side
È successo che mi sono seduto di fianco a lei a una riunione.
It happened that I sat next to her at a meeting.

1094 **entrata** - *nf*

entrance

	entrata	L'entrata in vigore del trattato di Lisbona ha confermato il diritto di petizione dinanzi al Parlamento europeo *The entry into force of the Treaty of Lisbon confirmed the right to petition the European Parliament*
1095	**furgone** - *nm* furgone	**van, pick-up truck** C'è un furgone rosso parcheggiato davanti a casa tua. *There's a red van parked in front of your house.*
1096	**amato** - *adj* amato	**beloved** Sei l'unica donna che io abbia mai amato davvero. *You're the only woman I've ever really loved.*
1097	**motore** - *adj; nm* motore	**motor; enginge, motor** Tom ha detto che non era mai stato su una barca a motore. *Tom said he'd never been in a motorboat.*
1098	**presentare** - *verb* prezentare	**to present, submit** Nella stessa risoluzione il Parlamento europeo ha chiesto al Consiglio e alla Commissione di presentare proposte per ridurre il volume dei rifiuti. *The European Parliament, in the same Resolution, requests the Council and the Commission to put forward proposals for cutting the volume of waste.*
1099	**ladro** - *adj* ladro	**thief** Sono entrati dei ladri nel nostro appartamento e hanno rubato la pelliccia di mia moglie. *Burglars broke into our apartment and stole my wife's fur coat.*
1100	**soluzione** - *nf* soluttsjone	**solution** Non aveva altra soluzione; non ha potuto far altro che abbandonare i suoi piani. *He could do nothing but give up his plan against his will.*
1101	**sguardo** - *nm* zgwardo	**look** Un semplice sguardo non è sufficiente per noi a distinguere l'uno dall'altro. *A mere glance is not enough for us to tell one from the other.*
1102	**fantasma** - *nf* fantasma	**ghost** Poi il fantasma riprese a parlare, e la sua voce assomigliava al sospiro del vento. *Then the ghost spoke again, and his voice sounded like the sighing of the wind.*
1103	**spiegare** - *verb*	**to explain**

spjegare — Venne dagli irlandesi con tutti i segni di un apostolo, e quando la gente gli chiese di spiegare la Santissima Trinità, si chinò a terra e prese un trifoglio.

He came to the Irish with all the signs of an apostle, and when the people asked him to explain the Blessed Trinity, he reached down to the ground and picked up a shamrock.

1104 **pioggia** - *nf*
pjoddʒa
rain
Dato che c'è nuvolo con possibilità di pioggia oggi, non dovremmo andare a fare surf.
Since it's cloudy with a chance of rain today, we shouldn't go surfing.

1105 **zero** - *adj; num*
dzero
zero
Il termometro ha registrato dieci gradi sotto zero la scorsa notte.
The thermometer registered ten degrees below zero last night.

1106 **eppure** - *conj*
eppure
and yet
"Una volta è come mai", sottintese la giovane donna. Eppure il ginecologo sottintese: "gemelli".
"Once is like never," implied the young lady. Yet the gynecologist implied: "twins."

1107 **potente** - *adj*
potente
powerful
L'America è il paese più ricco e più potente.
America is the richest and most powerful country.

1108 **sé** - *pron*
sˈe
himself, herself
L'illuminismo è l'uscita dell'uomo dallo stato di minorità che egli deve imputare a sé stesso.
Enlightenment is man's leaving his self-imposed immaturity.

1109 **famoso** - *adj*
famozo
famous
Il nome Campoformido è diventato famoso nel mondo per il trattato di pace tra Napoleone e l'Austria, ma la storia della località è molto più antica.
The name Campoformido is famous all over the world because of the peace treaty between Napoleon and Austria, but the history of this town is much older.

1110 **uccello** - *nm*
uttʃello
bird
Sai che la gru è un uccello migratore capace di sollevare fino a cento chili?
Did you know that the crane is a migratory bird and that it can lift up to one hundred kilograms?

1111 **accadere** - *verb*
akkadere

to happen
Povero ragazzo! Se solo avesse saputo allora le cose terribili che dovevano accadergli a causa della sua disobbedienza!
Poor boy! If he had only known then the dreadful things that were to happen to him on account of his disobedience!

1112 **giacca** - *nf*
dʒakka

jacket
Ha notato un buco nella sua giacca, ma ha provato a ignorarlo.
He noticed a hole in his jacket, but he tried to ignore it.

1113 **sbagliare** - *verb*
zbaʎʎare

to make a mistake
A lezione James era terrorizzato di sbagliare e di ricevere una nota.
James had a great fear of making mistakes in class and being reprimanded.

1114 **polvere** - *nf*
polvere

dust
Sopra i dizionari non c'è che della polvere, almeno sopra i miei.
On the dictionaries there's nothing but dust, at least on mine.

1115 **faro** - *nm*
faro

lighthouse, beacon, headlight
I secondo fattore decisivo è la creazione di un'università europea multiconfessionale a Sarajevo, che costituirà un faro di tolleranza e reciproca comprensione in Europa
The second decisive factor is the establishment of a European multi-faith university in Sarajevo, which will act as a European centre of tolerance and mutual understanding

1116 **università** - *nf*
universit'a

university
Questo non è molto logico per me, ma Tom ha deciso di non andare all'università.
It doesn't make much sense to me, but Tom has decided not to go to college.

1117 **pollo** - *nm*
pollo

chicken
Quando ha iniziato a mangiare il suo pollo, aveva un sapore un po' strano.
When he started to eat his chicken, it tasted a little funny.

1118 **gloria** - *nf*
glorja

glory
Giusta è la gloria, che è frutto del valore.
Just is the glory that is the fruit of bravery.

1119 **ovest** - *nm*

West

ovest | Il consumo di alcol è più alto nell'Europa dell'est che nell'Europa dell'ovest.

Alcohol consumption is higher in Eastern Europe than in Western Europe.

1120 **attendere** - *verb* | **to wait for**
attendere | Mi perdoni se l'ho lasciata attendere così a lungo.
I am sorry to have kept you waiting so long.

1121 **tedesco** - *adj, nm/f* | **German; German**
tedesko | La nipote del pittore tedesco Otto Dix ha accusato la Germania di non avere realmente affrontato la questione delle opere d'arte sequestrate dai nazisti.

The granddaughter of German painter Otto Dix accused Germany of never really having addressed the issue of works of art seized by the Nazis.

1122 **doppio** - *adj* | **double**
doppjo | Per questo lavoro ci vorrà il doppio di quello che mi aspettavo.
This job will take twice as long as I expected

1123 **coglione** - *nm* | **balls, nuts, asshole**
koʎʎone | Il tuo ex-fidanzato è un coglione.
Your ex-boyfriend is a jerk.

1124 **sei** - *adj; num* | **six**
sˈɛi | Le ci sono voluti sei anni per trovare il coraggio di dirgli che non le piaceva più.

It took her six years to get up the courage to tell him that she didn't like him anymore.

1125 **maiale** - *nm* | **pig, pork**
majale | Chi vuole essere felice per un giorno, deve ubriacarsi. Chi vuole essere felice per un mese, deve uccidere un maiale. Chi vuole essere felice per un anno deve sposarsi. Chi vuole essere felice per tutta la vita, deve amare il proprio lavoro.

Those who want to be happy for a day should get drunk. Those who want to be happy for a month, should slaughter a pig. Those who want to be happy for a year, should marry. Those who want to be happy for the whole life, must love their profession.

1126 **conoscenza** - *nf* | **knowledge**
konoʃʃentsa | Devi acquisire al più presto una buona conoscenza dell'inglese commerciale.

You have to acquire as soon as possible a good knowledge of business English.

1127 **telefonata** - *nf* telefonata

phone call

Dovresti essere abbastanza intelligente da sapere che non è il caso di fare telefonate nel cuore della notte.

You should know better than to call at midnight.

1128 **ammazzare** - *verb* ammattsare

to kill

Gli atleti erano seduti ad ammazzare il tempo, aspettando che la loro partita iniziasse.

The athletes sat around killing time, waiting for their game to start.

1129 **vacanza** - *nf* vakantsa

holiday, vacation

L'anno scorso hanno comprato una casa nel posto dove noi stiamo andando in vacanza.

They bought a house last year in the place where we're going on vacation.

1130 **medio** - *adj* medjo

average, medium, middle

La promozione dalla scuola elementare alla scuola media è vista da alcuni come il primo passo verso la maturità.

The graduation from elementary school to middle school is regarded by some as the first step towards adulthood.

1131 **grandioso** - *adj* grandjozo

great

Dalla via ferrata del Monte San Salvatore, un percorso di scalata artificiale su rocce verticali, si gode un panorama grandioso.

A splendid panoramic view can be enjoyed from the Monte San Salvatore via ferrata route, an artificial climbing route on vertical rocks.

1132 **atto** - *nm* atto

act

Non mi è mai passato per la mente che lui avrebbe veramente messo in atto la sua minaccia.

It never crossed my mind that he would actually carry out his threat.

1133 **nazionale** - *adj* nattsjonale

national

Ci siamo alzati dai nostri posti quando è stato suonato l'inno nazionale.

We rose from our seats when the national anthem was played.

1134 **aeroporto** - *nm*

airport

aeroporto — Quanto tempo ci vuole ad arrivare all'aeroporto con l'autobus aeroportuale?

How long does it take to get to the airport with the airport bus?

1135 **proteggere** - *verb* — **to protect**

proteddʒere — L'intero paese sta favorendo importanti tagli del bilancio che permetterebbero di proteggere l'educazione.

The whole county is favoring critical budget revisions which promise to protect education.

1136 **neppure** - *adv; conj* — **not even, neither**

neppure — "Tom da dove ottiene la sua capacità in francese? Non ha mai messo piede in un paese di lingua francese, e non ha neppure amici di lingua francese."

"Where does Tom get his ability in French? He's never set foot in a French-speaking country, and he has no French-speaking friends, either."

1137 **movimento** - *nm* — **movement**

movimento — Le conseguenze del movimento femminista hanno colpito sia gli uomini che le donne.

The changes resulting from the women's movement have affected both women and men.

1138 **pesante** - *adj* — **heavy**

pezante — Ho trasportato oggetti di ferro, ma non ho trovato niente di più pesante di un debito.

I carried iron, but didn't find anything heavier than debt.

1139 **quarto** - *adj; num; nm* — **fourth; quarter**

kwarto — Gennaio è il primo mese dell'anno, aprile è il quarto, novembre è l'undicesimo, dicembre è il dodicesimo.

January is the first month of the year, April is the fourth, November is the eleventh, and December is the twelfth.

1140 **taglio** - *nm* — **cut, cutting**

taʎʎo — I parametri di taglio opzionali sono determinati da un insieme di fattori, quali ad esempio la durezza del materiale, il feed rate, la velocità di rotazione del mandrino, la profondità di taglio e la capacità di taglio dell'utensile.

The optimal cutting parameters are determined by a balance of such factors as the hardness of the material, the feed rate, the spindle rotating speed, the cutting-in depth, and the capacity of the cutter.

1141 **assistente** - *adj; nm&f* — **assistant; assistant**

	assistente	Noi vogliamo un assistente, preferibilmente qualcuno con dell'esperienza. *We want an assistant, preferably someone with experience.*
1142	**scemo** - *adj* ʃemo	**fool** Ed eccomi qui, con tutta la mia tradizione, povero scemo, non più saggio di prima. *And here I stand, with all my lore, poor fool, no wiser than before.*
1143	**puzza** - *nf* puttsa	**stink** Questo tizio seduto di fianco a me sul treno puzza! *This guy sitting next to me on the train stinks!*
1144	**interesse** - *nm* interesse	**interest** Tenendo conto del suo interesse per i bambini, sono certo che l'insegnamento sia la carriera migliore per lei. *Given her interest in children, I am sure teaching is the right career for her.*
1145	**orecchio** - *nm* orekkjo	**ear** Avete mai notato che l'orecchio destro di Tom è molto più grande di quello sinistro? *Have you ever noticed that Tom's right ear is much larger than his left ear?*
1146	**regno** - *nm* reɲɲo	**kingdom** Se uno non è nato di nuovo, non può vedere il regno di Dio. *No one can see the kingdom of God unless he is born again.*
1147	**passato** - *adj* passato	**past** Fece una smorfia come se i ricordi del suo passato amaro si schiantassero come le onde dentro la sua testa. *He grimaced as if memories of his bitter past were crashing like waves inside his head.*
1148	**uovo** - *nm* wovo	**egg** Fa così caldo che si potrebbe cuocere un uovo sul cofano di una macchina. *It's so hot that you could cook an egg on the hood of a car.*
1149	**affrontare** - *verb* affrontare	**to face** Loro sono entrambi riusciti a trovare il problema più grave che abbia mai affrontato il nostro pianeta. *They have both failed to find the most serious problem that has ever faced our planet.*
1150	**neve** - *nf*	**snow**

neve
Il Canada, un paese coperto di neve e ghiacci otto mesi all'anno, abitata da barbari, orsi e castori.
Canada, a country covered with snows and ices eight months of the year, inhabited by barbarians, bears and beavers.

1151 **legale** - *adj; nm* — **legal; lawyer**
legale
Un matrimonio non è legale finché non vengono fatte certe dichiarazioni.
A marriage is not legal unless certain declarations are made.

1152 **sveglio** - *adj* — **awake**
zveʎʎo
Riesco a riaddormentarmi facilmente una volta che mi sono svegliato o poi sto sveglio a lungo senza prendere sonno?
Do I find it easy to get to sleep again after I have been woken, or do I then stay lying awake for long periods?

1153 **nervoso** - *adj* — **nervous**
nervozo
Questa è la mia prima confessione e ho ogni ragione di essere nervoso.
This is my first confession and I have every reason to be nervous.

1154 **richiesta** - *nf* — **request**
rikjesta
Se la leggi fra le righe, questa lettera è una richiesta di denaro.
If you read between the lines, this letter is a request for money.

1155 **preso** - *adj* — **took**
prezo
La mia gola fa male e il mio corpo sembra pesante. Sembra che abbia preso un raffreddore in qualche modo.
My throat hurts and my body feels heavy. It looks like I've caught a cold somehow.

1156 **lago** - *nm* — **lake**
lago
Sono appena arrivato in cima a una montagna. Questo è molto sorprendente, perché secondo la mia mappa qui deve essere un lago.
I've just arrived at the top of a mountain. That's really surprising, because according to my map, there should be a lake here.

1157 **teoria** - *nf* — **theory**
teorja
Vorrei fare alcune osservazioni prima di dedicarmi a un attento esame della teoria.
I would like to make a few remarks before turning to a close examination of the theory.

1158 **desiderare** - *verb* dezíderare

to wish

A causa dell'aggravarsi delle condizioni di salute, desidera dare le dimissioni.

He wishes to resign on the grounds that his health is failing.

1159 **distanza** - *nf* distantsa

distance

L'apprendimento delle lingue non è una gara a breve distanza; è una maratona.

Language learning isn't a short distance race; it's a marathon.

1160 **pista** - *nf* pista

track

Le condizioni della pista di prova o quelle dell'utente finale possono essere una vera sfida.

Conditions on the test track or in the hands of the end user can be very challenging.

1161 **solamente** - *adv* solamente

only

La sorgente di radiazioni può essere trasportata solamente con una pinza o un utensile prensile e va tenuta il più lontano possibile dal corpo.

The source must only be transported with pliers or a gripper and the distance to the body must be kept as large as possible.

1162 **nonostante** - *prep; conj; adv* nonostante

despite; altough; even though, nevertheless

Nonostante ciò la società è riuscita, come appena accennato e meglio descritto di seguito, a proseguire in tutte le attività.

Despite this, as has just been mentioned and as will be better described below, the company has managed to continue with all its activities.

1163 **dettaglio** - *nm* dettaʎʎo

detail

Tom rivelò i dettagli più intimi della sua relazione con Mary.

Tom revealed the most intimate details of his relationship with Mary.

1164 **dannare** - *verb* dannare

to damn

Ecco, finalmente un produttore che non ti fa dannare con un cavo del calibro di un doppino telefonico solo perchè hai comprato il suo prodotto più economico!

Lo and behold, finally a manufacturer emerges who does not damn you to telephone line caliber cable just beacuse you're buying their cheapest speaker!

1165 **moto** - *nm*

motion, motorbike

moto — se i componenti elettronici della moto non funzionassero, nemmeno la moto potrebbe gareggiare!

if the electronic components of the motorbike don't work, then neither does the motorbike!

1166 **prete** - *nm*
prete

priest

Non serve a nulla confessare i suoi peccati al prete se non pensa due volte prima di ripeterli.

It's no use confessing your sins to the priest if you don't think twice before repeating them.

1167 **ospite** - *nm*
ospite

guest, host

Quell'hotel fa ogni sforzo possibile, affinchè i suoi ospiti si sentano a casa.

That hotel really goes the extra mile to make sure their guests feel at home.

1168 **direttamente** - *adv*
direttamente

directly

Ho fatto il check-in in un motel e sono andata direttamente a dormire.

I checked into a motel and went right to sleep.

1169 **risolvere** - *verb*
rizolvere

to solve

Questo problema è difficile da risolvere. Quindi avresti fatto meglio a iniziare con quello.

This problem is hard to solve. So you had better begin with that one.

1170 **diretto** - *adj*
diretto

direct

È salito a bordo di un aereo diretto a Los Angeles.

He boarded a plane bound for Los Angeles.

1171 **sigaretta** - *nf*
sigaretta

cigarette

Quel tizio in piedi in un angolo laggiù riesce a finire una sigaretta in meno di un minuto.

That guy standing in the corner over there can finish a smoke in less than a minute.

1172 **pilotare** - *verb*
pilotare

to pilot, fly

Il timoniere è così in grado di pilotare tranquillamente il rimorchiatore.

The steersman can concentrate all his attention to pilot the tug.

1173 **presenza** - *nf*
prezentsa

presence

Ti avrei chiesto almeno il nome, ma la presenza di mio padre è stata un impedimento.

I would have at least asked you for the name, but my father's presence has been an impediment.

1174 **raggiungere** - *verb* raddʒundʒere

to reach

Riuscirono a raggiungere la vetta della montagna, ma ebbero un incidente mentre stavano scendendo.

They succeeded in reaching the mountain summit, but had an accident when coming back down.

1175 **trappola** - *nf* trappola

trap

Il topo è stato attirato nella trappola da un grosso pezzo di formaggio.

The mouse was lured into the trap by a big piece of cheese.

1176 **premio** - *nm* prˈɛmjo

prize

Madre Teresa usò i soldi del premio per il suo lavoro in India e in giro per il mondo.

Mother Teresa used the prize money for her work in India and around the world.

1177 **pietra** - *nf* pjetra

stone

Una casa in legno brucia più facilmente di una casa di pietra.

A house built of wood is more easily burnt than a house of stone.

1178 **pulito** - *adj* pulito

clean, clean

Se si verifica il contatto, pulire la superficie con un panno morbido e pulito appena possibile.

If contact occurs, wipe the surface with a clean, soft cloth as soon as possible.

1179 **pausa** - *nf* pauza

break

Ha lavorato senza pausa per mantenere i suoi figli fino a che si sono sposati.

She worked without a break to feed her children until they got married.

1180 **fastidio** - *nm* fastidjo

bother, annoyance, nuisance

Va bene se lei ride alle sue proprie battute. Mi dà fastidio quando lo fa Tom, ma è perché lui non è molto divertente.

It's okay if you laugh at your own jokes. It annoys me when Tom does, but that's because he isn't very funny.

1181 **gola** - *nf* gola

throat

Un esame completo orecchio-naso-gola dev'essere effettuato per il rilascio iniziale di un certificato medico di classe 1 e in seguito periodicamente, quando indicato clinicamente.

A comprehensive ear, nose and throat examination shall be undertaken for the initial issue of a class 1 medical certificate and periodically thereafter when clinically indicated.

1182 **tavola** - *nf*
tavola

table
Sedersi a tavola a Trieste diventa un vero e proprio viaggio tra sapori, odori e colori appartenenti a culture e modi di vivere diversi.
Sitting down to eat in Trieste becomes a real and proper journey on tastes, smells and colours belonging to different cultures and ways of living.

1183 **discutere** - *verb*
diskutere

to discuss
Le persone che introducono dati personali nelle discussioni non sanno come si discute.
People who bring personal details into arguments don't know how to argue.

1184 **perdono** - *nm*
perdono

pardon, forgiveness
Il perdono è una cosa tra loro e Dio, il mio compito è di organizzare l'incontro.
Forgiveness is between them and God, it's my job to arrange the meeting.

1185 **quartiere** - *nm*
kwartjere

district, neighbourhood, quarter
Se ti mostrassi la mia casa, il mio quartiere di allora, tu comprenderesti da dove vengo?
If I showed you my house, my neighborhood back then, would you understand where I am from?

1186 **venti** - *adj; num*
venti

twenty
Le licenze, concessioni, marchi e diritti simili sono ammortizzate in un periodo che varia da cinque a venti anni o, relativamente ad alcuni diritti, in base alla durata del contratto cui si riferiscono.
Licences, concessions, brand names and similar rights are amortized over periods varying from five to twenty years or, in some cases, over the duration of the relevant contract.

1187 **augurio** - *nm*
augurjo

wish, greeting, omen
La prossima volta che la vedi, falle i migliori auguri da parte mia.
Next time you see her, give her my best wishes.

1188 **lupo** - *nm*
lupo

wolf
Il ragazzo urlò: "Al lupo, al lupo!" e tutto il villaggio corse in suo aiuto.

The boy cried "Wolf, wolf!" and the villagers came out to help him.

1189 **carico** - *adj* kariko
load, freight
Il morso di un serpente a sonagli è carico di veleno.
A rattlesnake's bite is filled with poison.

1190 **cugino** - *nm/f* kudʒino
cousin
George ha due cugini; uno vive in Germania e l'altro in Svizzera.
George has two cousins; one lives in Germany and the other in Switzerland.

1191 **galera** - *nf* galera
jail
Sono passati 10 giorni da quando il mio fidanzato è andato in galera.
It's been 10 days since my boyfriend went to jail.

1192 **ragazzina** - *nf* ragattsina
little girl
Le fotografie e le lettere ci mostrano una ragazzina vivace e curiosa che inizialmente ha una vita normale.
Photos and letters in the exhibition reveal a vivacious and curious girl who lives a normal life

1193 **medicina** - *nf* meditʃina
medicine
I recenti progressi della medicina daranno inizio a una nuova era nel campo delle cure mediche.
Recent advances in medicine will usher in a new age in medical care.

1194 **violenza** - *nf* vjolentsa
violence
Si possono insegnare le buone maniere ai bambini senza ricorrere alla violenza.
You can teach good manners to children without resorting to punishment.

1195 **spaventare** - *verb* spaventare
to scare, frighten
Questa è la cosa che mi ha fatto spaventare di più.
This is the thing that frightened me the most.

1196 **amante** - *nm&f; adj* amante
lover; fond
Non dimenticherò mai la pelle morbida e umida della mia amante in quella notte d'estate.
I'll never forget the soft and moist skin of my lover on that summer night.

1197 **preparare** - *verb* preparare
to prepare
Il re, convinto, disse ai sarti di preparare un abito, ma neanche lui vedeva questa stoffa.

The king, convinced, told the tailors to prepare the outfit, but he also couldn't see this material.

1198 **mostra** - *nf* mostra

show

La Mostra internazionale d'arte cinematografica di Venezia è il più vecchio festival cinematografico del mondo.

The Mostra internazionale d'arte cinematografica di Venezia is the oldest film festival in the world.

1199 **superiore** - *adj* superjore

higher, superior

Il livello di istruzione delle persone contemporanee è di gran lunga superiore a quello che è stato in passato.

The level of education of contemporary people is far higher than it has been in the past.

1200 **accesso** - *nm* attʃesso

access

C'è un costo aggiuntivo all'albergo per l'accesso a Internet.

There's an extra charge at the hotel for Internet access.

1201 **disturbo** - *nm* disturbo

disorder

La cefalea a grappolo è considerata un disturbo del bioritmo, perché gli attacchi spesso avvengono con forte periodicità

Cluster headache is regarded as a biorhythmic disorder because the attacks often occur with a strong periodicity

1202 **trucco** - *nm* trukko

makeup, trick

Quella persona sembra giovane grazie al trucco, ma è già oltre ai 40 anni.

She looks young because of her makeup, but she is already more than forty years old.

1203 **sindaco** - *nm* sindako

mayor

Il sindaco ha riconosciuto i suoi servizi per la città.

The mayor acknowledged her services to the city.

1204 **responsabilità** - *nf* responsabilit'a

responsibility

Un capitano ha la responsabilità della propria nave e del suo equipaggio.

A captain is in charge of his ship and its crew.

1205 **uscita** - *nf* uʃʃita

exit

Se si deve abbandonare il treno in caso di emergenza, seguire le indicazioni per l'uscita di emergenza.

If leaving the train in the event of an emergency follow the emergency exit signs.

1206 **profondo** - *adj*

deep

profondo

Dopo avere ucciso Tom, Mary lo ha sepolto in una tomba poco profonda.

After killing Tom, Mary buried him in a shallow grave.

1207 **televisione (TV)** - *nf*
televizjone (tivv'u)

television

Io trovo la televisione molto educativa. Ogni volta che qualcuno la accende, io vado nell'altra stanza a leggere un libro.

I find television very educating. Every time somebody turns one on, I go into the other room and read a book.

1208 **opinione** - *nf*
opinjone

opinion

Tutto quello che sentiamo è un'opinione, non un fatto. Tutto ciò che vediamo è una prospettiva, non la verità.

Everything we hear is an opinion, not a fact. Everything we see is a perspective, not the truth.

1209 **perfettamente** - *adv*
perfettamente

perfectly

Tom ha detto che era tutto perfettamente normale, però non lo è.

Tom said it was all perfectly normal, but it isn't.

1210 **conte** - *nm*
konte

count

Il percorso termina con uno spazio dedicato al castello, sede del museo, e alla figura del conte Giuseppe di Ragogna, ultimo proprietario del maniero.

The tour ends with an area dedicated to the castle, seat of the museum and to the figure of count Giuseppe di Ragogna, last owner of the manor.

1211 **parco** - *nm;*
parko

park, parklan; frugal, sober

A me piace andare al parco, dai giochi, a vedere i bambini che si divertono.

I like to go to the park and watch the children in the playground enjoying themselves.

1212 **miracolo** - *nm*
mirakolo

miracle

Un miracolo è un evento descritto da coloro a cui è stato detto da persone che non l'hanno visto.

A miracle is an event described by those to whom it was told by people who did not see it.

1213 **mancato** - *adj*
maŋkato

failed, unsuccessful

(a) mancato rispetto delle condizioni d'uso contenute nella descrizione del Prodotto o nella documentazione;

(a) non-compliance with the conditions of use and operation contained in the Product description or the documentation;

1214 **rubare** - *verb*
rubare

to steal
Metterlo all'angolo durante una discussione è semplice come rubare le caramelle a un bambino.

Cornering him in an argument is easy - like taking candy from a baby.

1215 **castello** - *nm*
kastello

castle
Sullo sfondo di quel dipinto vi è raffigurato un castello.
There is a castle in the background of the picture.

1216 **pur** - *adv*
pur

while
Pur disponendo di più del 20% dei diritti di voto, non si ha influenza notevole nella società.

Even though it controls more than 20% of the voting rights, it does not exercise a significant influence on this company.

1217 **nazione** - *nf*
nattsjone

nation, country
Multiculturalismo: Israele è una nazione di immigranti, con la sua popolazione altamente qualificata proveniente da oltre 100 paesi dei cinque continenti.

Multiculturalism: Israel is a nation of immigrants, with its highly educated population hailing from over 100 countries across five continents.

1218 **vendetta** - *nf*
vendetta

vengeance
Avrò la mia vendetta su di lui a tutti costi domani.
I'll take my revenge on him at all costs tomorrow.

1219 **deserto** - *adj; nm*
dezerto

desert (food); desert
Si sedette sulla spiaggia deserta osservando le onde infrangersi una dopo l'altra. Il suo regalo è stato come la scoperta di un'oasi nel mezzo di un deserto.

She sat on the deserted beach watching the waves roll in one after the other. Your gift was like discovery of an oasis in the midst of a desert.

1220 **lancio** - *nm*
lantʃo

launch, throw, launching
Settantatrè secondi dopo il lancio il Challenger esplose. Tutti i sette astronauti, compresa la prima insegnante nello spazio,Christa McAuliffe, rimasero uccisi.

Seventy-three seconds after launch, Challenger exploded. All seven astronauts, including the first teacher in space, Christa McAuliffe, were killed.

1221 **magia** - *nf*
madʒa

magic
La strega maledetta ha eseguito una magia malvagia sull'uomo e lo ha trasformato in un insetto.

The wicked witch cast an evil spell on the man and turned him into an insect.

1222 **pazienza** - *nf*
pattsjentsa
patience
Con un po' più di pazienza avresti potuto risolvere questo problema.
You could have solved this puzzle with a little more patience.

1223 **college** - *nm*
kolledʒe
college
Qual è la ragione per cui vuoi entrare in questo college?
What is the reason you want to enter this college?

1224 **camicia** - *nf*
kamitʃa
shirt
Tom indossa la stessa camicia di flanella rossa ogni volta che va in campeggio.
Tom wears the same red flannel shirt every time he goes camping.

1225 **ultimamente** - *adv*
ultimamente
lately
Ultimamente ha ceduto anche questa attività al figlio Massimo e si è dedicato alla progettazione e realizzazione di nuove moto.
In the end he passed the running of the business on to his son Massimo and focussed on the design and construction of new motorcycles.

1226 **osso** - *nm*
osso
bone
Io mi sono quasi soffocato con un pezzo d'osso di pollo.
I almost choked on a piece of chicken bone.

1227 **universo** - *nm*
universo
universe
Inoltre è difficile spiegare in altro modo il perché di così tanto elio nell'universo.
It is, moreover, very difficult to explain in any other way why there should be so much helium in the universe.

1228 **studiare** - *verb*
studjare
to study
La Chiesa cattolica ha il dovere permanente di scoprire e studiare i segni dei tempi presenti ed interpretarli alla luce del Vangelo.
The Catholic Church has the permanent duty to discover and study the signs of the times and to interpret them in the light of the gospel.

1229 **praticare** - *verb*
pratikare
to practice
Salendo di livello scolastico, si riduce il tempo a disposizione dei giovani per praticare uno sport.

The higher the level of schooling, the less time there is for young people to be involved in sport.

1230 **togliere** - *verb*
toʎʎere
to remove, take off
Dite ai nostri nemici che potranno prendersi le nostre vite, ma non potranno mai toglierci la nostra libertà!
Tell our enemies that they may take our lives, but they'll never take our freedom!

1231 **gara** - *nf*
gara
race, competition
Nelle gare olimpiche la medaglia d'oro è per il primo posto, quella d'argento per il secondo, quella di bronzo per il terzo.
In Olympic competitions, a gold medal is for first place, a silver medal for second, and a bronze medal is for third place.

1232 **fidanzato** - *nm*
fidantsato
boyfriend
Il tuo fidanzato è una persona problematica, però questo non è un motivo sufficiente per arrendersi o per interrompere la vostra relazione.
Your boyfriend is a problematic person, but that's not a good enough reason to give up or break off your relationship.

1233 **tentare** - *verb*
tentare
to attempt, try, tempt
Non tentare mai di essere qualcun altro, non c'è meglio di te.
Never try to be someone else, there is no better than you.

1234 **amen** - *int*
amen
amen
Ed infine l'« amen » esprime la docilità allo Spirito santo nel pensare e decidere il futuro secondo il progetto di Dio.
And finally the "amen" expresses docility to the Holy Spirit in reflecting and deciding on one's future according to God's plan.

1235 **tomba** - *nf*
tomba
tomb
La tomba del re Dagoberto si trova nel luogo dove il sovrano fu sepolto nel 639, alla destra delle reliquie di Saint Denis.
King Dagobert's tomb is located where the monarch was buried in 639, to the right of Saint Denis's relics.

1236 **costruire** - *verb*
kostrwire
to build
Noi abbiamo iniziato a costruire la casa due mesi fa e la termineremo entro un anno.
We began to build the house two months ago and we'll end it within a year.

1237 **lentamente** - *adv*
slowly

lentamente

Il traffico e i passanti si sono fermati mentre salutavano lentamente dal piccolo villaggio.

Traffic and passers-by stopped as they were slowly seen off from the little village.

1238 **esplosione** - *nf*
esplozjone

explosion

Gli esperti non sono giunti a spiegare l'origine dell'esplosione.

Experts have failed to come up with an explanation of why the explosion happened.

1239 **fugare** - *verb*
fugare

to dispel

E' doveroso tuttavia fugare ogni equivoco per non proporre una grazia a buon prezzo

Nonetheless, it is right and proper to dispel all possibility of misunderstanding

1240 **privato** - *adj; nm*
privato

private; personal life, privacy

Non dovresti leggere le lettere private delle altre persone senza permesso.

You shouldn't read other people's private letters without permission.

1241 **scusa** - *nf*
skuza

sorry

"Quanto ci vuole ad arrivare a Vienna a piedi?" "Scusa, non sono di queste parti."

"How long does it take to get to Vienna on foot?" "Sorry, I'm a stranger here."

1242 **sorridere** - *verb*
sorridere

to smile

Perché gli esseri umani sorridono? Questa è una domanda molto difficile a cui rispondere.

Why do humans smile? This is a very difficult question to answer.

1243 **sospetto** - *adj; nm*
sospetto

suspected, suspicious; suspicion

Ci promettono la luna, ma ho il sospetto che per il compimento di quelle promesse potremmo aspettare che l'inferno geli.

They promise us the moon, but I suspect we can wait for the fulfillment of those promises till hell freezes over.

1244 **perdita** - *nf*
perdita

loss, leak, waste

Lui fallì molte volte, ma non aveva la sensazione che fosse una perdita di tempo.

He failed many times, but he had no feeling that it was a waste of time.

1245 **banda** - *nf* | **band, gang**
banda
La polizia ha arrestato dei membri di due bande criminali.
The police arrested members from two criminal gangs.

1246 **velocità** - *nf* | **speed**
velotʃitˈa
Anche se ci fosse vita in altre galassie, è impossibile per l'uomo viaggiare alla velocità della luce per studiarli.
Even if there is life in other galaxies, it is impossible for man to travel at the speed of light to study them.

1247 **pugno** - *nm* | **fist**
puɲɲo
In un momento di rabbia ho tirato un pugno al muro e mi sono rotto l'indice.
In a fit of anger I punched the wall and broke my index finger.

1248 **secolo** - *nm* | **century**
sekolo
Quelli che non hanno vissuto nel diciottesimo secolo prima della Rivoluzione non conoscono la dolcezza della vita.
Those who haven't lived in the eighteenth century before the Revolution do not know the sweetness of life.

1249 **minaccia** - *nf* | **threat**
minattʃa
Gli americani sono preoccupati che gli immigrati clandestini siano una minaccia per la cultura e l'economia della nazione.
Americans are worried that illegal migrants are threatening the nation's culture and economy.

1250 **stomaco** - *nm* | **stomach**
stomako
Tom ha uno stomaco di ferro. Lui riesce a mangiare praticamente di tutto.
Tom has a cast iron stomach. He can eat just about anything.

1251 **sopravvivere** - *verb* | **to survive**
sopravvivere
Se non fosse stato per il supporto del pubblico, il presidente non avrebbe potuto sopravvivere alla rivolta.
But for the support of the public, the President could not have survived the revolt.

1252 **attore** - *nm* | **actor**
attore
Il mio sogno è di diventare un attore di Hollywood.
My dream is to make it as an actor in Hollywood.

1253 **ruolo** - *nm* | **role**
rwolo
Frustrato di non essere più l'unico oggetto dei suoi desideri, Tom ha relegato Mary a un ruolo inferiore.

Frustrated of not being the exclusive object of her desires anymore, Tom relegated Mary.

1254 **russo** - *adj; nm/f* russo
Russian; Russian
Io non sto scrivendo in inglese. Questa lingua è il russo.
I am not writing in English. This language is Russian.

1255 **accusa** - *nf* akkuza
accusation, charge, prosecution
L'accusa di omicidio premeditato è stata ridotta a omicidio preterintenzionale.
The murder charge was reduced to manslaughter.

1256 **piantare** - *verb* pjantare
to plant
Siamo in grado di piantare un vasta scelta di coltivazioni e varietà.
We can plant a wide choice of crops and varieties .

1257 **sporco** - *adj* sporko
dirty, soiled
Tom si è tolto i vestiti sporchi e li ha messi direttamente nella lavatrice.
Tom took off his dirty clothes and put them directly into the washing machine.

1258 **praticamente** - *adv* pratikamente
practically
Dal 2008, anno in cui ha iniziato il suo processo di internazionalizzazione, praticamente l'80% delle vendite proviene da mercati esteri.
Since 2008, the year in which it initiated its internationalization process, practically 80% of sales come from foreign markets.

1259 **mancare** - *verb* maŋkare
to miss
È vero che lui è un uomo istruito, ma manca di buon senso.
It is true he is a learned man, but he lacks common sense.

1260 **completo** - *adj; nm* kompleto
complete, full; suit
Il guardaroba di una donna non è completo senza un piccolo vestito nero.
A woman's wardrobe isn't complete without a little black dress.

1261 **collegare** - *verb* kollegare
to connect, link
Come posso collegare il mio iPod all'impianto stereo di un'automobile?
How can I connect my iPod to a car stereo?

1262 **bugiardo** - *adj* budʒardo
liar
Puoi dire che è un bugiardo, ma non che sia un uomo cattivo.

You may call him a liar, but you cannot call him a bad man.

1263 **sonno** - *nm* sonno | **sleep**
Smith ha passato anni a studiare l'effetto del sonno e della mancanza di sonno sulla memoria e l'apprendimento.
Smith has spent years studying the effects of sleep and sleep loss on memory and learning.

1264 **termine** - *nm* termine | **term**
Assicuratevi di illustrare chiaramente l'impatto del progetto sui beneficiari e l'impatto a lungo termine sulla comunità auspicato.
Make sure to clearly explain the project's impact on the beneficiaries as well as its expected long-term impact on the community.

1265 **finora** - *adv* finora | **so far**
Molte persone che finora se la sono spassata spargendo soldi a destra e a manca ora devono fare maggiore attenzione al proprio denaro.
A lot of people who have up until now been spending money having a good time now need to be more careful with their money.

1266 **raccontare** - *verb* rakkontare | **to tell**
L'ultima persona a cui ho raccontato la mia idea ha pensato che io fossi pazza.
The last person I told my idea to thought I was nuts.

1267 **taglia** - *nf* taʎʎa | **size**
La taglia e altri fattori sono importanti nella selezione dei pazienti da trattare con questo ventilatore.
Patient size and other factors are important in the selection of patients to be treated using this ventilator.

1268 **merito** - *nm* merito | **merit**
Ma tu hai qualche merito pratico o ti sei limitato ad inculcare loro il vero spirito di educazione civica?
Do you actually have any practical merit or have you merely been trying to give them a sense of the true spirit of polite society?

1269 **ombra** - *nf* ombra | **shadow**
Christine è rimasta all'ombra per tutto il giorno perché non voleva bruciarsi col sole.
Christine stayed in the shade all day, because she didn't want to get a sunburn.

1270 **perfino** - *adv* | **even**

	perfino	Perfino una piccola goccia, continuando a cadere, trafora una montagna di granito. *Even small drops falling constantly will bore through a granite mountain.*
1271	**fidare** - *verb* fidare	**to trust** Non si fidi di un uomo di cui non conosce nulla sul suo passato. *Don't trust a man whose past you know nothing about.*
1272	**tuttavia** - *adv; conj* tuttavja	**however, nevertheless; but, yet** Tutti hanno diritto alla propria opinione. Tuttavia, a volte è meglio non dire a nessuno qual è quest'opinione. *Everybody has a right to his own opinion. However, sometimes it's better not to tell anybody what that opinion is.*
1273	**governatore** - *nm* governatore	**governor** Secondo il governatore di Laghman, sette combattenti stranieri erano entrati nella provincia portando con sé telefoni satellitari. *According to the governor of Laghman, seven foreign fighters entered the province and carried satellite phones.*
1274	**vergogna** - *nf* vergoɲɲa	**shame** Ciò che più preoccupa il minore e la famiglia è la vergogna di non essere in grado di pagare il debito, più che le conseguenze. *What worries most the child and the family most is the shame of not being able to pay the debt, rather than the consequences.*
1275	**mostrare** - *verb* mostrare	**to show** I pittori e gli scultori sotto i Nazisti rappresentavano spesso il nudo, ma era vietato loro mostrare qualunque difetto fisico. *Painters and sculptors under the Nazis often depicted the nude, but they were forbidden to show any bodily imperfections.*
1276	**tetta** - *nf* tetta	**tit** Le tette sono la prova che gli uomini riescono a concentrarsi su due cose alla volta! *Boobs are the proof that men can focus at two things at once!*
1277	**totale** - *adj; nm* totale	**total** Se richiederà una ristrutturazione totale, sono sicuro che saranno soddisfatti con il vecchio sistema.

If it's going to require a total restructuring, I'm sure they will be satisfied with the old system.

1278 **largo** - *adj* — **wide, large, loose**
largo
Il sole è circa 1.000.000 di volte più largo della terra.
The sun is about 1,000,000 times as large as the earth.

1279 **articolo** - *nm* — **article**
artikolo
In questa rivista c'è un interessante articolo sui problemi dell'educazione.
There's an interesting article in this magazine about education problems.

1280 **complimento** - *nm* — **compliment**
komplimento
Non so se prenderlo come complimento o come insulto.
I do not know whether to take it as a compliment or an insult.

1281 **foresta** - *nf* — **forest**
foresta
Due piccoli scoiattoli, uno scoiattolo bianco e uno scoiattolo nero, vivevano in una vasta foresta.
Two little squirrels, a white squirrel and a black squirrel, lived in a large forest.

1282 **appartenere** - *verb* — **to belong**
appartenere
Questo diario apparteneva alla ragazza che viveva nella Leningrado assediata.
This diary belonged to the girl who lived in besieged Leningrad.

1283 **rovinare** - *verb* — **to ruin**
rovinare
Con questo continuo lavorare di giorno e di notte finirai per rovinarti la salute.
If you work day and night, you will lose your health.

1284 **gratis** - *adv* — **free**
gratis
Gli studenti di questa scuola possono avere i libri gratis.
The students of this school can get textbooks for free.

1285 **riposo** - *nm* — **rest, rest period**
ripozo
Uno staff attento e discreto vi accoglie in un ambiente in cui dominano i colori beige, ocra e azzurro, che favoriscono il riposo e la prosperità.
An attentive and discreet staff will welcome you in a well-kept and intimist decoration, privileging the beige, ochre tones and the azure, favorable to the rest and to the prosperity.

1286 **mucchio** - *nm* — **pile**

mukkjo | sapevamo che gli errori di fabbricazione ci sarebbero costati un mucchio di tempo e denaro.
But we knew that manufacturing mistakes would cost us a lot of time and money.

1287 **funerale** - *nm* | **funeral**
funerale | Non è appropriato indossare una minigonna rossa a un funerale.
It's not appropriate to wear a red miniskirt to a funeral.

1288 **cima** - *nf* | **top**
tʃima | Se ci vogliono quattro ore per andare dai piedi alla cima della montagna, lasciamo perdere.
If it's going to take four hours from the foot of the mountain to the top, let's forget it.

1289 **spia** - *nf* | **light, spy, indication**
spja | Lui lavora come professore, ma in realtà è una spia.
He works as a teacher, but actually he is a spy.

1290 **assurdo** - *adj* | **absurd**
assurdo | Questa è la cosa più assurda che io abbia mai sentito.
This is the most absurd thing I have ever heard.

1291 **revisione** - *nf* | **review, revision**
revizjone | Mi è sembrato ovvio che il piano aveva bisogno di qualche revisione.
It seemed obvious to me that the plan needed a few revisions.

1292 **ala** - *nf* | **wing**
ala | Ho trovato un uccello la cui ala era severamente danneggiata.
I found a bird whose wing was severely damaged.

1293 **ovvio** - *adj* | **obvious**
ovvjo | Mi è sembrato ovvio che il piano aveva bisogno di qualche revisione.
It seemed obvious to me that the plan needed a few revisions.

1294 **scala** - *nf* | **ladder, scale, stairs**
skala | Ho mancato un gradino sulle scale e ho paura mi si sia slogata la caviglia.
I missed a step on the stairs and I'm afraid I sprained my ankle.

1295 **respiro** - *nm* | **breath**
respiro | Con nostra grande sorpresa, lei ha trattenuto il respiro per tre minuti.

To our great surprise, she held her breath for three minutes.

1296 **fabbrica** - *nf* fabbrika
factory
C'è un'alta percentuale di immigrati tra la manodopera di queste fabbriche.
One finds a large proportion of immigrants among the workforce in these factories.

1297 **infermiera** - *nf* infermjera
nurse
Ho capito solo ora che la donna che credevo un'infermiera è in realtà una dottoressa.
I now understand that the woman I thought was a nurse is a doctor.

1298 **bestia** - *nf* bestja
beast
La musica ha la proprietà magica di calmare una bestia feroce.
Music has charms to soothe the savage beast.

1299 **ebreo** - *adj; nm* ebreo
Jewish, Jew
Dustin Moskovitz è un imprenditore ebreo. È uno dei co-fondatori di Facebook.
Dustin Moskovitz is a Jewish entrepreneur. He is one of the co-founders of Facebook.

1300 **piatto** - *nm* pjatto
dish, plate
Aveva così fame che non esitò a mangiare tutto quello che c'era nel piatto.
He was so hungry that he didn't hesitate to eat everything on the plate.

1301 **impazzire** - *verb* impattsire
to go crazy
Il caos invernale mi sta facendo impazzire, però arriveranno presto le vacanze.
The winter chaos is driving me crazy, but soon the holidays will come.

1302 **pagina** - *nf* padʒina
page
Il mondo è un libro, e chi non viaggia non legge che una sola pagina.
The world is a book, and those who do not travel read only a page.

1303 **mondiale** - *adj* mondjale
world
Gerhard Schroeder è il primo cancelliere tedesco che non ha vissuto la seconda guerra mondiale.
Gerhard Schroeder is the first German chancellor not to have lived through World War II.

1304 **tasca** - *nf* **pocket**
taska
Tom ha tirato fuori dalla tasca una busta e l'ha messa nella cassetta della posta.
Tom took an envelope out of his pocket and put it into the mail slot.

1305 **calcio** - *nm* **football, soccer**
kaltʃo
L'Italia è l'unico paese che considera la guerra come una partita di calcio e una partita di calcio come se fosse una guerra.
Italy is the only country that regards war as a soccer game, and a soccer game as it is a war.

1306 **cieco** - *adj* **blind**
tʃeko
Devi essere cieco come una talpa se non sei riuscito a vederla.
You must be blind as a bat if you couldn't see it.

1307 **torre** - *nf* **tower**
torre
Galileo ha fatto cadere due palle di ferro dalla cima della torre.
Galileo dropped two iron balls from the top of the tower.

1308 **riso** - *nm* **rice**
rizo
Quando sono entrato in cucina, lei stava facendo del pollo al curry con riso.
When I entered the kitchen, she was making chicken curry with rice.

1309 **commettere** - *verb* **to commit**
kommettere
Ho dovuto impedire a Tom di commettere l'errore più grande della sua vita.
I had to stop Tom from making the biggest mistake in his life.

1310 **nota** - *nf* **note**
nota
Noi abbiamo tenuto nota di tutte le nostre spese mentre eravamo in Australia.
We kept track of all our expenses while we were in Australia.

1311 **comodo** - *adj* **comfortable**
komodo
I treni per pendolari sono meno comodi dei treni veloci.
The local train is less comfortable than the express train.

1312 **cazzata** - *nf* **crap**
kattsata
Prima che combini qualche altra cazzata dobbiamo trovarlo.
We've got to find him before he does something stupid.

1313 **crescere** - *verb* **to grow**

kreʃʃere | La popolazione della Russia, così come il suo progresso nella civilizzazione, è cresciuta considerevolmente in questi ultimi cento anni.

The population of Russia, as well as its progress in civilization, has considerably increased within these last hundred years.

1314 **perdonare** - *verb* | **to forgive**
perdonare | Io ho perdonato il ragazzo per aver rubato i soldi dalla cassaforte.
I forgave the boy for stealing the money from the safe.

1315 **battere** - *verb* | **to beat**
battere | Tom non è mai stato in grado di battermi a scacchi.
Tom has never been able to beat me at chess.

1316 **invitare** - *verb* | **to invite**
invitare | Non vorremmo mai venire a sapere che qualcuno non ci ha invitato alla sua festa.
We would never know that someone hadn't invited us to his party.

1317 **abito** - *nm* | **dress, suit, attire**
abito | Tutta la gente lodò l'abito dell'imperatore senza vederlo per non sembrare stupida, fino a quando un bambino disse: "Ma il re è nudo!"
The people all praised the emperor's clothes without telling him the truth so as not to seem stupid, until a little boy said, "The emperor is naked!"

1318 **fumare** - *verb* | **to smoke**
fumare | Jane è grassa, grezza e fuma troppo. Ma Ken pensa che sia bella e attraente. Ecco perché si dice che l'amore è cieco.
Jane is fat and rude, and smokes too much. However, Ken thinks she's lovely and charming. That's why they say love is blind.

1319 **respirare** - *verb* | **to breathe**
respirare | L'aria che respiriamo è inquinata dallo smog delle ciminiere delle fabbriche.
The very air we breathe is polluted with smog from the factory chimneys.

1320 **studente** - *nm* | **student**
studente | Nel sentire che sarebbe arrivato uno studente trasferito da fuori, la classe era tutta un bisbiglio di eccitazione.

Hearing that a transfer student was coming, the class buzzed with excitement.

1321 **criminale** - *adj nm&f* kriminale
criminal; criminal
Le attività criminali di suo figlio gli hanno causato grande dolore.
His son's criminal activities caused him great pain.

1322 **dirigere** - *verb* diridʒere
to direct
Il nostro aereo si dirige lentamente verso sud.
Our plane is flying slowly toward the south.

1323 **disastro** - *nm* dizastro
disaster
La Croce Rossa porta degli aiuti senza ritardo alle vittime di disastri.
The Red Cross gets help to disaster victims without delay.

1324 **mezzanotte** - *nf* mettsanotte
midnight
Lei mi ha fatto la promessa di tornare a casa prima di mezzanotte.
She made me a promise to return home before midnight.

1325 **dono** - *nm* dono
gift
L'uomo ha il dono della parola, che nessun animale ha.
Man has the gift of speech which no animal has.

1326 **colorare** - *verb* kolorare
to to color
Nell'originale scansionato, viene copiata un'area da colorare con il colore specifico, ed un 'area che deve essere nero su nero.
In the scanned original, an area judged to be color is copied with the specified color, and an area judged to be black in black.

1327 **creatura** - *nf* kreatura
creature
La maggior parte delle creature del mare sono colpite dall'inquinamento.
Most creatures in the sea are affected by pollution.

1328 **traccia** - *nf* trattʃa
track
Come fanno i controllori del traffico a tener traccia di così tanti aerei alla volta?
How are air traffic controllers able to keep track of so many planes at once?

1329 **spesa** - *nf* speza
expense
Tom ha perso la lista della spesa che sua madre gli aveva dato e ha comprato soltanto cose che voleva mangiare.

Tom lost the shopping list his mother had given him and just bought things he wanted to eat.

1330 **amaro** - *adj; nm* amaro

bitter; bitter, tonic liqour

Per esperienza personale so che qualsiasi incontro con lui lascerà l'amaro in bocca.

From personal experience, I know that any encounter with him will leave a bad taste in your mouth.

1331 **corda** - *nf* korda

rope

Mi sono tenuto alla corda saldamente in modo da non cadere.

I held on to the rope tightly so I wouldn't fall.

1332 **pensione** - *nf* pensjone

board, pension, retirement

Lui è un uomo in pensione che lavora come volontario per intrattenere i pazienti negli ospedali.

He is a retired man who volunteers to entertain patients in hospitals.

1333 **minimo** - *adj* minimo

minimum

Se hai il minimo problema, puoi contattarmi via e-mail, o se è davvero urgente, vieni che ci incontriamo nel mio ufficio.

If you have the least problem, you can contact me by email, or if it's really urgent, come and meet me in my office.

1334 **grazia** - *nf* grattsja

grace, pardon

Quest'uomo è pieno di grazia e verità. Il giudice gli ha concesso la grazia.

This man is full of grace and truth. The judge pardoned him.

1335 **velocemente** - *adv* velotʃemente

quickly

Correndo il più velocemente che ho potuto, sono stato in grado di raggiungere il mio amico.

Running as fast as I could, I was able to catch up with my friend.

1336 **istante** - *nm* istante

instant

Se n'è andato dalla stanza nell'istante in cui mi ha visto.

He left the room the moment he saw me.

1337 **maniera** - *nf* manjera

way, manner

Fino ad ora le sole persone che mi abbiano trattato in maniera educata siete voi.

You were the only person that was ever nice to me.

1338 **autorità** - *nf* autoritˈa

authority

Era una grande autorità in astronomia, ovvero la scienza dei corpi celesti.

He was a great authority on astronomy, or the science of the heavenly bodies.

1339 **esame** - *nm* ezame

exam, test

Questa volta, l'esame non era solo difficile, ma le domande erano anche ambigue.

This time, the exam was not just difficult, but also, the questions were ambiguous.

1340 **abbandonare** - *verb* abbandonare

to abandon sth, leave sth.

La necessità di abbandonare i suddetti Piani e il ricorso ad un nuovo strumento di incentivazione di lungo termine ha origine dal mutamento delle condizioni economico-finanziarie.

The need to abandon these Plans and take recourse in a new incentivised instrument for the longterm originated from the change in economic and financial conditions.

1341 **mosca** - *nf* moska

fly, Moscow

Tu hai visto il video in cui il Presidente Obama uccide una mosca a mani nude?

Did you see that video where President Obama kills a fly with his bare hands?

1342 **parecchio** - *adv; adj* parekkjo

a lot of, several; some

Il ticchettio dei tacchi a spillo mi da parecchio fastidio alle orecchie. Le persone che li indossano lo notano?

The clicking of high heels kind of hurts my ears. Do the people wearing them not notice?

1343 **pietà** - *nf* pjetˈa

pity

“Io non ho paura,” disse con fermezza “e chiederò all’angelo di avere pietà di voi”.

"I am not afraid," she said firmly, "and I will ask the angel to have mercy on you."

1344 **assieme [a]** - *adv* assjeme [a]

together [with]

Dobbiamo imparare a vivere assieme come fratelli, oppure moriremo assieme come folli.

We must learn to live together as brothers, or we will perish together as fools.

1345 **impressione** - *nf* impressjone

impression

Non hai mai una seconda occasione per fare una prima impressione.

You never have a second chance to make a first impression.

1346 **opportunità** - *nf*

opportunity

opportunit'a | Tom ha avuto certamente moltissime opportunità di andare a sentire concerti mentre era a Boston.

Tom certainly had plenty of opportunities to go to concerts while he was in Boston.

1347 **debito** - *nm* | **straight line, tuition, debt**
debito | I suoi debiti sono maggiori di quello che riesce a pagare.
Her debts amount to more than she can pay.

1348 **retta** - *nf* | **straight line; tuition**
retta | Dio è un cerchio la cui circonferenza è una linea retta.
God is a circle whose circumference is a straight line.

1349 **falso** - *adj* | **false**
falso | La verità è che niente è completamente vero o completamente falso.
The truth is that nothing is totally true or false.

1350 **fuggire** - *verb* | **to flee**
fuddʒire | Andrew Johnson ha dovuto fuggire da casa sua per salvare la vita.
Andrew Johnson had to flee his home to save his life.

1351 **risultato** - *nm* | **result**
rizultato | Ieri abbiamo raccolto quasi mezzo chilo di frammenti di vetro rotto sulla spiaggia per un'ora, il che è un risultato da record.
Yesterday we collected nearly half a kilo of pieces of broken glass on the beach within an hour, which was a record result.

1352 **cella** - *nf* | **cell**
tʃella | Noi non saremo in grado di uscire da questa cella.
We won't be able to get out of this cell.

1353 **marino** - *adj; nf* | **marine, sea; marina, marine, navy**
marino | Da lontano la piccola isola assomigliava a una tartaruga marina.
The small island looked like a tortoise from a distance.

1354 **amicizia** - *nf* | **friendship**
amitʃittsja | Tra uomini e donne non è possibile che ci sia amicizia. C'è passione, ostilità, adorazione e amore ma nessuna amicizia.

Between men and women there is no friendship possible. There is passion, enmity, worship, love, but no friendship.

1355 **chilometro** - *nm* | **kilometer**
kilometro | La distanza da casa mia a casa vostra è di due chilometri.
The distance from my home to yours is two kilometers.

1356 **centinaio** - *adj; num* | **hundred**

tʃentinajo

Diverse centinaia di anni fa, le epidemie di scarlattina uccisero migliaia di persone in tutto il continente.

Several hundred years ago, scarlet fever epidemics killed thousands of people throughout the continent.

1357 **pari** - *adv*
pari

equal

Di tutti gli album pubblicati nel 2009, solo il 2,1% ha registrato vendite pari ad almeno 5.000 copie.

Only 2.1 percent of the music albums released in 2009 sold 5,000 copies or more.

1358 **scomparire** - *verb*
skomparire

to disappear

Molte persone in Inghilterra vogliono vedere scomparire il finanziamento pubblico della monarchia.

Many in England want to see the public subsidy of the monarchy done away with.

1359 **giapponese** - *adj*
dʒapponeze

Japanese

Gli scienziati britannici hanno accertato che se si capovolge la bandiera giapponese, si ottiene la bandiera giapponese.

British scientists have established that if you turn the flag of Japan upside down, you get the Japanese flag.

1360 **punta** - *nf*
punta

tip, point

Gli istituti d'istruzione superiore europei devono continuare ad essere la punta di diamante dello sviluppo

European higher education institutions must remain at the leading edge of developments.

1361 **volontà** - *nf*
volontˈa

will

Un democratico è un libero cittadino che si sottomette alla volontà della maggioranza.

A democrat is a free citizen who yields to the will of the majority.

1362 **occhiali** - *nmpl*
okkjali

glasses

Ho cercato per mari e monti i miei occhiali ma non sono riuscito a trovarli.

I searched high and low for my glasses but couldn't find them.

1363 **specialmente** - *adv*
spetʃalmente

specially, particulary, especially

Da parte polacca – specialmente nell'era della Repubblica Popolare della Polonia – fu usato il concetto dei "territori riconquistati".

On the Polish side – especially in the era of the People's Republic of Poland – the concept of "regained territories" was used .

1364 **chiaramente** - *adv* kjaramente

clearly

La voce di Kate è chiaramente differente da quella delle altre ragazze.

Kate's voice is clearly different from the other girls'.

1365 **ginocchio** - *nm* dʒinokkjo

knee

Dopo l'operazione al ginocchio, riusciva a camminare senza dolore.

After his knee repair, he could walk without pain.

1366 **impronta** - *nf* impronta

footstep, imprint, impression, mark

Ho sentito che delle impronte di un abominevole uomo delle nevi sono state scoperte in Himalaya.

I heard that footprints of an abominable snowman have been discovered in the Himalayas.

1367 **ripetere** - *verb* ripetere

to repeat

Tom chiese a Mary di ripetere quello che aveva appena detto.

Tom asked Mary to repeat what she had just said.

1368 **coscienza** - *nf* koʃʃentsa

consciousness, conscience, awareness

La sua coscienza s'è improvvisamente risvegliata in lui.

His conscience suddenly awoke in him.

1369 **uguale** - *adv* ugwale

equal

Deve essere almeno uguale al numero di dispositivi attivi in modo che tutte le copie siano scritte su dischi diversi.

There must be at least that many active devices so that all of the copies can be distributed onto different disks.

1370 **lieto** - *adj* ljeto

happy

La maggior parte dei film di Hollywood ha un lieto fine.

Most Hollywood movies have a happy ending.

1371 **proprietà** - *nf* proprjetˈa

property

Ha disegnato una linea tratteggiata per mostrare dove finiva la proprietà.

She drew a broken line to show where the property ended.

1372 **personaggio** - *nm* personaddʒo

character

Che voi ci crediate o no, i cattivi non sono sempre i personaggi più contorti.

Believe it or not, villains aren't always the most twisted characters.

1373 **stagione** - *nf*
stadʒone

season
Molto tempo fa, la maggior parte delle persone vivevano in gruppi che si spostavano appena cambiavano le stagioni.
A long time ago, most people lived in groups that moved around as the seasons changed.

1374 **crisi** - *nf*
krizi

crisis
L'Italia è nella peggiore crisi economica della sua storia.
Italy is having the worst economical crisis in its history.

1375 **scalare** - *verb*
skalare

to climb
È necessario disporre di attrezzature speciali per scalare la montagna, o noleggiare attrezzature speciali da parte dell'impresa che esegue i servizi.
You have to have special equipment to climb the mountain, or rent special equipment from the business who is performing the services.

1376 **maledire** - *verb*
maledire

to curse
È meglio accendere una candela piuttosto che maledire il buio.
It is better to light a candle than to curse the darkness.

1377 **copia** - *nf*
kopja

copy
Io voglio comprare una copia del libro, ma è fuori stampa.
I want to buy a copy of the book, but it is out of print.

1378 **titolo** - *nm*
titolo

title
Per quanto ci provi, non riesco a ricordare il titolo di questa canzone.
No matter how hard I tried, I couldn't remember that song's title.

1379 **attorno** - *adv; prep*
attorno

about; around
Il rumore è il problema più grave per quelli che vivono attorno agli aeroporti.
Noise is the most serious problem for those who live around the airports.

1380 **stop** - *nm; int*
stop

stop
Stringere i manici dello strumento fino a quando lo stop di chiusura tocca il manico opposto.
Squeeze tool handles until closure stop touches opposite handle.

1381 **assicurare** - *verb*
assikurare

to ensure, insure
Quale parte anatomica di Betty Grable è stata notoriamente assicurata per un milione di dollari?

What part of Betty Grable's anatomy was famously insured for $1,000,000?

1382 **commissione** - *nf* kommissjone

commission, committee

Tom è diventato il presidente in carica della commissione.

Tom became the acting chairman of the committee.

1383 **seriamente** - *adv* serjamente

seriously

Il segnale indica situazioni di grave pericolo che, se trascurate, possono mettere seriamente a rischio la salute e la sicurezza delle persone.

This symbol indicates situations of danger which, if ignored, may result in serious injury to the operator.

1384 **levare** - *verb* levare

to upbeat

Una mela al giorno leva il medico di torno!

One apple a day keeps the doctor away!

1385 **passione** - *nf* passjone

passion

Non c'è una passione così fortemente radicata nel cuore umano come l'invidia.

There is not a passion so strongly rooted in the human heart as envy.

1386 **teste** - *nm* teste

witness

Il teste nel corso del suo esame è apparso pacificamente non attendibile ed incorerente.

The witness during his examination appeared unquestionably unreliable and incoherent.

1387 **trafficare** - *verb* traffikare

to trade, deal, traffic

Non devi ricordarti di salvarli in un posto particolare o trafficare con file e cartelle per trovare quel che ti serve.

You don't have to remember to upload your work to a special folder, or browse a cluttered file system to find it again.

1388 **scienza** - *nf* ʃentsa

science

Dalla fine della guerra, il Giappone ha fatto molti progressi nella scienza e nella tecnologia.

Since the war, Japan has advanced greatly in science and technology.

1389 **riposare** - *verb* ripozare

to rest

Mio padre è ammalato, è a letto a riposare e non può incontrarti.

Being sick in bed, my father can't see you.

1390 **tagliato** - *adj*

cut

	taʎʎato	Il profumo di erba tagliata mi fa riaffiorare l'immagine di caldi pomeriggi d'estate. *The smell of cut grass summons up images of hot summer afternoons.*
1391	**rete** - *nf* rete	**network, net** Il Regno Unito deve migliorare i problemi della sua rete ferroviaria. *The UK must improve the problems with its rail network.*
1392	**alba** - *nf* alba	**sunrise, dawn** Andavamo al lavoro all'alba e smettevamo di lavorare tra il tramonto e il calar delle tenebre. *We went to work at sunrise, and quit work between sundown and dark.*
1393	**prestito** - *nm* prestito	**loan** Tom mi sta evitando come come la peste da quando ha preso in prestito la mia macchina. *Tom has been avoiding me like the plague ever since he borrowed my car.*
1394	**morale** - *adj* morale	**moral** È un gioco da ragazzi per una ragazza di facile morale trovare un nuovo uomo. *It's duck soup for a girl of easy virtue to find a new man.*
1395	**becco** - *nm* bekko	**beak** Un pellicano riesce a contenere molti pesci nel suo becco. *A pelican can fit a lot of fish in its beak.*
1396	**onesto** - *adj* onesto	**honest** Ero stupito nel sentire che lei è morta di un'overdose da droga. Mi sembrava sempre una persona molto onesta. *I was flabbergasted to hear that she died of a drug overdose. She always seemed like such a straight arrow to me.*
1397	**artista** - *nm* artista	**artist** Io non so disegnare, però mia sorella è una grande artista. *I can't draw, but my sister is a great artist.*
1398	**rabbia** - *nf* rabbja	**anger** La rabbia che fino ad allora avevo accumulato in me svanì come nebbia colpita dal sole. *The anger that I had built up in me until then evaporated like a mist hit by the sun.*
1399	**attività** - *nf*	**activity**

attivit'a — Mio nonno fa attività fisica moderata ogni mattina, che è il motivo per cui è forte e sano.

My grandfather does moderate exercise every morning, which is why he is strong and healthy.

1400 **conversazione** - *nf*
konversattsjone
conversation
Abbiamo conversato fino a tarda notte, bevendo tè e mangiando la torta.
We conversed until late at night while eating cake and drinking tea.

1401 **stregare** - *verb*
stregare
to bewitch
Visitate il negozio e la boutique Rominger all'uscita del villaggio in direzione Bernina e lasciatevi stregare dalle meraviglie in legno.
Visit the shops and the Rominger Boutique as you leave the village in the direction of Bernina and allow yourself to be enchanted by the wooden creations.

1402 **mappa** - *nf*
mappa
map
Tom si perde sempre se non porta con sé una mappa.
Tom always gets lost if he doesn't carry a map.

1403 **fallito** - *adj*
fallito
failed
Lui ha fallito nel suo tentativo di attraversare a nuoto il fiume.
He failed in his attempt to swim the river.

1404 **sciocchezza** - *nf*
ʃokkettsa
foolishness
È stato stupido da parte sua sprecare soldi per tali sciocchezze.
It was foolish of him to waste his money on such trifles.

1405 **gusto** - *nm*
gusto
taste
Il vero gusto della vita non lo si trova nelle grandi cose, ma in quelle piccole.
The real taste of life is not found in great things, but in small ones.

1406 **risultare** - *verb*
rizultare
to to result
Se si registrano delle immagini vicino a trasmettitori radio o linee ad alta tensione, immagini e/o suoni potrebbero risultare disturbati.
If you record near radio transmitters or high-voltage lines, the recorded pictures and/or sound may be adversely affected.

1407 **ambulanza** - *nf*
ambulantsa
ambulance
Tom è morto prima che l'ambulanza arrivasse qui.

Tom died before the ambulance got here.

1408 **credito** - *nm*
kredito

credit

Ad esempio, a tutt'oggi è stato erogato solo un po' più di un quarto dei crediti di impegno

For example, to date, only a quarter of the commitment appropriations has been paid out.

1409 **protezione** - *nf*
protettsjone

protection

Dopo aver indossato il casco di protezione si è sentita molto più sicura.

She felt much safer once she'd put her helmet on.

1410 **affascinare** - *verb*
affaʃʃinare

to fascinate

Le opere d'arte luminose dell'americano James Turrell hanno lo straordinario potere di affascinare.

Works of art by the American light artist James Turrell have the extraordinary power to fascinate.

1411 **facilmente** - *adv*
fatʃilmente

easily

Il suo database è facilmente accessibile da svariati prodotti software di altri produttori.

Its DataBase is easily accessible by a range of third party software products.

1412 **materiale** - *adj; nm*
materjale

material

Tali impieghi come la guerra, la politica, il culto pubblico e il divertimento pubblico, sono avvertiti, in apprensione popolare, come diversi intrinsecamente dal mercato del lavoro che ha a che fare con l'elaborazione dei mezzi materiali della vita.

Such employments as warfare, politics, public worship, and public merrymaking, are felt, in the popular apprehension, to differ intrinsically from the labour that has to do with elaborating the material means of life.

1413 **coso** - *nm*
kozo

thing

Il Consiglio sottolinea che le presenti conclusioni definiscono una posizione di negoziato della Comunità per i negoziati in coso sul mandato di Berlino e non un impegno unilaterale

The Council stresses that these conclusions establish a Community negotiating position for the ongoing negotiations on the Berlin Mandate, not a unilateral commitment

1414 **carcere** - *nm*

prison

	kartʃere	Tom è stato un detenuto di un carcere di massima sicurezza per gli ultimi tre anni. *Tom has been an inmate of a high-security prison for the past three years.*
1415	**sistemare** - *verb* sistemare	**to fix** E' stato possibile o necessario sistemare l'aula in modo da simulare l'ambiente proposto dall'esercizio? *Has it been possible or necessary to adapt the classroom so as to replicate the environment posited by the simulation?*
1416	**scherzo** - *nm* skertso	**joke** Ho beccato mio figlio a fare scherzi telefonici a numeri di telefono casuali. *I caught my son making prank calls to random phone numbers.*
1417	**bersaglio** - *nm* bersaʎʎo	**target** Il suo comportamento era spesso bersaglio di critiche. *His behavior was often a target of criticism.*
1418	**salto** - *nm* salto	**leap, jump** Vorrei che tu riuscissi a fare un salto da me prima di tornare a casa tua. *I wish you could drop in at my house on your way home.*
1419	**membro** - *nm* membro	**member** Ogni individuo, in quanto membro della società, ha diritto alla sicurezza sociale, nonché alla realizzazione attraverso lo sforzo nazionale e la cooperazione internazionale ed in rapporto con l'organizzazione e le risorse di ogni Stato. *Every individual, as a member of society, has the right to social security and is entitled to realization, through national effort and international co-operation and in accordance with the organization and resources of each State.*
1420	**labbro** - *nm* labbro	**lip** Ha alzato il bicchiere alle labbra e l'ha vuotato tutto d'un fiato. *He raised the glass to his lips and drained it at one gulp.*
1421	**specchiare** - *verb* spekkjare	**to mirror** La nostra conoscenza avviene attraverso passaggi che ci danno la possibilità di riflettere, specchiare il reale, catalogarlo in simboli operativi per avere la reversibilità.

Our knowledge comes through passages that give us the chance to consider, to reflect the real, catalogue it in operative symbols to get reversibility.

1422 **proporre** - *verb* proporre

to propose, put forward

Se si vuole un uomo per proporre il matrimonio, gli si dà da mangiare bene.

If you want a man to propose marriage, feed him well.

1423 **senatore** - *nm* senatore

senator

La mia prima azione da Senatore è designarti come giullare ufficiale.

My first deed as Senator is designating you as the official jester.

1424 **maschio** - *adj; nm* maskjo

male

Il risultato è calcolato secondo la tabella di lettura generale creata dalla World Health Organization (WHO) - la stessa per maschio e femmina a prescindere dall'età.

The result is calculated according to general reading table created by World Health Organization (WHO) - the same for male and female regardless the age.

1425 **terreno** - *nm; adj* terreno

ground, soil; earthly

Comprendere come si comportano i prototipi ed i componenti dei veicoli sul terreno di prova aiuta ad garantire le prestazioni per tutta la vita del prodotto.

Understanding how prototype vehicles and components behave on the proving ground helps ensure through-life product performance.

1426 **bugia** - *nf* budʒa

lie, falsehood

La bugia lo ha messo nei guai quando il suo capo ha scoperto la verità.

The lie got him in trouble when his boss found out the truth.

1427 **proprietario** - *nm* proprjetarjo

owner, landlord

Faresti meglio a rimettere il libro sul tavolo, nel caso torni il proprietario.

You had better put the book back on the desk, for the owner will come back there.

1428 **modello** - *adj* modello

model

Io penso che sia improbabile che qualsiasi negozio venderebbe questo modello a quel prezzo.

I think it's unlikely that any store would sell this model for that price.

1429 **benzina** - *nf*
bentsina

petrol, gasoline
Non ho potuto incontrarlo alla stazione perché sono rimasto senza benzina.
I couldn't meet him at the station because my car ran out of gas.

1430 **panico** - *nm*
paniko

panic
Non c'è alcun motivo di andare nel panico... per ora.
There's no reason to panic... yet.

1431 **mentire** - *verb*
mentire

to lie
In verità, se avessi detto che non ho avuto rimpianti sulla mia decisione rapida, avrei mentito.
Truthfully, if I'd said I didn't have any regrets over my snap decision I'd have been lying.

1432 **giovanotto** - *nm*
dʒovanotto

young man
Nella corte, c'erano due giovanotti, uno di diciotto anni, l'altro di diciannove, che erano molto appassionati al gioco degli scacchi.
In the court, there were two young fellows, one of eighteen years old, the other of nineteen, who were very fond of playing chess.

1433 **suicidio** - *nm*
switʃidjo

suicide
Il suicidio è un atto di vendetta contro se stessi, e io personalmente non ho nulla contro di me.
Suicide is an act of revenge against yourself, and I personally have nothing against myself.

1434 **oceano** - *nm*
otʃano

ocean
Ciò che sappiamo è una goccia d'acqua. Ciò che ignoriamo è un oceano.
What we know is a drop. What we don't know is an ocean.

1435 **reparto** - *nm*
reparto

department, ward
Molti lavoratori stanno rischiando il posto di lavoro nel reparto di montaggio.
Many workers are facing the ax in the assembly department.

1436 **truppa** - *nf*
truppa

troop
Bush non ha inviato delle truppe per distruggere gli altri paesi.
Bush didn't send troops to annihilate other countries.

1437 **firmare** - *verb*
firmare

to sign
Sono state stampate due copie del contratto in corso e saranno firmate dalle due parti.

Two copies of the current agreement were printed and will be signed by the two sides.

1438 **socio** - *nm* sotʃo
partner
È importante che tutti i soci osservino queste regole.
It is necessary that every member observe these rules.

1439 **onda** - *nf* onda
wave
Un catamarano è improbabile che possa essere ribaltato dal vento, ma un'onda anomala abbastanza grande può farlo.
A catamaran is unlikely to be capsized by wind, but a big enough rogue wave can do it.

1440 **oggetto** - *nm* oddʒetto
object
È un oggetto di famiglia. È stato nella mia famiglia da diverse generazioni.
It's an heirloom. Been in my family for generations.

1441 **sciocco** - *adj* ʃokko
silly
È sciocco pensare che il fumo abbia poco a che fare con il cancro.
It's foolish to think that smoking has little to do with cancer.

1442 **cancro** - *nm* kaŋkro
cancer
Quell'uomo è morto per un cancro ai polmoni la settimana scorsa.
That man died of lung cancer a week ago.

1443 **tazza** - *nf* tattsa
cup
Quella sera lascia la mia mancia sottoo una tazza da caffè, che lasciai alla rovescia sul tavolo.
That evening I left my tip under a coffee cup, which I left upside down on the table.

1444 **felicità** - *nf* felitʃitˈa
happiness
In conclusione: le condizioni per la felicità possono essere identificate su base empirica; i dati disponibili sono già molto illuminanti.
Summing up: Conditions for happiness can be charted empirically; the available data is already very informative.

1445 **filo** - *nm* filo
wire
Tom si pulisce i denti con il filo interdentale più volte alla settimana.
Tom flosses his teeth several times a week.

1446 **ferro** - *nm*
iron

ferro — Milioni di persone, migliaia di edifici, io cammino attraverso questo labirinto, labirinto di cemento, cemento e ferro, asfalto e vetro.
Millions of people, thousands of buildings, I walk through that maze, maze of concrete, concrete and iron, asphalt and glass.

1447 **assegno** - *nm* — **check**
asseɲɲo
Ho compilato un assegno da 25 dollari e l'ho dato al commesso.
I made out a check for $25 and handed it to the salesperson

1448 **argomento** - *nm* — **topic, subject, argument**
argomento
È un argomento di cui non so niente a riguardo.
That's a subject I know nothing about.

1449 **anticipo** - *nm* — **advance, anticipation**
antitʃipo
Gli ospiti sono arrivati in anticipo, ma fortunamente avevo già finito di cucinare.
The guests have arrived early, but luckily I had already finished cooking.

1450 **negro** - *adj; nm* — **black, negro; negro, nigger**
negro
La parola "negro" è un termine offensivo.
The word "nigger" is an offensive term.

1451 **esperto** - *adj* — **expert**
esperto
Io non sono un esperto, quindi la mia risposta alla tua domanda è solo una stima ragionata.
I'm not an expert, so my answer to your question is just an educated guess.

1452 **chilo** - *nm* — **kilo**
kilo
Posso avere un chilo di petto di pollo, per favore?
Can I get a kilo of chicken breast please?

1453 **lacrima** - *nf* — **tear**
lakrima
La ragazza versò qualche lacrima alla morte del padre.
The girl shed some tears when her father died.

1454 **personalmente** - *adv* — **personally**
personalmente
Rispetto il fatto che abbiate atteso la nostra adesione e mi sento personalmente onorata di poter votare.
I respect the fact that you waited for us and I personally feel honoured that I am able to cast my vote.

1455 **offrire** - *verb* — **to offer**
offrire
La notte fonda e la luna piena ci offrivano da dono solo l'atmosfera.

The deep night and the full moon offered us only the atmosphere as a gift.

1456 **incubo** - *nm*
iŋkubo

nightmare
Purtroppo, quell'incubo è diventato una realtà ricorrente nel distretto scolastico di Grossmon
Sadly, that nightmare became a recurring reality at Grossmont Union School District

1457 **carro** - *nm*
karro

wagon
L'uomo primitivo ha fermato il suo carro: decide che quella sarà la sua terra.
Primitive man has brought his chariot to a stop, he decides that here shall be his native soil.

1458 **comportamento** - *nm*
komportamento

behavior
Quel tipo di comportamento non ha nulla a che fare con me.
That kind of behavior has nothing to do with me.

1459 **inverno** - *nm*
inverno

winter
Melbourne Winter Masterpieces è il nome di una serie annuale di mostre organizzate durante l'inverno nelle sedi culturali più rinomate di Melbourne.
Melbourne Winter Masterpieces is the name for an annual series of major exhibitions during winter at Melbourne's most renowned cultural venues.

1460 **elicottero** - *nm*
elikottero

helicopter
L'elicottero rimaneva sospeso in volo sopra l'edificio.
The helicopter hovered over the building.

1461 **virus** - *nm*
virus

virus
Molte persone non si rendono conto che gli antibiotici sono inefficaci contro i virus.
Many people don't realize that antibiotics are ineffective against viruses.

1462 **miseria** - *nf*
mizerja

misery
Alla fine della sua vita, Hokusai visse in miseria, solo con sua figlia, e lavorò fino alla sua morte.
At the end of his life, Hokusai lived in misery, alone with his daughter, and worked until his death.

1463 **coinvolgere** - *verb*
koinvoldʒere

to involve
C'è un tentativo di coinvolgere il pubblico con le traduzioni.
There's an attempt to involve the audience with translations.

1464 **eccellente** - *adj*

excellent

ettʃellente

Lei mi ricorda tanto la mia amica Marina, eccellente insegnante di russo.

You remind me so much of my friend Marina, a great teacher of Russian.

1465 **cavaliere** - *nm*
kavaljere

knight

Il coraggioso cavaliere fa un passo in avanti e bacia la dama sulla mano.

The brave knight steps forward and kisses the lady on the hand

1466 **follia** - *nf*
follja

madness

Chi vive senza follia non è così saggio come crede.

Who lives without folly is not so wise as he thinks.

1467 **toccato** - *adj*
tokkato

touched

Ma recatosi a Parigi per compiere gli studi, egli fu toccato dall'esigenza di riforma che si andava profilando nella chiesa.

While studying in Paris, he took to heart the need for reform that was becoming increasingly evident in the church.

1468 **dosso** - *nm*
dosso

back

Io non riesco a togliergli gli occhi di dosso.

I can't take my eyes off him.

1469 **marciare** - *verb*
martʃare

to march

Le tensioni a vuoto devono essere identiche su tutti gli alternatori destinati a marciare in parallelo tra loro.

The no-load voltages should be identical on all the alternators intended for parallel operation between each other.

1470 **sufficiente** - *adj*
suffitʃente

enough, sufficient

Tom aveva un sacco di cose in mente, così non prestava sufficiente attenzione alla sua guida.

Tom had a lot on his mind, so he wasn't paying enough attention to his driving.

1471 **cassetta** - *nf*
kassetta

cassette

C'è una cassetta delle lettere da qualche parte lungo questa strada.

There is a mailbox somewhere along this street.

1472 **pavimento** - *nm*
pavimento

floor

Ho chiamato la polizia appena ho visto il suo cadavere sul pavimento.

I called the police as soon as I saw his dead body on the floor.

1473 **licenziare** - *verb* litʃentsjare

to dismiss

Tom stava per essere trasferito a Boston, ma invece hanno deciso di licenziarlo.

Tom was going to be transferred to Boston, but they decided to fire him instead.

1474 **folle** - *adj* folle

crazy

Qual è la cosa più folle che hai fatto di recente?

What's the craziest thing you've done lately?

1475 **fattoria** - *nf* fattorja

farm

Perché, ovviamente, la gente non vuole la guerra. Perché qualche poveraccio in una fattoria vuole rischiare la sua vita in una guerra quando il meglio che può uscirne è tornare alla sua fattoria in un unico pezzo. Naturalmente, la gente comune non vuole la guerra; né in Russia, né in Inghilterra né in America, né del resto in Germania. Quello è capito.

Why, of course, the people don't want war. Why would some poor slob on a farm want to risk his life in a war when the best that he can get out of it is to come back to his farm in one piece. Naturally, the common people don't want war; neither in Russia nor in England nor in America, nor for that matter in Germany. That is understood.

1476 **moda** - *nf* moda

fashion, style

la pittura tradizionale cinese vive con la moda cinese, inglese, francese, italiana o spagnola.

traditional Chinese painting survives alongside Chinese, English, French, Italian and Spanish fashion.

1477 **bloccare** - *verb* blokkare

to block

Google è stato accusato di bloccare i concorrenti, come Microsoft, dai suoi risultati di ricerca.

Google has been accused of blocking competitors, like Microsoft, from its search results.

1478 **primavera** - *nf* primavera

spring

Non vedo l'ora che la primavera arrivi, così da poter sedermi sotto i ciliegi.

I can't wait for spring to come so we can sit under the cherry trees.

1479 **incendiare** - *verb* intʃendjare

to fire

Le case fatte di legno sono quelle che si possono incendiare più facilmente.

Houses made of wood are the easiest to catch on fire.

1480 **ambiente** - *nm* | **environmnent, room, ambience**
ambjente
Si pregha di pensare a l'ambiente - avete realmente bisogno di stampare questo messagio ?
Please consider the environment - do you really need to print this email?

1481 **ingresso** - *nm* | **entrance**
iŋgresso
Lei ha studiato duramente per non essere bocciata all'esame d'ingresso.
She studied hard in order not to fail the entrance exam.

1482 **piscina** - *nf* | **pool**
piʃʃina
Non vengo in piscina oggi pomeriggio perché ho il raffreddore e la tosse.
I'm not coming to the pool this afternoon because I have a cold and a cough.

1483 **partenza** - *nf* | **departure**
partentsa
Non ci resta altro da fare che di rimandare la nostra partenza.
There is nothing for it but to put off our departure.

1484 **presente** - *adj; nm* | **this, present; present**
prezente
L'uomo passa la vita a ragionare sul passato, a lamentarsi del presente, di temere il futuro.
Man spends his life in reasoning on the past, in complaining of the present, in fearing future.

1485 **quadro** - *nm* | **painting, picture, panel, square**
kwadro
"Ti piace questo quadro?" "Sì, ma credo che la cornice sia più cara della stampa. Dove l'hai comprato?"
"Do you like this painting?" "Yes, but I think the frame is more expensive than the picture. Where did you buy it?"

1486 **rapina** - *nf* | **robbery**
rapina
Lui è stato mandato in prigione per rapina a mano armata.
He was sent to prison for armed robbery.

1487 **spagnolo** - *adj; nm/f* | **Spanish; Spaniard**
spaɲɲolo
Non so parlare lo spagnolo, però son stato comunque in grado di farmi capire quando sono andato a Malaga l'anno scorso.
I can't speak Spanish but even so, I was able to make myself understood when I went to Malaga last year.

1488 **nastro** - *nm* | **tape**
nastro
La madre ha legato un nastro ai capelli della figlia.
The mother tied a ribbon in her daughter's hair.

1489 **venerdì** - *nm*
venerd'i

Friday
Il presidente della compagnia, a cui ti ho presentato venerdì scorso, vuole rivederti.
The president of the company, to whom I introduced you last Friday, wants to see you again.

1490 **coda** - *nf*
koda

queue, tail
La bella coda del pavone lo aiuta ad attirare le femmine.
The peacock's beautiful tail helps it attract females.

1491 **petto** - *nm*
petto

chest
Tom aveva un dolore al petto, quindi è andato all'ospedale.
Tom had a pain in his chest, so he went to the hospital.

1492 **giornalista** - *nm*
dʒornalista

journalist
In generale, i giornalisti investigativi non esitano a violare la privacy delle persone.
By and large, reporters don't hesitate to intrude on one's privacy.

1493 **profumo** - *nm*
profumo

perfume
Tom ha comprato una bottiglia di vodka e un po' di profumo al duty-free shop.
Tom bought a bottle of vodka and some perfume at the duty-free shop.

1494 **originale** - *adj; nm*
oridʒinale

original
L'originale e la copia sono facilmente distinguibili in quanto l'uno è molto più vivace rispetto all'altra.
The original and the copy are easily distinguished since the one is much more vivid than the other.

1495 **erba** - *nf*
erba

grass, pot, herb
Tom ama stare sdraiato sull'erba nelle giornate di sole.
Tom loves to lie in the grass on a sunny day.

1496 **risata** - *nf*
rizata

laugh
Molti dei progetti in mostra sono presentati in modo da suscitare un sogghigno o una risata, anche se riguardano temi potenzialmente seri in fatto di grattacieli e vita moderna.
Many projects on display are rigged to trigger smirks and laughter, even as they address the potentially serious topics of skyscrapers and our modern lives.

1497 **esterno** - *adj; nm*
esterno

external, outside, out; outside, exterior
Io ho visto Tom stare in piedi all'esterno di un motel economico.

I saw Tom standing outside a cheap motel.

1498 **tracciare** - *verb* trattʃare
to draw
Tracciare un bilancio può essere considerato un passo importante per dare contenuto al futuro modello sociale europeo.
Stocktaking can be seen as an important step in fleshing out the contents of a European social model for the future.

1499 **settore** - *nm* settore
sector
I lavoratori del settore dei trasporti hanno organizzato uno sciopero per protestare contro i tagli di paga.
Transportation workers staged a walkout to protest pay cuts.

1500 **croce** - *nf* krotʃe
cross
Lei fece molto lavoro volontario per la Croce Rossa.
She did a lot of voluntary work for the Red Cross.

1501 **eccoti** - *int* ekkoti
here you are
Selezionane una, immetti la password se necessario, ed eccoti pronto e connesso.
Just select one, enter a password if required, and you're up and running.

1502 **prigioniero** - *nm* pridʒonjero
prisoner
I prigionieri politici sono in sciopero della fame per avere condizioni migliori.
Political prisoners are on a hunger strike for better conditions.

1503 **ascensore** - *nm* aʃʃensore
lift, elevator
Tom e Mary hanno aspettato l'ascensore assieme.
Tom and Mary waited for the elevator together.

1504 **corridoio** - *nm* korridojo
aisle, hallway
La voce di corridoio non è vera per quello che so.
The rumor is not true as far as I know.

1505 **combattimento** - *nm* kombattimento
combat
Voleva assistere a un combattimento di tori, ma suo padre non glielo permetteva.
He wanted to see a bullfight, but his father wouldn't let him go.

1506 **passeggiare** - *verb* passeddʒare
to stroll, walk
Passeggiare alla luce della luna è un modo romantico per concludere un appuntamento.
Walking in the moonlight is a romantic way to end a date.

1507	**epoca** - *nf* epoka	**era** Penso che sia il più grande artista della nostra epoca. *I think he is the greatest artist of the time.*
1508	**valigia** - *nf* validʒa	**suitcase** Io sto morendo dalla voglia di sapere cosa c'è nella valigia di Tom. *I'm dying to know what's in Tom's suitcase.*
1509	**fonte** - *nf* fonte	**source, spring** Il gioco d'azzardo non era affatto la sua unica fonte di reddito. *Gambling was by no means his only source of income.*
1510	**falla** - *nf* falla	**leak** Ovviamente tutto questo non esclude che a un certo punto la ricerca possa giungere a rivelare una falla. *Though this is no guarantee that research will never reveal a deficiency.*
1511	**tratto** - *nm* tratto	**stretch** Quando riaprii gli occhi, tutto ad un tratto una signora sconosciuta era in piedi proprio davanti a me. *When I opened my eyes again, all of a sudden an unknown lady was standing right in front of me.*
1512	**tempestare** - *verb* tempestare	**to batter, besiege, annoy** Una delle tattiche della CSU consisteva nel tempestare l'avversario con accuse che dovevano essere confutate di volta in volta. *One of the CSU tactics consisted of constantly harassing the opponent with allegations which had to be disproved time and time again.*
1513	**dolcezza** - *nf* doltʃettsa	**sweetness, gentleness** Le cene svolte dal nostro capo Hassan sono famosi per la loro dolcezza e la loro qualità. *The dinners carried out by our Hassan chief are famous for their smoothness and their quality.*
1514	**furbo** - *adj* furbo	**sly, cunning** Il ladro furbo si nascose in un capanno degli attrezzi. *The crafty thief hid in a tool shed.*
1515	**bomba** - *nf* bomba	**bomb** La bomba atomica è una minaccia seria per l'umanità. *The atomic bomb is a grave threat to mankind.*
1516	**concerto** - *nm*	**extraordinary; overtime**

kontʃerto — Non ho mai immaginato che sarei stato in grado di fare un concerto a Boston.
I never imagined I'd be able to give a concert in Boston.

1517 **straordinario** - *adj* — **extraordinary; overtime**
straordinarjo — Le cose straordinarie non accadono mai in modo semplice e ordinario.
Extraordinary things never happen in simple and ordinary ways.

1518 **miliardo** - *adj; num* — **billion**
miljardo — 1,3 miliardi di persone in tutto il mondo non hanno accesso all'elettricità.
1.3 billion people around the world lack access to electricity.

1519 **tentativo** - *nm* — **attempt**
tentativo — Tom non pensava di avere una possibilità di successo, ma almeno ha voluto fare un tentativo.
Tom didn't think he had a chance to succeed, but he at least wanted to give it a shot.

1520 **decisamente** - *adv* — **definitely, decidedly**
detʃizamente — Le questioni politiche sono decisamente troppo serie per essere lasciate ai politici.
Political questions are far too serious to be left to the politicians.

1521 **costringere** - *verb* — **to force**
kostrindʒere — Tom mi costringe a fare quello che non vorrei fare.
Tom makes me do things I don't want to do.

1522 **splendido** - *adj* — **wonderful**
splendido — Andrà tutto bene, puoi farcela! Fidati di te! Sei già uno splendido nuotatore!
It'll be fine, you can do it! Trust yourself! You are already a splendid swimmer!

1523 **babbo** - *nm* — **dad, father**
babbo — Il babbo sarà di ritorno fra pochi giorni.
Father will be back in a few days.

1524 **simpatico** - *adj* — **nice, sympathetic**
simpatiko — L'antagonista è allo stesso tempo un diversivo per tutto ciò che l'autore odia e il personaggio più simpatico di diversi ordini di grandezza.
The antagonist is simultaneously a strawman for everything the author hates and the most likeable character by several orders of magnitude.

1525	**sopportare** - *verb* sopportare	**to bear** Ci sta che tu ti arrabbi con Dio. Lui è capace di sopportarlo. *It's OK to get angry with God. He can take it.*
1526	**rischio** - *nm* riskjo	**risk** Essere in una nave è essere in una prigione, con il rischio di annegare. *Being in a ship is being in a jail, with the chance of being drowned.*
1527	**autista** - *nf* autista	**driver, chauffeur** Quando il bus sbandò per evitare un gatto, l'autista disse, "C'è mancato poco!" *When the bus swerved to miss a cat, the driver said, "That was a close one!"*
1528	**serpe** - *nf* serpe	**snake** Quando io e lo zio Chen raggiungemmo i Giardini del Tempio di Giada, alcuni lavoratori stavano scolpendo un'enorme statua di giada chiamata Cuore della Serpe. *When Uncle Chen and I reached the temple grounds, workers were carving an enormous jade statue called the Serpent's Heart.*
1529	**confine** - *nm* konfine	**border, boundery** L'esercito protegge il confine tra la Francia e la Spagna. *The army is protecting the border between France and Spain.*
1530	**fan** - *nm* fan	**fan** A Maria piace la musica classica, mentre Tom è un fan dell'heavy metal. *Mary likes classical music while Tom's a heavy metal fan.*
1531	**meritare** - *verb* meritare	**to deserve** È quello che si ottiene a dare il proprio cuore a qualcuno che non lo meritava. *That's what you get for giving your heart to someone who never deserved it.*
1532	**contante** - *adj; nm* kontante	**cash** Io vorrei pagare in contanti. La colazione è inclusa nel prezzo? *I would like to pay with cash. Is breakfast included in the price?*
1533	**risposta** - *nf*	**answer**

	risposta	Non ho bisogno della sua risposta ora, ci pensi con calma e risponda tra qualche giorno. *I don't need your answer now, you can sleep on it and come back in a few days.*
1534	**weekend** - *nm* veekend	**weekend** Tom e Mary ci hanno invitati a trascorrere il weekend con loro. *Tom and Mary invited us to spend the weekend with them.*
1535	**poesia** - *nf* poezja	**poetry** La poesia non è solo tormento, la poesia è amore, è passione calda e sensuale, è rivoluzione, romanticismo e tenerezza. *Poetry is not just torment; poetry is love. It is warm and sensual passion; it is revolution, romance and tenderness.*
1536	**sbirro** - *nm* zbirro	**cop** Gli sbirri hanno lanciato delle granate lacrimogene nell'edificio. *The cops threw tear-gas bombs into the building.*
1537	**affittare** - *verb* affittare	**to rent** Loro hanno affittato la camera del primo piano a uno studente. *They rented the room on the second floor to a student.*
1538	**piacevole** - *adj* pjatʃevole	**pleasant** Tom ha detto a Mary che era molto piacevole sentire la sua voce. *Tom said to Mary that it was very pleasant to hear her voice.*
1539	**procuratore** - *nm* prokuratore	**attorney** Il procuratore del Tribunale penale internazionale ha presentato prove sostanziali contro i soggetti accusati di crimini di guerra. *The prosecutor of the International Criminal Court has presented substantial evidence against individuals accused of war crimes*
1540	**buttare** - *verb* buttare	**to throw** Si viene multati a Singapore se si butta della spazzatura in strada. *They fine you in Singapore if you throw trash in the streets.*
1541	**imbecille** - *nm; adj* imbetʃille	**imbecile** È meglio rimanere in silenzio ed essere considerati imbecilli che aprire bocca e togliere ogni dubbio.

Better to remain silent and be thought a fool than to speak out and remove all doubt.

1542 **sociale** - *adj* sotʃale

social

Le femministe credono nella parità politica, sociale ed economica di tutti i generi.

Feminists believe in the political, social, and economic equality of all genders.

1543 **italiano** - *adj; nm* italjano

Italian

L'italiano ha pagato il suo caffè in Germania con monete di euro greche.

The Italian paid for his coffee in Germany with Greek euro coins.

1544 **canto** - *nm* kanto

singing, song

Il suono della vostra voce è per me come il canto melodioso delle sirene.

The sound of your voice is like siren's song to me.

1545 **gelare** - *verb* dʒelare

to freeze

La condensa che si accumula durante l'esercizio deve essere eliminata senza che possa gelare.

Condensed water that forms during operation must be drained off frost-free.

1546 **patto** - *nm* patto

pact

Il 15 febbraio 2003 è stato pubblicato sul Corriere della Sera l'estratto di un patto parasociale

On 15 February 2003, the Italian newspaper Corriere della Sera published an excerpt of a shareholders' agreement

1547 **scrivania** - *nf* skrivanja

desk

Quando Tom si è svegliato, ha trovato Mary che leggeva un libro alla scrivania.

When Tom woke up, he found Mary reading a book at the desk.

1548 **sognare** - *verb* soɲɲare

to dream

Se vuoi ascoltare una storia spaventosa ti dirò di un sogno che ho fatto qualche settimana fa.

If you want to hear a scary story, I'll tell you about a dream I had a few weeks ago.

1549 **limite** - *nf* limite

limit

In città, il limite di velocità è di 50 km/h.

In towns, speed is limited to 50 km/h.

1550 **trattare** - *verb*

to treat

trattare | Il mio compagno di stanza è prodigo quando si tratta di spendere soldi per i film; li compra il giorno che escono, indipendentemente dal prezzo.

My roommate is prodigal when it comes to spending money on movies; he buys them the day they're released, regardless of price.

1551 **precedente** - *adj; nm* **previous, preceding; precedent**
pretʃedente
La precedente valuta italiana è la lira e il suo simbolo "£". Non è legata alla lira turca.
The former Italian currency was the lira and its symbol was "£". It's not related to the Turkish lira.

1552 **area** - *nf* **area**
area
I fenomeni meteorologici estremi al momento danneggiano le reti di trasporto in tutte le aree del paese; le proiezioni indicano che tali perturbazioni aumenteranno.
Extreme weather events currently disrupt transportation networks in all areas of the country; projections indicate that such disruptions will increase.

1553 **sparire** - *verb* **to disappear**
sparire
In Senegal ci sono molte specie che rischiano di sparire, come le ostriche o come i prodotti dell'orticoltura tradizionali.
In Senegal there are many species that are at risk of disappearance, like the oysters or the traditional garden crops.

1554 **disco** - *nm* **disc**
disko
Ascolta di nuovo il disco e poi dimmi se ti piace.
Listen to the album again and tell me later if you like it.0

1555 **divertimento** - *nm* **fun, entertainment**
divertimento
Noi non impariamo per la scuola, ma impariamo per divertimento.
We do not learn for school, but we learn for fun.

1556 **resistere** - *verb* **to resist**
rezistere
Io non guardo molti film, ma non riesco a resistere ad un buon documentario.
I don't watch a lot of movies, but I can't resist a good documentary.

1557 **prevedere** - *verb* **to foresee**
prevedere
Tom prevede di andare a trovare Mary a Boston uno di questi giorni.
Tom plans to go visit Mary in Boston one of these days.

1558 **tempio** - *nm*
tempjo

temple
Nel 1907 i resti architettonici di un tempio di marmo sono stati trovati insieme a decine di manufatti.
In 1907 the architectural remains of a marble temple were found along with dozens of artifacts.

1559 **soccorso** - *nm*
sokkorso

rescue
Stiamo seguendo un corso intensivo di primo soccorso prima di fare le nostre due settimane di trekking attraverso le montagne.
We're taking a crash course in first aid before our two-week trek through the mountains.

1560 **mestiere** - *nm*
mestjere

craft, skill, trade
Sappiamo di poter dimostrare così che continuiamo a fare bene il nostro mestiere, generando ricchezza e rafforzando la fiducia nel futuro.
We know that, in this way, we can demonstrate that we are continuing to do our craft well, generating wealth and strengthening confidence in the future.

1561 **cancello** - *nm*
kantʃello

gate
Il cancello è sufficientemente largo perché ci passi la macchina.
The gate is wide enough for the car to go through.

1562 **maschera** - *nf*
maskera

mask
Il mondo è un grande ballo in cui ognuno indossa una maschera.
The world is a grand ball in which everyone wears a mask.

1563 **tradire** - *verb*
tradire

to betray
Tradire la fiducia che i nostri clienti ripongono in noi può esporre Aon a pesanti sanzioni civili e penali.
Breaching the trust placed in us by our clients may expose Aon to severe civil and criminal penalties.

1564 **votare** - *verb*
votare

to vote
Tom non era in grado di decidere per chi avrebbe dovuto votare.
Tom was unable to decide who he should vote for.

1565 **attaccare** - *verb*
attakkare

to attack
I terroristi attaccarono il World Trade Center a New York nel 2001.
Terrorists attacked the World Trade Center in New York City in 2001

1566 **vergine** - *adj; nf*
verdʒine
virgin
Maria, Vergine dell'Orto e Madre di tutta la Famiglia Gianelliana, ci accompagni nel cammino, ci dia la forza di percorrerlo.
Mary, Virgin of Our Lady of the Garden and Mother of all the Gianellian Family, may accompany us on our journey, may strengthen us on our way.

1567 **racconto** - *nm*
rakkonto
(short) story
Lui è un autore famoso per i suoi romanzi e i suoi racconti.
He is an author famous for his novels and stories.

1568 **dubitare** - *verb*
dubitare
to doubt
Io dubito di tutto e di tutti, persino dei miei dubbi.
I doubt everything, even my own doubts.

1569 **sorprendere** - *verb*
sorprendere
to surprise
L'idea di sorprenderla mi è passata improvvisamente per la testa.
The idea of surprising her suddenly crossed my mind.

1570 **meraviglia** - *nf*
meraviʎʎa
wonder
Io l'ho sempre detto che la Croazia è il paese delle meraviglie.
I always said that Croatia is the land of wonders.

1571 **agenzia** - *nf*
adʒentsˈia
agency
Se ci si iscrive a Facebook, le informazioni verranno inviate alle agenzie di intelligence.
If you sign up to Facebook, your information will be sent to intelligence agencies.

1572 **stupendo** - *adj*
stupendo
wonderful
Il festival è un evento stupendo e io vorrei che durasse più a lungo.
The festival is a fantastic event and I wish it could last longer.

1573 **continuato** - *adj*
kontinwato
continued
Ha continuato a danzare in discoteca per tutta la notte.
She kept dancing at the disco all night.

1574 **sabbia** - *nf*
sabbja
sand
Si affaccia su una spiaggia di sabbia dorata che si estende fino a nord, formando la Costa de Maresme.
It looks out over a golden, sandy beach which stretches up to the north, forming the Costa de Maresme.

1575 **intanto** - *adv*
in the meantime

	intanto	Intanto c'è chi continua a predicare in modo fraudolento che siamo sulla buona via. *Meanwhile, there are those who continue to preach in a fraudulent manner that we are on the right track.*
1576	**resistenza** - *nf* rezistentsa	**resistance** Nei rapporti in America, la guerrilla di resistenza dei militari iracheni è chiamata terrorismo. *In reports in America, guerrilla resistance by the Iraq military is called terrorism.*
1577	**bosco** - *nm* bosko	**wood** Il cane da caccia si è diretto verso il bosco. *The hunting dog headed for the woods.*
1578	**fase** - *nf* faze	**phase** I lettori formulano delle aspettative su ciò che potrebbe accadere durante fasi successive di testi. *Readers formulate expectations as to what might be happening at subsequent stages of texts.*
1579	**copertura** - *nf* kopertura	**coverage** Lo squadrone rilevò un agguato e si arrampicò per avere una copertura. *The squadron encountered an ambush and scrambled for coverage.*
1580	**svelto** - *adj* zvelto	**quick, brisk, fast** Spero che ti passi alla svelta il raffreddore. *I hope you'll get over your cold soon.*
1581	**super** - *adj* super	**super** La grafica del Super Nintendo è sorprendente. È così migliore di quella del Nintendo originale. *The Super Nintendo's graphics are amazing. They're so much better than those of the original Nintendo.*
1582	**produzione** - *nf* produttsjone	**production, output** La produzione di acciaio ha raggiunto una stima di 100 milioni di tonnellate l'anno scorso. *Steel production reached an estimated 100 million tons last year.*
1583	**grasso** - *adj* grasso	**fat** È più grasso di quando l'ho visto per l'ultima volta. *He is fatter than when I last saw him.*
1584	**settembre** - *nm*	**September**

settembre | Nel 2015 a settembre Il tasso di disoccupazione in Giappone era del 3,4%.

The unemployment rate in Japan was 3.4 percent in September of 2015.

1585 **sessuale** - *adj* — **sexual**
sesswale
Dopo avere avuto un rapporto sessuale, la mantide religiosa solitamente divora il maschio.
After realizing copulation, praying mantis usually devours the male.

1586 **tagliare** - *verb* — **to cut**
taʎʎare
Non smontare, tagliare, aprire, rompere, piegare, deformare, forare o frantumare le celle o le batterie.
Do not dismantle, cut, open, crush, bend, deform, puncture, or shred cells or batteries.

1587 **zucchero** - *nm* — **sugar**
tsukkero
Lei ha rifiutato di bere una tazza di tè con molto zucchero.
She refused to drink a cup of coffee with a lot of sugar.

1588 **qualità** - *nf* — **quality**
kwalitˈa
Tom è incapace di capire la differenza tra un vino di qualità e uno da poco.
Tom can't tell the difference between expensive wine and cheap wine.

1589 **crudele** - *adj* — **cruel**
krudele
Non riesco a immaginare quanto fosse crudele a quel tempo.
I could not image how cruel he was at that time.

1590 **studiato** - *adj* — **studied**
studjato
In particolare essa ha studiato nuovi materiali e tecnologie innovative che le consentono di offrire soluzioni più efficienti in termini di produttività e risparmio energetico.
In particular, it has studied new materials and innovative technologies that enable it to offer solutions that are more efficient in terms of productivity and energy saving.

1591 **mancanza** - *nf* — **lack**
maŋkantsa
Tutti i fiori del giardino sono morti a causa della mancanza d'acqua.
All the flowers in the garden died for lack of water.

1592 **spazzatura** - *nf* — **trash**

spattsatura

Secondo Cooper, “le pile di spazzatura, come sacchetti di plastica e bottiglie, confezioni alimentari, pannolini sporchi e altri rifiuti, continuano ad accumularsi: un insulto alla memoria di tutti quelli che lottarono e morirono per il loro paese."

According to Cooper, "The piles of garbage, such as plastic bags and bottles, food wrappers, soiled diapers, and other trash is continuing to pile up -- an insult to the memory of all who fought and died there for their country."

1593 **incarico** - *nm* | **appointment**
iŋkariko

L'incarico è da consegnare entro due settimane a partire da oggi.

The assignment is due two weeks from today.

1594 **novità** - *nf* | **news**
novitˈa

La signora White scoppiò in lacrime quando le dissi la novità.

Mrs. White broke into tears when I told her the news.

1595 **vetro** - *nm* | **glass**
vetro

Il sensore di rottura del vetro utilizza l'analisi di un segnale digitale proveniente dal microfono ed è in grado di rilevare il caratteristico suono del vetro che si rompe fino a 9 metri di distanza.

Glass-break detector uses a digital signal analysis from the microphone and is able to detect a characteristic sound of the window breaking up to 9 meters away.

1596 **assassinare** - *verb* | **to assassinate**
assassinare

Alcune persone dicono che lui è stato assassinato, altre dicono che si è suicidato.

Some people say he was murdered, others say he killed himself.

1597 **dimostrare** - *verb* | **to show**
dimostrare

Penso ancora che sia improbabile che troveremo alcuna prova per dimostrare la colpevolezza di Tom.

I still think it's unlikely that we'll find any evidence to prove Tom's guilt.

1598 **civile** - *adj; nm* | **civil; civilian**
tʃivile

Non possiamo escludere che una guerra civile scoppi in questo paese.

We cannot rule out the possibility that civil war will break out in that country.

1599 **odiare** - *verb* | **to hate**

odjare | Odio i politici del mondo che mettono gli interessi personali davanti a quelli del loro Paese.

I hate the politicians of the world who put their personal interests before those of their country.

1600 **fiero** - *adj* **proud**
fjero
Io sono molto fiero del lavoro che ho scelto da solo.
I'm very proud of the job I chose myself.

1601 **lindo** - *adj* **clean, neat**
lindo
Si manteneva lindo e pulito; per quanto si sentisse stanco, non mancava mai di radersi.
He kept himself neat and tidy; no matter how tired he became, he never skipped a shave.

1602 **dodici** - *adj; num* **twelve**
dˈɔditʃi
Riesce a correre cento metri in meno di dodici secondi.
He can run 100 meters in less than twelve seconds.

1603 **assicurazione** - *nf* **insurance**
assikurattsjone
Tom non è più coperto dall'assicurazione sanitaria dei suoi genitori.
Tom is no longer covered by his parents' health insurance.

1604 **regista** - *nm* **director**
redʒista
Mi sono avvicinato al teatro, mondo che ho esplorato prima come scenografo e poi anche come drammaturgo e regista
I got closer to the theatre, a world I explored first as set designer and then also as dramatist and director.

1605 **puro** - *adj* **pure**
puro
Le sue gambe son colonne di marmo, fondate su basi d'oro puro.
His legs are as pillars of marble, set upon sockets of fine gold.

1606 **versione** - *nf* **version**
versjone
Se la frase è contenuta nei database otterremo subito la versione tradotta.
If the sentence is in the database, we'll obtain at once the translated version.

1607 **legno** - *nm* **wood**
leɲɲo
Io voglio un pezzo di legno per fare una marionetta. Me lo darai?
I want a piece of wood to make a marionette. Will you give it to me?

1608 **bibbia** - *nf* **Bible**

	bibbja	Secondo la Bibbia, i Re Magi sono stati condotti da Gesù da una stella luminosa. *According to the Bible, the Three Kings were guided to Jesus by a shining star.*
1609	**veleno** - *nm* veleno	**poison** In caso di sovradosaggio, consultare un medico di assistenza o di contattare un controllo centrale de veleno. *In case of overdose, get medical help or contact a Poison Control Center right away.*
1610	**raccomandare** - *verb* rakkomandare	**to recommend** Io sono felice che la pomata che ha raccomandato il medico funziona davvero. *I am happy the ointment the doctor has recommended really works.*
1611	**confondere** - *verb* konfondere	**to confound** Gli studenti d'inglese confondono spesso le parole 'lie' e 'lay'. *Students of English often mix up the words 'lie' and 'lay'.*
1612	**formaggio** - *nf* formaddʒo	**cheese** Qual è il tuo formaggio preferito da mangiare quando bevi del vino? *What's your favorite cheese to eat when drinking wine?*
1613	**territorio** - *nm* territorjo	**territory** Quando Colombo scoprì l'America, i bisonti (bufali americani) occupavano vasti territori. *When Columbus discovered America, bison (American buffalo) inhabited a wide-ranging area*
1614	**inventare** - *verb* inventare	**to invent** L'uomo può inventare tutto, tranne l'arte di essere felice. *Man may invent anything, save for the art of being happy.*
1615	**talmente** - *adv* talmente	**so** Una soluzione l'ho trovata, ma l'ho trovata talmente in fretta che non può essere giusta. *I found a solution, but I found it so fast that it can't be the right solution.*
1616	**eccellenza** - *nf* ettʃellentsa	**excellence** Debian è soprattutto popolare tra gli utenti esperti a causa della sua eccellenza tecnica.

Debian is especially popular among advanced users because of its technical excellence .

1617 **esplodere** - *verb* | **to explode**
esplodere
Gli ingegneri hanno fatto esplodere il ponte perché stava per collassare.
The engineers blew up the bridge because it was about to collapse.

1618 **abitare** - *verb* | **to live**
abitare
Tom era felice di non aver dovuto abitare a Boston per più di un anno.
Tom was glad he didn't have to live in Boston for more than a year.

1619 **divertire** - *verb* | **to entertain**
divertire
Stasera ci siamo divertiti a disegnare insieme il nostro albero genealogico.
Tonight, we had fun drawing up our family tree together.

1620 **preciso** - *adj* | **precise**
pretʃizo
Non utilizzi Google Translate per imparare delle frasi in un'altra lingua perché non è sempre preciso.
Don't use Google Translate to learn phrases in another language because it's not always accurate.

1621 **mordere** - *verb* | **to bite**
mordere
Il vecchio cane riesce ad abbaiare, però non riesce più a mordere.
The old dog can bark, but cannot bite anymore.

1622 **fiamma** - *nf* | **flame**
fjamma
Hanno dovuto chiamare i vigili del fuoco per spegnere le fiamme.
They had to call the firefighters to put out the flames.

1623 **nobile** - *adj* | **noble**
nobile
Si è trattato di un compromesso, certo, ma di un compromesso alto, nobile tra istanze, sensibilità ed interessi diversi.
The text was, indeed, a compromise, but a superior, noble compromise between different bodies, perspectives and interests.

1624 **richiamo** - *nm* | **recall**
rikjamo
Per la configurazione manuale si possono richiamare tutte le funzioni usando il pannello di controllo e indicazione.

The instrument can be fully computer-controlled; for manual settings you can call up all functions using a display and control panel.

1625 **cerimonia** - *nf* tʃerimonja
ceremony
La sposa e lo sposo si sono baciati quando la cerimonia si è conclusa.
The bride and groom kissed when the ceremony ended.

1626 **coraggioso** - *adj* koraddʒozo
courageous
Lei era coraggiosa e allegra, e ha sempre fatto poco dei suoi problemi.
She was brave and cheerful, and always made little of her troubles.

1627 **convenire** - *verb* konvenire
to agree
Possiamo convenire che le strutture sono impeccabili, solo che non si fa nulla.
The structures are superb, we can all agree on that. Except that they do nothing.

1628 **tunnel** - *nm* tunnel
tunnel
Thread the sample tubing nut into the fitting at the top of the probe and then tighten until the sample tubing nut is finger-tight.
Building a tunnel from Japan to China is out of the question.

1629 **apprezzare** - *verb* apprettsare
to appreciate
Ho davvero apprezzato la bistecca che ha servito, per non parlare degli altri piatti.
I really enjoyed the beefsteak you served, not to mention the other dishes.

1630 **topo** - *nm* topo
mouse
Un cane corre dietro a un gatto e il gatto corre dietro a un topo.
A dog runs after a cat, and the cat after a mouse.

1631 **potenza** - *nf* potentsa
power
Si dice che il Giappone sia la più grande potenza economica del mondo.
It is said that Japan is the greatest economic power in the world.

1632 **liceo** - *nm* litʃo
high school
Mi sarebbe piaciuto partire all'estero durante il liceo, ma i miei genitori non hanno voluto.
I would have gladly gone abroad during high school, but my parents didn't want me to.

1633 **totalmente** - *adv*
totalmente

totally
Posare il serbatoio totalmente vuoto sul letto di sabbia distribuito sul fondo dello scavo, riempire progressivamente il serbatoio con acqua e contemporaneamente rinfiancare con sabbia.
Place the totally empty tank on the bed of sand at the bottom of the hole, gradually fill the tank with water and at the same time support it by backfilling with sand.

1634 **canale** - *nm*
kanale

channel
La televisione si vede in sei canali in quella città.
TV may be seen on six channels in that city.

1635 **apposta** - *adj*
apposta

on purpose
Ti assicuro che lui non l'ha fatto apposta.
I assure you that I did not do it purposely.

1636 **attrice** - *nf*
attritʃe

actress
All'attrice venne regalato un mazzo di fiori dopo l'esibizione.
The actress was presented a bouquet of flowers after the performance.

1637 **pillola** - *nf*
pillola

pill
Tom ha preso una pillola dalla bottiglia e l'ha inghiottita.
Tom took a pill from the bottle and swallowed it.

1638 **prodotto** - *nm*
prodotto

product
Il prezzo di questo prodotto non copre il suo costo di fabbricazione.
The price of this article does not cover the cost of its manufacture.

1639 **museo** - *nm*
muzeo

museum
Dicono che c'è un Picasso e tre Renoir in quel museo. Il nostro museo è tra i dieci musei più rinomati del paese.
They say there's a Picasso and three Renoirs in that museum. Our museum is among the ten most renowned in the country.

1640 **cittadino** - *nm*
tʃittadino

citizen
Le leggi obbligano tutti i cittadini a pagare le tasse.
The laws oblige all citizens to pay taxes.

1641 **fotografia** - *nf*
fotografja

photography, photo
Lei voleva sapere se il fotografo poteva togliere il cappello dalla fotografia.
She wanted to know if the photographer could remove the hat from the picture.

1642 **recente** - *adj* retʃente

recent

I recenti progressi nel campo della medicina sono degni di nota.

The recent advances in medicine are remarkable.

1643 **vantaggio** - *nm* vantaddʒo

advantage

Quest'ultimo vantaggio è molto importante per noi, in quanto la personalizzazione è d'obbligo nel nostro campo e dobbiamo realizzare soluzioni più facili da configurare per diverse applicazioni", precisa de la Fuente.

This last advantage is very important to us, since customisation is a must in our business and we need to build solutions that can be configured more easily for different applications," de la Fuente specifies.

1644 **cammino** - *nm* kammino

path

Ci sono voluti solo dieci minuti di cammino per arrivare là.

It took only ten minutes to walk there.

1645 **mago** - *nm* mago

magician

Io non sono un mago, però so quello che tutti dicono su di me.

I'm not a wizard, but I know what everybody says about me.

1646 **lunedì** - *nm* luned'i

Monday

Il corso di tedesco si tiene due sere a settimana, il lunedì e il mercoledì.

German classes are held twice a week - on Mondays and Wednesdays.

1647 **frattempo** - *nm* frattempo

meanwhile, meantime

Ho dovuto fare i salti mortali perché, nel frattempo, mi sono iscritta a scuola.

I had to do all I could because, in the meantime, I started school.

1648 **ahi** - *int* ai

ouch

Ahi! Il mio computer si è ancora impiantato.

Argh! My computer froze up again.

1649 **beccare** - *verb* bekkare

to peck, catch

Noi abbiamo beccato Tom che stava provando a rubare il nostro cibo.

We caught Tom trying to steal our food.

1650 **alare** - *verb*

to andiron

alare | Protagoniste di questo spettacolo sono le aquile, che arrivano a pesare fino a sette chili e raggiungono i due metri e mezzo di apertura alare.

The protagonists of this awesome sight are eagles, some of which may weigh as much as seven kilos and have a wingspan of some two and a half meters.

1651 **visione** - *nf*
vizjone

vision
Per altri, si tratta di una visione di quello che potrebbe essere.
For others, it is a vision of what could be.

1652 **figurato** - *adj*
figurato

figurative
Bruto e Cassio, sono, a loro volta, pronti a tradire o addirittura a uccidere (sia in senso stretto che figurato).

Brutus and Cassius, are in turn ready to betray or even to kill (both in literally and figuratively).

1653 **figura** - *nf*
figura

figure, frame
Il triangolo, il quadrato, il rettangolo, il cerchio, il parallelogrammo ed il trapezio isoscele sono alcune importanti figure geometriche.
Some important geometric shapes are the triangle, the square, the rectangle, the circle, the parallelogram and the trapezium.

1654 **nascita** - *nf*
naʃʃita

birth
Ha detto sotto giuramento che il suo luogo di nascita è l'Italia.
He said under oath that his birthplace is Italy.

1655 **urlare** - *verb*
urlare

to scream
La smetta di urlare! Mi sta facendo venire il mal di testa.
Stop screaming! You're giving me a headache.

1656 **parente** - *nm*
parente

relative
La polizia pubblicherà il nome della vittima dopo averlo comunicato al suo parente più prossimo.

The police will release the victim's name after they have notified his next of kin.

1657 **essi** - *pron*
essi

they, them
Tutti gli esseri umani nascono liberi ed eguali in dignità e diritti. Essi sono dotati di ragione e di coscienza e devono agire gli uni verso gli altri in spirito di fratellanza.

All human beings are born free and equal in dignity and rights. They are endowed with reason and conscience and should act towards one another in a spirit of brotherhood.

1658 **indagine** - *nf* **investigation, survery, inquiry**
indadʒine
Abbiamo bisogno di fare indagini circa la data dell'esame.
We need to make inquiries about the date of the examination.

1659 **sete** - *nf* **thirst**
sete
Ha detto che aveva fame, poi ha aggiunto che aveva anche sete.
He said he was hungry, and then he added that he was also thirsty.

1660 **adatto** - *adj* **suitable**
adatto
Lui è l'ultima persona a essere adatta per il lavoro.
He is the last man that is suited for the job.

1661 **parlato** - *adj* **spoken**
parlato
Malgrado l'esame gli sia andato bene, il suo cinese parlato non è per forza migliore del tuo.
Although he did well in the exam, his spoken Chinese is not necessarily as good as yours.

1662 **seta** - *nf* **thirst**
seta
La lavorazione del vetro è arrivata fino a noi dalla Persia attraverso la Via della Seta.
Glasswork came from Persia by way of the Silk Road.

1663 **scimmia** - *nf* **ape, monkey**
ʃimmja
Lui si è spaventato quando la scimmia gli è saltata addosso.
He was scared when the monkey jumped at him.

1664 **voto** - *nm* **vote, grade**
voto
La mancanza di sonno può avere un impatto negativo enorme sui voti di uno studente.
Lack of sleep can have an enormous negative impact on a student's grades.

1665 **barba** - *nf* **beard**
barba
Lui si è fatto crescere la barba per sembrare più maturo.
He grew a beard to look more mature.

1666 **soffrire** - *verb* **to suffer**
soffrire
Durante la notte mia nonna è venuta a mancare, senza soffrire.
My grandmother went peacefully in the night.

1667 **fegato** - *nm* **liver**

	fegato	Tom è quasi morto dopo aver mangiato un po' di fegato crudo. *Tom nearly died after eating some raw liver.*
1668	**dichiarazione** - *nf* dikjarattsjone	**declaration** Le aziende spesso hanno un elenco di 5-10 "dichiarazioni di missione" presenti nei loro opuscoli, sui loro siti web o appesi nel loro ufficio esprimendo in dettaglio i valori in loro possesso, come una forma di comunicazione ai loro dipendenti, i clienti e il pubblico. *Businesses often have a list of 5-10 'mission statements' featured in their brochures, on their websites or hanging in their office detailing the values they hold as a form of communication to their employees, their clients and the public.*
1669	**consegna** - *nf* konseɲɲa	**delivery** In caso di ritardo nella consegna, abbiamo una speciale assicurazione sul ritardo. *In case the shipment is delayed, we have special delay insurance.*
1670	**cassa** - *nf* kassa	**cash, case** Tom ha aiutato Mary ad aprire la cassa. Tom scoprì che Mary stava rubando dal registro di cassa. *Tom helped Mary open the case. Tom found out Mary was stealing from the cash register.*
1671	**giudizio** - *nm* dʒudittsjo	**judgment** La bellezza è un potere che oscura spesso il nostro giudizio. *Beauty is a power that often clouds our judgement.*
1672	**esistenza** - *nf* ezistentsa	**existence** Sto provando a immaginare la mia esistenza senza te. *I've been trying to imagine my life without you.*
1673	**diamante** - *nm* djamante	**diamond** Tom non ha detto a nessuno che aveva comprato un anello di diamanti per Mary. *Tom didn't tell anyone that he'd bought a diamond ring for Mary.*
1674	**miele** - *nm* mjele	**honey** Non crederai a dove sono stati Tom e Mary per la loro luna di miele. *You won't believe where Tom and Mary went for their honeymoon.*
1675	**femmina** - *nf*	**female**

femmina

Il coccodrillo, che produce solo maschi giovani in un clima più caldo, potrebbe morire anche lui perché non ci saranno femmine per riprodursi.

The crocodile, which produces only male young in hotter weather, might die out too because there will be no females to breed.

1676 **ministero** - *nm*
ministero

ministry

Perché l'Agenzia della Difesa giapponese è stata promossa a Ministero della Difesa?

Why was the Japan Defense Agency upgraded to the Japanese Ministry of Defense?

1677 **divorzio** - *nm*
divortsjo

divorce

Tom mi ha detto che non poteva permettersi un altro divorzio.

Tom told me that he could afford another divorce.

1678 **brillante** - *adj; nm*
brillante

brilliant, bright; diamond

Io vidi qualcosa di molto brillante volare nel cielo notturno.

I saw something very bright fly across the night sky.

1679 **furto** - *nm*
furto

theft

La polizia arrestò un sospetto in relazione con il furto.

The police arrested a suspect in connection with the robbery.

1680 **federale** - *adj*
federale

federal

Konrad Adenauer è stato il primo cancelliere della Repubblica Federale di Germania.

Konrad Adenauer was the first chancellor of the Federal Republic of Germany.

1681 **sorgere** - *adj*
sordʒere

to arise, rise

Perché la Luna è così grande quando sorge e tramonta, rispetto a quando è alta nel cielo?

Why is the Moon larger when it rises and sets, than when it is high in the sky?

1682 **vendita** - *nf*
vendita

sale, selling

Tom pensò che lanciare un sito di vendita pop-corn sarebbe stata una buona idea.

Tom thought it would be a good idea to start a website that sold nothing but popcorn.

1683 **uniforme** - *adj*
uniforme

uniform

I poliziotti della città di New York portano un'uniforme blu scuro.

New York City policemen wear dark blue uniforms.

1684 **chiacchiera** - *nf* kjakkjera

gossip

La storia di Michael Jackson e del tredicenne divenne un'immensa montatura pubblicitaria e una chiacchiera inconsistente

The story of Michael Jackson and the 13-year-old boy became a frenzy of hype and unsubstantiated rumor

1685 **scopare** - *verb* skopare

to sweep, fuck

Appuntamento, ma per se stesso più di Dio, e poi scopare per imparare da Dio?

Appointment, but for himself more than God, then fuck to learn from God?

1686 **blocco** - *nm* blokko

block

Ogni autore soffre del blocco dello scrittore di tanto in tanto.

Every author suffers from writer's block from time to time.

1687 **discussione** - *nf* diskussjone

discussion

Le registrazioni delle nostre discussioni sono conservate dalla segretaria.

The records of our discussions are kept by the secretary.

1688 **ella** - *pron* ella

she

Ella nascose la lettera con cura, in modo che nessuno la vedesse.

She hid the letter carefully so that no one should see it.

1689 **volentieri** - *adv* volentjeri

willingly

Viaggiavo volentieri e viaggerei ancora, ma i viaggi costano molto e io non guadagno più come una volta.

I certainly enjoyed traveling, and I still would if I could, but traveling is expensive and I don't earn as much as I used to.

1690 **rivoluzione** - *nf* rivoluttsjone

revolution

Dopo la caduta della cortina di ferro e la rivoluzione del 1989, la Romania ha iniziato la sua transizione verso la democrazia e l'economia capitalista.

After the fall of the Iron Curtain and the 1989 Revolution, Romania started its transition towards democracy and a capitalist market economy.

1691 **complicare** - *verb* komplikare

to complicate

Se la situazione si complica, chiamami al numero di telefono che ti ho dato ieri.

If things get out of hand, you should call me at the number I gave you yesterday.

1692 **bastone** - *nm* | **stick**
bastone
Sapete come fare un fuoco utilizzando solo bastoni di legno?
Do you know how to start a fire using just sticks of wood?

1693 **azienda** - *nf* | **company, business**
addzjˈɛnda
Le aziende percepiscono come concorrenti una gamma ristretta del mondo degli affari; ci sono molti casi in cui non capiscono i loro veri rivali.
Businesses perceive as competitors a narrow range of the business world; there are many cases where they don't understand their real rivals.

1694 **bagaglio** - *nm* | **luggage**
bagaʎʎo
Ho molti bagagli, quindi non riesco ad andare a casa a piedi.
I have a lot of baggage, so I can't walk home.

1695 **caspita** - *int* | **good heavens**
kaspita
E dice: 'Non c'è tempo', e caspita, ciò è terribilmente vicino all'essere vero.
He says, 'There is no time' and boy, that is awfully close to being true.

1696 **pesca** - *nf* | **fishing, catch, peach**
peska
Nell'Unione Europea, i sussidi per la pesca vengono utilizzati per l'ammodernamento delle navi o la loro demolizione
In the EU, fisheries subsidies are used to pay for vessel modernisation or scrapping.

1697 **improvvisamente** - *adv* | **suddenly**
improvvizamente
Dopo che mia madre è morta improvvisamente, mio padre si è preso cura di me tutto da solo.
After my mother died suddenly, my father looked after me all by himself.

1698 **urgente** - *adj* | **urgent**
urdʒente
Coloro che soffrono la fame in Africa hanno bisogno d'aiuto urgente.
Those who are suffering from hunger in Africa need urgent help.

1699 **pagano** - *nm* | **pagan, heathen**
pagano
Di suo padre, sappiamo solo che era un pagano, e pertanto non era circonciso.
Of his father, we know only that he was a pagan and that is why he wasn't circumcised.

1700 **augurare** - *verb* | **to wish**

	augurare	Auguro a tutti voi un buon Natale e felice anno nuovo. *I wish you all a merry Christmas and a happy new year.*
1701	**glielo (di glie e lo)** - *pron*	**it to him**
	ʎelo (di ʎe e llo)	Ha detto che se avesse conosciuto il suo indirizzo, gliel'avrebbe scritto. *He said that if he knew her address, he would write to her.*
1702	**pancia** - *nf* pantʃa	**belly** Il dolore di stomaco è comunemente confuso con dolore alla pancia. *Stomachache is usually mistaken with bellyache.*
1703	**vicenda** - *nf* vitʃenda	**event** Tuttavia, la Commissione seguirà la vicenda e, se opportuno, avvierà un dialogo con le autorità tunisine in stretta collaborazione con gli Stati membri. *However, the Commission will follow the situation, and if opportune, open the dialogue with Tunisian Authorities in close co-operation with the Member States.*
1704	**rivedere** - *verb* rivedere	**to review, revise** Io penso che sia molto improbabile rivedere la mia moto rubata. *I think it's highly unlikely that I'll ever see my stolen motorcycle again.*
1705	**volante** - *nm; adj* volante	**steering wheel; flying** Questa mattina, sono andata a un bancone di vendita di pesce e il pesce volante era molto fresco e anche in vendita. *This morning, I went to a fish selling counter and the flying fish was very fresh and also on sale.*
1706	**leggenda** - *nf* leddʒenda	**legend** La leggenda racconta che la valle dell'Hasli, nell'Oberland bernese, era abitata dagli gnomi *According to legend, in days gone by, the Bernese Oberland's Haslital (Hasli Valley) was a favourite haunt of dwarves*
1707	**guadagnare** - *verb* gwadaɲɲare	**to earn, gain** Potenzialmente ogni piccolo miglioramento fatto alla vettura può contribuire alla velocità e alla fine può far guadagnare punti in campionato.

Every small improvement made to the car has the potential to contribute to the speed and ultimately the gaining of championship points.

1708 **junior** - *adj* dʒunjor

junior
Il mio nome completo è Ricardo Vernaut Junior.
My full name is Ricardo Vernaut, Junior.

1709 **tecnologia** - *nf* teknolodʒa

technology
Mi piacerebbe sapere di più sulla tecnologia che è stata utilizzata nella costruzione delle piramidi egizie.
I would like to know more about the technology which was used in the construction of the Egyptian pyramids.

1710 **mistero** - *nm* mistero

mystery
Ieri è storia, domani è un mistero, ma oggi è un dono. Per questo è chiamato "presente".
Yesterday is history, tomorrow is a mystery, but today is a gift. That is why it is called the "present".

1711 **accomodare** - *verb* akkomodare

to accommodate
Per accomodare il bambino è possibile ripiegare la maniglia di trasporto dietro il seggiolino in 2 posizioni, premendo entrambi i pulsanti.
To position your child, you can fold the carrying handle behind the seat in 2 positions, by pressing both handle release buttons.

1712 **palco** - *nm* palko

stage
A Roger piaceva scrivere canzoni. Gli piaceva anche eseguire le sue canzoni sul palco.
Roger liked writing songs. He also liked to perform his own songs on the stage.

1713 **stringere** - *verb* strindʒere

to tighten
Non spanare o stringere troppo il dado di fissaggio o il tubo può fuoriuscire.
Do not cross-thread or over-tighten the retaining nut or the tubing may leak.

1714 **eccoli** - *int* ekkoli

here they are (eccolo/i (m), eccola/e (f)
Avete detto che volevate delle prove. Beh, eccole.
You said you wanted proof. Well, here it is.

1715 **ritornare** - *verb*

to return

ritornare

Con il pulsante 1.23 si può passare direttamente al menu per la rimozione della protezione contro la cancellazione, o da qui ritornare indietro.

You can use button 1.23 to switch directly to the menu for canceling protection or to return from that menu.

1716 **disgustoso** - *adj*
dizgustozo

disgusting

Voglio comprare una macchina per il caffè, non riesco più a bere il caffè solubile, è disgustoso.

I want to buy a coffee maker, I can't drink instant coffee any longer, it's disgusting.

1717 **superare** - *verb*
superare

to exceed

Non pensavo che Tom ce l'avrebbe fatta a superare la notte, così sono rimasta al suo capezzale.

I didn't think Tom would make it through the night, so I stayed by his bedside.

1718 **nuotare** - *verb*
nwotare

to swim

Tom vive vicino a una spiaggia, quindi va a nuotare quasi ogni giorno d'estate.

Tom lives near a beach, so he goes swimming almost every day in the summer.

1719 **dimentico** - *adj*
dimentiko

oblivious

Un mondo, sempre più dimentico del passato e insanamente proteso al nuovo, è facile preda di chi vuol distruggere.

A world that tends to forget its past more and more, and that unhealthily tends towards the new, is easy prey for those who wish to destroy.

1720 **atmosfera** - *nf*
atmosfera

atmosphere

Il linguaggio formalmente educato, in un certo senso, rovina un'atmosfera informale.

Polite language, in a sense, spoils a casual atmosphere.

1721 **cameriere** - *nm&f*
kamerjere

waiter, butler / waitress, maid

Al cameriere ossequioso viene solitamente assegnato il tavolo migliore perché cerca sempre di ingraziarsi il suo manager e i suoi superiori.

The obsequious waiter is usually assigned the best table because he always curries favor with his manager and superiors.

1722 **impegno** - *nm*

commitment

	impeɲɲo	Quando, un giorno, i computer si impegneranno a tradurre opere letterarie, sarà la fine della letteratura come noi la conosciamo. *When, one day, computers undertake to translate literary works, it will be the end of literature as we know it.*
1723	**regale** - *adj* regale	**kingly** Gesù ritornerà sul trono regale della sua gloria, per dare compimento a quella sua parola. *Jesus will return on the royal throne of His glory, to bring to fulfillment that word of His.*
1724	**robot** - *nm* robot	**robot** I robot non si ammalano o si lamentano mai e riescono a lavorare 24 ore al giorno. *The robots never get sick or complain and they can work 24 hours a day.*
1725	**imperatore** - *nm* imperatore	**Emperor** L'imperatore Adriano ha fatto costruire il Vallo di Adriano. *Emperor Hadrian had Hadrian's Wall built.*
1726	**festeggiare** - *verb* festeddʒare	**to celebrate** Tom e Mary hanno festeggiato il loro primo anniversario con una cena romatica. *Tom and Mary had a romantic dinner to celebrate their first anniversary together.*
1727	**danzare** - *verb* dantsare	**to dance** Yoko ha danzato con tanta eleganza che ci ha sorpreso noi tutti. *Yoko danced with a grace that surprised us.*
1728	**benedire** - *verb* benedire	**to bless** Grazie. Che Dio vi benedica. E che Dio benedica gli Stati Uniti d'America. *Thank you. God bless you. And may God bless the United States of America*
1729	**appunto** - *adv* appunto	**just** Quel che unisce noi tutti è appunto il senso dell'appartenenza all'Europa, come patrimonio comune di valori e di idee *What unites us all is precisely the sense of belonging to Europe, seen as a common heritage of values and ideas, traditions*
1730	**fresco** - *adj*	**fresh, cool**

	fresko	Tom ha detto che aveva bisogno di prendere un po' d'acqua fresca. *Tom said that he needed to take a bit of fresh water.*
1731	**sincero** - *nm* sintʃero	**sincere** Mi piace non perché è gentile, ma perché è sincero. *I like him not because he is kind but because he is honest.*
1732	**gestire** - *verb* dʒestire	**to handle, manage** L'ufficio Etica può dispensare consigli per gestire le situazioni difficili tra colleghi? *Can the Office of Ethics provide advice on how to handle difficult situations with colleagues?*
1733	**parcheggio** - *nm* parkeddʒo	**parking, park** Anch'io ho già pagato qualche volta multe per divieto di parcheggio. *I've paid parking fines a number of times myself.*
1734	**rifugio** - *nm* rifudʒo	**refuge** La coerenza è l'ultimo rifugio delle persone senza immaginazione. *Consistency is the last refuge of the unimaginative.*
1735	**sposo** - *nm* spozo	**groom** E poi la sposa e lo sposo vengono lasciati soli. *and then the bride and bridegroom are left alone.*
1736	**telecamera** - *nf* telekamera	**camera** Tom mi ha mostrato come usare la sua telecamera. *Tom showed me how to use his camera.*
1737	**equipaggio** - *nm* ekwipaddʒo	**crew** L'equipaggio dovette abbandonare la nave che affondava. *The crew had to abandon the sinking ship.*
1738	**organizzare** - *verb* organiddzare	**to organize, arrange** Grazie per avermi aiutata ad organizzare la festa di compleanno di Tom. *Thank you for helping me organize Tom's birthday party.*
1739	**cola** - *adv* kola	**there (form)** Il soggiorno colà è tanto più piacevole quanto più è elevato; e ai confini del piano mentale lo spirito trova quiete, poiché già attratto dall'alto. *The higher up, the more pleasant the stay; and on the border of the mental plane the spirit can rest, because there the spirit is already subject to lofty attractions.*
1740	**penna** - *nf*	**pen**

penna | Mi sono piegato per raccogliere la penna che mi era caduta sul pavimento.

I bent over to pick up my pen which had fallen on the floor.

1741 **nozze** - *nfpl* | **wedding**

nottse | Il mio anello di nozze è stato realizzato da un orafo specializzato.

My wedding ring was crafted by a skilled goldsmith.

1742 **biblioteca** - *nf* | **library**

bibljoteka | Apparentemente in questa biblioteca ci sono dei libri preziosi che i soldi non possono comprare.

Apparently in this library are precious books that money can't buy.

1743 **pregare** - *verb* | **to pray**

pregare | Ti prego di accettare le mie condoglianze per la morte di tuo padre.

Please accept my condolences on the death of your father.

1744 **frase** - *nf* | **phrase, sentence**

fraze | Ci sono delle frasi la cui traduzione in alcune lingue non ha senso e, quindi, devono essere evitate.

There are sentences whose translation into certain languages doesn't make sense and, therefore, should be avoided.

1745 **ricominciare** - *verb* | **to recommence**

rikomintʃare | Cancella fino all'inizio del discorso o del testo; togli il soggetto o ricomincia da capo.

Erase to the start of discourse or text; drop the subject or start over.

1746 **pulire** - *verb* | **to clean**

pulire | A me piacerebbe ridurre drasticamente la quantità di tempo che mi ci vuole per pulire la casa.

I would like to drastically decrease the amount of time it takes me to clean the house.

1747 **bruciare** - *verb* | **to burn**

brutʃare | Maria, che è appena stata nominata Coordinatrice Nazionale contro l'estremismo violento, ha partecipato a una manifestazione, in cui hanno ritualmente bruciato la bandiera elboniana.

Maria, who has just been appointed as National Coordinator against violent extremism, participated in a demonstration, in which they ritually burned the Elbonian flag.

1748 **leone** - *nm* | **lion**

leone | I suoi capelli erano lunghi e spettinati, simili alla criniera di un leone.
His long and untidy hair was similar to a lion's mane.

1749 **istruzione** - *nf* | **instruction, education**
istruttsjone | I genitori hanno diritto di priorità nella scelta del genere di istruzione da impartire ai loro figli.
Parents have a prior right to choose the kind of education that shall be given to their children.

1750 **cambiamento** - *nm* | **change**
kambjamento | Il Gruppo ha iniziato con determinazione un importante processo di cambiamento ponendo al centro la performance industriale e commerciale.
The Group has begun to implement with determination an important process of change, focusing all of its efforts on its industrial and commercial performance.

1751 **cimitero** - *nm* | **cemetery**
tʃimitero | Ho sepolto il mio cane nel cimitero per animali da compagnia.
I buried my dog at the pet cemetery.

1752 **reazione** - *nf* | **reaction**
reattsjone | Osservate la sua reazione del viso quando parliamo di un prezzo.
Observe his facial reaction when we mention a price.

1753 **realmente** - *adv* | **really**
realmente | Tom non aveva realmente voglia di andare in campeggio con John e Mary.
Tom didn't really feel like going camping with John and Mary.

1754 **cioccolato** - *nm* | **chocolate**
tʃokkolato | Questa è la migliore mousse al cioccolato che io e i miei ospiti abbiamo mai mangiato.
This is the best chocolate mousse that my guests and myself have ever eaten.

1755 **orgoglio** - *nm* | **pride**
orgoʎʎo | Il mio orgoglio mi ha impedito di prendere in prestito del denaro da lui.
My pride prevented me from borrowing money from him.

1756 **combinare** - *verb* | **to combine**
kombinare | Non è facile combinare i passatempi con i profitti.
It is not easy to combine hobbies with profits.

1757 **giocatore** - *nm* — **player, gambler**

dʒokatore

L'allenatore ha detto ai giocatori di non mangiare troppo prima della partita.

The coach told the players not to eat too much before the game.

1758 **cretino** - *adj; nm* — **stupid; cretin**

kretino

Grazie per avermi spiegato il motivo per cui tutti mi prendono per un cretino.

Thanks for having explained to me at last why people take me for an idiot.

1759 **disporre** - *verb* — **to have**

disporre

A tal fine, tutti gli Stati membri devono disporre dei poteri necessari per prendere tempestivamente, se necessario, le misure idonee.

To this end, all the Member States must have the necessary powers to take the relevant measures, where appropriate.

1760 **golf** - *nm* — **golf, sweater, jersey**

golf

Tom ha fatto finire la sua macchina da golf in un banco di sabbia.

Tom drove his golf cart into a sand bank.

1761 **ara** - *nf* — **macaw, altar**

ara

Il Nuovo Spazio Espositivo dell'Ara Pacis è lo spazio dedicato alle mostre del museo.

The New Temporary Exhibition Space of the Ara Pacis is the space that hosts the exhibitions of the museum.

1762 **capacità** - *nf* — **capacity**

kapatʃitˈa

La capacità di lavorare duro è una caratteristica ammirevole, ma la capacità di rilassarsi non è meno importante.

The ability to work hard is an admirable characteristic but the ability to relax is not less important.

1763 **spostare** - *verb* — **to move**

spostare

Preferisco spostarmi con la metro piuttosto che con il treno.

I prefer to go by subway, rather than by train.

1764 **perduto** - *adj* — **lost**

perduto

Purtroppo il seme andò perduto a causa dello scarso interesse manifestato dagli allevatori e dal governo

Unfortunately, the semen were lost due to lack of interest by breeders and the government

1765 **bandiera** - *nf* — **flag**

	bandjera	I colori della bandiera italiana sono il bianco, il rosso e il verde. *The colors of Italian flag are white, red and green.*
1766	**saggiare** - *verb* sadd ʒare	**to test** Una volta qui è d'obbligo saggiare la cucina prelibata tipica che va dai piatti di riso e frutti di mare ai primi e secondi. *Once here one must try the excellent typical cuisine, with their succulent rice and seafood dish first courses.*
1767	**indossare** - *verb* indossare	**to wear, put on** Mia sorella indossa sempre i jeans, ma in questo momento sta comprando una gonna per la festa di Tom. *My sister always wears jeans, but now she's buying a skirt for Tom's party.*
1768	**contea** - *nf* kontea	**county** Celebra l'inizio del bellissimo periodo di fioritura dei meli con diversi eventi nella contea irlandese di Orchard. *Celebrate the start of the beautiful apple blossom season with a range of events in Ireland's Orchard County.*
1769	**umanità** - *nf* umanitˈa	**humanity** Ai suoi occhi, il predominio della lingua inglese, non soltanto costituisce una minaccia per il patrimonio dell'umanità, ma è carico di un rischio ben più grave. *In his view, the domination by the English language is a threat to the heritage of humanity. It poses an even worse risk.*
1770	**professionista** - *adj; nm&f; nm* professjonista	**professional; professional; expert** La ragazza indiana nel film non è un'attrice professionista. *The Indian girl in the film isn't a professional actress.*
1771	**calore** - *nm* kalore	**heat** Sono andati a Edimburgo per fuggire dal calore estivo. *They went to Edinburgh to escape from the summer heat.*
1772	**orgoglioso** - *adj* orgoʎʎozo	**proud** Io ero molto orgoglioso quando mio figlio ha vinto il primo premio al concorso. *I was very proud when my son won first prize at the competition.*
1773	**disposizione** - *nf* dispozittsjone	**arrangement** Ogni attività che volete compiere prenderà più tempo di quanto ne avete a disposizione.

Any activity you need to accomplish will take more time than you have.

1774 **negativo** - *adj* negativo
negative
La mancanza di sonno può avere un impatto negativo enorme sui voti di uno studente.
Lack of sleep can have an enormous negative impact on a student's grades.

1775 **delitto** - *nm* delitto
crime
Sui giornali è stato scritto che si trattava di un delitto passionale.
It said in the newspapers that it was a crime of passion.

1776 **impegnare** - *verb* impeɲɲare
to commit
Se vuoi conseguire buoni risultati a scuola, devi impegnarti nello studio a più non posso.
If you are to do well in school, you must study hard.

1777 **umore** - *nm* umore
mood, humor
Io non penso che Tom sia dell'umore giusto per lavorare in questo momento.
I don't think Tom is in the mood to work right now.

1778 **superficie** - *nf* superfitʃe
surface
Gli ultimi raggi del sole si riflettono sulla superficie del mare infinito.
The last rays of the sun are reflected on the infinite sea.

1779 **divano** - *nm* divano
sofa
Tom ha raccolto le monete che erano cadute dietro il divano.
Tom picked up the coins that had fallen behind the sofa.

1780 **cabina** - *nf* kabina
cabin
Il futuro pilota è addestrato in una cabina di pilotaggio finta.
The future pilot is trained in a mock cockpit.

1781 **saluto** - *nm* saluto
greeting
Questo infatti è il saluto che Gesù ha rivolto agli apostoli riuniti nel Cenacolo: “Pace a voi!
In fact, this is the greeting Jesus directed to the apostles assembled at the Last Supper: “May Peace be with you!

1782 **raggio** - *nm* raddʒo
radius, spoke, beam, range, ray
Gli ultimi raggi del sole si riflettono sulla superficie del mare infinito.
The last rays of the sun are reflected on the infinite sea.

1783 **fiato** - *nm*
breath

fjato | Lei si è nascosta dietro la porta e ha trattenuto il fiato.
She hid behind the door and held her breath.

1784 **colui** - *pron* | **he**
kolwi | Colui che è in grado di definire un problema, ne ha già risolto metà.
The one that is able to define a problem, already solved half of it.

1785 **girato** - *adj* | **endorsed, turned (moved around axis), shot (movie)**
dʒirato | Abbiamo girato tutte le scene con riprese master e modificato gli assi quando eravamo soddisfatti della performance degli attori.
We filmed all the scenes in master shots and changed axes when we were satisfied with the actors' performance.

1786 **ritmo** - *nm* | **rhythm**
ritmo | A questo ritmo, è una questione di tempo prima che mi becchino.
At this rate, it's a matter of time before I get caught.

1787 **costo** - *nm* | **cost**
kosto | Non c'è alcun costo d'ingresso per i bambini al di sotto dei cinque anni.
There is no admission fee for children under five.

1788 **imbarazzante** - *adj* | **embarrassing**
imbarattsante | Dopo un imbarazzante silenzio, Bill la prese per mano e la trascinò di sopra.
After an awkward pause, Bill took her by the hand and dragged her upstairs.

1789 **pubblicità** - *nf* | **advertising**
pubblitʃitˈa | La pubblicità on-line, grazie all'ampio raggio di diffusione, gode di un maggior grado di fiducia rispetto alla pubblicità classica.
Due to their extensive reach, more confidence is placed in online advertisements than in traditional advertising.

1790 **sport** - *nm* | **sport, sports**
sport | Il rugby è uno sport che non viene mai interrotto per la pioggia.
Rugby is a sport which is never called off by rain.

1791 **eccitante** - *adj; nm* | **exciting; stimulate, upper**
ettʃitante | Era tremendamente eccitante essere a Boston in quel periodo.
It was tremendously exciting to be in Boston at that time.

1792 **zuppa** - *nf* | **soup**

tsuppa

All'ombra della torre pendente di Pisa siede il cantore della città, mangiando un piatto di zuppa di piselli. Dopodiché egli racconterà ai bambini la fiaba "La principessa sul pisello".

In the shadow of the Leaning Tower of Piza sits the storyteller of the town, eating a plate of pea soup. After that he tells some children the fairy tale "The Princess and the Pea".

1793 **diario** - *nm*
djarjo
diary
Tom scrive qualcosa nel suo diario ogni sera, non importa quanto stanco sia.

Tom writes something in his diary every evening, no matter how tired he is.

1794 **cavo** - *nm; adj*
kavo
cable, wire; hollow
La settimana prossima l'elettricista viene a riparare i cavi.
Next week the electrician is coming to fix the wires.

1795 **salutare** - *adj; verb*
salutare
healthy; to greet, say goodbye to
"Dove sei andato?" "Sono andato in stazione per salutare un amico che partiva."

"Where have you been?" "I have been to the station to see a friend off."

1796 **collina** - *nf*
kollina
hill
Dalla collina su cui sorge la mia casa, si ha una vista su tutta la città.
The hill on which my house stands commands a full view of the city.

1797 **attraversare** - *verb*
attraversare
to cross
Mia madre mi ha insegnato a guardare entrambi i lati prima di attraversare la strada.

My mother taught me to always look both to the left and to the right before crossing the street.

1798 **coprire** - *verb*
koprire
to cover
Il suo nuovo taglio di capelli le copre le orecchie.
Her new hairstyle covers her ears.

1799 **struttura** - *nf*
struttura
structure
Tutti gli elementi di una struttura dati sono pubblici per impostazione predefinita.

All the elements of a data structure are public by default.

1800 **attraente** - *adj*
attraente
attractive
Bello, intelligente e attraente - questo descrive ciò che lui non è.

Beautiful, intelligent and hot - this describes what he is not.

1801 **riserva** - *nf* rizerva
reserve, reservation
Sfortunatamente, le riserve di cibo finirono prima della fine dell'inverno.
Unfortunately, the food supplies gave out before the end of winter.

1802 **analisi** - *nf* analizi
analysis
Le decisioni efficaci si basano sull'analisi di dati e informazioni.
Effective decisions are based on the analysis of data and information.

1803 **florido** - *adj* florido
florid
Un viale bordato da filari di cipressi accompagna gli ospiti lungo il curatissimo e florido giardino
A driveway bordered by rows of cypresses takes guests through the well-kept, blooming garden.

1804 **cintura** - *nf* tʃintura
belt
Dobbiamo sempre indossare la cintura di sicurezza nel caso ci capiti un incidente.
We should always wear a seatbelt in case we have an accident.

1805 **condannare** - *verb* kondannare
to convict
L'Iran condannò gli attacchi di Israele contro la Siria.
Iran condemned the attacks of Israel against Syria.

1806 **patata** - *nf* patata
potato, pussy (coll)
Nostra sorella ha comprato alcune melanzane, delle patate, delle zucchine e del cavolo cinese al mercato.
Our sister bought some eggplants, potatoes, zucchinis and Chinese cabbage at the market.

1807 **sforzo** - *nm* sfortso
effort
I processi politici del nostro paese sono tali che, se una regola della ragione non si applica in questo sforzo, perderemo tutto - anche un possibile cambiamento drastico nella Costituzione.
The political processes of our country are such that if a rule of reason is not applied in this effort, we will lose everything — even to a possible and drastic change in the Constitution.

1808 **scrittore** - *nm* skrittore
writer
Io non dimenticherò mai l'incontro con quel famoso scrittore l'anno scorso.

I will never forget meeting that popular writer last year.

1809 **reputazione** - *nf; nm*
reputattsjone
reputation; credit, standing
Il comportamento non ha fatto bene alla sua reputazione.
The behavior did his reputation no good.

1810 **spiegazione** - *nf*
spjegattsjone
explanation
In realtà, la spiegazione è un po' più complicata di così, ma si ottiene il succo del discorso.
In reality, the explanation is a bit more complicated than this, but you get the gist.

1811 **armato** - *adj*
armato
armed
Tom si è armato con una pistola e un coltello.
Tom armed himself with a gun and a knife.

1812 **religione** - *nf*
relidʒone
religion
La religione è considerata vera dalla gente comune, falsa dai saggi e utile dai governanti.
Religion is regarded by the common people as true, by the wise as false, and by the rulers as useful.

1813 **eccezionale** - *adj*
ettʃettsjonale
exceptional, outstanding
Il festival è stato teatro di un eccezionale grande concorso di pubblico.
The festival witnessed an unusually large attendance.

1814 **rinforzo** - *nm*
rinfortso
reinforcement
I pannelli vengono utilizzati come elementi portanti e di rinforzo ma anche come elementi non portanti.
The panels are used for load-bearing and bracing, but also for non-structural elements.

1815 **conseguenza** - *nf*
konsegwentsa
result, consequence
La conseguenza di una traduzione errata a volte può essere catastrofica.
The consequence of a wrong translation can sometimes be catastrophic.

1816 **ebbene** - *conj*
ebbene
so, well
Ebbene, la cooperazione allo sviluppo ha proprie leggi, norme, criteri, strumenti e istituzioni
Well, development cooperation has its own laws, rules, criteria, tools and institutions

1817 **evento** - *nm*
evento
event
L'evento ha luogo sia che piova sia che ci sia il sole.
The event takes place rain or shine.

1818 **traditore** - *adj; nm* | **treacherousl.; traitor**
traditore
Gli italiani dicono che i traduttori sono dei traditori.
The Italians say that translators are traitors.

1819 **proiettile** - *nm* | **bullet, projectile**
projettile
Un dottore ha provato a rimuovere il proiettile dalla sua schiena.
A doctor tried to remove the bullet from his back.

1820 **costume** - *nm* | **costume, custom, suit**
kostume
I russi copiano i costumi francesi, ma sempre a cinquant'anni di distanza.
The Russians copy the French ways, but always fifty years later.

1821 **torcere** - *verb* | **to twist**
tortʃere
Durante il confezionamento non torcere il cavo rispetto al connettore.
Do not twist the cable during assembly.

1822 **accompagnare** - *verb* | **to accompany**
akkompaɲɲare
Lui e il suo compagno mi hanno chiesto di accompagnarli.
He and his companion asked me to come along with them.

1823 **nudo** - *adj* | **naked**
nudo
Una scheggia di legno, quasi invisibile a occhio nudo, ha causato una dolorosa infezione a uno delle dita di Tom.
A splinter of wood, barely visible to the naked eye, caused a very painful infection in one of Tom's fingers.

1824 **vasca** - *nm* | **tub**
vaska
Tom ha riempito la vasca da bagno con dell'acqua calda.
Tom filled the bathtub with hot water.

1825 **giuria** - *nf* | **jury**
dʒurja
La Giuria, riunita in sessione plenaria, procede alla valutazione dei bilanci.
The Jury then meets in plenary session and examines the financial reportings.

1826 **sfida** - *nf* | **challenge**
sfida
Emergono sempre sfide nella vita, alcuni le chiamano problemi, gli altri opportunità di crescita.
Again and again there are challenges in our life. Some call them problems, others call them growth opportunities.

1827 **catena** - *nf* | **chain**
katena
L'Italia ha due catene montuose, le Alpi e gli Appennini.
Italy has two mountain ranges, the Alps and the Apennines.

1828 **schiavo** - *nm*
skjavo
slave
Mi rifiuto di essere trattato come uno schiavo da te.
I refuse to be treated like a slave by you.

1829 **accetto** - *adj*
attʃetto
acceptable
Naturalmente, chiunque (inclusi gli xilofonisti Jazz sperimentali...) è più che ben accetto ad entrare a far parte della schiera di utenti di Ditto Looper!
Of course, everyone (including experimental Jazz xylophone players...) is more than welcome to use Ditto Looper!

1830 **beva(anda)** - *nf*
bevaanda)
drink
L'uomo, per vivere, ha bisogno di alimenti, che consistono in cibi e in bevande.
In order to stay alive, humans need alimentation, which consists of foods and beverages.

1831 **febbre** - *nf*
febbre
temperature, fever
Io ho la febbre e il mal di testa. Penso che mi sto ammalando.
I have a fever and a headache. I think I'm getting ill.

1832 **curioso** - *adj*
kurjozo
curious
Lei è curiosa di scoprire chi le ha inviato i fiori.
She's curious to find out who sent the flowers.

1833 **tragedia** - *nf*
tradʒedja
tragedy
Questa è una tragedia per questa famiglia, è una tragedia per questa comunità, è una tragedia per la città.
This is a tragedy for this family, it's a tragedy for this community, it's a tragedy for the city.

1834 **monte** - *nm*
monte
mountain, mount
Il Monte Etna ha eruttato, spedendo pennacchi di lava e cenere nel cielo siciliano.
Mount Etna has erupted, sending lava and ash plumes into the Sicilian sky.

1835 **pochino** - *adv*
pokino
a little
Io dovrei dire che certamente lui è un pochino arrabbiato.
I should say he is surely a little angry.

1836 **olio** - *nm*
oljo
oil
"Qual è il motivo della tua allergia questa volta? È l'olio d'oliva nell'insalata?" "No, sono i pomodori."
"What's the reason for your allergy this time? Is it the olive oil in the salad?" "No, it's the tomatoes."

1837 **barone** - *nm*
barone

baron
Negli ultimi anni della sua vita Revoltella si dedicò a opere di mecenatismo e nel 1867 l'Impero gli conferì il titolo di barone.
Revoltella dedicated the final years of his life to patronage, and was ennobled as Baron by the Austrian Empire in 1867.

1838 **pizza** - *nf*
piddza

pizza
Chi stavo provando a ingannare quando ho tagliato quella fetta di pizza a metà?
Who was I trying to fool when I cut that slice of pizza in half?

1839 **legare** - *verb*
legare

to tie
Tom ha legato le sue piante di pomodoro a dei pali con dello spago.
Tom tied his tomato plants to stakes with twine.

1840 **accusare** - *verb*
akkuzare

to accuse
Il poliziotto mi ha accusato di avere ignorato le regole del traffico.
The policeman blamed me for ignoring traffic rules.

1841 **antico** - *adj*
antiko

ancient
L'astronomia è al tempo stesso la scienza più antica e la più moderna.
Astronomy is at the same time the most ancient and the most modern science.

1842 **capo** - *nm*
kapo

boss
Stephen viaggia più del suo capo.
Stephen travels more than his boss.

1843 **clinico** - *adj*
kliniko

clinical
Le cartelle cliniche nella maggior parte degli ospedali sono tenuti in ordine alfabetico.
The clinical records in most hospitals are kept in alphabetical order.

1844 **carattere** - *nm*
karattere

character
Tom non riesce più a sopportare il carattere di Mary.
Tom can't put up with Mary's behavior anymore.

1845 **ricompensare** - *verb*
rikompensare

to reward
La certificazione viene a ricompensare il lavoro iniziato nel novembre del 2007 dall'insieme dello staff e dalla direzione.
This certification endorses the work initiated in November 2007 by the entire staff and management .

1846 **fila** - *nf*

row, line

	fila	C'erano delle file di alberi su entrambi i lati della strada. *There were rows of trees on either side of the road.*
1847	**pene** - *nm* pene	**penis** Il pene dell'elefante nano può raggiungere il mezzo metro di lunghezza. *The penis of a dwarf elephant can reach the half meter in length.*
1848	**probabile** - *adj* probabile	**likely** È molto meno probabile che un Macintosh abbia un virus rispetto ad un computer con Windows. *It's a lot less likely for a Macintosh computer to have a virus than a computer running Windows.*
1849	**raccogliere** - *verb* rakkoʎʎere	**to gather** Tom ha fatto del volontariato per aiutare a raccogliere soldi per un nuovo orfanotrofio. *Tom volunteered to help raise money for a new orphanage.*
1850	**petrolio** - *nm* petroljo	**oil, petroleum** I prodotti petrolchimici sono dei prodotti chimici derivati dal petrolio. *Petrochemicals are chemical products derived from petroleum.*
1851	**schermo** - *nm* skermo	**screen, monitor** Lo scopo di questo gioco è di fare esplodere tutte le bombe sullo schermo. *The aim of this game is to explode all the bombs on the screen.*
1852	**familiare** - *adj* familjare	**familiar** Lei sembra più o meno familiare con il soggetto. *He seems more or less familiar with the subject.*
1853	**onde** - *adv; conj; pron* onde	**hence, whence; so that, so as; of which, whose** Indica informazioni importanti da memorizzare, incluse precauzioni quali la visualizzazione di allarmi onde evitare di danneggiare i dispositivi. *Indicates important information that should be memorized, including precautions such as alarm displays to avoid damaging the devices.*
1854	**gentiluomo** - *nm* dʒentilwomo	**gentleman** Si veste come un gentiluomo, ma parla e si comporta come un pagliaccio.

His dress is that of gentleman, but his speech and behavior are those of a clown.

1855 **argento** - *nm* ardʒento
silver
Come dice il proverbio: il silenzio è d'oro, la parola d'argento.
As the saying goes: Speech is silver, silence is gold.

1856 **orso** - *nm* orso
bear
In realtà, a muoversi a qualsiasi velocità l'orso polare utilizza il doppio dell'energia della maggior parte degli altri mammiferi.
In fact, to move at any speed the polar bear uses twice as much energy as do most other mammals.

1857 **fico** - *nm* fiko
fig
Il fico ha messo i suoi ficucci, e le viti fiorite esalano il loro profumo.
The fig tree hath put forth her green figs: the vines in flower yield their sweet smell.

1858 **romantico** - *adj* romantiko
romantic
In questo caso è meglio limitarsi alla corrispondenza romantico - ci sono sempre persone che vogliono sentire l'amore virtuale!
In this case it's better to limit yourself to romantic correspondence – there are always people who wish to feel virtual love!

1859 **ripresa** - *nf* ripreza
recovery
Negli ultimi anni, c'è stata una ripresa di interesse nella danza swing.
In recent years, there has been a revival of interest in swing dancing.

1860 **circo** - *nm* tʃirko
circus
In estate, diversi festival musicali, spettacoli all'aperto o sul lago con fuochi d'artificio, così come un circo animano questa città.
In summer, several music festivals, performances in the open air or on the Lake with Fireworks, as well as a circus animate this city.

1861 **organizzazione** - *nf* organiddzattsjone
organization
L'Organizzazione Mondiale della Sanità dice che l'abuso di alcol è la terza causa di morte e disabilità nel mondo.
The World Health Organization says alcohol abuse is the third leading cause of death and disability in the world.

1862 **tassa** - *nf*
fee, tax

tassa | Il 2005 include il rimborso della tassa portuale da parte della Agenzia delle Dogane di Siracusa per gli anni dal 1994 al 2001.
Figures for 2005 include the port fees repaid by the Syracuse Customs Department for the years from 1994 to 2001.

1863 **arabo** - *adj; nm/f* **Arabic; Arab**
arabo
Il Golfo Persico si trova tra l'Iran (Persia) e la Penisola Arabica.
The Persian Gulf is located between Iran (Persia) and the Arabian Peninsula.

1864 **indiano** - *adj; nm/f* **Indian; Indian**
indjano
La nuova situazione rende più difficile per il governo indiano la lotta contro la diffusione del virus dell'AIDS.
The new situation makes it harder for the Indian government to combat the spread of the AIDS virus.

1865 **tappeto** - *nm* **carpet**
tappeto
Noi abbiamo bisogno di comprare un nuovo tappeto per questa camera.
We need to buy a new rug for this room.

1866 **massa** - *nf* **mass**
massa
La massa di Cerere corrisponde a un terzo della massa della fascia degli asteroidi.
Ceres contains one-third of the mass found in the asteroid belt.

1867 **viaggiare** - *verb* **to travel**
vjaddʒare
Per viaggiare nel Croazia in macchina avete bisogno di carta verde e valida guida di patente.
For traveling to Croatia by car you will need a green card and a valid driving license.

1868 **indovinare** - *verb* **to guess**
indovinare
Non avrei mai indovinato che Tom parla così bene francese.
I would never have guessed that Tom could speak French so well.

1869 **file** - *nm* **file (set of records)**
file
Il file selezionato è protetto e il simbolo della funzione verrà visualizzato sul monitor.
The selected file is protected and the symbol appears on the screen.

1870 **terapia** - *nf* **therapy**

terapja — La domanda di terapia occupazionale è lievitata negli ultimi anni.
Demand for occupational therapy has surged in recent years.

1871 **catturare** - *verb*
katturare
to capture
Con la sua macchina fotografica, Tom ha catturato un tornado in azione.
With his camera, Tom captured a tornado in action.

1872 **soggetto** - *nm*
soddʒetto
subject
Per realizzare grandi cose non è sufficiente agire, bisogna anche sognare; non è sufficiente calcolare, bisogna credere.
To accomplish great things we must not only act, but also dream; not only plan, but also believe.

1873 **assumere** - *verb*
assumere
to take, assume
I ragazzi tendono ad assumere un'aria di superiorità rispetto alle sorelle minori.
Boys tend to look down on their younger sisters.

1874 **punizione** - *nf*
punittsjone
punishment
Mary impose delle punizioni draconiane al figlio per aver commesso anche le più piccole infrazioni.
Mary imposed draconian punishments on her son for committing even the smallest infractions.

1875 **considerare** - *verb*
konsiderare
to consider
In Europa e in America si considera il cane come un membro della famiglia.
In Europe and America they regard the dog as a member of the family.

1876 **immaginazione** - *nf*
immadʒinattsjone
imagination
C'era davvero un'Alice, ma il Paese delle Meraviglie è un frutto dell'immaginazione.
There really was an Alice, but Wonderland is a figment of the imagination.

1877 **geloso** - *adj*
dʒelozo
jealous
Io sono sempre stata un po' gelosa della vostra amicizia con Tom.
I've always been a little jealous of your friendship with Tom.

1878 **botto** - *nf; nm*
botto
blow, hit; explosion
Proprio in quel momento la porta si aprì e una creatura con un lungo becco infilò la testa e disse. "Nessuno entri fino alla prossima settimana." E la porta si chiuse con un botto.

Just then the door opened a little way, and a creature with a long beak put its head out for a moment and said: "No admittance till the week after next!" and shut the door again with a bang.

1879 **difficoltà** - *nf*
diffikolt'a
difficulties, difficulty, trouble
Alcuni bambini imparano le lingue facilmente e altri con difficoltà.
Some children learn languages easily and others with difficulty.

1880 **spegnere** - *verb*
speɲɲere
to switch off, turn off
Mary ha chiesto a Tom di spegnere il computer e preparare la cena.
Mary asked Tom to turn off the computer and prepare dinner.

1881 **motel** - *nc*
motel
motel
Un motel è come un albergo, solo più piccolo, ed è usato soprattutto da persone che viaggiano in macchina.
A motel is like a hotel only much smaller and is used mostly by people traveling by automobile.

1882 **luglio** - *nm*
luʎʎo
July
Prima della fine di luglio avranno messo il pannello pubblicitario sulla facciata di quell'edificio.
They will have placed the billboard on that building's facade before July ends.

1883 **gioiello** - *nm*
dʒojello
jewel
Lei prende in prestito dei gioielli dai suoi amici.
You borrow jewels from your friends.

1884 **adorabile** - *adj*
adorabile
adorable
È possibile che conosca anch'io questa persona adorabile di cui stai parlando?
Is it possible I also know this lovely person you're speaking of?

1885 **cultura** - *nf*
kultura
culture
Sono in grado di relazionarmi con persone di diversa nazionalità e cultura grazie all'esperienza maturata all'estero.
I can relate with people from different nations and culture thanks to my foreign experience.

1886 **botte** - *nf*
botte
barrel, cask
Non puoi avere la botte piena e la moglie ubriaca.
You cannot eat your cake and keep it.

1887 **fedele** - *adj* fedele

faithful

Vi saluto, o tutte le anime fedeli, i cui corpi qui e ovunque riposino in terra.

Hail all faithful souls, whose bodies here and everywhere do rest in the dust.

1888 **poiché** - *conj* poik'e

as, because, for

Preferisco un cane a un gatto, poiché il primo è più fedele del secondo.

I like a dog better than a cat, for the former is more faithful than the latter.

1889 **gomma** - *nf* gomma

rubber, gum, tire

Mio padre mi ha fatto cambiare una gomma della sua macchina.

My father had me change a tire on his car.

1890 **reverendo** - *adj* reverendo

reverend

Arrivò, dunque, la vigilia del grande giorno e il reverendo fece riunire tutti i bambini in chiesa.

The eve of the great day arrived, and the priest sent word that all the children were to go to the church.

1891 **impresa** - *nf* impreza

firm, enterprise

La nostra impresa ha il progetto di costruire una nuova fabbrica chimica in Russia.

Our company is planning to build a new chemical plant in Russia.

1892 **perso** - *adj* p'ɛrso

lost

Tom ha perso così tanto peso che uno dei suoi amici ha tirato dritto davanti a lui in strada, senza riconoscerlo.

Tom lost so much weight that one of his friends walked straight past him in the street, without recognising him.

1893 **geniale** - *adj* dʒenjale

ingenious

E non solo era un brillante pittore, ma anche un geniale uomo d'affari!

He was not only a brilliant painter but a genius as a businessman!

1894 **pazzesco** - *adj* pattsesko

crazy

Questo premio speciale è riservato al giocatore con il punteggio più pazzesco in un livello specifico

This special award goes to the player with the most staggering score in a specific level

1895 **completare** - *verb*

to complete

	kompletare	Poiché questa settimana molta gente era assente, non abbiamo potuto completare il progetto. *With so many people absent this week, we weren't able to complete the project.*
1896	**sorveglianza** - *nf* sorveʎʎantsa	**surveillance** Infine è stato deciso che i negozi saranno forniti di telecamere di sorveglianza. *Eventually it was decided that the stores be equipped with surveillance cameras.*
1897	**patrio** - *adj* patrjo	**patrio** In nome dell' amor patrio sono stati commessi crimini orribili *Many horrible crimes have been committed in the name of love for one's homeland*
1898	**scambio** - *nm* skambjo	**exchange** Un trattato di libero scambio tra Europa e Stati Uniti è in corso di negoziato. *A free-trade agreement between Europe and the United States is currently under negotiation.*
1899	**grato** - *adj* grato	**grateful** Ho svolto una serie di riunioni sulla relazione con la Commissione, le Presidenze dei Paesi Bassi e del Lussemburgo, [...] il segretariato del Parlamento, il governo del Regno Unito e i miei colleghi, e sono grato a tutti per i loro contributi. *I had a number of meetings about the report with the Commission, the Netherlands and Luxembourg presidencies, [...] Parliament's Secretariat, the United Kingdom Government and my colleagues, and I am grateful to everyone for their contributions.*
1900	**indovino** - *nm* indovino	**fortune-teller** Lungo il percorso si trova un altro rifugio, Aronte, che prende nome da una leggenda su un indovino della zona. *Along the way lies another refuge, Aronte, which takes its name from the legend of a soothsayer of the region.*
1901	**coincidenza** - *nf* kointʃidentsa	**coincidence** Guarda che stupefacente coincidenza! Tom ha le mie stesse impronte digitali. *Look, what an amazing coincidence! Tom has the same fingerprints as me.*

1902 **gabbia** - *nf* gabbja

cage

L'orso sta camminando su e giù per la gabbia.

The bear is walking up and down in the cage.

1903 **duca** - *nm* duka

duke

Una ciliegia avvelenata può uccidere un duca.

A poisoned cherry may kill a duke.

1904 **sebbene** - *conj; adv* sebbene

although, though; even though

Sebbene abbia corso più veloce che potesse, la ragazza non riuscì a prendere l'autobus in tempo.

Running as fast as she could, she still failed to catch the bus.

1905 **comitato** - *nm* komitato

committee

Tom non riesce più ad essere un membro del nostro comitato.

Tom can no longer be a member of our committee.

1906 **magazzino** - *nm* magattsino

warehouse, magazine

Ha insistito per andare al grande magazzino con la madre.

He insisted on going to the department store with his mother.

1907 **misura** - *nf* mizura

measure

Le misure di austerità che molti governi cittadini hanno implementato sono estremamente impopolari.

The austerity measures that many city governments have implemented are hugely unpopular.

1908 **disegno** - *nm* dizeɲɲo

drawing

Lui avrà la spina dorsale di pronunciarsi contro il disegno di legge?

Will he have the backbone to speak out against the bill?

1909 **tacere** - *verb* tatʃere

to be silent

Nella vita reale si può tacere andare con una persona, e ancora è la comunicazione che è insolito per gli utenti quando si incontrano in internet.

In real life we can keep silent going with a person, and still it’s communication which is unusual for users when meeting in the internet.

1910 **riprendere** - *verb* riprendere

to resume

Ci son volute quasi due settimane a John per riprendersi dalla sua malattia.

It took John about two weeks to get over his illness.

1911 **fisico** - *adj; nm*

physical (fisica= physics)

	fiziko	È un fisico famoso non solo in Giappone ma anche nel resto del mondo. *He is a famous physicist not only in Japan, but in the world.*
1912	**episodio** - *nm* epizodjo	**episode** Parlando seriamente, l'episodio 21 mi ha quasi fatta piangere dal ridere. *Seriously though, episode 21 made me almost cry while laughing.*
1913	**illegale** - *adj* illegale	**illegal** Uccidere elefanti, tigri e altre specie in via di estinzione non è soltanto crudele; è anche illegale. *Murdering elephants, tigers and other endangered species is not just cruel; it's also illegal.*
1914	**accorto** - *adj* akkorto	**shrewd** Deve continuare a svolgere un ruolo accorto ed intransigente, per garantire che si affrontino tutte le cause all'origine *It must continue to play a shrewd and uncompromising role in ensuring that all the underlying causes of poverty are dealt*
1915	**sfortunatamente** - *adv* sfortunatamente	**unfortunately** Sfortunatamente il mio viaggio in Indonesia non è riuscito ad avvenire perché non sono riuscito a risparmiare abbastanza soldi. *Unfortunately, my trip to Indonesia fell through because I couldn't save enough money.*
1916	**sapore** - *nm* sapore	**flavor, taste** Il frutto è simile a un'arancia come forma e a un ananas come sapore. *The fruit is similar to an orange in shape and to a pineapple in taste.*
1917	**confusione** - *nf* konfuzjone	**confusion** In un certo senso, io riesco a capire la sua grande confusione. *In a sense, I can understand his great confusion.*
1918	**essa** - *pron* essa	**it** Qualsiasi sia la lingua che studi, essa richiede del tempo. *Whatever language you study, it takes time.*
1919	**drago** - *nm* drago	**dragon** I draghi sono creature lunghe come serpenti, alate come gli uccelli e sagge come gli uomini.

Dragons are creatures long like snakes, winged like birds, and wise like man.

1920 **valle** - *nf* valle

Valley

Gira voce che nella valle sia stato trovato l'oro.

There is a rumor that gold has been found in the valley.

1921 **giallo** - *adj* dʒallo

yellow

Lo descriverei come un uomo di mezza età con una giacca gialla, una cravatta arancione e una camicia rosa.

I'd describe him as a middle-aged man in a yellow jacket, orange tie and a pink shirt.

1922 **gesto** - *nm* dʒesto

gesture

L'atto eroico è un gesto di un uomo spaventato dalla morte.

The heroic deed is an act of the man frightened to death.

1923 **bimbo** - *nm* bimbo

baby, child

A causa della tempesta, non potemmo continuare le ricerche del bimbo scomparso.

The storm hindered us from searching for the missing child.

1924 **sacro** - *adj* sakro

sacred

Come inizio ho visitato Gerusalemme - un luogo sacro per tre religioni principali.

For a start, I visited Jerusalem - a sacred place for three major religions.

1925 **circostanza** - *nf* tʃirkostantsa

circumstance

Noi dobbiamo adattare il nostro piano a queste nuove circostanze.

We must adapt our plan to these new circumstances.

1926 **estremamente** - *adv* estremamente

extremely

Una musica a volume estremamente alto interruppe la loro conversazione.

Extremely loud music interrupted their conversation.

1927 **villa** - *nf* villa

villa

Ci sono non più di una dozzina di camere da letto in questa villa.

There are no fewer than a dozen bedrooms in this mansion.

1928 **centesimo** - *adj; nm* tʃentezimo

hundredth; cent

È morto pochi giorni prima del suo centesimo compleanno.

He died a few days before his hundredth birthday.

1929 **percorso** - *nm*

route

	perkorso	L'attuale crisi finanziaria ed economica ci offre la rara opportunità di fermarci a riflettere sulla strada che abbiamo percorso e sul dove stiamo andando. *The current financial and economic crisis affords us a rare opportunity to pause and reflect on where we have been going and where it leads.*
1930	**sperimentare** - *verb* sperimentare	**to experiment, experience** Allo stand di Zumtobel dell'EuroShop i visitatori hanno potuto esperimentare direttamente soluzioni di luce su misura per la presentazione e la vendita. *Zumtobel simulated dynamic lighting solutions for all retail areas in real situations at the stand.*
1931	**terrore** - *nm* terrore	**terror** Il silenzio irreale ha messo il terrore nei loro cuori. *The eerie silence struck terror into their hearts.*
1932	**affetto** - *nm; adj* affetto	**affection, love; affected** Per mantenere un'amicizia ci dev'essere affetto reciproco. *To maintain a friendship, there must be mutual affection.*
1933	**attentamente** - *adv* attentamente	**carefully** Arrivarono a una grossa pietra, e qui il vecchio si fermò, si guardò attentamente intorno, fece un fischio acuto e pestò tre volte a terra con il piede sinistro. *They came to a large stone, and here the old fellow stopped, looked carefully round, gave a sharp whistle, and stamped three times on the ground with his left foot.*
1934	**tocco** - *nm* tokko	**touch** Nella modalità mouse, il tocco della penna funziona come il pulsante sinistro del mouse. *In the mouse mode, touching with it functions as a "left button of mouse.*
1935	**deposito** - *nm* depozito	**deposit** Io ho in banca un deposito di 500.000 yen. *I have a deposit of 500,000 yen at the bank.*
1936	**coniglio** - *nm* koniʎʎo	**rabbit** La coda di una volpe è più lunga di quella di un coniglio. *The tail of a fox is longer than that of a rabbit.*
1937	**sanare** - *verb* sanare	**to heal** Il loro giubileo mi offrì inoltre l'occasione per pronunciare un forte invito a sanare gli squilibri economici e sociali esistenti nel mondo.

That Jubilee gathering also gave me the opportunity to voice a strong call to correct the economic and social imbalances present in the world.

1938 **preparato** - *adj; nm* preparato
prepared; specimen, compound
Verificare che il campione sia stato preparato correttamente.
Confirm that the sample was prepared correctly.

1939 **schifoso** - *adj* skifozo
lousy (fa schifo= it sucks)
Fa schifo, ma è quello che ognuno di noi ha scelto.
It sucks, but it's what each of us has chosen.

1940 **pasto** - *nm* pasto
meal
Mary fu piacevolmente sorpresa quando tornò a casa dal lavoro per scoprire che Tom aveva già preparato il pasto serale.
Mary was pleasantly surprised, when she got home from work, to find that Tom had already prepared the evening meal.

1941 **garage** - *nm; nf* garadʒe
garage (box); garage (autoparking)
È abbastanza comune in Nord America che una casa abbia un garage per una o due auto.
It is quite common in North America for homes to have a one or two-car garage.

1942 **coronare** - *verb* koronare
to crown
San Marino Rugby Club riuscì a crescere tecnicamente e coronare il sogno di entrare a far parte alla grande famiglia del rugby giocato
the San Marino Rugby Club was able to grow technically and realize its dream of joining the grand family of rugby played.

1943 **visita** - *nf* vizita
visit
L'unico sito web che Tom visita almeno una volta al giorno è questo.
The only website Tom visits at least once a day is this one.

1944 **mezzogiorno** - *nm* mettsodʒorno
noon, midday
Noi abbiamo una pausa di un'ora per pranzo da mezzogiorno all'una.
We have an hour's recess for lunch from twelve to one.

1945 **caos** - *nm* kaos
chaos
Se non ci fossi io, questo ufficio sarebbe nel caos nel giro di tre giorni.
If I wasn't here, this office would be in chaos in three days.

1946 **causare** - *verb*
to cause

	kauzare	I gabbiani causano tutti i tipi di disturbo schiamazzando fragorosamente, sporcando di guano, lacerando sacchi della spazzatura e attaccando per ottenere cibo. *Seagulls cause all types of disturbances by cackling loudly, spreading guano, tearing up garbage bags and attacking to get food.*
1947	**cappotto** - *nm* kappotto	**coat** Lei stava indossando un cappotto verde con una minigonna in tinta. *She was wearing a green coat with a matching mini-skirt.*
1948	**succo** - *nm* sukko	**juice** Anche se ti piacciono pomodori, non ti piace il succo di pomodoro, giusto? *Even though you like tomatoes, you dislike tomato juice, right?*
1949	**combattuto** - *adj* kombattuto	**hard-fought** Hanno combattuto una battaglia ad armi pari con il nemico. *They fought a fair battle with the enemy.*
1950	**positivo** - *adj* pozitivo	**positive** Penso che la globalizzazione abbia degli effetti negativi e anche positivi. *I think that globalization has negative effects as well as positive.*
1951	**marco** - *nm* marko	**mark** il Marco tedesco per alcuni anni è stato la banconota preferita dalla criminalità in gran parte d'Europa *the Deutschmark has for some years been the banknote of choice for criminals across large parts of Europe*
1952	**armadio** - *nm* armadjo	**wardrobe, closet** Tom tirò fuori dall'armadio una delle sue magliette e la indossò. *Tom took one of the shirts out of the closet and put it on.*
1953	**ideale** - *adj; nm* ideale	**ideal; ideal** Sono troppo impegnati a litigare tra loro per occuparsi di ideali comuni. *They are too busy fighting against each other to care for common ideals.*
1954	**occorrere** - *verb* okkorrere	**to take** In generale occorre avere un passaporto per partire all'estero.

When you travel abroad, you usually need a passport.

1955 **espressione** - *nf* espressjone
expression
Il tenersi per mano può essere espressione di amore tra due persone.
Holding hands can express love between two people.

1956 **piazza** - *nf* pjattsa
square, plaza
Dopo le ore dieci il parcheggio è proibito in questa piazza.
Parking in this plaza after ten o'clock is prohibited.

1957 **annunciare** - *verb* annuntʃare
to announce
Il premier ha annunciato la sua intenzione di intraprendere riforme drastiche in parlamento.
The premier announced his intention to undertake drastic reforms in parliament.

1958 **telefonare** - *verb* telefonare
to call, telephone
Volevo telefonarti, ma pensando che tu non volessi, alla fine ho rinunciato a chiamarti.
I wanted to phone you, but I thought you wouldn't get it so I didn't phone you in the end.

1959 **principiare** - *verb* printʃipjare
to principiare
Appena che Pinocchio fu entrato nel letto, si addormentò a colpo e principiò a sognare.
As soon as Pinocchio was in bed, he fell fast asleep and began to dream.

1960 **vice** - *nm* vitʃe
vice, deputy
Il Vice Presidente è scelto fra i Rappresentanti nominati dalla Assemblea col voto degli Associati Fondatori.
The Vice President is selected among the representatives appointed by the Assembly through a vote by the Founder Members.

1961 **ammettere** - *verb* ammettere
to admit
Tom non aveva il coraggio di ammettere che aveva commesso un errore.
Tom didn't have the courage to admit that he had made a mistake.

1962 **tatto** - *nm* tatto
(sense) touch, tact
I ciechi leggono con il tatto, usando un sistema di punti in rilievo chiamato braille.
Blind people read by touching, using a system of raised dots called Braille.

1963 **rovina** - *nf*
ruin, ruination

	rovina	Non possiamo starcene qui immobili a guardare la città che cade in rovina. *We can't just look on dejectedly while this city continues to go into decline.*
1964	**esso** - *pron* esso	**it, he** Non si poteva dire che era un piano con qualsiasi senso di realtà associato ad esso. *You couldn't say that was a plan with any sense of reality to it.*
1965	**dopotutto** - *adv* dopotutto	**after all** Non ridere mai delle scelte di tua moglie, perché dopotutto tu sei una di esse. *Don't ever laugh at your wife's choices, because after all you're one of them.*
1966	**passeggero** - *nm* passeddʒero	**passenger** Tom si è sporto e ha aperto la portiera dal lato del passeggero. *Tom leaned over and opened the passenger-side door.*
1967	**riconoscere** - *verb* rikonoʃʃere	**to recognize** Essere pronti per il futuro significa gestire i rischi e riconoscere e cogliere le opportunità. *Being ready for the future means managing risks and recognizing and cultivating opportunities.*
1968	**deludere** - *verb* deludere	**to disappoint** Temo che dovrò deluderti. Non mi va di partecipare a questa discussione. *I'm afraid I'll have to disappoint you. I don't feel like participating in this discussion.*
1969	**cognome** - *nm* koɲɲome	**last name** Tom e Mary hanno lo stesso cognome, però non sono imparentati. *Tom and Mary have the same last name, but they aren't related.*
1970	**licenza** - *nf* litʃentsa	**license** A febbraio è stata annunciata la firma di un accordo di licenza semiesclusiva con Menarini, primo gruppo farmaceutico italiano *In February a semi-exclusive licensing agreement was entered into with Menarini*
1971	**suono** - *nm*	**sound**

	swono	La prima cosa che si sente quando si arriva a Las Vegas sono i suoni delle slot machine. *The first things that you hear when you arrive at Las Vegas are the dings of the slot machines.*
1972	**abbassare** - *verb* abbassare	**to lower** Potresti abbassare un po' il volume della TV per favore? *Would you please turn down the TV a little?*
1973	**patire** - *verb* patire	**to suffer** Ancora oggi Cristo continua a patire nel suo corpo che è la Chiesa! *Still today, Christ continues to suffer in his body which is the Church!*
1974	**nucleare** - *adj* nukleare	**nuclear** Quando una nazione cerca di impossessarsi di un'arma militare, il rischio di attacco nucleare aumenta per tutte le nazioni. *When one nation pursues a nuclear weapon, the risk of nuclear attack rises for all nations.*
1975	**cantina** - *nf* kantina	**cellar, basement, winery** Bravo che sei venuto a trovarmi: scendo in cantina a prendere una bottiglia di vino rosso. *That's nice you came to visit me: I'll go get a bottle of red wine from the cellar.*
1976	**identità** - *nf* identitˈa	**identity** Una tabella oraria è una carta d'identità per il tempo, solamente, se non si ha una tabella oraria, il tempo non c'è. *A schedule is an identity card for time, but, if you don't have a schedule, the time isn't there.*
1977	**coro** - *nm* koro	**choir** Per iscriverti al coro, devi essere capace di leggere la musica. *To join the choir, you have to be able to read music.*
1978	**busta** - *nf* busta	**envelope** Ho scordato di scrivere l'indirizzo sulla busta. *I forgot to write the address on the envelope.*
1979	**ottobre** - *nm* ottobre	**October** Le ricordiamo che tutti i libri della biblioteca devono essere restituiti entro il 15 ottobre. *We remind you that all library books are due to be returned by 15th October.*
1980	**temperatura** - *nf*	**temperature**

	temperatura	Il latte bolle a una temperatura più alta rispetto all'acqua. *Milk boils at a higher temperature than water.*
1981	**bambola** - *nf* bambola	**doll** Da bambina, a Elisa piaceva giocare alle infermiere con le bambole. *As a girl, Elisa loved to play nurse with her dolls.*
1982	**ruotare** - *verb* rwotare	**to rotate** Chiedere perché sono a favore dell'esperanto è come chiedere a Galileo perché è a favore del fatto che la terra ruota attorno al sole. *To ask why I'm in favour of Esperanto is like asking Galileo why he's in favour of the earth revolving around the sun.*
1983	**stufo** - *adj* stufo	**fed up, sick and tired** Sei stufo del traffico e dello stress per correre in aeroporto il giorno della tua partenza? *Are you tired of traffic jams and the stress of rushing to the airport on the day of your departure?*
1984	**gigante** - *adj* dʒigante	**giant** Quando il sole della cultura cala, anche i nani sembrano giganti. *When the sun of culture sets, the dwarfs too look like giants.*
1985	**cucinare** - *verb* kutʃinare	**to cook** Nonostante tutti i programmi di cucina che ho guardato, non sono ancora bravo a cucinare. *In spite of all the cooking shows I've watched, I'm still not good at cooking.*
1986	**istituto** - *nm* istituto	**institute** Ho comprato un poster all'Istituto del Mondo Arabo di Parigi e l'ho fatto incorniciare. *I bought a poster at the Arab World Institute in Paris and I had it framed.*
1987	**trasferire** - *verb* trasferire	**to transfer** Quando si eseguono grosse modifiche, quando si spostano o copiano rung, o quando si inseriscono o cancellano blocchi di programma, modificare offline e poi trasferire il programma. *When making large changes, when moving or copying rungs, or when inserting or deleting block programs, edit offline, then transfer the program.*
1988	**partner** - *nm*	**partner**

partner | Accogliamo i clienti e i loro partner dall'Europa, America, Australia, Asia and Africa fornendo loro una gamma completa di servizi in Italia.
We welcome customers and our clients from Europe, America, Australia, Asia and Africa, providing them with full range services in Italy.

1989 **acciaio** - *nm* | **steel**
attʃajo | Nonostante avesse dominato l'industria dell'acciaio, non ha mai ottenuto un monopolio completo.
Though he long dominated the steel industry, he never achieved a complete monopoly.

1990 **passaporto** - *nm* | **passport**
passaporto | Mentre altre aziende possono richiedere per voi di avere un visto gli altri possono non necessariamente chiedere questo documento una volta che
avete dato il vostro passaporto
While other companies may demand for you to have a visa others may not necessarily ask this document once you have given your passport.

1991 **unione** - *nf* | **union**
unjone | Tom non conosce la differenza tra l'Europa e l'Unione Europea..
Tom doesn't know the difference between Europe and the European Union.

1992 **noioso** - *adj* | **boring**
nojozo | Il tuo ordine può essere un processo noioso, perché ogni offerte componenti distinti deve essere richiesto a singoli produttori.
Your order can be a tedious process, because each component separate bids must be sought from the individual manufacturers.

1993 **DNA** - *abbr* | **DNA**
dna | I risultati non erano definitivi, però sono sicura che il DNA abbia una corrispondenza.
The results were not definitive, but I'm sure the DNA's a match

1994 **tigre** - *nf* | **tiger**
tigre | È stato durante l'era glaciale che la tigre dai denti a sciabola si è estinta.
It was during the ice age that the saber-toothed tiger became extinct.

1995 **continuamente** - *adv* kontinwamente

continuously, continually

Tom se la prendeva continuamente con Mary quando erano alle elementari.

Tom used to pick on Mary all the time when they were in elementary school.

1996 **accendere** - *verb* attʃendere

to switch, turn on

Hai l'abitudine di accendere la televisione, non appena arrivi a casa?

Do you have the habit of turning on the television as soon as you get home?

1997 **arto** - *nm* arto

limb

L'invalidità funzionale totale o parziale di un arto o un organo equivale alla sua perdita totale o parziale.

Total or partial functional disability of a limb or organ is treated as its total or partial loss.

1998 **spingere** - *verb* spindʒere

to push

Provò ad aprire la porta spingendo con tutte le sue forze.

He tried with all his might to push the door open.

1999 **partecipare** - *verb* partetʃipare

to take part

Tom aggiunse il proprio nome alla lista di persone che volevano partecipare al ballo.

Tom added his name to the list of people who wanted to attend the dance.

2000 **ooh** - *int* oo

ooh

Sordo è balenato tra la folla con il motore rombante e lasciandosi dietro una scia di ghiaia e polvere, si è levata una serie di "ooh" e "aaah".

Sordo flashed past the crowd, engine roaring and tyres spitting out dust and pebbles in his wake.

2001 **informato** - *adj* informato

informed

L'Organizzazione deve tenermi informato circa la presenza di eventuali osservazioni/segnalazioni pervenute dalle autorità

The organisation must keep me informed of any observations/remarks from national or local authorities

2002 **avvertire** - *verb* avvertire

to warn

L'insegnante ci ha avvertiti che il test sarebbe stato difficile.

The teacher warned us that the test would be hard.

2003 **intervista** - *nf*

interview

intervista | Durante un'intervista dopo la partita, l'allenatore ha espresso il suo malcontento verso l'arbitro.

During an interview after the game, the coach voiced his discontent towards the umpire.

2004 **cortesia** - *nf* | **courtesy**
kortezja | Il Presidente mi ha fatto la cortesia di rispondere alla mia lettera.
The President did me the courtesy of replying to my letter.

2005 **linguaggio** - *nm* | **language, speech**
liŋgwaddʒo | Koko conosce e utilizza più di 500 parole nel linguaggio dei segni, la lingua dei sordi.
Koko knows and uses more than 500 words in sign language, the language of deaf people.

2006 **squalo** - *nm* | **shark**
skwalo | Uno squalo è un pesce, mentre un delfino è un mammifero.
A shark is a fish while a dolphin is a mammal.

2007 **offendere** - *verb* | **to offend**
offendere | Faresti meglio a invitarli altrimenti si offenderanno.
You had better invite them or they will be offended.

2008 **premiare** - *verb* | **to reward**
premjare | Il nostro processo di valutazione ci aiuta a raggiungere l'obiettivo di premiare i migliori.
Our relative rating process helps to achieve our goal of rewarding our strongest performers.

2009 **convincere** - *verb* | **to convince**
konvintʃere | Tom non voleva mangiare e Mary non riusciva a convincerlo a farlo.
Tom didn't want to eat and Mary couldn't persuade him to.

2010 **noto** - *adj* | **known**
noto | I personaggi creati da Walt Disney sono noti ai bambini di tutto il mondo.
The characters created by Walt Disney are known by kids from all the world.

2011 **internet** - *nm* | **Internet**
internet | Il problema con le citazioni su Internet è che non sai mai se sono autentiche.
The trouble with quotes on the Internet is that you never know whether or not they are genuine.

2012 **conferenza** - *nf* | **conference**

	konferentsa	Lei l'ha incontrato per la prima volta a una conferenza a Boston. *She first met him at a conference in Boston.*
2013	**romanzo** - *nm* romandzo	**novel, romance** Mary, la famosa psicologa e scrittrice forense, è stata ispirata da Tatoeba per scrivere un romanzo su Tom, il serial killer da Boston *Mary, the famous forensic psychologist and writer, was inspired by Tatoeba to write a novel about Tom, the serial killer from Boston.*
2014	**avventurarsi** - *verb* avventurarsi	**to venture** Le arti sono un mondo di possibilità, dove ognuno è padrone di se stesso e dove ci si può avventurare a nuove esperienze e nuove prospettive. *Arts are a world of possibilities where everyone is his own master and where one can venture to new experiences and new perspectives.*
2015	**litigare** - *verb* litigare	**to quarrel** Io non posso litigare con Taninna. Lei è la moglie di mio zio. *I cannot argue with Taninna. She's my uncle's wife.*
2016	**chitarra** - *nf* kitarra	**guitar** A me piace il modo in cui Tom suona la chitarra. *I like the way Tom plays the guitar.*
2017	**sin** - *conj* sin	**since** Io suono il pianoforte sin da quand'ero bambino. *I've played the piano ever since I was a boy.*
2018	**congresso** - *nm* koŋgresso	**congress** Ai bambini è permesso entrare nella sala congressi solo in quel giorno. *The hall allows children in only on that day.*
2019	**pazzia** - *nf* pattsja	**madness** L'amore è una pazzia temporanea curabile con il matrimonio o con la rimozione del paziente dalle influenze sotto cui ha subito il disordine. *Love is a temporary insanity curable by marriage or by removal of the patient from the influences under which he incurred the disorde.*
2020	**brindisi** - *nm* brindizi	**toast (social drinking), pledge** Vorrei fare un brindisi per il nostro caro amico Michael. *I would like to have a toast for our dear friend, Michael.*
2021	**appetito** - *nm*	**appetite, hunger**

appetito | L'appetito vien mangiando, ma la sete se ne va bevendo.
Appetite comes with eating, but the thirst goes away with drinking.

2022 **fango** - *nm* | **mud, dirt**
faŋgo | Il cane era ricoperto di fango dalla testa ai piedi.
The dog was covered in mud from head to foot.

2023 **elegante** - *adj* | **elegant**
elegante | Porta un vestito elegante per andare a teatro o a una festa.
Bring one elegant dress to go to the theater or to a party.

2024 **profondamente** - *adv* | **deeply**
profondamente | Il profilo e le irregolarità della superficie della terraferma o marina influenzano profondamente il vento.
The profile and unevenness of the surface of the dry land or of the sea deeply affect the wind.

2025 **tendere** - *verb* | **to stretch**
tendere | La ragazza voleva monopolizzare l'affetto del padre e tendeva a vedere la madre come una rivale.
The girl wanted to monopolize her father's affection and tended to view her mother as a competitor.

2026 **disponibile** - *adj* | **available**
disponibile | C'è grande differenza nella qualità di shampoo disponibili sul mercato.
There is big difference in the quality of shampoos available in the market.

2027 **fantasia** - *nf* | **fantasy**
fantazja | I matematici sono dei poeti, a parte il fatto che devono dimostrare ciò che crea la loro fantasia.
Mathematicians are poets, except that they have to prove what their fantasy creates.

2028 **secco** - *adj* | **dry**
sekko | Ho fatto il pane per la prima volta, ma mi è venuto troppo secco e poco buono.
I tried baking bread for the first time, but it's dry and not tasty.

2029 **roccia** - *nf* | **rock**
rottʃa | Lui è caduto e ha sbattuto la testa contro una roccia.
He fell and hit his head on a rock.

2030 **lancia** - *nf* | **spear**

lantʃa | La lancia, l'arco, l'arma da fuoco e infine il missile teleguidato gli avevano dato armi di portata infinita e di una quasi infinita potenza.
The spear, the bow, the gun, and finally the guided missile had given him weapons of infinite range and all but infinite power.

2031 **recuperare** - *verb* | **to recover, retrieve**
rekuperare | È necessario che nel dispositivo sia definito un punto di accesso Internet dati cellulare per recuperare i dati di assistenza.
You must have a mobile data internet access point defined in the device to recover assistance data.

2032 **guerriero** - *adj* | **warrior**
gwerrjero | Il kendo è un'antica arte marziale giapponese che risale all'epoca dei guerrieri samurai.
Kendo is an ancient Japanese martial art that dates back to the time of the samurai warriors.

2033 **femminile** - *adj* | **female**
femminile | "Michael" è un nome maschile, però "Michelle" è un nome femminile.
"Michael" is a man's name, but "Michelle" is a woman's name.

2034 **badare** - *verb* | **to look after**
badare | Jane si è offerta di badare ai nostri bambini mentre siamo fuori.
Jane offered to take care of our children when we were out.

2035 **frutta** - *nf* | **fruit**
frutta | Ho sentito dire che le persone che mangiano verdure e frutta ogni giorno hanno meno rischi di avere un attacco cardiaco.
I've heard that people who eat vegetables and fruit every day are less likely to have a heart attack.

2036 **clacson** - *nm* | **horn (automotive)**
klakson | Tom continuava a suonare il clacson.
Tom continued to honk the horn.

2037 **influenzare** - *verb* | **to influence**
inflwentsare | Non si rilevano eventi successivi alla chiusura dell'esercizio 2010 tali da influenzare la redditività della Banca o aumentarne l'esposizione al rischio.

No other events likely to influence the Bank's profitability or increase its exposure to risk have occurred since the end of 2010.

2038 **emozione** - *nf* emottsjone
emotion
Ha espresso le sue emozioni per la natura in una poesia.
She expressed her feelings for nature in a poem.

2039 **quaggiù** - *adv* kwaddʒu
hither
Voi siete di quaggiù; io sono di lassù; voi siete di questo mondo; io non sono di questo mondo.
You are from below; I am from above. You are of this world; I am not of this world.

2040 **vincitore** - *adj* vintʃitore
winner
Il vincitore dei biglietti per il primo volo e il suo accompagnatore devono esibire un documento di identità prima di iniziare il volo.
The winner of the tickets for the flight and his or her companion must provide proof of identity before boarding the flight.

2041 **lanciare** - *verb* lantʃare
to launch
Lei mi lanciava acini d'uva e io provato a prenderli con la bocca.
She tossed me grapes and I tried to catch them with my mouth.

2042 **ridurre** - *verb* ridurre
to reduce
Disinfezione: procedura utilizzata per ridurre il numero di microrganismi vitali su un prodotto fino a un livello precedentemente specificato come adeguato che consente un'ulteriore manipolazione o utilizzo.
Disinfection: process used to reduce the number of viable microorganisms on a product to a level previously specified as appropriate for its further handling or use.

2043 **munizione** - *nf* munittsjone
munition
Il cacciatore ha messo delle munizioni nella pistola.
The hunter put ammunition in the gun.

2044 **shock (choc)** - *adj* sokk (kok)
shock
La notizia dell'incidente è stata un grande shock per me.
The news of the accident was a great shock to me.

2045 **coperto** - *adj* koperto
covered
Quando Maria entrò in cucina il pavimento era coperto di acqua.

When Mary entered the kitchen, the floor was covered in water.

2046 **quassù** - *prep* kwassu

up here

Quassù, gli ostelli offrono molto di più di un semplice letto pulito e confortevole in cui passare la notte.

Up here, hostels offer so much more than a comfy, clean bed for the night.

2047 **corretto** - *nm* korretto

correct

La lettera che avete scritto deve essere corretta e ricopiata anche se l'avete già rifatta più volte.

The letter you wrote must be corrected and transcribed, even if you already refined it many times.

2048 **dovunque** - *adv* dovuŋkwe

anywhere

Ho cercato dovunque, ma non trovo il mio libro.

I've looked everywhere, but I can't find my book.

2049 **chiappa** - *nf* kjappa

(colll) butt cheek, bottom, backside

Tra una chiazza di birra e dei pezzetti di tofu piccante appiccicati tra le lettere, lessi che aveva finalmente alzato le chiappe e se n'era andato dal birrificio.

Between the ale stains and bits of spicy tofu splattered across the parchment, I learned that he'd finally gotten off his butt and left the brewery.

2050 **maresciallo** - *nm* mareʃʃallo

marshal

Questo monumento fu eretto in onore del maresciallo che prese parte all'assalto di Koenigsberg durante la Seconda Guerra Mondiale.

This monument was erected in honour of the marshall who took part in the storming of Koenigsberg during the World War II.

2051 **mortale** - *adj; adv* mortale

mortal; deadly, fatal; deathly

La maggior parte delle punture di medusa non sono mortali, ma molte sono comunque abbastanza dolorose.

Most jellyfish stings aren't deadly, but many are pretty painful nonetheless.

2052 **abitante** - *nm* abitante

inhabitant

Il divertimento a questa città è che questa città ha più barche per abitante di qualsiasi altra città del mondo.

The fun at this city is that this city has more boats per inhabitant than any other city in the world.

2053 **addestramento** - *nm*

training

	addestramento	La chiave per trasformare ogni soldato in un grande guerriero è rafforzare l'addestramento. *The key to raising every soldier into a great warrior is in strengthening training.*
2054	**brusio** - *nm* bruzjo	**buzz** Spero che il brusio che ha accompagnato il mio intervento sia soltanto l'espressione di un'approvazione generale *I hope that the commotion accompanying my speech is only the expression of widespread approval*
2055	**distretto** - *nm* distretto	**district** Tom è il direttore delle vendite di distretto per una società di software. *Tom is the district sales manager for a software company.*
2056	**nervo** - *nm* nervo	**nerve** Il nervo sciatico è il nervo più lungo del corpo umano. *The sciatic nerve is the longest nerve in the human body.*
2057	**flotta** - *nf* flotta	**fleet** I Romani costruirono una flotta di trecento navi. *The Romans built a fleet of three hundred ships.*
2058	**branco** - *nm* braŋko	**herd, pack, flock** Sto cominciando a pensare che i leader religiosi sono popolari perché assecondano i pregiudizi del branco che chiamano loro gregge. *I'm beginning to think that religious leaders are popular because they pander to the prejudices of the pack they call their flock.*
2059	**tecnico** - *adj; nm* tekniko	**technical; technician** Per ottenere aiuto, consultare il rivenditore o un tecnico esperto di radio o televisori. *Consult the dealer or an experienced radio or television technician for help.*
2060	**merce** - *nf* mertʃe	**goods, wares, merchandise** Esse si basavano su merci che i membri di una società riconoscevano come aventi valore. *They were based on goods which the members of a society recognized as having value.*
2061	**sconosciuto** - *adj; nm* skonoʃʃuto	**unknown; stranger, unkown** I padri avvertono i figli di non mangiare i cibi che vengono dati loro dagli sconosciuti.

Parents warn their children not to eat food given to them by strangers.

2062 **stivale** - *nm*
stivale
boot
Io pulisco gli stivali ed esco — il vecchio sporco cederà il passo al nuovo.
I polish my boots and go out — the old dirt will give way to the new.

2063 **campanello** - *nm*
kampanello
bell
Io avevo appena finito di pranzare quando suonò il campanello.
I had just finished eating lunch when my doorbell rang.

2064 **confermare** - *verb*
konfermare
to confirm
Abbiamo bisogno che confermiate la vostra presenza perché i posti sono limitati.
We need you to confirm your attendance because places are limited.

2065 **veicolo** - *nm*
veikolo
vehicle
Il parabrezza è l'ampia finestra di vetro nella parte anteriore di un veicolo.
The windscreen is the large glass window at the front of a vehicle.

2066 **preghiera** - *nf*
pregjera
prayer
Il salmo offre all'anima e allo spirito la possibilità di una preghiera intima e personale.
The psalm offers to the soul and the spirit the possibility of an intimate and personal prayer.

2067 **biscotto** - *nm*
biskotto
cookie, biscuit
Tom ha preso un biscotto zuccherato dal piatto che era sul tavolo di cucina.
Tom grabbed a sugar cookie from the dish on the kitchen table.

2068 **ammiraglio** - *nm*
ammiraʎʎo
admiral
L`ammiraglio Nelson ha perso la vita nella fase finale della battaglia sulla nave Victory.
Admiral Nelson died on his ship during the final stages of the battle.

2069 **moneta** - *verb*
moneta
money, coin, currency
La moneta d'oro aveva un valore molto maggiore di quanto si supponesse.
The gold coin had a much higher value than you would expect

2070	**ambasciatore** - *nm* ambaʃʃatore	**ambassador** Ho visto adesso che l'ambasciatore dell'Arabia Saudita ha dato le dimissioni. *I've seen just now that the ambassador of Saudi Arabia has resigned.*
2071	**delizioso** - *adj* delittsjozo	**delicious** I fiori d'arancio hanno un effetto rilassante e un profumo delizioso. *Orange blossoms have a relaxing effect and a delightful scent.*
2072	**alcol** - *nm* alkol	**alcohol** Quando è venuto e mi ha trovato, tutto il suo corpo puzzava di alcol. *When he came and found me, his whole body reeked of alcohol.*
2073	**trasmissione** - *nf* trasmissjone	**transmission** Ci potrebbe esser stato un errore durante la trasmissione. *There might have been an error during transmission.*
2074	**verme** - *nm* verme	**worm, maggot** Le parole di quella donna mi fecero sentire un "verme" e decisi di restare. *The words of that woman made me feel like a "worm" and I decided to stay.*
2075	**quindici** - *adj; num* kwinditʃi	**fifteen** Non fece più ritorno da quando lasciò casa all'età di quindici anni. *He left his hometown at the age of fifteen never to return.*
2076	**tono** - *nm* tono	**tone** C'è stato un cambiamento improvviso nel suo tono. *There was a sudden change in her tone.*
2077	**incastrare** - *verb* iŋkastrare	**to fit** Lui è stato incastrato con un'accusa di omicidio. *He was framed on a murder charge.*
2078	**straniero** - *adj; nm/f* stranjero	**foreign, alien; foreigner** È sorprendente come l'umile tentativo di uno straniero di formare una frase russa, infine, risulti dal fatto che due madrelingua russi sono entrati in una vivace discussione circa la loro propria lingua. *It's simply surprising, how a modest attempt by a foreigner to compose a Russian sentence ultimately leads to two*

Russian speakers engaging in a lively discussion about their native language.

2079 **divisione** - *nf*
divizjone

division
Il terrorismo è il fattore più importante per la divisione del paese e la creazione di regioni autonome.
Terrorism is the most important factor for the division of a country and the creation of autonomous regions.

2080 **acquisto** - *nm*
akkwisto

buy, purchase
"Questa casetta è vostra?" "Sì, è nostra, l'abbiamo acquistata l'anno scorso."
"Is this small house yours?" "Yes, it's ours, we bought it last year."

2081 **produttore** - *nm*
produttore

producer
Il sud-est è un importante produttore di energia del carbone, petrolio greggio e gas naturale.
The Southeast is a major energy producer of coal, crude oil, and natural gas.

2082 **elettrico** - *adj*
elettriko

electric, electrical
Gli squali sono sensibili agli impulsi elettrici, così come al suono.
Sharks are sensitive to electrical impulses as well as sound.

2083 **bionda** - *nf/m; adj*
bjonda

blonde
Lei è una bella ragazza con i capelli biondi e occhi blu cielo.
She is a beautiful girl with blonde hair and blue eyes.

2084 **infelice** - *adj*
infelitʃe

unhappy
Variante: Per un gruppo avanzato l'insegnante può tentare con combinazioni avverbioaggettivo: "disperatamente infelice", "ragionevolmente equo", etc.
Variation: For an advanced group the teacher may try adverb-adjective combinations: "desperately miserable", "reasonably fair", etc.

2085 **batteria** - *nf*
batterja

battery, drums
Tom ha iniziato a suonare la batteria quando aveva tredici anni.
Tom started playing drums when he was thirteen.

2086 **picchiare** - *verb*
pikkjare

to beat
La bambina è scappata di casa perché i suoi genitori la picchiavano.

The child ran away because her parents beat her.

2087 **cravatta** - *nf* kravatta

necktie

Tom deve indossare obbligatoriamente un completo e una cravatta al lavoro.

Tom is required to wear a suit and tie to work.

2088 **cessare** - *verb* tʃessare

to cease

La neve cesserà presto di scendere, penso.

It'll stop snowing soon, I think.

2089 **giugno** - *nm* dʒuɲɲo

June

A proposito, oggi è l'8 giugno - il compleanno di mia moglie.

By the way, today is the 8th of June — my wife's birthday.

2090 **risorgere** - *verb* rizordʒere

to rise again

Significativa è la posa del pontefice, rappresentato nell'atto di risorgere dal sarcofago come per destarsi dal torpore della morte fisica.

The pose of the pontiff is important, he is portrayed in the act of rising from the sarcophagus as if awakening from the torpor of physical death

2091 **procedura** - *nf* protʃedura

procedure

Il documento spiega chiaramente la procedura corretta per affrontare lamentele.

The document clearly spells out the correct procedure for dealing with complaints.

2092 **osare** - *verb* ozare

to dare

Se dobbiamo diventare un'economia competitiva, la più competitiva al mondo entro il 2010, non dovremmo osare nuovi metodi?

If we are to become this competitive economy, the worldâ™s most competitive by 2010, should we also dare to try new ways?

2093 **infanzia** - *nf* infantsja

childhood

Noi avevamo l'abitudine di fare il bagno in questo fiume durante la nostra infanzia.

We used to bathe in this river in our childhood.

2094 **aumento** - *nm* aumento

increase

Le bevande contenenti zucchero non hanno alcun valore nutritivo, e contribuiscono notevolmente all'aumento di peso.

Sugary drinks have no nutritional value and contribute significantly to weight gain.

2095 **stretto** - *adj; nm*
stretto

strict, strait; narrow
Il capo della polizia della prefettura tentò di rendere più stretta la disciplina dei propri agenti.
The prefectural police chief tried to tighten his police officers' discipline.

2096 **avvicinare** - *verb*
avvitʃinare

to approach
Il mio capo mi ha detto che è difficile avvicinarsi a me.
My boss told me it's hard to approach me.

2097 **internazionale** - *adj*
internattsjonale

international
La sua vittoria a questa età in una competizione internazionale è una buona indicazione di un futuro luminoso.
His victory at this age in an international competition is a good indication of a bright future.

2098 **distruzione** - *nf*
distruttsjone

destruction
Il tornado ha lasciato una scia di distruzione al suo passaggio.
The tornado left a trail of destruction in its wake.

2099 **vedovo** - *nm/f*
vedovo

widower, widow
In caso di decesso dell'agente la vedova, il vedovo e le persone a carico hanno diritto al rimborso delle spese di viaggio alle stesse condizioni.
In the event of the death of an official, the widow, widower and dependants shall be entitled to reimbursement of travel expenses under the same conditions.

2100 **eccetto** - *prep*
ettʃetto

except
Si può fare qualunque cosa con le maionesi, eccetto sedercisi sopra.
You can do anything with mayonnaise, except sit on it.

2101 **tramite** - *nm; prep*
tramite

means, medium; through
Non tutto quello che si trova sul web può essere trovato tramite Google.
Not everything on the web can be found through Google.

2102 **fermata** - *nf*
fermata

stop
Se si viaggia sempre con la metropolitana, raramente si va in superficie al di fuori della propria fermata.
If you always travel by subway, you seldom surface other than at your stop.

2103 **rifiutare** - *verb*

to refuse

rifjutare | Robert era così impegnato che ha dovuto rifiutare un invito a giocare a golf.

Robert was so busy he had to turn down an invitation to play golf.

2104 **registrazione** - *nf* | **registration**
redʒistrattsjone | La registrazione dei valori minimi e massimi permette di riconoscere immediatamente se il trasduttore è stato sovraccaricato.
The recording of the minimum and maximum values permits you to recognize immediately whether your transducer has been overloaded.

2105 **sinceramente** - *adv* | **sincerely**
sintʃeramente | Per lui è una questione di principio rispondere sinceramente alle tue domande.

It is a matter of principle with him to answer your questions honestly.

2106 **terrorista** - *nf* | **terrorist**
terrorista | I terroristi hanno attaccato il World Trade Center a New York nel 2001.
Terrorists attacked the World Trade Center in New York City in 2001.

2107 **eterno** - *adj* | **eternal**
eterno | Il vero amore è eterno, infinito, e sempre come se stesso.
True love is eternal, infinite, and always like itself.

2108 **servo** - *nm* | **servant**
servo | Facendo eco alle parole del Papa Paolo VI, il Servo di Dio Giovanni Paolo II ha riaffermato il desiderio della Chiesa di rinnovare il dialogo e la collaborazione con gli artisti.

Echoing the words of Pope Paul VI, the Servant of God Pope John Paul II restated the Church"s desire to renew dialogue and cooperation with artists.

2109 **rinunciare** - *verb* | **to give up**
rinuntʃare | Ho rinunciato all'idea di visitare le attrazioni della città a causa del maltempo.

I gave up the idea of seeing the sights of the city because of the bad weather.

2110 **tema** - *nf* | **theme, topic**
tema | Una rivista studentesca in lingua inglese ha invitato i lettori a inviare un articolo sul tema dello shock culturale.

An English language students' magazine has invited readers to submit an article on the theme of culture shock.

2111 **ragionevole** - *adj*
radʒonevole
reasonable
Un uomo ragionevole non direbbe una cosa del genere in pubblico.
A sensible man wouldn't say such a thing in public.

2112 **carburante** - *nm*
karburante
fuel
Per l'arrivo anticipato dell'inverno di quest'anno, le autorità si aspettano scarsità di carburante per il riscaldamento.
Due to the early onset of winter this year, authorities are forecasting shortages of heating oil.

2113 **sfortuna** - *nf*
sfortuna
bad luck
Lui era la persona più suscettibile che io abbia avuto la sfortuna di conoscere!
He was the angriest man I've ever had the misfortune to meet!

2114 **mollare** - *verb*
mollare
to give
Tom è completamente ossessionato dal cibo. Non c'è da meravigliarsi che Mary lo abbia mollato!
Tom is utterly obsessed with food. No wonder Mary dumped him!

2115 **accento** - *nm*
attʃento
accent
Io potevo dire dal suo accento che lui era un francese.
I could tell from his accent that he was a Frenchman.

2116 **materia** - *nf*
materja
matter
La fisica può essere definita come la scienza della materia, del moto e dell'energia.
Physics can be defined as the science of matter, motion, and energy.

2117 **registrare** - *verb*
redʒistrare
to record
Io non voglio che ciò che sto per dire venga registrato.
I don't want what I'm about to say to be recorded.

2118 **mentale** - *adj*
mentale
mental
Tom e Mary si preoccupano molto di loro figlio che ha problemi di salute mentale.
Tom and Mary are worried sick about their son, who has mental health problems.

2119 **demonio** - *nm*
demonjo
devil, demon
Sembrava una creatura posseduta, in lotta contro uno spirito o un demonio che avesse assunto il dominio del suo corpo.

He seemed to be a thing possessed, struggling against some spirit or demon who had taken over control of his body.

2120 **recitare** - *verb*
retʃitare
to recite
La sua tecnica è superba, ma deve recitare con più espressività.
Her technique is superb, but she needs to play with more expression.

2121 **simbolo** - *nm*
simbolo
symbol
La Statua della Libertà è il simbolo degli Stati Uniti.
The Statue of Liberty is the symbol of the United States.

2122 **orario** - *nm; adj*
orarjo
time, hours, timetable; hourly
I lavoratori presso l'azienda di Tom stanno chiedendo una riduzione dell'orario di lavoro.
The workers at Tom's company are demanding shorter working hours.

2123 **peggiorare** - *verb*
peddʒorare
to worsen
Per peggiorare le cose, lui non si rende neanche conto di infastidire i suoi vicini.
To make matters worse, he isn't even conscious of annoying his neighbors.

2124 **ossigeno** - *nm*
ossidʒeno
oxygen
Una molecola d'acqua è composta da tre atomi: due di idrogeno e uno di ossigeno.
A water molecule is composed by three atoms: two hydrogen and one oxygen.

2125 **giovedì** - *nm*
dʒoved'i
Thursday
Tutti a parte la famiglia Anderson andranno alla festa giovedì sera.
Everybody except the Anderson family is going to the party next Thursday evening.

2126 **sospirare** - *verb*
sospirare
to sigh
Smettete di piangere e sospirare quando parlate delle prove.
Do away with sighing and tearful faces when speaking about tests.

2127 **bacio** - *nm*
batʃo
kiss
Gli gnocchi di Salisburgo sono dolci come l'amore e teneri come un bacio.
Salzburg dumplings are sweet as love and tender as a kiss.

2128 **pallottola** - *nf*
bullet

pallottola | La pallottola uccide una figura di aspirante suicida, raddrizza un'antenna e arriva a penetrare un corpo di donna.

The bullet kills a would-be suicide, straightens an antenna, and penetrates the body of a woman.

2129 **spesare** - *verb*
spezare

to pay the expenses

I costi relativi all'acquisizione interamente spesati a conto economico sono stati pari a 11 migliaia di euro.

The costs relating to the acquisition entirely expensed to the income statement amounted to Euro 11 thousand.

2130 **richiedere** - *verb*
rikjedere

to request

La riduzione dei sussidi al settore del Patrimonio Culturale richiede l'adozione di un nuovo paradigma.

The reduction of subsidies to the Cultural Heritage sector requires the adoption of a new paradigm.

2131 **maglietta** - *nf*
maʎʎetta

t-shirt

Voglio scoprire se Tom indosserà la maglietta che gli ho regalato.
I want to find out if Tom is going to wear the new shirt I gave him.

2132 **procedere** - *verb*
protʃedere

to continue

Potrebbe essere vantaggioso per me procedere in questo modo.
It may be advantageous to me to proceed in this way.

2133 **segretario** - *nm/f*
segretarjo

secretary

Il segretario generale sta facendo un ultimo disperato tentativo per negoziare un trattato di pace tra le due fazioni in guerra.
The Secretary General is making a last-ditch effort to negotiate a peace treaty between the two warring factions.

2134 **banco** - *nm*
baŋko

bench, counter, bank, desk

Ci sono una lavagna, una lampada, una porta, due finestre, dodici sedie e un banco; ci sono anche molti studenti.

There are a blackboard, a lamp, a door, two windows, twelve chairs and a desk; there are many students as well.

2135 **fatica** - *nf*
fatika

fatigue

Sto facendo fatica a scaricare delle canzoni sul mio iPod.
I'm having a hard time downloading songs to my iPod.

2136 **elemento** - *nm*
elemento

element

Ci sono degli elementi più complessi nelle conversazioni più lunghe.

There are more complex elements in longer conversations.

2137 **ostaggio** - *nm* **hostage**
ostaddʒo
Fai arrivare qualcosa da mangiare o ucciderò un ostaggio.
Send in something to eat or I'll kill a hostage.

2138 **adulto** - *adj* **adult**
adulto
Anche se Arina ha sedici anni, imita bene una donna adulta.
Although Arina is 16 years old, she imitates an adult woman well.

2139 **pastore** - *nm* **shepherd, pastor**
pastore
Il pastore conta le pecore: "Una, due, tre, quattro, cinque... cento".
The shepherd counts the sheep: "One, two, three, four, five ... one hundred."

2140 **salvatore** - *nm* **savior**
salvatore
A Betlemme Maria dà alla luce Gesù, il figlio di Dio, il Salvatore
Mary gives birth to Jesus, the Son of God, the Saviour, in Bethlehem

2141 **rappresentare** - *verb* **to represent**
rapprezentare
Insieme, voi rappresentate l'armonia tra la tradizione e il progresso.
Together, you represent the harmony between tradition and progress.

2142 **confronto** - *nm* **comparison**
konfronto
I condomini sono piccoli in confronto ai grattacieli di New York.
The buildings are small in comparison with the skyscrapers in New York.

2143 **palestra** - *nf* **gym**
palestra
In qualità di ospiti potrete rilassarvi nella sauna, nella vasca idromassaggio o nella sala vapore oppure allenarvi nella moderna palestra e nella piscina coperta.
Guests can relax in the sauna, spa bath or steam room, or exercise in the modern gym and indoor swimming pool.

2144 **origine** - *nf* **origin, source**
oridʒine
È meglio se si può leggere il materiale di origine prima di vedere un film.
It's best if you can read the source material before seeing a movie.

2145 **empero** - *verb* **empire**

empero | L'Albania ha ottenuto la sua indipendenza dall'Impero Ottomano nel 1912.

Albania gained its independence from Ottoman Empire in 1912.

2146 **spettare** - *verb* spettare | **to belong**

Spetta a ciascuno di noi capire che le sottospecie sono un concetto biologico, privo della specie Homo sapiens sapiens.

It's up to each one of us to understand that subspecies is a biological concept, lacking in the species Homo sapiens sapiens.

2147 **istinto** - *nm* istinto | **instinct**

I nostri istinti, a quanto pare, ci guidano e ci proteggono.

It seems our instincts guide and protect us.

2148 **burro** - *nm* burro | **butter**

Tritate la cipolla e mettetela in una casseruola con il burro e l'olio.

Chop the onions and put them in a casserole with butter and oil.

2149 **grilletto** - *nm* grilletto | **trigger**

Io non voglio rischiare il nostro piano solo perché hai il grilletto facile!

I don't want to risk our plan just because you are trigger-happy!

2150 **abitudine** - *nf* abitudine | **habit**

La noia, l'abitudine, la mancanza di curiosità sono le grandi nemiche del nostro cervello.

Boredom, routine, and lack of curiosity are the greatest enemies of our brain.

2151 **imbarazzo** - *nm* imbarattso | **embarrassment**

Gli alunni misero in imbarazzo l'insegnante con domande sciocche.

The students bothered the teacher with silly questions.

2152 **trenta** - *adj* trenta | **thirty**

Tom ha comprato un computer con uno sconto del trenta percento rispetto al prezzo di listino.

Tom bought a computer at thirty percent off the list price.

2153 **maggio** - *nm* maddʒo | **May**

Finirò il lavoro in una settimana, cioè il 5 maggio.

I'll finish the work in a week, that is, on May 5th.

2154 **marte** - *nm* | **Mars**

	marte	Il Sistema Solare ha quattro pianeti terrestri o tellurici: Mercurio, Venere, Terra e Marte. *The Solar System has four terrestrial or telluric planets: Mercury, Venus, Earth, and Mars.*
2155	**addirittura** - *adv* addirittura	**even** Lui non beve nemmeno la birra, per non parlare addirittura del whisky. *He doesn't even drink beer, not to mention whiskey.*
2156	**sofferenza** - *nf* sofferentsa	**suffering** L'amicizia raddoppia le gioie e divide a metà la sofferenza. *Friendship redoubles joy and cuts grief in half.*
2157	**giurato** - *adj; nm* dʒurato	**swon; juror** Il giurato nota le sue osservazioni eventuali nello spazio riservato, firma la scheda e la restituisce o convalida la sua scelta. *The taster can make possible observations in the appropriate space, signs the sheet and then he/she can submit the sheet*
2158	**eroina** - *nf* eroina	**heroin, heroine** Il suo rosso inconfondibile ben si addice all'elegante sensualità della nostra eroina e insieme a lei ci accompagna in un sogno lungo dodici mesi. *Its unmistakable red hue is the perfect partner for our heroine's elegant sensuality and accompanies us in a dream that lasts for 12 months.*
2159	**sordo** - *adj* sordo	**deaf** La gentilezza è la lingua che il sordo riesce a sentire e che il cieco riesce a vedere. *Kindness is the language which the deaf can hear and the blind can see.*
2160	**possedere** - *verb* possedere	**to own** L'obiettivo di Mary è possedere una casa prima di avere trent'anni. *Mary's goal is to own a home before she's thirty.*
2161	**agio** - *nm* adʒo	**ease** Io non mi sento mai a mio agio in sua compagnia. *I never feel at ease in his company.*
2162	**custodia** - *nf* kustodja	**custody** La polizia trovò dell'attrezzatura per produrre droga nell'appartamento di Tom e lo prese in custodia.

Police found drug paraphernalia in Tom's flat and took him into custody.

2163 **magico** - *adj*
madʒiko
magical
Questa sarà un'altra serata magica con la nostra famiglia estesa.
This will be another magical evening with our extended family.

2164 **droga** - *nf*
droga
drug
La polizia trovò dell'attrezzatura per produrre droga nell'appartamento di Tom e lo prese in custodia.
Police found drug paraphernalia in Tom's flat and took him into custody.

2165 **storto** - *adv*
storto
awry
Dammi un po' di tempo per capire che cos'è andato storto.
Give me some time to figure out what went wrong.

2166 **temporale** - *adj; nm*
temporale
temporal; (thunder) storm
Nel bel mezzo della partita improvvisamente è scoppiato un temporale con tanto di tuoni.
During the game, it suddenly began to rain and it thundered, too.

2167 **comportare** - *verb*
komportare
to involve
Penso che Tom si stia comportando in un modo un po' sospetto.
I think Tom is acting a little suspicious.

2168 **ione** - *nm*
jone
ion
l'energia impartita a uno ione dal campo elettrico è irrilevante in confronto all'energia termica dello ione.
the energy imparted to an ion by the electric field is small in comparison with the thermal energy of the ion.

2169 **tramontare** - *verb*
tramontare
to set
Il sole sta per tramontare, e prima di congedarci, gli insegnanti ci consegnano le letterine che hanno preparato le bimbe per i loro sostenitori.
The sun is about to set, and before we say goodbye the teachers give us letters that the girls have prepared for their sponsors.

2170 **aggiungere** - *verb*
addʒundʒere
to add
Se il tuo caffè è troppo forte, aggiungi dello zucchero.
If your coffee is too strong, add some sugar.

2171 **economia** - *nf*
economy, economics

ekonomja | In un momento in cui la nostra economia è in crescita, le nostre imprese stanno creando posti di lavoro al ritmo più veloce dagli anni '90, e i salari stanno iniziando a salire di nuovo, noi dobbiamo fare delle scelte sul tipo di paese che vogliamo essere.
At a moment when our economy is growing, our businesses are creating jobs at the fastest pace since the 1990s, and wages are starting to rise again, we have to make some choices about the kind of country we want to be.

2172 **intervento** - *nm*
intervento

intervention
Soltanto un intervento immediato può salvare la vita del paziente.
Only an immediate operation can save the patient's life.

2173 **miniera** - *nf*
minjera

mine
La città di Charleroi ha anche molti musei, come il sito di miniera di Bois du Cazier, il Museo di fotografia, il Museo archeologico o il Museo di belle arti.

The city of Charleroi also has many museums such as the Bois du Cazier mine site, the Museum of photography, the archaeological museum or the Museum of fine arts.

2174 **capitale** - *adj*
kapitale

capital
Lui è andato a Parigi, che è la capitale della Francia.
He went to Paris, which is the capital of France.

2175 **campionare** - *verb*
kampjonare

to sample
A seguito di analisi strategica e di rischio i tempi di verifica e i siti da campionare potrebbero essere modificati rispetto a quanto definito in fase di riesame contratto.

As a result of the strategic and risk analysis, the verification times and sites to be sampled may be modified compare to those defined in the contract review.

2176 **scortare** - *verb*
skortare

to escort
Il 6 agosto 1916 il Colonnello ordinò che fossi scortato presso il suo ufficio.

At August 6, 1916, the Colonnel ordered that I were escorted to his place.

2177 **legame** - *nm*
legame

bond, tie, link, connection
Gli Stati Uniti d'America hanno un legame stretto con il Messico.
The United States has close ties to Mexico.

2178 **insetto** - *nm*

insect, bug

	insetto	Gli scoiattoli mangiano semi e noci, così come insetti e funghi. *Squirrels eat seeds and nuts, as well as insects and mushrooms.*
2179	**concentrato** - *adj* kontʃentrato	**concentrated** Il comparto uffici in Italia è ancora concentrato prevalentemente sul mercato della compravendita, che compone circa l'80% del totale. *The office sector in Italy is still predominantly focused on the purchase-sale market, which makes up 80% of the total.*
2180	**occupato** - *adj* okkupato	**busy** Sto provando a mettermi in contatto con il Signor Jones da questa mattina, ma la sua linea è sempre occupata. *I have been trying all morning to get in touch with Mr Jones, but his line is always busy.*
2181	**metodo** - *nm* metodo	**method** Conoscere le loro lingue non è sufficiente per comunicare in modo efficace, perché i metodi di comunicazione sono determinati dalle loro culture. *Knowing their languages is not enough to communicate effectively, because the methods of communication are determined by their cultures.*
2182	**oscuro** - *adj* oskuro	**dark, obscure** Ognuno è una luna, e ha un lato oscuro che non mostra mai a nessuno. *Everyone is a moon, and has a dark side which he never shows to anybody.*
2183	**rispettare** - *verb* rispettare	**to respect** Lui ha sottolineato la realizzazione delle promesse fatte al popolo, ma non è riuscito a rispettare molti impegni. *He emphasised carrying out promises made to the people, but he failed to uphold many commitments.*
2184	**tensione** - *nf* tensjone	**tension, voltage** Provo tensione ed agitazione quando ho troppo lavoro da fare. *I feel tense and agitated when I have too much work to do.*
2185	**trono** - *nm* trono	**throne** Uno dei re d'Inghilterra ha abdicato dal trono per sposare una cittadina comune.

One of England's kings abdicated the throne in order to marry a commoner.

2186 **giungla** - *nf*
dʒunʎʎa
jungle
Le tigri vivono nella giungla, i leoni vivono nella savana.
Tigers live in the jungle, lions in the savanna.

2187 **consegnare** - *verb*
konseɲɲare
to deliver
Lui sarà in grado di consegnare il suo rapporto domani.
He will be able to hand in his report tomorrow.

2188 **soddisfare** - *verb*
soddisfare
to satisfy
Io sono ancora lontano da quel risultato che potrebbe soddisfarmi.
I am far from satisfied with the result.

2189 **caporale** - *nm*
kaporale
corporal
Allo stesso modo, il soldato israeliano, caporale Shalit, che è prigioniero in Palestina, dev'essere immediatamente rilasciato.
Equally, the Israeli soldier Corporal Shalit, who is being held in Palestine, must be released immediately.

2190 **tradimento** - *nm*
tradimento
betrayal, treason, treachery
È un atto di tradimento vendere i segreti militari ai nemici del vostro paese.
It is an act of treason to sell military secrets to your country's enemies.

2191 **eccome** - *int*
ekkome
all right!, I´ll say!
Sì, ci saranno le imposte europee, eccome se ci saranno.
Yes, there will be European taxes, indeed there will.

2192 **sommo** - *adj*
sommo
highest
Dovrà essere convocato, da coloro a cui compete, il Conclave per l'elezione del nuovo Sommo Pontefice.
A Conclave to elect the new Supreme Pontiff will have to be convoked by those whose competence it is.

2193 **pozzo** - *nm*
pottso
well
Devo sempre controllare nel cortile per vedere che non ci siano delle pozze d'acqua stagnante, affinché le zanzare non si riproducano.
I always have to check my yard for stagnant pools of water so mosquitoes don't breed there.

2194 **possesso** - *nm*
possesso
possession
Adam ha passato 3 anni in prigione per possesso di droga.
Adam spent 3 years in jail for drug possession.

2195 **demone** - *nm* demone | **demon**
Se gli uomini sono dei lupi allora le donne sono dei demoni.
If men are wolves then women are devils.

2196 **diamine** - *int* djamine | **heck**
Ho letto la recensione e ho pensato, oh che diamine?
I read the review and I though, oh what the heck?

2197 **vomitare** - *verb* vomitare | **to throw up, puke**
Aveva i conati di vomito e poi ha iniziato a vomitare.
He retched and then started puking.

2198 **mobile** - *adj; nm* mobile | **mobile; furniture**
Non c'era assolutamente nessun mobile in quella stanza.
There was absolutely no furniture in that room.

2199 **medaglia** - *nf* medaʎʎa | **medal**
La squadra giapponese ha vinto la medaglia d'oro in questa competizione.
The Japanese team won the gold medal for this competition.

2200 **onestamente** - *adv* onestamente | **honestly**
Posso onestamente dire che questo è il caffè migliore che io abbia mai bevuto.
I can honestly say this is the best coffee I've ever had.

2201 **atteggiamento** - *nm* atteddʒamento | **attitude**
Il suo volto e il suo atteggiamento mostravano il disprezzo che provava.
His face and attitude showed the scorn he felt.

2202 **rientrare** - *verb* rjentrare | **to re-enter**
Tutto sommato, penso che dovresti rientrare a casa e aiutare i tuoi vecchi genitori.
All things considered, I think you should go back home and support your old parents.

2203 **sito** - *adj* sito | **place, website**
Sono preso dalla coltivazione delle erbe e il suo sito mi è di grande aiuto.
I am absorbed in growing herbs and your Web pages are a great help to me.

2204 **sentiero** - *nm* sentjero | **pathway, trail**
Il sentiero di montagna si trovava sotto una coperta di foglie, morbida e facile da percorrere.
The mountain path was under a blanket of leaves, soft and easy to walk on.

2205 **rifiuto** - *nm*
rifjuto

refusal, rejection, waste
Come possiamo giustificare il rifiuto di inviare medicinali a persone che ne hanno bisogno, e che vivono in paesi politicamente osteggiati dagli Stati Uniti?
How can we justify not sending medicine to people in need who live in places that are out of political favor with the United States?

2206 **imputare** - *verb*
imputare

to attribute sth to
Sta accadendo la stessa cosa, e non sappiamo a cosa imputare tutte queste trasferte né dove finiranno questi fondi.
The same thing is happening again, and we do not know what so much travel attributes to, and where these funds are going to end.

2207 **missile** - *adj*
missile

missile
La folla inferocita ha lanciato dei missili contro la polizia.
The angry crowd threw missiles at the police.

2208 **salsa** - *nf*
salsa

sauce
Se aggiungi della salsa al riso al curry, il sapore sarà più denso.
If you add sauce to curry rice, the taste will be more dense.

2209 **altrettanto** - *adv; adj; pron*
altrettanto

as; as much; just as many
Lei gioca molto bene a tennis ma io so giocare altrettanto bene.
She can play tennis very well, but I can play as well as she can.

2210 **monaco** - *nm&f*
monako

monk
Madre Teresa era una monaca cattolica che viveva e lavorava a Calcutta, in India.
Mother Teresa was a Catholic nun who lived and worked in Calcutta, India.

2211 **vario** - *adj*
varjo

various, varied
Oltre a prestare libri, le biblioteche offrono vari altri servizi.
Besides lending books, libraries offer various other services.

2212 **dichiarare** - *verb*
dikjarare

to declare, claim
Ha sempre dichiarato di essere stata soltanto un'altra delle sue vittime.
She always claimed to have been just another one of his victims.

2213 **fune** - *nm; nf*

cable, wire; rope, linen

fune | Tommaso ha legato la fune col cappio fra due alberi
Tom strung a clothesline between the two trees.

2214 **inviato** - *nm*
invjato
envoy, correspondent
Esigo che tu cessi e desista dall'inviare delle e-mail indesiderate.
I demand that you cease and desist from sending unsolicited emails.

2215 **evidente** - *adj*
evidente
evident
Il suo gusto eclettico era evidente dall'insolito arredamento della stanza.
Her eclectic taste was evident from the unusual decor of the room.

2216 **stipendio** - *nm*
stipendjo
salary
Anche se non ricevo uno stipendio alto, io non sono disposto ad abbandonare questo modo di guadagnarsi da vivere.
Even if I don't get a high salary, I'm not willing to quit this way of making a living.

2217 **comunità** - *nf*
komunitˈa
community
Questa è una tragedia per questa famiglia, è una tragedia per questa comunità, è una tragedia per la città.
This is a tragedy for this family, it's a tragedy for this community, it's a tragedy for the city.

2218 **inizio** - *nm*
inittsjo
beginning
Non importa quale strumento musicale tu voglia imparare, la cosa più importante è di non fare alcun errore fin dall'inizio, poiché gli errori si fissano nella memoria sempre meglio di tutto ciò che hai fatto bene.
No matter which musical instrument you want to learn to play, the most important thing is not to make any mistakes from the beginning on, because mistakes are always imprinted on your mind more easily than everything you do right.

2219 **varo** - *nm*
varo
launch, launching
Il Consiglio europeo chiede il varo di un piano europeo per l'innovazione.
The European Council calls for the launching of a European plan for innovation.

2220 **vigliacco** - *adj*
viʎʎakko
coward
Da ora molti omuncoli non potranno fare più i vigliacchi.

From now on many petty men will not be able to be cowards anymore.

2221 **assicurato** - *adj*
assikurato

secured, assured, insured
Si è assicurata che la porta sia chiusa a chiave?
Have you made sure the door is locked?

2222 **ritrovato** - *nm*
ritrovato

finding, discovery
Ultimo ritrovato in fatto di tecnologia multimediale digitale, il DVD garantisce una qualità d'immagine impareggiabile.
The latest in multimedia digital technology, DVD guarantees second-to-none picture quality.

2223 **manuale** - *adj; nm*
manwale

manual
Non utilizzare il sistema diversamente da come è specificato in questo manuale di istruzioni.
Do not use the system in any other manner than specified in this instruction manual.

2224 **sacrificio** - *nm*
sakrifitʃo

sacrifice
Fare una scelta significa sempre fare un sacrificio, rinunciare ad una cosa per un'altra.
Making a choice always means making a sacrifice, giving up one thing for another.

2225 **divenire** - *verb*
divenire

to become
Dopo che l'aveva visto, è caduto in una enorme confusione dei pensieri, era divenuto immobile e, in breve, trasformato in pietra.
After having caught sight of her, he fell into a huge confusion of thoughts, was motionless and, in one word, turned to stone.

2226 **popolare** - *adj; verb*
popolare

populair; to populate
Io penso che Twitter non sia molto popolare in Germania. 140 caratteri sono circa due parole in tedesco.
I think Twitter is not very popular in Germany. 140 characters is approx two words in German.

2227 **investire** - *verb*
investire

to invest
È la prima volta che investo un cane con la mia macchina.
This is the first time I've ever knocked a dog down with my car.

2228 **nascosto** - *adj*
naskosto

hidden
Applicare ulteriori analisi ai documenti e ai file che corrispondono alle parole chiave e trovare la verità nascosta è "conoscenza".

To apply further analysis to documents and files matching the keywords and find the hidden truth is "knowledge".

2229 **franco** - *adj; nm* frаŋko
frank, free; franc
Il valore esterno del franco era sensibilmente salito dallo scoppio della crisi finanziaria internazionale nell'agosto 2007.
The Swiss franc had gained markedly in value since the onset of the international financial crisis in August 2007.

2230 **altrove** - *adv* altrove
elsewhere
I libri sono per la gente che spera di essere altrove.
Books are for people who wish they were somewhere else.

2231 **infine** - *adv* infine
finally, at last
Infine ha fissato, quale regola di comportamento interna, che siano sottoposte alla sua approvazione le operazioni finanziarie.
Lastly, the Board of Directors adopted an internal rule of conduct whereby its approval is required for financial transactions.

2232 **lira** - *nf* lira
lira
Le sue idee non gli hanno mai reso una lira.
His ideas never earned him a dime.

2233 **pelo** - *nm* pelo
hair, fur, coat
Il pelo del nostro gatto ha perso la sua lucentezza.
Our cat's fur has lost its luster.

2234 **sesto** - *adj; num* sesto
sixth
La gravità della Luna è un sesto di quella della Terra.
The gravity of the moon is one-sixth of that of the earth.

2235 **trasporto** - *nm* trasporto
transport
Qualora da analisi risulti che il difetto sia stato cagionato da uso improprio o ricada nelle esclusioni previste nelle condizioni di garanzia, l'importo della riparazione e del trasporto verrà addebitato all'utente.

If the defect is found to be due to improper use or falls in the exclusions provided for in the warranty conditions, the costs incurred for the component repair and carriage shall be charged to the user.

2236 **cassaforte** - *nf* kassaforte
safe, strongbox
È chiaro che lui ha rubato i soldi dalla cassaforte.
It's clear that he stole money from the safe.

2237 **capitolo** - *nm*
chapter

kapitolo | Prima di andare a dormire ho letto qualche altro capitolo.
I read a couple of more chapters before I went to sleep.

2238 **cifrare** - *verb* **to encipher**
tʃifrare
Questa operazione deve essere ripetuta per ogni partizione da cifrare.
This will be repeated for each partition to be encrypted.

2239 **tara** - *nf* **tare, defect, faint**
tara
Per calcolo della tara si intende la sottrazione del peso del contenitore in modo da visualizzare solo il peso degli oggetti all'interno del contenitore (peso netto).
Taring refers to the action of allowing for the weight of a container so that only the weight of objects held in the container (net weight) is displayed.

2240 **commerciale** - *adj* **commercial, trade**
kommertʃale
Mia madre è andata al centro commerciale per fare qualche acquisto.
My mother went to the department store to do some shopping.

2241 **sodo** - *adj* **hard**
sodo
Generalmente gli studenti del liceo studiano più sodo degli studenti del college.
Generally speaking, high school students study harder than college students.

2242 **tubo** - *nm* **tube, pipe**
tubo
Quando nel tubo di alimentazione gas è presente aria (es. nel caso di nuova installazione) può essere necessario ripetere più tentativi di accensione.
When the gas supply tube is filled with air (e.g. in case of new installation) it may be necessary to repeat the ignition cycle several times.

2243 **nuvoloso** - *adj* **overcast, cloudy**
nuvolozo
L'errore più comune è la mancanza dell'orizzonte libero a causa di eventuali ostacoli o di cielo estremamente nuvoloso, che impedisce la ricezione dei segnali dei satelliti.
Most common error is not having a clear view of the sky, or being under very cloudy conditions, when a satellite signal may not be received.

2244 **codardo** - *adj; nm/f* **cowardly; coward**
kodardo
John è in apparenza coraggioso, però in realtà è un codardo.
John is brave in appearance, but is in reality a coward.

2245	**riparo** - *nm* riparo	**shelter** Quando scende il buio, i babbuini ritornano agli alberi per dormire, al riparo dai predatori notturni. *When darkness falls, the baboons return to the trees to sleep, safe from night prowlers.*
2246	**tradizione** - *nf* tradittsjone	**tradition** Cristo nostro Signore, nella Sacra Scrittura dell'uno e dell'altro Testamento e nella Tradizione, ha affidato alla sua Chiesa l'unico deposito della Rivelazione. *Christ our Lord in the sacred Scripture of the Old and New Testaments and in Tradition has entrusted to his Church the one deposit of divine revelation.*
2247	**martedì** - *nm* marted'i	**Tuesday** Tom mi ha detto che può andare in qualsiasi giorno tranne il martedì. *Tom told me that he could come on any day but Tuesday.*
2248	**sofferto** - *adj* sofferto	**suffered** L'umanità ha sofferto perdite a causa della guerra di più negli ultimi cento anni che mai prima d'ora. *Humanity has suffered more from war in this century than ever before.*
2249	**gonna** - *nf* gonna	**skirt** Lei stava indossando delle mutandine rosa sotto la gonna. *She was wearing pink panties under the skirt.*
2250	**mucca** - *nf* mukka	**cow** Le mucche sono più utili di qualsiasi altro animale in questo paese. *Cows are more useful than any other animal in this country.*
2251	**siccome** - *conj* sikkome	**since** Siccome era la prima volta che siamo entrati a scuola in ritardo, la nostra professoressa non ci ha puniti. *Since it was the first time we arrived late at school, our teacher didn't give us detention.*
2252	**educazione** - *nf* edukattsjone	**education** Se pensate che l'educazione sia cara, aspettate e vedrete quanto vi costa cara l'ignoranza. *If you think education is expensive, wait till you see what ignorance costs you.*
2253	**sospeso** - *adj*	**suspended**

sospezo | La figlia di Tom fu sospesa per avere portato della marijuana a scuola.
Tom's daughter was suspended for taking marijuana to school.

2254 **undici** - *adj; num* **eleven**
unditʃi
Questo aeroporto offre
servizi di volo diretto undici che includono sei destinazioni nazionali e cinque destinazioni internazionali.

This airport offers eleven direct flight services that include six domestic destinations and five international destinations.

2255 **motorio** - *adj* **motor**
motorjo
Facilitare il trasporto di persone con limitazioni di tipo motorio è uno dei modi più efficienti per promuovere attività sociali per tutti.
Facilitating transportation of mobility impaired people is one of the most efficient ways to promote social activities for everyone.

2256 **assoluto** - *adj* **absolute**
assoluto
Tom è stato il primo ragazzo in assoluto ad aver baciato Mary.
Tom was the first boy that ever kissed Mary.

2257 **prezioso** - *adj* **precious**
prettsjozo
Ho un sacco di libri antichi. Un paio di loro sono abbastanza prezioso.
I have a lot of old books. A couple of them are quite valuable.

2258 **rapire** - *verb* **to kidnap**
rapire
Ogni anno molti bambini vengono rapiti da membri delle loro famiglie.
Each year many children are kidnapped by members of their own families.

2259 **presso** - *prep; adv; adj* **at,in; near; close**
presso
Irene Pepperberg, una ricercatrice presso la Northwestern University, sta scoprendo che un pappagallo può non solo imitare le persone, ma anche imparare il significato delle parole.
Irene Pepperberg, a researcher at Northwestern University, is discovering that a parrot can not only mimic people but also learn the meaning of words.

2260 **mail** - *nf* **email**

mail — Tom ha digitalizzato una vecchia foto di famiglia e l'ha inviata via e-mail a sua madre.

Tom digitized an old family photo and emailed it to his mother.

2261 **dipingere** - *verb* — **to paint**
dipindʒere
Lei era in piedi su una scala a dipingere il soffitto.
She was standing on a ladder painting the ceiling.

2262 **condotto** - *adj; nm* — **conducted; duct, conduit, canal**
kondotto
Il condotto uditivo invia le onde sonore al timpano.
The ear canal sends sound waves to the eardrum.

2263 **professionale** - *adj* — **professional**
professjonale
L'istruzione tecnica e professionale deve essere messa alla portata di tutti.
Technical and professional education shall be made generally available.

2264 **strumento** - *nm* — **tool**
strumento
Quando si tratta di strumenti musicali, più si fa pratica, più si diventa abili.
When it comes to musical instruments, the more you practice, the more skilled you become.

2265 **bentornato** - *int; nm* — **Welcome back!; welcome**
bentornato
Salve gente e bentornati per un altro aggiornamento sulle sessioni a Reglan !
Howdy Folks welcome back for another Raglan sessions update!

2266 **cremare** - *verb* — **to cremate**
kremare
Erano un po ' i primi a costruire strumenti di pietra, cremare i loro morti, e dipingere rappresentazioni di se stessi.
They were some the first people to make stone tools, cremate their dead, and paint representations of themselves.

2267 **mollo** - *adj* — **soaked, flabby**
mollo
Il giorno successivo unire al riso freddo i 4 tuorli, il lievito, la farina, il vinsanto e l'uvetta precedentemente messa a mollo.
The next day, combine the cold rice with 4 egg yolks, baking powder, flour, raisins (soaked previously) and vinsanto.

2268 **impattare** - *verb* — **to impact**

impattare | Piaggio ha cercato e cerca di fronteggiare tale rischio, che potrebbe impattare negativamente sulla situazione economica e finanziaria
Piaggio has tried to tackle this risk, which could have a negative impact on the financial position and performance of the Group

2269 **proibire** - *verb* | **to prohibit**
proibire | Se si proibisce agli studenti cinesi di pensare, cosa ci si aspetta da loro esattamente?
If we ban Chinese students from thinking, what exactly do we expect from them?

2270 **popolazione** - *nf* | **population**
popolattsjone | La popolazione curda dell'Iran, dell'Iraq, della Turchia e della Siria chiede da molto tempo una patria unificata.
The Kurdish people of Iran, Iraq, Turkey and Syria have long sought a unified homeland.

2271 **liberare** - *verb* | **to release**
liberare | Il senato stabilì che il console facesse un nuovo arruolamento e liberasse la patria dai nemici.
The Senate decreed that a new consul be chosen and the country be delivered from the enemies.

2272 **giudicare** - *verb* | **to judge**
dʒudikare | Si può facilmente giudicare la maturità di una banana dal colore della sua buccia.
You can easily judge the ripeness of a banana by the color of its peel.

2273 **manager** - *nm* | **manager**
manadʒer | Il manager non c'era, così ho lasciato un messaggio alla segretaria.
The manager was out, so I left a message with his secretary.

2274 **quinto** - *adj; num* | **fifth**
kwinto | In America il riso può essere comprato a un quinto di quello che costa in Giappone.
In America, rice can be bought for a fifth of what it costs in Japan.

2275 **quota** - *nf* | **quota, share, quote**
kwota | Una quota sempre crescente della popolazione non è in grado di utilizzare appieno la potenza espressiva della lingua tedesca.

An increasingly greater part of the population is not capable of fully utilizing the power of expression of the German language.

2276 **porno** - *adj; nm* porno — **porn**
A me piace guardare i video porno di lesbiche.
I like watching lesbian porn.

2277 **euro** - *nm* euro — **Euro**
Noi abbiamo mangiato al ristorante a dieci euro a persona.
We ate at the restaurant for ten euros per person.

2278 **pacchetto** - *nm* pakketto — **package**
Pensavo che avessimo mangiato tutto quello che c'era in casa, ma poi ho trovato un altro pacchetto di cracker.
I thought we had eaten everything in the house, but I found another box of crackers.

2279 **polso** - *nm* polso — **wrist, pulse**
Sapevo di essermi rotto il polso nel momento in cui sono caduto.
I knew I'd broken my wrist the moment I fell.

2280 **fratellino** - *nm* fratellino — **(younger) brother (coll)**
Il mio fratellino dice che ieri notte ha fatto un brutto sogno.
My little brother says that he had a dreadful dream last night.

2281 **produrre** - *verb* produrre — **to produce**
Ho un orologio prodotto in Giappone che tiene il tempo molto bene.
I have a watch of Japanese make, which keeps very good time.

2282 **rigare** - *verb* rigare — **to scratch**
Con questo addestramento i bambini imparavano, non ad essere se stessi, ma a “rigare dritto”.
With this training children learned not to be themselves, but to behave themselves .

2283 **sospettare** - *verb* sospettare — **to suspect**
Tom non aveva alcuna ragione di sospettare che Mary stava mentendo.
Tom had no reason to suspect that Mary was lying.

2284 **intelligenza** - *nf* intellidʒentsa — **intelligence**
Qualcuno di famoso ha detto che l'immaginazione è più importante dell'intelligenza.

Someone famous said that imagination is more important than intelligence.

2285 **confessione** - *nf* konfessjone

confession

Sono nato di confessione ebraica, ma invecchiando mi sono convertito al narcisismo. La vendetta è una confessione di dolore.

I was born into the Hebrew persuasion, but when I got older I converted to narcissism. Revenge is a confession of pain.

2286 **abituare** - *verb* abitware

to accustom

Se vuoi diventare ambidestro, prova a lavarti i denti con la mano non dominante. All'inizio sarà complicato, ma molto presto ti ci abituerai.

If you want to become ambidextrous, try brushing your teeth with your non-dominant hand. It'll be hard at first, but you'll get used to it in no time.

2287 **spendere** - *verb* spendere

to spend

Non volevo più spendere altro tempo a cercare di convincere Tom a studiare il francese.

I didn't want to spend any more time trying to convince Tom to study French.

2288 **scommessa** - *nf* skommessa

bet

Non mi andrà bene con questa scommessa.

I won't have it good with this bet.

2289 **bruno** - *adj* bruno

brown, dark

Lo slogan per la giornata contro gli estremismi era "multicolorato invece di bruno."

The slogan for the day against extremism was, "multicolored instead of brown"

2290 **denuncia** - *nf* denuntʃa

complaint

Per risolvere il problema né denunce né lacrime possono contribuire.

To solve the problem neither complaints nor tears can contribute.

2291 **bucare** - *verb* bukare

to puncture

Se si cucina carne con la pelle che con l'effetto della pressione può gonfiarsi, non bucare la carne finché la pelle è gonfia: ciò potrebbe provocare scottature.

A sharp object may puncture the battery which may present a risk of fire, chemical burn, electrolyte leak, and/or injury.

2292 **assomigliare** - *verb*

to look like, resemble

assomiʎʎare

Quando si comincia ad assomigliare alla propria foto nel passaporto, è ora di andare in vacanza.

When you start to look like the photo in your passport, it's time to go on vacation.

2293 **seno** - *nf*
seno

breast

Questa è la prima volta che mi capita di allattare al seno il mio bambino.

This is the first time I've ever breast-fed my baby.

2294 **gemere** - *verb*
dʒemere

to moan

Il vento errava gemendo attorno al castello come un'anima in pena.

The wind wandered moaning round the house like a lost soul.

2295 **pacco** - *nm*
pakko

pack, parcel

Tom ha incartato il pacco e lo ha legato con del filo.

Tom wrapped the package and tied it with strings.

2296 **comunista** - *adj; nm*
komunista

communist

Il comunismo era il sistema politico nell'Unione delle Repubbliche Socialiste Sovietiche, ma che si è fermato nel 1993.

Communism was the political system in the Union of Soviet Socialist Republics, but that stopped in 1993.

2297 **attuale** - *adj*
attwale

current

Leggete il giornale tutti i giorni, altrimenti perderete il contatto con il mondo attuale.

Read the newspaper every day, or you will get behind the times.

2298 **mela** - *nf*
mela

apple

Tom ha acquistato un sacchetto di mele e ne ha mangiate un terzo in un giorno.

Tom bought a bag of apples and he ate a third of them in one day.

2299 **carrozza** - *nf*
karrottsa

carriage

Le ultime tre carrozze del treno sono state pesantemente danneggiate.

The last three coaches of the train were badly damaged.

2300 **extra** - *adj*
ekstra

extra

Abbiamo già avuto alcuni extra, come il cesto di frutta e ha chiesto una sedia a sdraio, che abbiamo ricevuto dopo aver disegnato su di essa tre volte.

We previously had a few extras, such as fruit basket and a lawn chair asked, which we received only after we had drawn on it three times.

2301 **scienziato** - *nm* ʃentsjato

scientist

Uno scienziato americano di nome William Keeton fece un esperimento interessante per risolvere questo mistero.

One American scientist, William Keeton, used a very interesting experiment to solve this mystery.

2302 **sottovoce** - *adv* sottovotʃe

whisper

Di giorno dobbiamo camminare in punta di piedi e parlare sottovoce perché nel magazzino non devono sentirci.

We have to whisper and tread lightly during the day, otherwise the people in the warehouse might hear us.

2303 **lento** - *adv* lento

slow

Poi cuocilo a fuoco lento per 30 minuti, ed sarà pronto.

After, cook it on a low flame for 30 minutes and you're done.

2304 **novembre** - *nm* novembre

November

A Chicago tende a nevicare verso la fine di novembre.

Snow is apt to fall in Chicago in late November.

2305 **rapidamente** - *adv* rapidamente

quickly

Io avevo paura del palcoscenico in un primo momento, ma l'ho superata rapidamente.

I had stage fright at first, but I got over it quickly.

2306 **apertura** - *nf* apertura

opening

L'open source è una filosofia che incoraggia l'apertura, la condivisione e la modificabilità.

Open source is a philosophy that encourages openness, sharing, and modification.

2307 **amministrazione** - *nf* amministrattsjone

administration

Io non mi fido dell'amministrazione.

I don't trust the administration.

2308 **riportare** - *verb* riportare

to report, take back

Devo riportare i miei libri in biblioteca prima del 25 gennaio.

I've got to take my library books back before January 25th.

2309 **malapena** - *adv* malapena

barely

Tom è messo davvero male. Riesco a sentire a malapena il suo battito.

Tom's really bad. I can barely feel his pulse.

2310 **anniversario** - *nm*

anniversary

anniversarjo — Tom e Mary hanno festeggiato il loro primo anniversario con una cena romatica.

Tom and Mary had a romantic dinner to celebrate the first anniversary of their being together.

2311 **cacciatore** - *nm* — **hunter**
kattʃatore
Le depredazioni dei cacciatori umani sono ritenute di essere state il fattore chiave che ha spinto molte specie all'estinzione.
The depredations of human hunters are thought to have been the key factor that pushed many species to extinction.

2312 **complesso** - *adj; nm* — **complex, whole; complex**
komplesso
La finanza moderna sta diventando sempre più complessa e sofisticata.

Modern finance is becoming increasingly complicated and sophisticated.

2313 **ipotesi** - *nf* — **hypothesis, speculation, assumption**
ipotezi
Ma questi ipotesi sono ancora oggetto di discussione nel mondo scientifico.

But those hypotheses are still an object of discussion in the world of science.

2314 **hall** - *nf* — **hall, lobby**
all
La sala da pranzo è direttamente adiacente alla hall, o piuttosto, da dove siete, è a soli tre passi?

The dining hall is directly adjacent to the lobby, or rather, from where you are, it's just three steps away?

2315 **agosto** - *nm* — **August**
agosto
Il quindici di agosto migliaia di persone fanno volare degli aquiloni.
On the fifteenth of August, thousands of people fly kites.

2316 **violento** - *adj* — **violent**
vjolento
Lui pronunciò il suo giudizio su un comportamento così violento.
He pronounced his judgment over such vehement behaviour.

2317 **estero** - *nm* — **abroad**
estero
Ho parlato con i miei genitori del mio progetto di andare a studiare all'estero.

I talked with my parents about my studying abroad.

2318 **asilo** - *nm* — **asylum, kindergarten, nursery (school)**
azilo
Loro sono diventati cittadini dopo aver ricevuto asilo politico.

They became citizens after receiving political asylum.

2319 **ciascuno** - *adj; pron* tʃaskuno

each, all, every; everyone, everybody

In molte parti del mondo, non c'è abbastanza cibo per soddisfare i bisogni di ciascuno.

In many parts of the world, there is not enough food to meet everyone's needs.

2320 **supporto** - *nm* supporto

support

A mia sorella Maya, a mia sorella Alma, a tutti i miei altri fratelli e sorelle, grazie mille per tutto il supporto che mi avete dato. Sono grato a loro.

To my sister Maya, my sister Alma, all my other brothers and sisters, thank you so much for all the support that you've given me. I'm grateful to them.

2321 **generazione** - *nf* dʒenerattsjone

generation

I genitori pensano la nuova generazione come una generazione lontana dalla realtà e occupata a rincorrere sogni non realizzabili.

Parents look to the new generation as a generation that is far from reality and busy running after unrealistic dreams.

2322 **nebbia** - *nf* nebbja

fog, mist

In caso di inalazione dell'aerosol o nebbia se necessario consultare un medico.

In the case of inhalation of aerosol/mist consult a physician if necessary.

2323 **salita** - *nf* salita

climb

Il percorso richiede ottimo allenamento, con una salita lunga e tratti difficili da compiere in sella; la discesa è ripida.

The route requires excellent training, with a long climb and stretches hard to cycle on; the descent is steep.

2324 **controllato** - *adj* kontrollato

checked

Ho controllato due volte per sincerarmi che non abbiamo commesso errori.

I checked twice to make certain we hadn't made any mistakes.

2325 **volume** - *nm* volume

volume

Per calcolare il volume, moltiplica la lunghezza con la larghezza e la profondità.

To calculate the volume, multiply the length by the width by the depth.

2326 **tipico** - *adj*

typical

tipiko — Ha vissuto in una casa con tipico stile giapponese.

He lived in a typical Japanese-style house.

2327 **spaventoso** - *adj* — **frightening, scary**

spaventozo — Non ho mai sentito prima d'ora una storia così spaventosa.

I've never heard of such a frightening story before.

2328 **comunicazione** - *nf* — **communication**

komunikattsjone — Una comunicazione efficace e il rispetto reciproco sono elementi essenziali del lavoro di squadra di successo.

Effective communication and mutual respect are essential elements of successful teamwork.

2329 **egoista** - *adj; nm* — **selfish; egoist**

egoista — Il mondo contemporaneo è freddo, egoista, consumista e violento, disumanizzato.

he contemporary world is cold, selfish, consumerist and violent, dehumanized.

2330 **ufficialmente** - *adv* — **officially**

uffitʃalmente — Gli Stati Uniti hanno ufficialmente concluso le sanzioni economiche contro la Birmania.

The United States has officially ended economic sanctions against Burma.

2331 **disperato** - *adj* — **desperate**

disperato — Lui era disperato, quando è tornato a casa.

He was desperatem when he returned home.

2332 **spiritoso** - *adj* — **humorous**

spiritozo — Sono in grado di esprimermi nelle lettere in modo ironico, ambiguo o spiritoso.

In a letter I can express myself in a consciously ironical, ambiguous and humorous way.

2333 **patatina** - *nf* — **french fry, potato chip, plump little girl (coll), pussy (coll)**

patatina — Io non ho mangiato tutte le patatine fritte perché erano troppo unte.

I didn't eat all the fries because they were too oily.

2334 **contadino** - *adj* — **farmer**

kontadino — Il contadino ha arato il suo campo per tutto il giorno.

The farmer ploughed his field all day.

2335 **minore** - *adj* — **less, minor, lower, lesser, smaller**

minore — La mia sorella minore ha due figli, il che significa che io ho due nipoti.

My younger sister has two sons, which means I have two nephews.

2336 **sensibile** - *adj*
sensibile

sensible
Mary è sensibile alla luce, per cui indossa degli occhiali da sole.
Mary is sensitive to light, so she wears sunglasses.

2337 **copione** - *nm*
kopjone

script
Lo sappiamo tutti che vai al cinema a vedere "Twilight" per via del suo "copione brillante" e non per via dei suoi attori.
We all know you go to the cinema to watch "Twilight" because of its "brilliant script" and not because of its actors.

2338 **coma** - *nm*
koma

coma
Nel frattempo, il suo compagno era uscito dal coma e veniva curato per le fratture (lei non gli aveva ancora detto della perdita del bambino), e il piccolo Major stava gradualmente riacquistando conoscenza.
In the meantime her partner had come out of his coma and was being treated for his fractures (she still had not told him about the loss of his son) and little Major was slowly regaining consciousness.

2339 **giungere** - *verb*
dʒundʒere

to reach
Le presidenze cercheranno anche di giungere all'adozione definitiva della decisione.
The Presidencies will also seek final adoption of the Decision.

2340 **lama** - *nf; nm*
lama

blade; llama
Questo coltello ha una lama affilata e taglia bene.
This knife has a fine edge and cuts well.

2341 **statua** - *nf*
statwa

statue
Una statua vivente poggia su una panchina e due statue della libertà parlano con i turisti.
A living statue rests on a bench and two statues of liberty talk with tourists.

2342 **infinito** - *adj*
infinito

Infinity
Solo due cose sono infinite: l'universo e la stupidità umana, ma non sono sicuro della prima.
Only two things are infinite, the universe and human stupidity, and I'm not sure about the former.

2343 **record** - *nm*
rekord

record
Per ulteriori informazioni sulla gestione dei record, consultare la Guida per la gestione dei record aziendali (Corporate Office Records Management Guide) e le politiche di gestione dei record specifiche di ciascuna business unit.

For more information regarding records management, please see the Corporate Office Records Management Guide and records management policies for each Business Unit.

2344 **astronave** - *nf* astronave
spaceship
Il gioco in Modalità Completa termina quando ogni giocatore umano è morto o ha lasciato l'astronave.
The game ends when every Human player has either been eliminated or has safely left the spaceship.

2345 **operaio** - *nm; adj* operajo
worker; working, labouring
Loro hanno detto che io ero il loro operaio migliore.
They said I was their best worker.

2346 **concetto** - *nm* kontʃetto
concept
Abbiamo bisogno di una chiara definizione del concetto di diritti umani.
We need a clear definition of the concept of human rights.

2347 **precedere** - *verb* pretʃedere
to precede
Giovanni il Battista è stato inviato per precedere la prima venuta di Cristo.
John the Baptist was sent to forerun the first coming of Christ.

2348 **regalare** - *verb* regalare
to give
Lui non le ha regalato un ramo di rose però l'ha invitata a prendere un caffè e ha parlato con lei.
He didn't give her a bucket of roses, but he took her out for a coffee and talked to her.

2349 **bara** - *nf* bara
coffin
Foto di bare coperte da bandiere andarono su tutti i giornali.
Pictures of coffins covered with flags went all over the papers.

2350 **esagerare** - *verb* ezadʒerare
to exaggerate
Ti stai impegnando molto, ma stai attento a non esagerare.
You're working hard, eh. But don't push yourself too hard.

2351 **autore** - *nm* autore
author
Agatha Christie è uno dei tuoi autori preferiti di tutti i tempi?
Is Agatha Christie one of your all-time favorite authors?

2352 **macchiare** - *verb* makkjare
to sully
Non utilizzare detergenti aggressivi o prodotti abrasivi, spugne abrasive e neppure oggetti appuntiti, perché potrebbero macchiare l'apparecchio.

Do not use aggressive or abrasive cleaning products, scourers that scratch surfaces or sharp objects, since stains may appear.

2353 **condividere** - *verb* kondividere

to share
Io devo condividere questa stanza con il mio amico al momento.
I have to share this room with my friend at present.

2354 **concedere** - *verb* kontʃedere

to grant
Puoi concedermi qualche minuto? Vorrei scambiare due parole con te.
Can you spare me a few minutes? I'd like to have a word with you.

2355 **psichiatra** - *nm* psikjatra

psychiatrist
È prevista la presenza di uno psichiatra in grado di gestire un'ampia serie di malattie mentali.
A psychiatrist works with a wide range of mental health illnesses.

2356 **generoso** - *adj* dʒenerozo

generous
Sono grato a ciascuno per l'impegno generoso e qualificato.
I thank you all for your so generous and qualified efforts.

2357 **vietato** - *adj* vjetato

forbidden
In molti paesi comprare o fumare cannabis è vietato dalla legge.
In many countries, buying or smoking cannabis is forbidden by law.

2358 **autunno** - *nm* autunno

autumn, fall
Le giornate stanno diventando notevolmente più corte ora che è arrivato l'autunno.
The days are getting noticeably shorter now that autumn has arrived.

2359 **ambasciata** - *nf* ambaʃʃata

embassy
Mia sorella lavora all'ambasciata degli Stati Uniti a Londra.
My sister works at the United States Embassy in London.

2360 **quantità** - *nf* kwantitˈa

amount
I semi di mela sono velenosi, ma sono pericolosi per la salute solo se consumati in grandi quantità.
Apple seeds are poisonous, but are only dangerous to health when consumed in large quantities.

2361 **impiegato** - *adj* impjegato

office worker, employee
Mio padre era un impiegato statale, e anche mia madre non stava facendo niente.

My father was a civil servant, and my mother wasn't doing anything either.

2362 **standard** - *adj*
standard
standard
L'articolo che hai scritto non è in conformità con gli standard del nostro giornale.
The article you wrote is not in compliance with our journal's standards.

2363 **dispiaciuto** - *adj*
dispjatʃuto
sorry
Devo ammettere che stavo cominciando a sentirmi un po' dispiaciuto per me stesso.
I have to admit I was starting to feel a little sorry for myself.

2364 **collezione** - *nf*
kollettsjone
collection
Tom ha la migliore collezione di monete che io abbia mai visto.
Tom has the best coin collection I've ever seen.

2365 **evviva** - *int*
evviva
cheers, hoorah
Evviva l'intuizione artistica, il piacere e il desiderio di creare, la qualità e la generosità!
Hurray to artistic intuition, pleasure, the desire to create, quality, and generosity!

2366 **detestare** - *verb*
detestare
to loathe
Detesto i cosiddetti corsi di lingue in "trenta giorni".
I hate so-called "30 days" language courses.

2367 **infarto** - *nm*
infarto
infarct
Gli indicatori in relazione ai processi delle cure fornite ai pazienti con infarto miocardico non dovrebbero per ora essere introdotti.
Consequently, indicators relating to the treatment of an acute myocardial infarction should not be introduced at present.

2368 **rallentare** - *verb*
rallentare
to decelerate
Sembra che Tom stia cercando di rallentare i negoziati.
It looks as if Tom is trying to slow down the negotiations.

2369 **invisibile** - *adj*
invizibile
invisible
La maggior parte di essi è invisibile senza l'aiuto di un microscopio.
Most of them are invisible without the help of a microscope.

2370 **normalmente** - *adv*
normalmente
normally
Nei viaggi all'estero, il presidente è normalmente accompagnato dalla moglie.

The President is usually accompanied by his wife when he goes abroad.

2371 **vampiro** - *nm* vampiro | **vampire**
Lui lavora come insegnante, però in realtà è un vampiro.
He works as a teacher, but actually he's a vampire.

2372 **murare** - *verb* murare | **to wall**
Si racconta che il marito avesse fatto murare viva la duchessa in una parete del castello.
Legend has it that the Duchess was walled up alive in a wall of the castle.

2373 **cortile** - *nm* kortile | **courtyard, yard**
Io ho permesso a Tom di campeggiare nel nostro cortile.
I permitted Tom to camp in our backyard.

2374 **allenatore** - *nm* allenatore | **coach**
L'allenatore mi ha detto che avevo bisogno di esercitarmi più duramente.
The coach told me I needed to practice harder.

2375 **eliminare** - *verb* eliminare | **to eliminate**
Non eliminerei la possibilità di trasferirmi in un altro paese se ottenessi una buona offerta di lavoro.
I wouldn't rule out the possibility of moving to another country if I get a good job offer.

2376 **scudo** - *nm* skudo | **shield**
Telecamere a cupola fisse sono racchiusi in una cupola a forma di scudo.
Fixed dome cameras are enclosed in a dome-shaped shield.

2377 **sviluppo** - *nm* zviluppo | **development**
Lo sviluppo economico del dopoguerra delle nazioni vinte può essere rapido se non vengono saccheggiate dai vincitori. Per ciò ci sono due motivi.
The post-war economic development of vanquished nations can be rapid if they are not looted by the victors. For this there are two reasons.

2378 **autostrada** - *nf* autostrada | **motorway, highway**
Molte auto sfrecciano su questa autostrada notte e giorno.
A lot of cars speed by on this expressway day and night.

2379 **gettare** - *verb* dʒettare | **to throw**
Avevo un solo obiettivo quando ho gettato via ogni cosa per gestire questo ristorante.

I had only one aim in throwing everything away to run this restaurant.

2380 **elenco** - *nm* eleŋko

list, directory

Tom sta facendo un elenco di cose che devono essere fatte.

Tom is making a list of things that need to be done.

2381 **matematico** - *adj; nm* matematiko

mathematical; mathemactician

Non è piacevole vedere che un matematico più ferrato di me non riesce a spiegarsi chiaramente.

I don't like it when mathematicians who know much more than I do can't express themselves explicitly.

2382 **collegamento** - *nm* kollegamento

connection, link

Io ho dei collegamenti all'interno del governo.

I have connections in the government.

2383 **fucilare** - *verb* futʃilare

to shoot

Oggi ricorre il settantesimo anniversario dell'ordine di Stalin di fucilare più di 20 000 ufficiali dell'esercito polacco.

Today marks the 70thÂ anniversary of the issue of the order by Stalin to shoot over 20Â 000 Polish Army officers.

2384 **autorizzazione** - *nf* autoriddzattsjone

authorization

Hai la nostra autorizzazione a includere il nostro software a condizione che ci invii una copia del prodotto finale.

You have our permission to include our software on condition that you send us a copy of the final product.

2385 **aprile** - *nm* aprile

April

Gennaio, febbraio, marzo, aprile, maggio, giugno, luglio, agosto, settembre, ottobre, novembre e dicembre sono i dodici mesi dell'anno.

January, February, March, April, May, June, July, August, September, October, November and December are the twelve months of the year.

2386 **francamente** - *adv* fraŋkamente

frankly

Informi francamente chi sei e che ti piacerebbe incontrare.

Please tell frankly who you are and whom you'd like to meet.

2387 **insalata** - *nf* insalata

salad

A Tom piace il modo in cui Mary fa l'insalata di patate.

Tom likes the way Mary makes potato salad.

2388 **sepolto** - *adj* sepolto

buried

Si dice che ci sia un tesoro sepolto qua attorno.

It is said that there is a treasure buried around here.

2389 **sceneggiatura** - *nf*

screenplay

ʃeneddʒatura | Lei è diventata famosa dopo aver scritto la sceneggiatura di quel film.
She became famous after having written the screenplay for that movie.

2390 **diviso** - *adj* | **divided**
divizo | Ha diviso un milione di dollari tra i suoi cinque figli.
He divided one million dollars among his five sons.

2391 **classico** - *adj* | **classic**
klassiko | A proposito di musica classica, qual è il suo compositore preferito?
Talking of classical music, who is your favorite composer?

2392 **pessimo** - *adj* | **very bad, terrible**
pessimo | Il suo comportamento, per come mi ricordo, è stato pessimo.
His behavior, as I remember, was very bad.

2393 **spento** - *adj* | **off, turned off**
spento | Assicurati che le luci siano spente prima che tu vada.
Make sure that the lights are turned off before you leave.

2394 **cartello** - *nm* | **cartel, sign**
kartello | Non c'è nessun cartello che indica che questa è una sala riunioni.
There is no sign indicating that this is a meeting room.

2395 **scordare** - *verb* | **to forget**
skordare | Non riesco a trovare i miei occhiali. Potrei averli scordati sul treno.
I can't find my glasses. I may have left them behind on the train.

2396 **vacca** - *nf* | **cow**
vakka | Il latte di vacca è più saporito del latte di soia.
Cow's milk is tastier than soy milk.

2397 **ansia** - *nf* | **anxiety**
ansja | Abbiamo avuto parecchi momento di ansia, ma alla fine è andato tutto bene.
We had a good many anxious moments, but everything turned out all right in the end.

2398 **preside** - *nm* | **dean, principal**
prezide | Il trofeo è stato presentato al Preside di ogni scuola e sarò consegnato per la prima volta alla fine dell'anno scolastico corrente.

The trophy was presented to the Principal of each school and will be awarded for the first time at the end of this school year.

2399 **equilibrio** - *nm*
ekwilibrjo
equilibrium
La musica è in equilibrio con la struttura del film.
The music is in balance with the structure of the movie.

2400 **contenere** - *verb*
kontenere
to contain
Questa bottiglia è in grado di contenere due litri di acqua calda.
This bottle is able to contain two liters of hot water.

2401 **unghia** - *nf*
uŋgja
nail
Se ti mangi le unghie, prima o poi ti farai sanguinare le dita.
If you bite your fingernails, sooner or later you will make your fingers bleed.

2402 **fica (figa)** - *nf*
fika (figa)
fanny, pussy (both used: fanny,pussy, fig)
Secondo Vladimir Chizhov, la parola "figa" è indecente.
According to Vladimir Chizhov, the word "pussy" is indecent.

2403 **lusso** - *nm*
lusso
luxury
A quell'epoca, il pane bianco e la carne erano considerati un lusso.
At that time, white bread and meat were considered a luxury.

2404 **panare** - *verb*
panare
to bread, dip in breadcrumbs
Disporre i filetti di pesce nello stampo in porcellana unto e 3 coprirli con la panata.
Put the fillets of fish into the greased porcelain dish and spread 3 the breadcrumb coating over them.

2405 **metallo** - *nm*
metallo
metal
Tom mise i diamanti in una piccola scatola di metallo.
Tom put the diamonds in a small metal box.

2406 **personalità** - *nf*
personalit'a
personality
Lui non è un uomo che riesce a non manifestare la sua personalità.
He knows how to assert himself.

2407 **portafoglio** - *nm*
portafoʎʎo
portfolio, wallet
Tom ha preso dei soldi dal suo portafoglio e li ha dati a Maria.
Tom took some money out of his wallet and gave it to Mary.

2408 **canna** - *nf*
kanna
cane, barrel, rod
La canna da zucchero è un frutto o una verdura?

Is sugar cane a fruit or a vegetable?

2409 **pisciare** - *verb* pi∫∫are
to piss
Pisciare da seduti non è poi così male.
Peeing sitting down is not all that bad.

2410 **lavoratore** - *nm; adj* lavoratore
worker; hard-working
Tutti i lavoratori hanno un rapporto con un fornitore od un cliente.
Any employee has a relationship with a supplier or a custome.

2411 **spinto** - *adj* spinto
pushed
Diversi motivi hanno spinto ognuno di noi all'atteso appuntamento.
Various were the reasons that brought us together.

2412 **orrore** - *nm* orrore
dread, terror
Tom e Mary hanno deciso di andare a vedere un film dell'orrore.
Tom and Mary decided to go see a scary movie.

2413 **reato** - *nm* reato
crime
Quando uscii di prigione, non avevo intenzione di commettere un altro reato.
When I got out of jail, I had no intention of committing another crime.

2414 **riparare** - *verb* riparare
to repair
Tom mi ha dato il nome di un tizio che probabilmente riesce a riparare il mio orologio.
Tom gave me the name of a guy who can probably repair my watch.

2415 **comunicare** - *verb* komunikare
to communicate
Tom e Mary devono imparare a comunicare meglio tra di loro.
Tom and Mary need to learn to communicate with each other better.

2416 **pattugliare** - *verb* pattuʎʎare
to patrol
Il personale di sicurezza deve pattugliare queste aree quando sono aperte al pubblico.
Security staff shall patrol these areas when open to the public.

2417 **alieno** - *adj* aljeno
alien
Questo non è un alieno. È solo uno strano animale.
This is not an alien, it's just a strange animal.

2418 **curare** - *verb*
to treat

kurare

Questo capitolo illustra come riporre e curare la manutenzione del sistema così da poter godere delle sue prestazioni per numerosi anni a venire.

This chapter explains how to store and maintain your system so that it continues to give pleasure for many years to come.

2419 **testamento** - *nm*
testamento

will

Il patto successorio (come il testamento pubblico) è redatto da un pubblico ufficiale e sottoscritto alla presenza di due testimoni.

Like public wills, a testamentary contract is drawn up by a certifying officer and signed in the presence of two witnesses.

2420 **satana** - *nm*
satana

Satan

Bush non è il migliore amico di Satana. Lui non lo sa nemmeno chi è Satana.

Bush is not Satan's best friend. He doesn't even know who Satan is.

2421 **galleria** - *nf*
gallerja

gallery

Dopo una lunga ispezione, la galleria è stata riaperta al traffico.

After a lengthy inspection, the tunnel was reopened to traffic.

2422 **distintivo** - *adj*
distintivo

distinctive

Il Gruppo ha sempre considerato la solidità patrimoniale come un importante elemento distintivo nel panorama competitivo nazionale.

The Group has always considered its capital strength to be one of the most distinctive competitive factors in the national banking scene.

2423 **migliorare** - *verb*
miʎʎorare

to improve

Mentre ero intento a migliorare il mio modo di parlare, mi sono imbattuto in un libro di grammatica inglese.

While I was intent on improving my language skill, I came upon an English grammar book.

2424 **riuscita** - *nf*
rjuʃʃita

success

Il risultato dell'operazione apparirà su schermo in modo da controllare la riuscita dell'invio del lavoro.

The result of the operation will be displayed for you to check that the work has been sent successfully.

2425 **esecuzione** - *nf*

execution

ezekuttsjone

Durante l'esecuzione di un'operazione al cervello, sia i dottori che le infermiere devono trattare il paziente con cautela, senza sacrificare la velocità di esecuzione.

While a brain operation is being performed, both doctors and nurses must handle the patient with kid gloves and yet with all speed practical.

2426 **bicicletta (bici)** - *nf*
bitʃikletta (bitʃi)

bicycle, (bike)

Tom usa ancora la bicicletta che gli hanno dato i suoi genitori quando aveva tredici anni.

Tom still rides the bicycle that his parents gave him when he was thirteen years old.

2427 **scavare** - *verb*
skavare

to dig

Gli oritteropi sono incredibili! Possono scavare e nascondersi nella sporcizia in meno di un minuto!

Aardvarks are amazing! They can dig and hide in the dirt in less than one minute!

2428 **colloquio** - *nm*
kollokwjo

(job) interview, talk, meeting

Ho fatto qualche colloquio, però non ho mai ottenuto un impiego.

I had a few auditions, but never got a job.

2429 **elezione** - *nf*
elettsjone

election

La campagna elettorale ebbe successo e lei vinse le elezioni

The campaign succeeded and she won the election.

2430 **umorismo** - *nm*
umorismo

humor, sense of humor

Attraverso una particolare pedagogia, basata sull'umorismo e il gioco, il bambino avrà la possibilità di stimolare la propria sensibilità, curiosità e creatività.

The young children will have the opportunity to stimulate their sensitivity, curiosity and creativity via a particular educational approach based on humour and play.

2431 **percento** - *nm*
pertʃento

per cent

Da sei anni a questa parte per la prima volta il tasso di disoccupazione è scieso sotto il sei percento.

For the first time in more than 6 years, the unemployment rate is below 6%.

2432 **assistenza** - *nf*
assistentsa

assistance

Lui ha visitato un istituto per l'assistenza all'infanzia.

He visited a children's home in Texas.

2433 **patetico** - *adj*

pathetic

	patetiko	Jason non è un tizio cattivo, ma piuttosto un patetico perdente. *Jason is no bad guy, but rather a pitiable loser.*
2434	**muso** - *nm* muzo	**muzzle, nose, face** Un cavallo entra in un bar. Il barista gli chiede: "Come mai quel muso lungo?" *A horse walks into a bar. The bartender asks, "Why such a long face?"*
2435	**comprendere** - *verb* komprendere	**to understand** L'inglese è troppo difficile da comprendere per me. *English is too difficult for me to understand.*
2436	**spedire** - *verb* spedire	**to send** Quand'è stata l'ultima volta che hai spedito una lettera all'estero? *When was the last time you sent a letter abroad?*
2437	**fallimento** - *nm* fallimento	**failure, bankruptcy** A prima vista sembra che questa idea è destinata al fallimento. *At first sight it seems that this idea is doomed to fail.*
2438	**martello** - *nm* martello	**hammer** Questo è un martello. Non è mio; l'ho preso in prestito da un amico. *This is a hammer. It's not mine; I borrowed it from a friend.*
2439	**falsare** - *verb* falsare	**to distort** si cercava una tenuta per valvole che garantisse la vita utile più lunga possibile senza falsare il gusto delle bevande. *what was required was a valve seal which guarantees maximum service life and which does not adulterate the individual taste.*
2440	**assassinio** - *nm* assassinjo	**murder, assasination** Dopo l'assassinio, ebbero una conversazione intima. *After the murder, they had an intimate conversation.*
2441	**selvaggio** - *adj* selvaddʒo	**wild** Il cavallo selvaggio è stato finalmente domato dall'addestratore paziente. *The wild horse was finally broken by the patient trainer.*
2442	**industria** - *nf* industrja	**industry** L'oratore ritiene che le industrie cosmetiche si comportano sempre in modo etico.

The speaker believes that cosmetic industries always behave in an ethical way.

2443 **indizio** - *nm* indittsjo | **clue, indication**
L'assassino ha appena ucciso la quattordicesima vittima e siamo ancora senza indizi sulla sua identità.
The killer has just taken his fourteenth victim, and we still have no lead on his identity.

2444 **sorellina** - *nf* sorellina | **litte sister, younger sister, baby sister**
La mia sorellina dipinse un quadro di un pupazzo di neve.
My little sister painted a picture of a snowman.

2445 **appellare** - *verb* appellare | **to appeal**
Per vincere le elezioni devi appellarti all'opinione pubblica.
You must appeal to public opinion to win the election.

2446 **preda** - *nf* preda | **prey**
Come può un serpente a sonagli localizzare la preda e seguirla fra le erbe e i cespugli dopo averla ferita, se è del tutto sordo?
How can rattlesnakes localise their prey and track it through grass and bushes, after they wound it, if they're fully deaf?

2447 **guadagno** - *nm* gwadaɲɲo | **gain**
Ci stiamo assicurando che nessuno si stia approfittando del popolo americano per un proprio guadagno a breve termine
We're going to make sure that no one is taking advantage of the American people for their own short-term gain.

2448 **diversamente** - *adv* diversamente | **otherwise**
Se solo lo avessi conosciuto! Poi le cose sarebbero andate diversamente, e sarebbe meglio per lui ora.
If only you had known him! Then things would have turned out differently, and it would be better for him now.

2449 **disagio** - *nm* dizadʒo | **discomfort**
Mi sono sempre sentito a disagio in compagnia di mio padre.
I always felt ill at ease in my father's company.

2450 **prostituta** - *nf* prostituta | **prostitute**
Una certa ragazza era una prostituta, ma non voleva che sua nonna lo sapesse.
A certain girl was a prostitute but didn't want her grandma to know.

2451 **asso** - *nm* asso | **ace**
Tom voltò la carta e vide che era l'asso di spade.

Tom flipped over the card and saw that it was the ace of spades.

2452 **stadio** - *nm* stadjo

stadium, stage

Una grande luce si è diffusa sopra lo stadio di baseball.

A great light was diffused over the baseball stadium.

2453 **chiusa** - *nf* kjuza

close, lock, sluice

Se una strada lungo il percorso è chiusa, è possibile effettuare una deviazione.

If a road on your route is closed, you can take a detour.

2454 **ribelle** - *adj* ribelle

rebel

Per parlare di alcuni casi faremo l'esempio di Maria, una ragazza adolescente rumena, ribelle che non sopportava le regole della sua famiglia.

To show an example of one of the cases we can use that of Maria, a teenage Romanian girl, a rebel, who could not stand the rules laid down by her family.

2455 **serpente** - *nm* serpente

snake, serpent

Aveva la testa di donna, il corpo di leone, le ali di uccello, e la coda di serpente.

It had the head of a woman, the body of a lion, the wings of a bird, and the tail of a serpent.

2456 **giunto** - *nm; adj* dʒunto

joint, coupling; joined

Giunto a casa al № 46-48 di Oak Street, in centro; mi tolsi il cappotto ed i guanti e mi sedetti davanti alla finestra.

Joined at home 46-48 Oak street, down city, and took off coat and cloves.

2457 **perla** - *nf* perla

pearl

Ci si riferisce spesso alle Hawaii come "la perla del Pacifico".

Hawaii is often referred to as "The Pearl of the Pacific."

2458 **comandare** - *verb* komandare

to command

Non ho bisogno di lui e non mi aspetto niente da lui, e non mi faccio comandare da lui

I do not need him and I expect nothing from him and I do not allow myself to be commanded by him

2459 **mammina** - *nf* mammina

mummy

Amava l'eucaristia e chiamava la Vergine "mammina" e noi siamo certi che la Madonna lo stesse aspettando a braccia aperte.

He loved the Eucharist and called the Virgin "dear mother", and we are sure that Our Lady was waiting for him with open arms.

2460 **microfono** - *nm* mikrofono

microphone

Rileva automaticamente il rumore del vento (disturbo del vento) catturato dal microfono, e sopprime il suono se il vento è troppo forte.

With this mode, wind noise captured by the microphone can be detected and suppressed when it gets too loud.

2461 **poetare** - *verb* poetare

to poetize

Il poetare è, sempre secondo il nostro poeta, "la più innocente delle occupazioni".

Making verses, according to our poet, is "the most innocent of all occupations"

2462 **malvagio** - *adj* malvadʒo

evil, wicked

La principessa è stata catturata da un malvagio stregone.

The princess was captured by an evil wizard.

2463 **meta** - *nf* meta

goal, destination

La nostra meta non è mai un luogo, ma piuttosto un nuovo modo di vedere le cose.

One's destination is never a place but rather a new way of looking at things.

2464 **piovere** - *verb* pjovere

to rain

Da principio m'ero preparato per venire quest'oggi in spiaggia, ma ha cominciato a piovere all'improvviso.

I was planning on going to the beach today, but then it started to rain.

2465 **trasferimento** - *nm* trasferimento

transfer

Per il trasferimento del carico il pontile è attrezzato, sul lato destro, con tre bracci di scarico.

To unload the cargo, the right-hand side of the pier is equipped with three unloading arms.

2466 **stress** - *nm* stress

stress

Il mestiere di controllore aereo è un mestiere che procura enormemente dello stress.

Air traffic controller is an extremely high pressure job.

2467 **alt** - *int* alt

halt

Potete usare anche la scorciatoia da tastiera Ctrl+Alt+R.

You can also use the Ctrl+Alt+R keyboard shortcut.

2468 **scelto** - *adj*

chosen

ʃelto | Il loro arredamento è stato scelto per l'utilità piuttosto che per lo stile.

Their furniture was chosen for utility rather than style.

2469 **scopata** - *nf* — **sweep, fuck, shag**
skopata
"Ei, sei proprio una bella gnocca, perché non sali da me e non ci facciamo una bella scopata? "

"Hey, you're a beautiful chick, why don't you come to my place to get laid? "

2470 **radar** - *adj* — **radar**
radar
Il radar ottico funziona usando la luce, anziché le onde radio come il radar normale.

Optical radars use light, rather than radio waves as normal radars.

2471 **singolo** - *adj; nm* — **single**
siŋgolo
Google Translate non riesce a tradurre frasi o dare definizioni delle singole parole.

Google Translate can't translate phrases or give definitions of individual words.

2472 **carità** - *nf* — **charity**
karitˈa
La Chiesa non può mai essere dispensata dall'esercizio della carità come attività organizzata dei credenti.

The Church can never be exempted from practising charity as an organized activity of believers.

2473 **consigliere** - *nm* — **advisor, councilor**
konsiʎʎere
Mio padre ha ottenuto quello ed altro in quattro parole, il che ha fatto sì che citare Shakespeare risultasse tanto efficace quanto potrebbe desiderare qualunque consigliere d'affari.
My father achieved that and more in four words, which made quoting Shakespeare as effective as any business adviser could wish.

2474 **spasso** - *nm* — **fun**
spasso
Il tragitto da Rotenboden dura circa dai cinque ai dieci minuti ed è un vero spasso per persone di tutte le età.

he downhill toboggan journey from Rotenboden lasts between five and ten minutes – and is great fun for all ages.

2475 **promessa** - *nf* — **promise**
promessa
Ci sono circostanze in cui rompere una promessa o dire una bugia sono ammissibili.

There are conditions under which breaking a promise or telling a lie are acceptable.

2476 **cioccolata** - *nf* tʃokkolata

chocolate

Io non mangio della cioccolata da quando avevo tredici anni

I haven't eaten chocolate since I was thirteen.

2477 **affinché** - *conj* affiŋkˈe

so that, in order to

Dovemmo chiudere le finestre affinché non entrassero le zanzare.

We had to close the windows so that the mosquitoes wouldn't come in.

2478 **applauso** - *nm* applauzo

applause

L'applauso crebbe fino a un ruggito quando Pinocchio, il famoso asino, apparve nel circo.

The applause grew to a roar when Pinocchio, the famous donkey, appeared in the circus ring.

2479 **ritrattare** - *verb* ritrattare

to retract, recant

Gli oneri nucleari derivano principalmente dalla necessità di ritrattare o stoccare e infine smaltire il combustibile nucleare esaurito.

Nuclear liabilities arise primarily from the need to reprocess or store and ultimately dispose of spent nuclear fuel.

2480 **dicembre** - *nm* ditʃembre

December

Lui sarà di ritorno nell'arco di una settimana, vale a dire il 10 dicembre.

He will be back a week from today, that is, on December 10.

2481 **identificare** - *verb* identifikare

to identify

Il ragazzo che era scomparso è stato identificato dai suoi vestiti.

The boy who had been missing was identified by his clothes.

2482 **civiltà** - *nf* tʃiviltˈa

civilization

Tra gli esseri umani, la sottomissione delle donne è molto più completa ad un certo livello di civiltà di quello che è tra i selvaggi. E la sudditanza è sempre rinforzata dalla morale.

Among human beings, the subjection of women is much more complete at a certain level of civilisation than it is among savages. And the subjection is always reinforced by morality.

2483 **funzione** - *nf* funtsjone

function

È il modulo di iscrizione che non funziona o è la mia connessione a Internet che non funziona correttamente?

Is the entry form not working or is my Internet connection not working right?

2484 **incredibilmente** - *adv* iŋkredibilmente

incredibilmente

I prezzi scenderanno a livelli incredibilmente bassi.

Prices went to amazingly low levels.

2485 **valigetta** - *nf* validʒetta

briefcase

Non conservare il computer in un ambiente con ridotta ventilazione, come una custodia chiusa o una valigetta, mentre è in esecuzione.

Do not store your portable computer in a low-airflow environment, such as a carrying case or a closed briefcase, while the computer is turned on.

2486 **movimentare** - *verb* movimentare

to ship, move, handle

Movimentare ed appoggiare delicatamente il variatore nella zona adibita per lo scarico, avendo cura di non provocare brusche oscillazioni durante lo spostamento.

Move the speed variator to the unloading area and lower it gently into position, taking care not to cause sudden oscillations while moving it.

2487 **sostegno** - *nm* sosteɲɲo

support

Tycho Brahe ha beneficiato notevolmente del generoso sostegno di Re Fredrik.

Tycho Brahe benefited greatly from King Fredrik's generous support.

2488 **protetta** - *nf* protetta

protection

La famiglia è il nucleo naturale e fondamentale della società e ha diritto ad essere protetta dalla società e dallo Stato.

The family is the natural and fundamental group unit of society and is entitled to protection by society and the State.

2489 **movimentato** - *adj* movimentato

lively, busy

Ieri notte abbiamo avuto una festa movimentata. Abbiamo una serata movimentata davanti a noi.

We had a lively party last night. We have a busy evening ahead of us.

2490 **ingegnere** - *nm* indʒeɲɲere

engineer

Le sette domande che deve farsi un ingegnere sono: chi, cosa, quando, dove, perché, come e quanto.

The seven questions that an engineer has to ask himself are: who, what, when, where, why, how and how much.

2491 **autorizzare** - *verb*

to permit, authorize

autoriddzare

Addirittura alla fine del diciannovesimo secolo, i marinai della Marina Britannica non erano autorizzati ad usare coltelli o forchette, perché era considerato come un segno di debolezza.
Even at the end of the nineteenth century, sailors in the British Navy were not permitted to use knives and forks because using them was considered a sign of weakness.

2492 **targa** - *nf*
targa

plate, nameplate
Ha cambiato il numero di targa del suo veicolo.
He changed the number plate of his vehicle.

2493 **particolarmente** - *adv*
partikolarmente

particolarmente
Nel primo semestre del 2012 l'andamento delle vendite è stato particolarmente positivo in America e nell'area Resto del mondo e duty free.
Sales were particularly strong in the first half of 2012 in the Americas and the rest of the world and duty free.

2494 **considerazione** - *nf*
konsiderattsjone

consideration
La prima cosa che si deve prendere in considerazione è il tempo.
The first thing you have to take into consideration is time.

2495 **repubblica** - *nf*
repubblika

republic
Nella Repubblica Ceca, le organizzazioni coinvolte sono state due: il Ministero del Lavoro e degli Affari Sociali.
In the Czech Republic, the organisations involved were the Ministry of Labour and the one of Social Affairs

2496 **esperimento** - *nm*
esperimento

experiment
Dopo anni di esperimenti falliti, posso dire di aver finalmente scoperto l'unico, assolutamente infallibile, rimedio istantaneo contro il singhiozzo!
After years of failed experiments, I can say I've finally discovered the only and absolutely flawless, instant cure for hiccups!

2497 **lavare** - *verb*
lavare

to wash
Estrarre elettrodo e sonda di temperatura dalla soluzione tampone, lavare accuratamente il tutto in acqua corrente.
Remove the electrode and the temperature probe from the buffer solution and wash them accurately with running water.

2498 **cucciolo** - *nm*

puppy

kuttʃolo "Che cucciolo carino. Perché si chiama Panda?" "Perché il suo volto assomiglia a un panda."

"What a cute puppy. Why is he called Panda?" "Because his face looks like a panda."

2499 **muscolo** - *nm* **muscolo**
muskolo Il muscolo più largo nel corpo umano è il gluteus maximus.
The largest muscle in the human body is the gluteus maximus.

2500 **udienza** - *nf* **hearing, audience**
udjentsa Si rifiutò di ricevere 4.000 cattolici tradizionalisti di tutto il mondo, ma ricevette in udienza, invece, un gruppo di Rabbini Talmudici e il Patriarca dei Bonzi.

He refused to receive 4,000 traditional Catholics from around the
world, but received at an audience, however, a group of Talmudic Rabbis and the Patriarch of the Bonzes.

2501 **riflettere** - *verb* **to reflect**
riflettere Riflettete sulle vostre benedizioni presenti - di cui ogni uomo ne ha molte - non sulle disgrazie del passato, di cui tutti gli uomini ne hanno un po'.

Reflect upon your present blessings — of which every man has many — not on your past misfortunes, of which all men have some.

A. Adjectives

Rank	Italian - *Part of Speech*	English
2	**che** - *conj; pron; adj*	that; which, who; what
24	**questo** - *adj; pron*	this; such, this one
26	**bene** - *adj; adv; nm*	very; well, good; good, asset
31	**solo** - *adj*	only
34	**più** - *adj; adv*	more, most
36	**ne** - *adj; pron*	any; of it, of them
39	**fatto** - *nm; adj*	fact, event; made, done
52	**molto** - *adv; adj*	very, much
58	**tuo** - *adj*	your
64	**primo** - *num; adj*	first
66	**due** - *adj; num*	two
81	**certo** - *adj; adv*	certain; of course;
91	**altro** - *adj; pron*	other, another, more
95	**proprio** - *adj; nm; pron; adv*	one's own; own; its; just, exactly
104	**nessuno** - *adj; pron*	no; nobody, no one, none, anyone
117	**ogni** - *adj*	every
124	**qualche** - *adj; pron*	to displeasure, dislike, be sorry
129	**grande** - *adj*	great, great
139	**tre** - *adj; num*	three
143	**nuovo** - *adj*	new
158	**giusto** - *adj; adv*	right, just, fair; correctly
166	**bello (bel)** - *adj; nm/f*	nice,beautiful; handsome, hunk/ beautiful woman
169	**sicuro** - *adj*	sure, safe, secure
179	**morto** - *adj*	dead, died
181	**pronto** - *adj; adv*	ready
182	**buono** - *adj; nm*	good; voucher, coupon
187	**stesso** - *adj; pron*	same; itself
201	**fino** - *prep; adv; adj*	till; even; fine, subtle
212	**fine** - *nm; nf; adj*	purpose; end; fine
213	**secondo** - *prep; nm; adv; adj*	according to; second
217	**piano** - *nm; adj*	plan, floor, piano; plane, flat
219	**meno** - *adv; adj; prep; conj*	less; less; unless; no so (much as)
222	**quale** - *adj; pron; conj*	what, which; which; as
229	**salvo** - *prep; adj*	save, but; safe
240	**nessun** - *adj*	no
242	**minuto** - *adj; nm*	minute
243	**finito** - *adj*	finished, over
249	**piccolo** - *adj*	little, small
252	**forte** - *adj; nm; adv*	strong; forte; loudly
253	**bravo** - *adj; nm*	good, fine, clever; bravo
261	**felice** - *adj*	happy
262	**vecchio** - *adj; nm/f*	old; old (wo)man
267	**dietro** - *prep; nm; adj; adv*	behind; back, rear; after; after
270	**importante** - *adj*	important
274	**poco** - *adj; adv; nm*	little; a litte, not much; bit
277	**migliore** - *adj*	best
278	**quattro** - *adj; num*	four
280	**cinque** - *adj; num*	five
290	**possibile** - *adj*	possible
292	**vicino** - *adj; adv*	close, near
297	**ultimo** - *adj*	last, latest
313	**serio** - *adj*	serious

314	**mezzo** - *nm; adj*	half, middle, means; half, middle
316	**difficile** - *adj*	difficult
323	**strano** - *adj*	strange
334	**davanti** - *adj; adv; prep*	front; in front
351	**vivo** - *adj*	alive, live
352	**andato** - *adj*	gone
358	**unico** - *adj*	alone, single, unique
360	**fantastico** - *adj*	fantastic
366	**caro** - *adj; nm*	dear, expensive; dear
370	**facile** - *adj*	easy
371	**giovane** - *adj*	young
372	**divertente** - *adj*	funny, humorous
373	**generale** - *adj; nm*	general
376	**lungo** - *prep; adj; nm*	long; along; length
377	**gran** - *adj*	great
378	**esatto** - *adj*	exact
384	**scritto** - *adj*	written
387	**attento** - *adj*	careful
391	**chiaro** - *adj*	clear; light
392	**lontano** - *adj*	far
394	**pazzo** - *adj*	crazy
397	**perfetto** - *adj*	perfect
398	**sbagliato** - *adj*	mistaken, incorrect, wrong
399	**dieci** - *adj; num*	ten
401	**stupido** - *adj*	stupid
405	**prossimo** - *adj*	next
406	**alcuni** - *pron; adj*	some, several; few, any
407	**fermo** - *adj; nm*	still, firm; stop, arrest
417	**milione** - *adj; num*	million
424	**zitto** - *adj*	silent, quiet
429	**idiota** - *adj; nmf*	idiotic, stupid; idiot
442	**alto** - *adj*	high, tall
447	**deciso** - *adj*	decided
451	**fondo** - *nm; adj*	background, bottom, fund; deep
459	**qualunque** - *adj*	any
460	**futuro** - *adj*	future
469	**semplice** - *adj*	simple
471	**brutto** - *adj; nm*	ugly, bad, nasty; bad, ugliness
473	**speciale** - *adj*	special
479	**incidente** - *nm; adj*	accident, incident; incident
480	**radio** - *adj; nm*	radio
481	**aereo** - *adj; nm*	air, aerial; plane, airplane
485	**ottimo** - *adj*	excellent
486	**solito** - *adj; nm*	usual
491	**gentile** - *adj*	kind, gentle
495	**incredibile** - *adj*	unbelievable
498	**spesso** - *adv; adj*	often; thick
499	**entrambi** - *adj*	both, either
500	**veloce** - *adj*	fast, quick
504	**provato** - *adj*	tried
508	**sette** - *adj; num*	seven
510	**pieno** - *adj*	full
514	**grosso** - *adj*	big, thick
516	**freddo** - *adj*	cold
518	**santo** - *adj; nm/f*	holy; saint
519	**libero** - *adj*	free
529	**sinistro** - *adj*	left
531	**scoperto** - *adj; nm*	uncovered, open, bare; overdraft
542	**terribile** - *adj*	terrible
544	**otto** - *adj; num*	eight
545	**pubblico** - *adj*	public
548	**tranquillo** - *adj*	quiet
550	**destro** - *adj*	right

552	**nero** - *adj*	black
553	**mille** - *adj*	one thousand
554	**diritto** - *nm; adj; adv*	right, law; straight; straight
556	**peggio** - *adj*	worse
560	**diverso** - *adj*	different
562	**impossibile** - *adj*	impossible
570	**governo** - *nm; adj*	government; governmental
572	**normale** - *adj*	normal, regular
574	**sorpreso** - *adj*	surprised
578	**chiuso** - *adj*	closed
582	**san** - *adj*	St., saint
584	**duro** - *adj*	hard
589	**personale** - *adj*	staff
592	**interessante** - *adj*	interesting
596	**caldo** - *adj; nm*	hot; heat
601	**dolce** - *adj; nm*	sweet, fresh; sweet, dessert
603	**lunare** - *adj*	lunar, moon
605	**medico** - *adj*	(medical) doctor
611	**inglese** - *adj; nmf*	English; English(wo)man
623	**simile** - *adj*	similar, alike
634	**contento** - *adj*	happy
646	**bianco** - *adj*	white
656	**leggero** - *adj*	light
667	**necessario** - *adj*	necessary
668	**umano** - *adj*	human
669	**rosso** - *adj*	red
674	**rubato** - *adj*	stolen
675	**carino** - *adj*	cute, nice, pretty
683	**benvenuto** - *adj; int; nm*	welcome
690	**triste** - *adj*	sad
705	**pericoloso** - *adj*	dangerous
714	**povero** - *adj; nm*	poor; the poor
729	**nemico** - *adj; nm*	enemy
738	**reale** - *adj*	real, actual
743	**aperto** - *adj*	open
745	**nove** - *adj; num*	nine
749	**intero** - *adj; nm*	entire, full, whole; whole
763	**ufficiale** - *adj; nm*	official
766	**animale** - *nm; adj*	animal
772	**francese** - *adj*	French
776	**americano** - *adj; nm/f*	American; American
786	**scorso** - *adj*	last
792	**alcun** - *adj*	any
794	**inutile** - *adj*	useless, unnecessary
807	**intelligente** - *adj*	intelligent, clever, smart
808	**blu** - *adj*	blue
812	**fortunato** - *adj*	lucky
818	**stanco** - *adj*	tired
826	**interno** - *adj; nm*	internal; interior, inside
835	**meraviglioso** - *adj*	wonderful
836	**pago** - *adj*	content, statisfied
841	**grave** - *adj*	serious, severe
846	**comune** - *adj; nm*	common; community, town
851	**terzo** - *adj; nm*	third
852	**massimo** - *adj; nm*	maximum
853	**miglior** - *adj*	best
854	**buio** - *adj; nm*	dark; dark
856	**matto** - *adj; nm*	crazy; madman
858	**cellulare** - *adj*	cell phone
861	**corto** - *adj*	short
872	**responsabile** - *adj; nm*	responsible; person in charge
873	**enorme** - *adj*	huge
874	**ex** - *adj; nmf*	former; ex
879	**verde** - *adj*	green
882	**locale** - *adj; nm*	local; club
895	**dubbio** - *adj; nm*	doubtful; doubt

899	**malato** - *adj*	ill, sick
903	**orribile** - *adj*	horrible
906	**portato** - *adj*	brought
910	**capace** - *adj*	capable, able
911	**calmo** - *adj*	calm
933	**basso** - *adj; nm*	low, bottom, lower; bass
943	**incinta** - *adj*	pregnant
947	**continuo** - *adj*	continuous
948	**mosso** - *adj*	blurred, rough, wavy, moved
953	**centrale** - *adj; nf*	central; main office, (nuclear) power station
957	**video** - *adj*	video
967	**torto** - *adj*	injustice
971	**particolare** - *adj*	particular
973	**campione** - *nm; adj*	sample, champion; champion
975	**politico** - *adj; nm*	political; politician
976	**colpevole** - *adj*	guilty
979	**utile** - *adj; nm*	helpful, useful; profit
982	**dato** - *adj; nm*	given; fact, datum
983	**ridicolo** - *adj*	ridiculous
995	**magnifico** - *adj*	magnificent
997	**ubriaco** - *adj*	drunk
998	**mentito** - *adj*	false, deceptive
1001	**principale** - *adj*	main
1013	**naturale** - *adj*	natural
1019	**cento** - *adj; num*	hundred
1023	**militare** - *adj; nm*	military; soldier
1025	**convinto** - *adj*	convinced
1026	**innocente** - *nm; adj*	innocent
1027	**finale** - *adj; nm/f*	final; final, ending, finish/final (sports)
1029	**innamorato** - *adj; nm*	in love; lover
1030	**breve** - *adj*	short
1033	**improvviso** - *adj*	sudden
1039	**preoccupato** - *adj*	worried
1040	**ricco** - *adj*	rich
1056	**paziente** - *adj; nm&f*	patient
1059	**debole** - *adj*	weak
1064	**vissuto** - *adj*	lived
1066	**cattivo** - *adj; nm/f*	bad; baddie, bad person
1067	**cinese** - *adj; nmf*	Chinese
1071	**preferito** - *adj*	favorite
1073	**dritto** - *adj; adv*	straight, upright; right
1074	**ferito** - *adj*	injured
1077	**sposato** - *adj*	married
1078	**migliaio** - *adj; num*	thousand
1083	**vuoto** - *adj*	empty
1089	**smesso** - *adj*	stopped
1096	**amato** - *adj*	beloved
1097	**motore** - *adj; nm*	motor; enginge, motor
1099	**ladro** - *adj*	thief
1105	**zero** - *adj; num*	zero
1107	**potente** - *adj*	powerful
1109	**famoso** - *adj*	famous
1121	**tedesco** - *adj, nm/f*	German; German
1122	**doppio** - *adj*	double
1124	**sei** - *adj; num*	six
1130	**medio** - *adj*	average, medium, middle
1131	**grandioso** - *adj*	great
1133	**nazionale** - *adj*	national
1138	**pesante** - *adj*	heavy
1139	**quarto** - *adj; num; nm*	fourth; quarter
1141	**assistente** - *adj; nm&f*	assistant; assistant
1142	**scemo** - *adj*	fool

1147	**passato** - *adj*	past
1151	**legale** - *adj; nm*	legal; lawyer
1152	**sveglio** - *adj*	awake
1153	**nervoso** - *adj*	nervous
1155	**preso** - *adj*	took
1170	**diretto** - *adj*	direct
1178	**pulito** - *adj*	clean, clean
1186	**venti** - *adj; num*	twenty
1189	**carico** - *adj*	load, freight
1196	**amante** - *nm&f; adj*	lover; fond
1199	**superiore** - *adj*	higher, superior
1206	**profondo** - *adj*	deep
1213	**mancato** - *adj*	failed, unsuccessful
1219	**deserto** - *adj; nm*	desert (food); desert
1240	**privato** - *adj; nm*	private; personal life, privacy
1243	**sospetto** - *adj; nm*	suspected, suspicious; suspicion
1254	**russo** - *adj; nm/f*	Russian; Russian
1257	**sporco** - *adj*	dirty, soiled
1260	**completo** - *adj; nm*	complete, full; suit
1262	**bugiardo** - *adj*	liar
1277	**totale** - *adj; nm*	total
1278	**largo** - *adj*	wide, large, loose
1290	**assurdo** - *adj*	absurd
1293	**ovvio** - *adj*	obvious
1299	**ebreo** - *adj; nm*	Jewish, Jew
1303	**mondiale** - *adj*	world
1306	**cieco** - *adj*	blind
1311	**comodo** - *adj*	comfortable
1321	**criminale** - *adj nm&f*	criminal; criminal
1330	**amaro** - *adj; nm*	bitter; bitter, tonic liqour
1333	**minimo** - *adj*	minimum
1342	**parecchio** - *adv; adj*	a lot of, several; some
1349	**falso** - *adj*	false
1353	**marino** - *adj; nf*	marine, sea; marina, marine, navy
1356	**centinaio** - *adj; num*	hundred
1359	**giapponese** - *adj*	Japanese
1370	**lieto** - *adj*	happy
1390	**tagliato** - *adj*	cut
1394	**morale** - *adj*	moral
1396	**onesto** - *adj*	honest
1403	**fallito** - *adj*	failed
1412	**materiale** - *adj; nm*	material
1424	**maschio** - *adj; nm*	male
1425	**terreno** - *nm; adj*	ground, soil; earthly
1428	**modello** - *adj*	model
1441	**sciocco** - *adj*	silly
1450	**negro** - *adj; nm*	black, negro; negro, nigger
1451	**esperto** - *adj*	expert
1464	**eccellente** - *adj*	excellent
1467	**toccato** - *adj*	touched
1470	**sufficiente** - *adj*	enough, sufficient
1474	**folle** - *adj*	crazy
1484	**presente** - *adj; nm*	this, present; present
1487	**spagnolo** - *adj; nm/f*	Spanish; Spaniard
1494	**originale** - *adj; nm*	original
1497	**esterno** - *adj; nm*	external, outside, out; outside, exterior
1514	**furbo** - *adj*	sly, cunning
1517	**straordinario** - *adj*	extraordinary; overtime
1518	**miliardo** - *adj; num*	billion

1522	**splendido** - *adj*	wonderful
1524	**simpatico** - *adj*	nice, sympathetic
1532	**contante** - *adj; nm*	cash
1538	**piacevole** - *adj*	pleasant
1541	**imbecille** - *nm; adj*	imbecile
1542	**sociale** - *adj*	social
1543	**italiano** - *adj; nm*	Italian
1551	**precedente** - *adj; nm*	previous, preceding; precedent
1566	**vergine** - *adj; nf*	virgin
1572	**stupendo** - *adj*	wonderful
1573	**continuato** - *adj*	continued
1580	**svelto** - *adj*	quick, brisk, fast
1581	**super** - *adj*	super
1583	**grasso** - *adj*	fat
1585	**sessuale** - *adj*	sexual
1589	**crudele** - *adj*	cruel
1590	**studiato** - *adj*	studied
1598	**civile** - *adj; nm*	civil; civilian
1600	**fiero** - *adj*	proud
1601	**lindo** - *adj*	clean, neat
1602	**dodici** - *adj; num*	twelve
1605	**puro** - *adj*	pure
1620	**preciso** - *adj*	precise
1623	**nobile** - *adj*	noble
1626	**coraggioso** - *adj*	courageous
1635	**apposta** - *adj*	on purpose
1642	**recente** - *adj*	recent
1652	**figurato** - *adj*	figurative
1660	**adatto** - *adj*	suitable
1661	**parlato** - *adj*	spoken
1678	**brillante** - *adj; nm*	brilliant, bright; diamond
1680	**federale** - *adj*	federal
1681	**sorgere** - *adj*	to arise, rise
1683	**uniforme** - *adj*	uniform
1698	**urgente** - *adj*	urgent
1705	**volante** - *nm; adj*	steering wheel; flying
1708	**junior** - *adj*	junior
1716	**disgustoso** - *adj*	disgusting
1719	**dimentico** - *adj*	oblivious
1723	**regale** - *adj*	kingly
1730	**fresco** - *adj*	fresh, cool
1758	**cretino** - *adj; nm*	stupid; cretin
1764	**perduto** - *adj*	lost
1770	**professionista** - *adj; nm&f; nm*	professional; professional; expert
1772	**orgoglioso** - *adj*	proud
1774	**negativo** - *adj*	negative
1785	**girato** - *adj*	endorsed, turned (moved around axis), shot (movie)
1788	**imbarazzante** - *adj*	embarrassing
1791	**eccitante** - *adj; nm*	exciting; stimulate, upper
1794	**cavo** - *nm; adj*	cable, wire; hollow
1795	**salutare** - *adj; verb*	healthy; to greet, say goodbye to
1800	**attraente** - *adj*	attractive
1803	**florido** - *adj*	florid
1811	**armato** - *adj*	armed
1813	**eccezionale** - *adj*	exceptional, outstanding
1818	**traditore** - *adj; nm*	treacherousl.; traitor
1823	**nudo** - *adj*	naked
1829	**accetto** - *adj*	acceptable
1832	**curioso** - *adj*	curious
1841	**antico** - *adj*	ancient
1843	**clinico** - *adj*	clinical
1848	**probabile** - *adj*	likely
1852	**familiare** - *adj*	familiar
1858	**romantico** - *adj*	romantic
1863	**arabo** - *adj; nm/f*	Arabic; Arab

1864	**indiano** - *adj; nm/f*	Indian; Indian
1877	**geloso** - *adj*	jealous
1884	**adorabile** - *adj*	adorable
1887	**fedele** - *adj*	faithful
1890	**reverendo** - *adj*	reverend
1892	**perso** - *adj*	lost
1893	**geniale** - *adj*	ingenious
1894	**pazzesco** - *adj*	crazy
1897	**patrio** - *adj*	patrio
1899	**grato** - *adj*	grateful
1911	**fisico** - *adj; nm*	physical (fisica= physics)
1913	**illegale** - *adj*	illegal
1914	**accorto** - *adj*	shrewd
1921	**giallo** - *adj*	yellow
1924	**sacro** - *adj*	sacred
1928	**centesimo** - *adj; nm*	hundredth; cent
1932	**affetto** - *nm; adj*	affection, love; affected
1938	**preparato** - *adj; nm*	prepared; specimen, compound
1939	**schifoso** - *adj*	lousy (fa schifo= it sucks)
1949	**combattuto** - *adj*	hard-fought
1950	**positivo** - *adj*	positive
1953	**ideale** - *adj; nm*	ideal; ideal
1974	**nucleare** - *adj*	nuclear
1983	**stufo** - *adj*	fed up, sick and tired
1984	**gigante** - *adj*	giant
1992	**noioso** - *adj*	boring
2001	**informato** - *adj*	informed
2010	**noto** - *adj*	known
2023	**elegante** - *adj*	elegant
2026	**disponibile** - *adj*	available
2028	**secco** - *adj*	dry
2032	**guerriero** - *adj*	warrior
2033	**femminile** - *adj*	female
2040	**vincitore** - *adj*	winner
2044	**shock (choc)** - *adj*	shock
2045	**coperto** - *adj*	covered
2051	**mortale** - *adj; adv*	mortal; deadly, fatal; deathly
2059	**tecnico** - *adj; nm*	technical; technician
2061	**sconosciuto** - *adj; nm*	unknown; stranger, unkown
2071	**delizioso** - *adj*	delicious
2075	**quindici** - *adj; num*	fifteen
2078	**straniero** - *adj; nm/f*	foreign, alien; foreigner
2082	**elettrico** - *adj*	electric, electrical
2083	**bionda** - *nf/m; adj*	blonde
2084	**infelice** - *adj*	unhappy
2095	**stretto** - *adj; nm*	strict, strait; narrow
2097	**internazionale** - *adj*	international
2107	**eterno** - *adj*	eternal
2111	**ragionevole** - *adj*	reasonable
2118	**mentale** - *adj*	mental
2122	**orario** - *nm; adj*	time, hours, timetable; hourly
2138	**adulto** - *adj*	adult
2152	**trenta** - *adj*	thirty
2157	**giurato** - *adj; nm*	swon; juror
2159	**sordo** - *adj*	deaf
2163	**magico** - *adj*	magical
2166	**temporale** - *adj; nm*	temporal; (thunder) storm
2174	**capitale** - *adj*	capital
2179	**concentrato** - *adj*	concentrated
2180	**occupato** - *adj*	busy
2182	**oscuro** - *adj*	dark, obscure
2192	**sommo** - *adj*	highest
2198	**mobile** - *adj; nm*	mobile; furniture
2203	**sito** - *adj*	place, website

2207	**missile** - *adj*	missile
2209	**altrettanto** - *adv; adj; pron*	as; as much; just as many
2211	**vario** - *adj*	various, varied
2215	**evidente** - *adj*	evident
2220	**vigliacco** - *adj*	coward
2221	**assicurato** - *adj*	secured, assured, insured
2223	**manuale** - *adj; nm*	manual
2226	**popolare** - *adj; verb*	populair; to populate
2228	**nascosto** - *adj*	hidden
2229	**franco** - *adj; nm*	frank, free; franc
2234	**sesto** - *adj; num*	sixth
2240	**commerciale** - *adj*	commercial, trade
2241	**sodo** - *adj*	hard
2243	**nuvoloso** - *adj*	overcast, cloudy
2244	**codardo** - *adj; nm/f*	cowardly; coward
2248	**sofferto** - *adj*	suffered
2253	**sospeso** - *adj*	suspended
2254	**undici** - *adj; num*	eleven
2255	**motorio** - *adj*	motor
2256	**assoluto** - *adj*	absolute
2257	**prezioso** - *adj*	precious
2259	**presso** - *prep; adv; adj*	at,in; near; close
2262	**condotto** - *adj; nm*	conducted; duct, conduit, canal
2263	**professionale** - *adj*	professional
2267	**mollo** - *adj*	soaked, flabby
2274	**quinto** - *adj; num*	fifth
2276	**porno** - *adj; nm*	porn
2289	**bruno** - *adj*	brown, dark
2296	**comunista** - *adj; nm*	communist
2297	**attuale** - *adj*	current
2300	**extra** - *adj*	extra
2312	**complesso** - *adj; nm*	complex, whole; complex
2316	**violento** - *adj*	violent
2319	**ciascuno** - *adj; pron*	each, all, every; everyone, everybody
2324	**controllato** - *adj*	checked
2326	**tipico** - *adj*	typical
2327	**spaventoso** - *adj*	frightening, scary
2329	**egoista** - *adj; nm*	selfish; egoist
2331	**disperato** - *adj*	desperate
2332	**spiritoso** - *adj*	humorous
2334	**contadino** - *adj*	farmer
2335	**minore** - *adj*	less, minor, lower, lesser, smaller
2336	**sensibile** - *adj*	sensible
2342	**infinito** - *adj*	Infinity
2345	**operaio** - *nm; adj*	worker; working, labouring
2356	**generoso** - *adj*	generous
2357	**vietato** - *adj*	forbidden
2361	**impiegato** - *adj*	office worker, employee
2362	**standard** - *adj*	standard
2363	**dispiaciuto** - *adj*	sorry
2369	**invisibile** - *adj*	invisible
2381	**matematico** - *adj; nm*	mathematical; mathemactician
2388	**sepolto** - *adj*	buried
2390	**diviso** - *adj*	divided
2391	**classico** - *adj*	classic
2392	**pessimo** - *adj*	very bad, terrible
2393	**spento** - *adj*	off, turned off
2410	**lavoratore** - *nm; adj*	worker; hard-working
2411	**spinto** - *adj*	pushed
2417	**alieno** - *adj*	alien
2422	**distintivo** - *adj*	distinctive
2433	**patetico** - *adj*	pathetic
2441	**selvaggio** - *adj*	wild
2454	**ribelle** - *adj*	rebel

2456 **giunto** - *nm; adj* joint, coupling; joined

2462 **malvagio** - *adj* evil, wicked

2468 **scelto** - *adj* chosen

2470 **radar** - *adj* radar

2471 **singolo** - *adj; nm* single

2489 **movimentato** - *adj* lively, busy

B. Adverbs

Rank	Italian - *Part of Speech*	English
1	**non** - *adv*	not, non
18	**no** - *adv*	no, not
25	**qui** - *adv; conj*	here; where
26	**bene** - *adj; adv; nm*	very; well, good; good, asset
32	**tutto** - *adv; nm*	all
34	**più** - *adj; adv*	more, most
38	**quando** - *adv; conj*	when
40	**perché** - *conj; adv*	because, why; why
42	**ora** - *adv; conj; nf*	now; now; now, time, hour
45	**mai** - *adv*	never
48	**così** - *adv; conj*	so, thus; that
51	**anche** - *adv; nf*	also, even; anchor
52	**molto** - *adv; adj*	very, much
57	**dove** - *adv*	where
59	**allora** - *adv*	then
62	**prima** - *adv; art*	first, before; before
67	**ancora** - *adv; conj*	to displeasure, dislike, be sorry
69	**fa** - *adv*	ago
72	**su** **sul, sullo, sulll', sulla, sui, sugli, sulle - adv; prep*	on,up; on, about
74	**sempre** - *adv*	always
76	**vi** - *pron; adv*	you; there
81	**certo** - *adj; adv*	certain; of course;
84	**forse** - *adv*	perhaps
85	**adesso** - *adv*	now
86	**fuori** - *adv*	out, outside
88	**davvero** - *adv*	really
90	**poi** - *adv*	then
93	**via** - *prep; adv; nf*	via, by; away; street, way
95	**proprio** - *adj; nm; pron; adv*	one's own; own; its; just, exactly
102	**quanto** - *adv; conj*	as, how much; than
106	**dopo** - *prep; adv*	after
111	**già** - *adv*	already
112	**meglio** - *adv*	better, best
119	**ecco** - *adv*	here
122	**male** - *adv; nm*	bad, evil
123	**troppo** - *adv*	too much
126	**tanto** - *adv*	much, so
133	**quindi** - *adv*	then
149	**oggi** - *adv; nm*	today
158	**giusto** - *adj; adv*	right, just, fair; correctly
160	**avanti** - *adv*	forward, ahead, on
162	**subito** - *adv*	immediately, at once
167	**lì** - *adv*	there
174	**appena** - *adv*	just, (as) soon (as)
175	**sotto** - *adv; prep*	under, below; under
181	**pronto** - *adj; adv*	ready
183	**presto** - *adv*	soon, early
190	**insieme** - *adv; nm*	together; set, whole
194	**domani** - *adv; nm*	tomorrow
200	**qua** - *adv*	here
201	**fino** - *prep; adv; adj*	till; even; fine, subtle
213	**secondo** - *prep; nm; adv; adj*	according to; second
219	**meno** - *adv; adj; prep; conj*	less; less; unless; no so (much as)

221	**neanche** - *adv; conj*	not even, neither; not even
224	**là** - *adv*	there
228	**quasi** - *adv*	almost, nearly
236	**indietro** - *adv*	back
237	**contro** - *adv; prep*	against, counter; against, versus
241	**abbastanza** - *adv*	enough
245	**tardi** - *adv*	late
246	**veramente** - *adv*	really
251	**nemmeno** - *adv; conj*	not even, neither
252	**forte** - *adj; nm; adv*	strong; forte; loudly
254	**giù** - *adv*	down
256	**comunque** - *adv; conj*	anyway; though
267	**dietro** - *prep; nm; adj; adv*	behind; back, rear; after; after
268	**invece** - *adv*	instead
274	**poco** - *adj; adv; nm*	little; a litte, not much; bit
281	**almeno** - *adv*	at least
283	**però** - *conj; adv*	but, yet; however
292	**vicino** - *adj; adv*	close, near
298	**qual** - *adv; pron*	everytime, whenever; what, which
302	**pure** - *adv*	also
317	**sopra** - *adv; prep*	above, on
320	**ieri** - *adv; nm*	yesterday
327	**magari** - *adv*	maybe, perhaps, even
331	**qualsiasi** - *adv*	any
334	**davanti** - *adj; adv; prep*	front; in front
342	**sacco** - *nm; adv*	bag, sack; a lot
379	**probabilmente** - *adv*	probably
389	**esattamente** - *adv*	exactly
416	**benissimo** - *adv*	very well, fine
421	**soltanto** - *adv*	only, solely
427	**durante** - *prep; adv*	during, in, over; while
454	**ormai** - *adv*	by now, almost, by then
455	**piuttosto** - *adv*	rather, quite, pretty
456	**oltre** - *adv; prep*	over; over, more than, beyond
458	**circa** - *adv; prep*	about
483	**finalmente** - *adv*	finally
484	**assolutamente** - *adv*	absolutely
498	**spesso** - *adv; adj*	often; thick
501	**intorno** - *adv*	around, round
530	**completamente** - *adv*	completely
538	**laggiù** - *adv*	over there, down there
554	**diritto** - *nm; adj; adv*	right, law; straight; straight
559	**stanotte** - *adv*	tonight
579	**manco** - *adv*	even, not even (with negative verb form)
594	**altrimenti** - *adv; conj*	otherwise
604	**semplicemente** - *adv*	simply
614	**attraverso** - *adv; prep*	through, across
616	**perciò** - *conj; adv*	therefore; accordingly
632	**naturalmente** - *adv*	naturally
637	**insomma** - *adv*	in short
657	**cioè** - *adv*	i.e., that is, namely
660	**certamente** - *adv*	of course

676	**dunque** - *adv*	therefore
695	**affatto** - *adv*	at all, quite
724	**ovunque** - *adv*	everywhere, whereever
727	**tale** - *adv; pron; art*	such; such; a, an
730	**ovviamente** - *adv*	obviously
736	**sicuramente** - *adv*	certainly
801	**immediatamente** - *adv*	immediately
815	**accanto** - *adv*	next
842	**infatti** - *adv*	indeed
859	**soprattutto** - *adv*	mostly
867	**persino** - *adv*	even
894	**chissà** - *int; adv*	who knows!; perhaps
923	**dappertutto** - *adv*	everywhere
935	**stavolta** - *adv*	this time
954	**lassù** - *adv*	up there, above, yonder
963	**domattina** - *adv*	tomorrow morning
964	**anzi** - *adv*	rather
972	**inoltre** - *adv*	sample, champion; champion
1028	**purtroppo** - *adv*	unfortunately
1050	**po' (pò)** - *adv*	bit
1073	**dritto** - *adj; adv*	straight, upright; right
1136	**neppure** - *adv; conj*	not even, neither
1161	**solamente** - *adv*	only
1162	**nonostante** - *prep; conj; adv*	despite; altough; even though, nevertheless
1168	**direttamente** - *adv*	directly
1209	**perfettamente** - *adv*	perfectly
1216	**pur** - *adv*	while
1225	**ultimamente** - *adv*	lately
1237	**lentamente** - *adv*	slowly
1258	**praticamente** - *adv*	practically
1265	**finora** - *adv*	so far
1270	**perfino** - *adv*	even
1272	**tuttavia** - *adv; conj*	however, nevertheless; but, yet
1284	**gratis** - *adv*	free
1335	**velocemente** - *adv*	quickly
1342	**parecchio** - *adv; adj*	a lot of, several; some
1344	**assieme [a]** - *adv*	together [with]
1357	**pari** - *adv*	equal
1363	**specialmente** - *adv*	specially, particulary, especially
1364	**chiaramente** - *adv*	clearly
1369	**uguale** - *adv*	equal
1379	**attorno** - *adv; prep*	about; around
1383	**seriamente** - *adv*	seriously
1411	**facilmente** - *adv*	easily
1454	**personalmente** - *adv*	personally
1520	**decisamente** - *adv*	definitely, decidedly
1575	**intanto** - *adv*	in the meantime
1615	**talmente** - *adv*	so
1633	**totalmente** - *adv*	totally
1689	**volentieri** - *adv*	willingly
1697	**improvvisamente** - *adv*	suddenly
1729	**appunto** - *adv*	just
1739	**cola** - *adv*	there (form)
1753	**realmente** - *adv*	really
1835	**pochino** - *adv*	a little
1853	**onde** - *adv; conj; pron*	hence, whence; so that, so as; of which, whose
1904	**sebbene** - *conj; adv*	although, though; even though

1915	**sfortunatamente** - *adv*	unfortunately
1926	**estremamente** - *adv*	extremely
1933	**attentamente** - *adv*	carefully
1965	**dopotutto** - *adv*	after all
1995	**continuamente** - *adv*	continuously, continually
2024	**profondamente** - *adv*	deeply
2039	**quaggiù** - *adv*	hither
2048	**dovunque** - *adv*	anywhere
2051	**mortale** - *adj; adv*	mortal; deadly, fatal; deathly
2105	**sinceramente** - *adv*	sincerely
2155	**addirittura** - *adv*	even
2165	**storto** - *adv*	awry
2200	**onestamente** - *adv*	honestly
2209	**altrettanto** - *adv; adj; pron*	as; as much; just as many
2230	**altrove** - *adv*	elsewhere
2231	**infine** - *adv*	finally, at last
2259	**presso** - *prep; adv; adj*	at,in; near; close
2302	**sottovoce** - *adv*	whisper
2303	**lento** - *adv*	slow
2305	**rapidamente** - *adv*	quickly
2309	**malapena** - *adv*	barely
2330	**ufficialmente** - *adv*	officially
2370	**normalmente** - *adv*	normally
2386	**francamente** - *adv*	frankly
2448	**diversamente** - *adv*	otherwise
2484	**incredibilmente** - *adv*	incredibilmente
2493	**particolarmente** - *adv*	particolarmente

C. Conjunctions

Rank	Italian - *Part of Speech*	English
2	**che** - *conj; pron; adj*	that; which, who; what
3	**e, ed** - *conj*	and
14	**ma** - *conj*	but
20	**se** - *conj*	if
25	**qui** - *adv; conj*	here; where
28	**di** *del, dello, dell', della, dei, degli, delle -prep*	of, to; than, and
38	**quando** - *adv; conj*	when
40	**perché** - *conj; adv*	because, why; why
42	**ora** - *adv; conj; nf*	now; now; now, time, hour
43	**o** - *conj*	or
48	**così** - *adv; conj*	so, thus; that
67	**ancora** - *adv; conj*	yet, still, more; more
102	**quanto** - *adv; conj*	as, how much; than
120	**senza** - *conj*	without
219	**meno** - *adv; adj; prep; conj*	less; less; unless; no so (much as)
221	**neanche** - *adv; conj*	not even, neither; not even
222	**quale** - *adj; pron; conj*	to displeasure, dislike, be sorry
231	**mentre** - *conj*	while, as, whereas
251	**nemmeno** - *adv; conj*	not even, neither
256	**comunque** - *adv; conj*	anyway; though
283	**però** - *conj; adv*	but, yet; however
409	**finché** - *conj*	until, till
423	**né** - *conj*	neither, nor
594	**altrimenti** - *adv; conj*	otherwise
616	**perciò** - *conj; adv*	therefore; accordingly
639	**oppure** - *conj*	or, or else
1106	**eppure** - *conj*	and yet
1136	**neppure** - *adv; conj*	not even, neither
1162	**nonostante** - *prep; conj; adv*	despite; altough; even though, nevertheless
1272	**tuttavia** - *adv; conj*	however, nevertheless; but, yet
1816	**ebbene** - *conj*	so, well
1853	**onde** - *adv; conj; pron*	hence, whence; so that, so as; of which, whose
1888	**poiché** - *conj*	as, because, for
1904	**sebbene** - *conj; adv*	although, though; even though
2017	**sin** - *conj*	since
2251	**siccome** - *conj*	since
2477	**affinché** - *conj*	so that, in order to

D. Interjections

Rank	Italian - Part of Speech	English
10	**sì** - *int*	yes, yeah
50	**oh** - *int*	oh
56	**grazie** - *int*	thank you
77	**ehi** - *int*	Hey
97	**ok** - *int*	ok
98	**beh, be** - *int*	well!
100	**ciao** - *int*	hello, bye
114	**cazzo** - *nm; int*	dick; fuck
127	**prego** - *int*	please, you're welcome
150	**ah** - *int*	ha
161	**eh** - *int*	huh
199	**okay** - *int*	okay
306	**buongiorno** - *int*	good morning
482	**buonanotte** - *int*	good night
512	**arrivederci** - *int*	goodbye
536	**uh** - *int*	uh
619	**salute** - *nf; int*	to displeasure, dislike, be sorry
663	**maledizione** - *nf; int*	curse; damn
682	**vaffanculo** - *int*	fuck off
683	**benvenuto** - *adj; int; nm*	welcome
691	**buonasera** - *int*	good evening
722	**ehm** - *int*	hum
894	**chissà** - *int; adv*	who knows!; perhaps
897	**sissignore** - *int*	Yes sir
1034	**fanculo** - *int*	fuck
1234	**amen** - *int*	amen
1380	**stop** - *nm; int*	stop
1501	**eccoti** - *int*	here you are
1648	**ahi** - *int*	ouch
1695	**caspita** - *int*	good heavens
1714	**eccoli** - *int*	here they are (eccolo/i (m), eccola/e (f)
2000	**ooh** - *int*	ooh
2191	**eccome** - *int*	all right!, I´ll say!
2196	**diamine** - *int*	heck
2265	**bentornato** - *int; nm*	Welcome back!; welcome
2365	**evviva** - *int*	cheers, hoorah
2467	**alt** - *int*	halt

E. Nouns

Rank	**Italian** - *Part of Speech*	English
16	**cosa** - *pron; nf*	what; thing
26	**bene** - *adj; adv; nm*	very; well, good; good, asset
32	**tutto** - *adv; nm*	all
39	**fatto** - *nm; adj*	fact, event; made, done
42	**ora** - *adv; conj; nf*	now; now; now, time, hour
51	**anche** - *adv; nf*	also, even; anchor
55	**niente** - *pron; nm*	nothing, anything, none
61	**potere** - *verb; nm*	to be able; power
68	**casa** - *nf*	house, home
70	**qualcosa** - *nf*	something, anything
71	**vero** - *nm*	true
73	**saio** - *nm*	habit
78	**dovere** - *verb; nm*	to have to, muste, should; duty, obligation
79	**signore** - *nm/f*	Mr. / Mrs.
80	**tempo** - *nm*	time, weather
83	**vita** - *nf*	life, waist
89	**anno** - *nm*	to displeasure, dislike, be sorry
92	**dio** - *nm*	God
93	**via** - *prep; adv; nf*	via, by; away; street, way
95	**proprio** - *adj; nm; pron; adv*	one's own; own; its; just, exactly
96	**parte** - *nf*	part
99	**credo** - *nm*	creed, credo
101	**volta** - *nf*	time, turn, vault
103	**uomo** - *nm*	man
105	**padre** - *nm*	father
107	**amico** - *nm/f*	friend
109	**lavoro** - *nm*	work, job
113	**giorno** - *nm*	day
114	**cazzo** - *nm; int*	dick; fuck
116	**bisogno** - *nm*	need
122	**male** - *adv; nm*	bad, evil
125	**mamma** - *nf*	mom
128	**modo** - *nm*	way, manner
132	**favore** - *nm*	favor
135	**soldo** - *nm*	money
138	**gente** - *nm*	people
140	**madre** - *nf*	mother
141	**momento** - *nm*	moment
144	**successo** - *nm*	success
145	**mondo** - *nm*	world
148	**forza** - *nf*	power
149	**oggi** - *adv; nm*	today
151	**figlio** - *nm*	son
153	**ragazzo** - *nm/f*	boy, boyfriend / girl. girlfriend
155	**accordo** - *nm*	agreement, deal
156	**fossa** - *nf*	pit, dich, gravel
157	**donna** - *nf*	woman
159	**nome** - *nm*	name
163	**signora** - *nf*	lady, Mrs.
165	**notte** - *nm*	night
166	**bello (bel)** - *adj; nm/f*	nice,beautiful; handsome, hunk/ beautiful woman
170	**testa** - *nf*	head
171	**faccia** - *nf*	face
173	**persona** - *nf*	person
177	**merda** - *nf*	shit
178	**tipo** - *nm*	type, kind
180	**paura** - *nf*	fear

182	**buono** - *adj; nm*	good; voucher, coupon
184	**moglie** - *nf*	wife
188	**problema** - *nf*	problem
189	**amore** - *nm*	(my) love
190	**insieme** - *adv; nm*	together; set, whole
191	**papà** - *nm*	dad, daddy
194	**domani** - *adv; nm*	tomorrow
195	**tesoro** - *nm*	treasure
196	**caso** - *nm*	case
197	**ragione** - *nm*	reason
198	**storia** - *nf*	history, story
202	**nulla** - *nf; pron*	nothing; nothing, anything
205	**mano** - *nm*	hand
207	**famiglia** - *nf*	family
208	**terra** - *nf*	land, earth
209	**fratello** - *nm*	brother
212	**fine** - *nm; nf; adj*	purpose; end; fine
213	**secondo** - *prep; nm; adv; adj*	according to; second
215	**aiuto** - *nm*	help
216	**polizia** - *nf*	police
217	**piano** - *nm; adj*	plan, floor, piano; plane, flat
218	**diavolo** - *nm*	Devil
225	**strada** - *nf*	(large) street, road
226	**occhio** - *nm*	eye
227	**giro** - *nm*	tour
232	**bambino** - *nm/f*	child, baby, boy/girl
233	**sera** - *nf*	evening
234	**film** - *nm*	movie
239	**acqua** - *nf*	water
242	**minuto** - *adj; nm*	minute
248	**guerra** - *nf*	war
250	**cuore** - *nm*	heart, core
252	**forte** - *adj; nm; adv*	strong; forte; loudly
253	**bravo** - *adj; nm*	good, fine, clever; bravo
255	**stasera** - *nf*	tonight, this evening
257	**numero** - *nm*	number
258	**punto** - *nm*	point
259	**roba** - *nf*	stuff, things
260	**scuola** - *nf*	school
262	**vecchio** - *adj; nm/f*	old; old (wo)man
265	**città** - *nf*	city
267	**dietro** - *prep; nm; adj; adv*	behind; back, rear; after; after
271	**figlia** - *nf*	daughter
274	**poco** - *adj; adv; nm*	little; a litte, not much; bit
275	**verso** - *prep; nm*	to, towards; direction, way
276	**marito** - *nm*	husband
279	**puttana** - *nf*	whore
282	**ricordo** - *nm*	memory
284	**sangue** - *nm*	blood
285	**settimana** - *nf*	week
287	**fata** - *nf*	fairy, femme fatale
288	**colpa** - *nf*	fault, guilt; blame
289	**dottore** - *nm*	doctor, Dr.
291	**piede** - *nm*	foot
293	**amo** - *nm*	hook, bait
295	**media** - *nf*	media, average
299	**andata** - *nf*	going
303	**stanza** - *nf*	room
304	**telefono** - *nm*	phone, telephone
309	**musica** - *nf*	music
310	**conto** - *nm*	bill
311	**corpo** - *nm*	body
312	**culo** - *nm*	ass
314	**mezzo** - *nm; adj*	half, middle, means; half, middle
320	**ieri** - *adv; nm*	yesterday

321	**genere** - *nm*	gender, kind, genre
322	**fuoco** - *nm*	fire
324	**paese** - *nm*	country, village
325	**signorina** - *nf*	young lady
326	**parola** - *nf*	word
328	**fortuna** - *nf*	luck
329	**mese** - *nm*	month
330	**gioco** - *nm*	game
332	**resto** - *nm*	rest
333	**sorella** - *nf*	sister
335	**re** - *nm*	king
336	**foto** - *nm*	photo
337	**domanda** - *nf*	demand, question
338	**parere** - *verb; nm*	to think, seem; opinion
339	**pace** - *nm*	peace
341	**mente** - *nm*	mind
342	**sacco** - *nm; adv*	bag, sack; a lot
343	**auto** - *nm*	car
345	**verità** - *nf*	truth
346	**paio** - *nm*	pair
347	**cane** - *nm*	dog
348	**attimo** - *nm*	moment, instant
349	**senso** - *nm*	direction, sense, meaning
353	**attenzione** - *nm*	caution
355	**pistola** - *nf*	gun
356	**festa** - *nf*	party
357	**presidente** - *nm*	president
359	**bere** - *nm*	drinking
361	**affare** - *nm*	deal, bargain, business, affair
362	**cielo** - *nm*	sky
363	**coraggio** - *nm*	courage
365	**ufficio** - *nm*	office
366	**caro** - *adj; nm*	dear, expensive; dear
373	**generale** - *adj; nm*	general
374	**controllo** - *nm*	control
375	**voce** - *nm*	entry, voice, item
376	**lungo** - *prep; adj; nm*	long; along; length
381	**libro** - *nm*	book
383	**squadra** - *nf*	team
385	**cristo** - *nm*	Christ
386	**cerca** - *nf*	search
388	**voglia** - *nf*	desire
390	**cura** - *nf*	care
393	**tratta** - *nf*	section, trade, bill, draft
395	**stronzo** - *nm*	shit, asshole
396	**ordine** - *nm*	order
402	**aria** - *nf*	air
403	**passo** - *nm*	passage, step, pace, stride
404	**motivo** - *nm*	reason
407	**fermo** - *adj; nm*	still, firm; stop, arrest
408	**viaggio** - *nm*	travel, trip, journey
411	**aspetto** - *nm*	appearance, look, aspect
412	**campo** - *nm*	field
413	**papa** - *nm*	Pope
414	**arrivo** - *nm*	arrival
415	**camera** - *nf*	room
419	**ospedale** - *nm*	hospital
420	**zio** - *nm*	uncle
422	**bocca** - *nf*	mouth
426	**bagno** - *nm*	bathroom
429	**idiota** - *adj; nmf*	idiotic, stupid; idiot
430	**colpo** - *nm*	hit
431	**fretta** - *nf*	hurry
432	**causa** - *nf*	cause
436	**arma** - *nf*	weapon
437	**bastardo** - *nm*	bastard
438	**gruppo** - *nm*	group, band
439	**genitore** - *nm*	parent
440	**situazione** - *nm*	situation

441	**denaro** - *nm*	money
444	**onore** - *nm*	honor
445	**sogno** - *nm*	dream
446	**giornata** - *nf*	day
448	**capello** - *nm*	hair
449	**pezzo** - *nm*	piece
450	**addio** - *nm*	goodbye, farewell
451	**fondo** - *nm; adj*	background, bottom, fund; deep
452	**traduzione** - *nm*	translation
457	**matrimonio** - *nm*	marriage, wedding
461	**sicurezza** - *nf*	safety, security
462	**scelta** - *nf*	choice
463	**odio** - *nm*	hatred
464	**cibo** - *nm*	food
465	**fame** - *nm*	hunger
466	**prigione** - *nm*	prison
467	**guaio** - *nm*	trouble
468	**mattina** - *nf*	morning
471	**brutto** - *adj; nm*	ugly, bad, nasty; bad, ugliness
476	**sistema** - *nf*	system
477	**natale** - *nf*	Christmas
478	**messaggio** - *nm*	message
479	**incidente** - *nm; adj*	accident, incident; incident
480	**radio** - *adj; nm*	radio
481	**aereo** - *adj; nm*	air, aerial; plane, airplane
486	**solito** - *adj; nm*	usual
487	**avvocato** - *nm*	lawyer
488	**compagnia** - *nf*	company
490	**nave** - *nm*	ship
493	**servizio** - *nm*	service, report
494	**scena** - *nf*	scene
496	**tv** - *nm*	TV
497	**specie** - *nf*	species, kind
503	**parto** - *nm*	birth, childbirth
506	**calma** - *nf*	calm
507	**tizio** - *nm*	someone, person, guy, chap
509	**segreto** - *nm*	secret
513	**ritardo** - *nm*	delay, retardation
515	**esercito** - *nm*	army
517	**vestito** - *nm*	dress, dressed
518	**santo** - *adj; nm/f*	holy; saint
520	**centro** - *nm*	center
522	**lettera** - *nf*	letter
523	**cavallo** - *nm*	horse
524	**grado** - *nm*	degree
525	**chiave** - *nf*	key
526	**fallo** - *nm*	foul
527	**mare** - *nm*	sea, seaside
528	**treno** - *nm*	train
531	**scoperto** - *adj; nm*	uncovered, open, bare; overdraft
532	**caffè** - *nm*	coffee, café
533	**rumore** - *nm*	noise
534	**sesso** - *nm*	sex
537	**intenzione** - *nf*	intention
539	**rapporto** - *nm*	relationship
541	**maestro** - *nm*	master, teacher, meastro
543	**fronte** - *nf*	front, forehead
546	**cervello** - *nm*	brain
549	**rispetto** - *nm*	respect
554	**diritto** - *nm; adj; adv*	right, law; straight; straight
555	**accidente** - *nf*	accident, fit, incident, damn
557	**realtà** - *nf*	reality
558	**consiglio** - *nm*	advice, council, board
561	**dolore** - *nm*	ache, pain
563	**anima** - *nf*	soul
564	**prova** - *nf*	test
565	**omicidio** - *nm*	murder

570	**governo** - *nm; adj*	government; governmental
571	**linea** - *nf*	line, figure
573	**tenente** - *nm*	lieutenant
575	**colonnello** - *nm*	colonel
577	**guardia** - *nf*	guard
580	**cavolo** - *nm*	cabbage, kale
581	**base** - *nf*	basis
585	**chiamata** - *nf*	(telephone) call
587	**riguardo** - *nm*	regard, respect
588	**luogo** - *nm*	place
590	**incontro** - *nm*	meeting, encounter
593	**sergente** - *nm*	sergeant
595	**posizione** - *nf*	position
596	**caldo** - *adj; nm*	hot; heat
597	**nonno** - *nm*	grandfather
599	**inferno** - *nm*	hell
600	**nonna** - *nf*	grandmother
601	**dolce** - *adj; nm*	sweet, fresh; sweet, dessert
602	**notizia** - *nf*	news
607	**esempio** - *nm*	example
608	**zona** - *nf*	area
609	**proposito** - *nm*	purpose, intention
611	**inglese** - *adj; nmf*	English; English(wo)man
612	**errore** - *nm*	error
615	**programma** - *nf*	program
618	**gamba** - *nf*	leg
619	**salute** - *nf; int*	health; cheers, bless you
620	**birra** - *nf*	beer
621	**comandante** - *nm*	commander
622	**assassino** - *nm/f*	killer, murderer
624	**possibilità** - *nf*	possibility
627	**poliziotto** - *nm*	policeman
628	**questione** - *nf*	question
629	**carta** - *nf*	paper, card, map

631	**spettacolo** - *nm*	show, spectacle, performance
638	**chiesa** - *nf*	church
640	**carne** - *nf*	meat
641	**pranzo** - *nm*	lunch
642	**studio** - *nm*	office, study
644	**appuntamento** - *nm*	appointment
645	**pena** - *nf*	penalty
647	**missione** - *nf*	mission
648	**uso** - *nf*	use, usage
651	**forma** - *nf*	form
652	**compleanno** - *nm*	birthday
653	**palla** - *nf*	ball
654	**barca** - *nf*	boat
655	**nord** - *nm*	north
658	**braccio** - *nm*	arm
659	**informazione** - *nf*	information
661	**direttore** - *nm*	director, (senior) manager
662	**canzone** - *nf*	song
663	**maledizione** - *nf; int*	curse; damn
664	**scarpa** - *nf*	shoe
666	**schifo** - *nm*	disgust
670	**soldato** - *nm*	soldier
671	**don** - *nm*	Don (title of respect/religious title)
673	**regalo** - *nm*	gift, present
677	**bar** - *nm*	bar, caffé
678	**figliolo** - *nm*	son, boy (affectuos or patronizing)
679	**classe** - *nf*	class, classroom
680	**stronzata** - *nf*	bullshit
683	**benvenuto** - *adj; int; nm*	welcome
684	**banca** - *nf*	bank
685	**negozio** - *nm*	shop, store

686	**sud** - *nm*	south
687	**spalla** - *nf*	shoulder
688	**mostro** - *nm*	monster
692	**attacco** - *nm*	attack
699	**metro(politana)** - *nm; (nf)*	meter; tape measure; (underground, metro)
701	**professore** - *nm*	teacher, professor
704	**comando** - *nm*	command
706	**dannazione** - *nf*	damn
708	**occasione** - *nf*	opportunity
709	**metà** - *nf*	half
710	**spazio** - *nm*	space
711	**regola** - *nf*	rule
712	**contatto** - *nm*	contact
713	**spirito** - *nm*	spirit
714	**povero** - *adj; nm*	poor; the poor
715	**appartamento** - *nm*	flat, apartment
716	**pelle** - *nf*	skin
717	**cucina** - *nf*	kitchen
720	**pomeriggio** - *nm*	afternoon
721	**pianeta** - *nf*	planet
728	**fiume** - *nm*	river
729	**nemico** - *adj; nm*	enemy
732	**lingua** - *nf*	tongue, language
733	**borsa** - *nf*	bag
734	**vino** - *nm*	wine
735	**destino** - *nm*	destiny
740	**urlo** - *nm*	yell, cry, shout
744	**ritorno** - *nm*	return
747	**principe** - *nm*	prince
748	**lista** - *nf*	list
749	**intero** - *adj; nm*	entire, full, whole; whole
750	**popolo** - *nm*	people
751	**passaggio** - *nm*	passage
752	**finestra** - *nf*	window
753	**ricerca** - *nf*	search, research
754	**differenza** - *nf*	difference
756	**tornio** - *nm*	lathe
757	**tavolo** - *nm*	table
759	**codice** - *nm*	code, codex
760	**vento** - *nm*	wind
761	**speranza** - *nf*	hope
762	**posto** - *nm*	place, spot, location
763	**ufficiale** - *adj; nm*	official
766	**animale** - *nm; adj*	animal
767	**libertà** - *nf*	freedom
769	**pesce** - *nm*	fish
770	**serata** - *nf*	evening
771	**società** - *nf*	society
774	**livello** - *nm*	level
775	**stazione** - *nf*	station
776	**americano** - *adj; nm/f*	American; American
777	**computer** - *nm*	computer
779	**detective** - *nmf*	detective
780	**lato** - *nm*	side
781	**hotel** - *nm*	hotel
782	**sezione** - *nf*	section, department
784	**regina** - *nf*	queen
788	**naso** - *nm*	nose
789	**padrone** - *nm/f*	boss, master, owner, host/mistress, hostess
793	**fiore** - *nm*	flower
795	**danno** - *nm*	damage
796	**casino (casinò)** - *nm*	mess (casino)
798	**natura** - *nf*	nature
799	**cliente** - *nm*	customer
802	**guida** - *nf*	guide, driving
803	**biglietto** - *nm*	ticket
804	**zia** - *nf*	aunt

805	**razza** - *nf*	race, breed, stingray
806	**stamattina** - *nf*	this morning
809	**effetto** - *nm*	effect
810	**cambio** - *nm*	change
811	**taxi** - *nm*	taxi
813	**corso** - *nm*	course
814	**giudice** - *nm*	judge
816	**villaggio** - *nm*	village
817	**cinema** - *nm*	cinema, movie theater
819	**lezione** - *nf*	lesson
820	**decisione** - *nf*	decision
821	**bordo** - *nm*	edge
822	**segno** - *nm*	sign
823	**ponte** - *nm*	bridge
824	**club** - *nm*	club
825	**muro** - *nm*	wall
826	**interno** - *adj; nm*	internal; interior, inside
827	**energia** - *nf*	energy
828	**spada** - *nf*	sword
830	**processo** - *nm*	process
832	**segnale** - *nm*	signal, sign
834	**battaglia** - *nf*	battle
837	**porco** - *nm*	pig
838	**ascolto** - *nm*	listening
840	**prezzo** - *nm*	price
843	**eroe** - *nm*	hero
845	**documento** - *nm*	document
846	**comune** - *adj; nm*	common; community, town
847	**dente** - *nm*	tooth
848	**pensata** - *nf*	thought
849	**memoria** - *nf*	storage
850	**data** - *nf*	date
851	**terzo** - *adj; nm*	third
852	**massimo** - *adj; nm*	maximum
854	**buio** - *adj; nm*	dark; dark
855	**colore** - *nm*	color
856	**matto** - *adj; nm*	crazy; madman
857	**cerchio** - *nm*	circle; rim
863	**maledetto** - *nm*	accursed, damn
864	**opera** - *nf*	opera
865	**partito** - *nm*	party
869	**fede** - *nf*	faith, wedding ring
870	**esperienza** - *nf*	experience
872	**responsabile** - *adj; nm*	responsible; person in charge
874	**ex** - *adj; nmf*	former; ex
875	**fiducia** - *nf*	confidence
877	**periodo** - *nm*	period
878	**albero** - *nm*	tree
880	**azione** - *nf*	action
881	**odore** - *nm*	smell
882	**locale** - *adj; nm*	local; club
883	**latte** - *nm*	milk
884	**bellezza** - *nf*	beauty
885	**vittima** - *nf*	victim
886	**congratulazione** - *nf*	congratulation
888	**colazione** - *nf*	breakfast, lunch
889	**isola** - *nf*	island
891	**contrario** - *nm*	contrary
893	**legge** - *nf*	law
895	**dubbio** - *adj; nm*	doubtful; doubt
896	**camion** - *nm*	truck
898	**stella** - *nf*	star
902	**pressione** - *nf*	pressure
904	**edificio** - *nm*	building
905	**progetto** - *nm*	project
907	**età** - *nf*	age
912	**principessa** - *nf*	princess
913	**sale** - *nm*	salt
914	**scopo** - *nm*	purpose
917	**stampa** - *nf*	press, printing
918	**viso** - *nm*	face
922	**pensiero** - *nm*	thought

924	**ristorante** - *nm*	restaurant
925	**giornale** - *nm*	newspaper, journal
926	**test** - *nm*	test
927	**gatto** - *nm*	cat
928	**giustizia** - *nf*	justice
930	**albergo** - *nm*	hotel
931	**tiro** - *nm*	shot, shooting, throw
932	**relazione** - *nf*	report
933	**basso** - *adj; nm*	low, bottom, lower; bass
934	**compagno** - *nm/f*	companion, mate
936	**crimine** - *nm*	crime
937	**angolo** - *nm*	angle, corner
938	**cappello** - *nm*	hat
939	**operazione** - *nf*	operation
940	**estate** - *nf*	summer
941	**desiderio** - *nm*	desire
942	**mercato** - *nm*	market
945	**arte** - *nf*	art
946	**coltello** - *nm*	knife
949	**macchina** - *nf*	machine
951	**vite** - *nf*	screw, grapevine, vine
952	**buco** - *nm*	hole
953	**centrale** - *adj; nf*	central; main office, (nuclear) power station
955	**carriera** - *nf*	career
956	**anello** - *nm*	ring
958	**stile** - *nm*	style
959	**contratto** - *nm*	contract
960	**compito** - *nm*	task
961	**paradiso** - *nm*	paradise
966	**riunione** - *nf*	meeting, reunion, assembly
968	**troia** - *nf*	slut
969	**faccenda** - *nf*	affair
973	**campione** - *nm; adj*	sample, champion; champion
974	**agente** - *nm*	agent
975	**politico** - *adj; nm*	political; politician
977	**ghiaccio** - *nm*	ice
978	**fucile** - *nm*	rifle, gun
979	**utile** - *adj; nm*	helpful, useful; profit
980	**ispettore** - *nm*	inspector
981	**autobus** - *nm*	bus
982	**dato** - *adj; nm*	given; fact, datum
984	**altezza** - *nf*	height
987	**sottofondo** - *nm*	background
988	**valore** - *nm*	value
989	**campagna** - *nf*	countryside, country
990	**tè** - *nm*	tea
993	**scatola** - *nf*	box
994	**peso** - *nm*	weight
996	**ragazzino** - *nm*	little boy, sonny (condenscending)
1000	**sensazione** - *nf*	sensation
1002	**schiena** - *nf*	back
1004	**orologio** - *nm*	clock, watch
1006	**sbaglio** - *nm*	mistake
1008	**maestà** - *nf*	majesty
1011	**angelo** - *nm*	angel
1014	**importanza** - *nf*	importance
1015	**baby** - *nmf*	baby
1016	**fumo** - *nm*	smoke
1017	**domenica** - *nf*	Sunday
1018	**ucciso** - *nm/f*	victim, killed person
1020	**rotta** - *nf*	route
1021	**nipote** - *nm*	grandson, granddaughter, nephew, niece
1022	**teatro** - *nm*	theater
1023	**militare** - *adj; nm*	military; soldier

1024	**palazzo** - *nm*	palace
1026	**innocente** - *nm; adj*	innocent
1027	**finale** - *adj; nm/f*	final; final, ending, finish/final (sports)
1029	**innamorato** - *adj; nm*	in love; lover
1031	**turno** - *nm*	round, shift
1032	**emergenza** - *nf*	emergency
1035	**tetto** - *nm*	roof
1036	**montagna** - *nf*	mountain
1037	**bottiglia** - *nf*	bottle
1038	**pane** - *nm*	bread
1041	**discorso** - *nm*	speech
1044	**immagine** - *nf*	image
1045	**ministro** - *nm*	minister
1047	**giardino** - *nm*	garden
1051	**retro** - *nm*	back, rear
1052	**bicchiere** - *nm*	(drinking) glass
1053	**pantalone** - *nm*	trousers
1054	**tribunale** - *nm*	court
1055	**gioia** - *nf*	joy
1056	**paziente** - *adj; nm&f*	patient
1058	**genio** - *nm*	genius
1060	**coppia** - *nf*	couple
1062	**allarme** - *nm*	alarm
1063	**est** - *nm*	East
1065	**condizione** - *nf*	condition
1066	**cattivo** - *adj; nm/f*	bad; baddie, bad person
1067	**cinese** - *adj; nmf*	Chinese
1068	**malattia** - *nf*	disease, illness
1069	**dito** - *nm*	finger
1070	**laboratorio** - *nm*	laboratory
1072	**vittoria** - *nf*	victory
1075	**unità** - *nf*	unit
1076	**direzione** - *nf*	direction, management
1080	**sabato** - *nm*	Saturday
1081	**mattino, mattina** - *nm*	morning
1082	**sentimento** - *nm*	feeling
1084	**spiaggia** - *nf*	beach
1085	**testimone** - *nm*	witness
1086	**gas** - *nm*	gas
1087	**dipartimento** - *nm*	department
1088	**miglio** - *nm*	mile
1090	**sedia** - *nf*	chair
1091	**cadavere** - *nm*	dead body
1092	**obiettivo** - *nm*	target, objective
1093	**fianco** - *nm*	side
1094	**entrata** - *nf*	entrance
1095	**furgone** - *nm*	van
1097	**motore** - *adj; nm*	motor; enginge, motor
1100	**soluzione** - *nf*	solution
1101	**sguardo** - *nm*	look
1102	**fantasma** - *nf*	ghost
1104	**pioggia** - *nf*	rain
1110	**uccello** - *nm*	bird
1112	**giacca** - *nf*	jacket
1114	**polvere** - *nf*	dust
1115	**faro** - *nm*	lighthouse, beacon, headlight
1116	**università** - *nf*	university
1117	**pollo** - *nm*	chicken
1118	**gloria** - *nf*	glory
1119	**ovest** - *nm*	West
1121	**tedesco** - *adj, nm/f*	German; German
1123	**coglione** - *nm*	balls, nuts, asshole
1125	**maiale** - *nm*	pig, pork
1126	**conoscenza** - *nf*	knowledge
1127	**telefonata** - *nf*	phone call
1129	**vacanza** - *nf*	holiday, vacation
1132	**atto** - *nm*	act
1134	**aeroporto** - *nm*	airport
1137	**movimento** - *nm*	movement

1139	**quarto** - *adj; num; nm*	fourth; quarter
1140	**taglio** - *nm*	cut, cutting
1141	**assistente** - *adj; nm&f*	assistant; assistant
1143	**puzza** - *nf*	stink
1144	**interesse** - *nm*	interest
1145	**orecchio** - *nm*	ear
1146	**regno** - *nm*	kingdom
1148	**uovo** - *nm*	egg
1150	**neve** - *nf*	snow
1151	**legale** - *adj; nm*	legal; lawyer
1154	**richiesta** - *nf*	request
1156	**lago** - *nm*	lake
1157	**teoria** - *nf*	theory
1159	**distanza** - *nf*	distance
1160	**pista** - *nf*	track
1163	**dettaglio** - *nm*	detail
1165	**moto** - *nm*	motion, motorbike
1166	**prete** - *nm*	priest
1167	**ospite** - *nm*	guest, host
1171	**sigaretta** - *nf*	cigarette
1173	**presenza** - *nf*	presence
1175	**trappola** - *nf*	trap
1176	**premio** - *nm*	prize
1177	**pietra** - *nf*	stone
1179	**pausa** - *nf*	break
1180	**fastidio** - *nm*	bother, annoyance, nuisance
1181	**gola** - *nf*	throat
1182	**tavola** - *nf*	table
1184	**perdono** - *nm*	pardon, forgiveness
1185	**quartiere** - *nm*	district, neighbourhood, quarter
1187	**augurio** - *nm*	wish, greeting, omen
1188	**lupo** - *nm*	wolf
1190	**cugino** - *nm/f*	cousin
1191	**galera** - *nf*	jail
1192	**ragazzina** - *nf*	little girl
1193	**medicina** - *nf*	medicine
1194	**violenza** - *nf*	violence
1196	**amante** - *nm&f; adj*	lover; fond
1198	**mostra** - *nf*	show
1200	**accesso** - *nm*	access
1201	**disturbo** - *nm*	disorder
1202	**trucco** - *nm*	makeup, trick
1203	**sindaco** - *nm*	mayor
1204	**responsabilità** - *nf*	responsibility
1205	**uscita** - *nf*	exit
1207	**televisione (TV)** - *nf*	television
1208	**opinione** - *nf*	opinion
1210	**conte** - *nm*	count
1211	**parco** - *nm;*	park, parklan; frugal, sober
1212	**miracolo** - *nm*	miracle
1215	**castello** - *nm*	castle
1217	**nazione** - *nf*	nation, country
1218	**vendetta** - *nf*	vengeance
1219	**deserto** - *adj; nm*	desert (food); desert
1220	**lancio** - *nm*	launch, throw, launching
1221	**magia** - *nf*	magic
1222	**pazienza** - *nf*	patience
1223	**college** - *nm*	college
1224	**camicia** - *nf*	shirt
1226	**osso** - *nm*	bone
1227	**universo** - *nm*	universe
1231	**gara** - *nf*	race, competition
1232	**fidanzato** - *nm*	boyfriend
1235	**tomba** - *nf*	tomb
1238	**esplosione** - *nf*	explosion
1240	**privato** - *adj; nm*	private; personal life, privacy

1241	**scusa** - *nf*	sorry, excuse
1243	**sospetto** - *adj; nm*	suspected, suspicious; suspicion
1244	**perdita** - *nf*	loss, leak, waste
1245	**banda** - *nf*	band, gang
1246	**velocità** - *nf*	speed
1247	**pugno** - *nm*	fist
1248	**secolo** - *nm*	century
1249	**minaccia** - *nf*	threat
1250	**stomaco** - *nm*	stomach
1252	**attore** - *nm*	actor
1253	**ruolo** - *nm*	role
1254	**russo** - *adj; nm/f*	Russian; Russian
1255	**accusa** - *nf*	accusation, charge, prosecution
1260	**completo** - *adj; nm*	complete, full; suit
1263	**sonno** - *nm*	sleep
1264	**termine** - *nm*	term
1267	**taglia** - *nf*	size
1268	**merito** - *nm*	merit
1269	**ombra** - *nf*	shadow
1273	**governatore** - *nm*	governor
1274	**vergogna** - *nf*	shame
1276	**tetta** - *nf*	tit
1277	**totale** - *adj; nm*	total
1279	**articolo** - *nm*	article
1280	**complimento** - *nm*	compliment
1281	**foresta** - *nf*	forest
1285	**riposo** - *nm*	rest, rest period
1286	**mucchio** - *nm*	pile
1287	**funerale** - *nm*	funeral
1288	**cima** - *nf*	top
1289	**spia** - *nf*	light, spy, indication
1291	**revisione** - *nf*	review, revision
1292	**ala** - *nf*	wing
1294	**scala** - *nf*	ladder, scale, stairs
1295	**respiro** - *nm*	breath
1296	**fabbrica** - *nf*	factory
1297	**infermiera** - *nf*	nurse
1298	**bestia** - *nf*	beast
1299	**ebreo** - *adj; nm*	Jewish, Jew
1300	**piatto** - *nm*	dish, plate
1302	**pagina** - *nf*	page
1304	**tasca** - *nf*	pocket
1305	**calcio** - *nm*	football, soccer
1307	**torre** - *nf*	tower
1308	**riso** - *nm*	rice
1310	**nota** - *nf*	note
1312	**cazzata** - *nf*	crap
1317	**abito** - *nm*	dress, suit, attire
1320	**studente** - *nm*	student
1321	**criminale** - *adj nm&f*	criminal; criminal
1323	**disastro** - *nm*	disaster
1324	**mezzanotte** - *nf*	midnight
1325	**dono** - *nm*	gift
1327	**creatura** - *nf*	creature
1328	**traccia** - *nf*	track
1329	**spesa** - *nf*	expense
1330	**amaro** - *adj; nm*	bitter; bitter, tonic liqour
1331	**corda** - *nf*	rope
1332	**pensione** - *nf*	board, pension, retirement
1334	**grazia** - *nf*	grace, pardon
1336	**istante** - *nm*	instant
1337	**maniera** - *nf*	way, manner
1338	**autorità** - *nf*	authority
1339	**esame** - *nm*	exam, test
1341	**mosca** - *nf*	fly, Moscow
1343	**pietà** - *nf*	pity
1345	**impressione** - *nf*	impression
1346	**opportunità** - *nf*	opportunity
1347	**debito** - *nm*	straight line, tuition, debt

1348	**retta** - *nf*	straight line; tuition
1351	**risultato** - *nm*	result
1352	**cella** - *nf*	cell
1353	**marino** - *adj; nf*	marine, sea; marina, marine, navy
1354	**amicizia** - *nf*	friendship
1355	**chilometro** - *nm*	kilometer
1360	**punta** - *nf*	tip, point
1361	**volontà** - *nf*	will
1362	**occhiali** - *nmpl*	glasses
1365	**ginocchio** - *nm*	knee
1366	**impronta** - *nf*	footstep, imprint, impression, mark
1368	**coscienza** - *nf*	consciousness, conscience, awareness
1371	**proprietà** - *nf*	property
1372	**personaggio** - *nm*	character
1373	**stagione** - *nf*	season
1374	**crisi** - *nf*	crisis
1377	**copia** - *nf*	copy
1378	**titolo** - *nm*	title
1380	**stop** - *nm; int*	stop
1382	**commissione** - *nf*	commission, committee
1385	**passione** - *nf*	passion
1386	**teste** - *nm*	witness
1388	**scienza** - *nf*	science
1391	**rete** - *nf*	network, net
1392	**alba** - *nf*	sunrise, dawn
1393	**prestito** - *nm*	loan
1395	**becco** - *nm*	beak
1397	**artista** - *nm*	artist
1398	**rabbia** - *nf*	anger
1399	**attività** - *nf*	activity
1400	**conversazione** - *nf*	conversation
1402	**mappa** - *nf*	map
1404	**sciocchezza** - *nf*	foolishness
1405	**gusto** - *nm*	taste
1407	**ambulanza** - *nf*	ambulance
1408	**credito** - *nm*	credit
1409	**protezione** - *nf*	protection
1412	**materiale** - *adj; nm*	material
1413	**coso** - *nm*	thing
1414	**carcere** - *nm*	prison
1416	**scherzo** - *nm*	joke
1417	**bersaglio** - *nm*	target
1418	**salto** - *nm*	leap, jump
1419	**membro** - *nm*	member
1420	**labbro** - *nm*	lip
1423	**senatore** - *nm*	senator
1424	**maschio** - *adj; nm*	male
1425	**terreno** - *nm; adj*	ground, soil; earthly
1426	**bugia** - *nf*	lie, falsehood
1427	**proprietario** - *nm*	owner, landlord
1429	**benzina** - *nf*	petrol, gasoline
1430	**panico** - *nm*	panic
1432	**giovanotto** - *nm*	young man
1433	**suicidio** - *nm*	suicide
1434	**oceano** - *nm*	ocean
1435	**reparto** - *nm*	department, ward
1436	**truppa** - *nf*	troop
1438	**socio** - *nm*	partner
1439	**onda** - *nf*	wave
1440	**oggetto** - *nm*	object
1442	**cancro** - *nm*	cancer
1443	**tazza** - *nf*	cup
1444	**felicità** - *nf*	happiness
1445	**filo** - *nm*	wire
1446	**ferro** - *nm*	iron
1447	**assegno** - *nm*	check
1448	**argomento** - *nm*	topic, subject, argument
1449	**anticipo** - *nm*	advance, anticipation

1450	**negro** - *adj; nm*	black, negro; negro, nigger
1452	**chilo** - *nm*	kilo
1453	**lacrima** - *nf*	tear
1456	**incubo** - *nm*	nightmare
1457	**carro** - *nm*	wagon
1458	**comportamento** - *nm*	behavior
1459	**inverno** - *nm*	winter
1460	**elicottero** - *nm*	helicopter
1461	**virus** - *nm*	virus
1462	**miseria** - *nf*	misery
1465	**cavaliere** - *nm*	knight
1466	**follia** - *nf*	madness
1468	**dosso** - *nm*	back
1471	**cassetta** - *nf*	cassette
1472	**pavimento** - *nm*	floor
1475	**fattoria** - *nf*	farm
1476	**moda** - *nf*	fashion, style
1478	**primavera** - *nf*	spring
1480	**ambiente** - *nm*	environmnent, room, ambience
1481	**ingresso** - *nm*	entrance
1482	**piscina** - *nf*	pool
1483	**partenza** - *nf*	departure
1484	**presente** - *adj; nm*	this, present; present
1485	**quadro** - *nm*	painting, picture, panel, square
1486	**rapina** - *nf*	robbery
1487	**spagnolo** - *adj; nm/f*	Spanish; Spaniard
1488	**nastro** - *nm*	tape
1489	**venerdì** - *nm*	Friday
1490	**coda** - *nf*	queue, tail
1491	**petto** - *nm*	chest
1492	**giornalista** - *nm*	journalist
1493	**profumo** - *nm*	perfume
1494	**originale** - *adj; nm*	original
1495	**erba** - *nf*	grass, pot, herb
1496	**risata** - *nf*	laugh
1497	**esterno** - *adj; nm*	external, outside, out; outside, exterior
1499	**settore** - *nm*	sector
1500	**croce** - *nf*	cross
1502	**prigioniero** - *nm*	prisoner
1503	**ascensore** - *nm*	lift, elevator
1504	**corridoio** - *nm*	aisle, hallway
1505	**combattimento** - *nm*	combat
1507	**epoca** - *nf*	era
1508	**valigia** - *nf*	suitcase
1509	**fonte** - *nf*	source, spring
1510	**falla** - *nf*	leak
1511	**tratto** - *nm*	stretch
1513	**dolcezza** - *nf*	sweetness, gentleness
1515	**bomba** - *nf*	bomb
1516	**concerto** - *nm*	concert
1519	**tentativo** - *nm*	attempt
1523	**babbo** - *nm*	dad, father
1526	**rischio** - *nm*	risk
1527	**autista** - *nf*	driver, chauffeur
1528	**serpe** - *nf*	snake
1529	**confine** - *nm*	border, boundery
1530	**fan** - *nm*	fan
1532	**contante** - *adj; nm*	cash
1533	**risposta** - *nf*	answer
1534	**weekend** - *nm*	weekend
1535	**poesia** - *nf*	poetry
1536	**sbirro** - *nm*	cop
1539	**procuratore** - *nm*	attorney
1541	**imbecille** - *nm; adj*	imbecile
1543	**italiano** - *adj; nm*	Italian
1544	**canto** - *nm*	singing, song
1546	**patto** - *nm*	pact
1547	**scrivania** - *nf*	desk

1549	**limite** - *nf*	limit
1551	**precedente** - *adj; nm*	previous, preceding; precedent
1552	**area** - *nf*	area
1554	**disco** - *nm*	disc
1555	**divertimento** - *nm*	fun, entertainment
1558	**tempio** - *nm*	temple
1559	**soccorso** - *nm*	rescue
1560	**mestiere** - *nm*	craft, skill, trade
1561	**cancello** - *nm*	gate
1562	**maschera** - *nf*	mask
1566	**vergine** - *adj; nf*	virgin
1567	**racconto** - *nm*	(short) story
1570	**meraviglia** - *nf*	wonder
1571	**agenzia** - *nf*	agency
1574	**sabbia** - *nf*	sand
1576	**resistenza** - *nf*	resistance
1577	**bosco** - *nm*	wood
1578	**fase** - *nf*	phase
1579	**copertura** - *nf*	coverage
1582	**produzione** - *nf*	production, output
1584	**settembre** - *nm*	September
1587	**zucchero** - *nm*	sugar
1588	**qualità** - *nf*	quality
1591	**mancanza** - *nf*	lack
1592	**spazzatura** - *nf*	trash
1593	**incarico** - *nm*	appointment
1594	**novità** - *nf*	news
1595	**vetro** - *nm*	glass
1598	**civile** - *adj; nm*	civil; civilian
1603	**assicurazione** - *nf*	insurance
1604	**regista** - *nm*	director
1606	**versione** - *nf*	version
1607	**legno** - *nm*	wood
1608	**bibbia** - *nf*	Bible
1609	**veleno** - *nm*	poison
1612	**formaggio** - *nf*	cheese
1613	**territorio** - *nm*	territory
1616	**eccellenza** - *nf*	excellence
1622	**fiamma** - *nf*	flame
1624	**richiamo** - *nm*	recall
1625	**cerimonia** - *nf*	ceremony
1628	**tunnel** - *nm*	tunnel
1630	**topo** - *nm*	mouse
1631	**potenza** - *nf*	power
1632	**liceo** - *nm*	high school
1634	**canale** - *nm*	channel
1636	**attrice** - *nf*	actress
1637	**pillola** - *nf*	pill
1638	**prodotto** - *nm*	product
1639	**museo** - *nm*	museum
1640	**cittadino** - *nm*	citizen
1641	**fotografia** - *nf*	photography, photo
1643	**vantaggio** - *nm*	advantage
1644	**cammino** - *nm*	path
1645	**mago** - *nm*	magician
1646	**lunedì** - *nm*	Monday
1647	**frattempo** - *nm*	meanwhile, meantime
1651	**visione** - *nf*	vision
1653	**figura** - *nf*	figure, frame
1654	**nascita** - *nf*	birth
1656	**parente** - *nm*	relative
1658	**indagine** - *nf*	investigation, survery, inquiry
1659	**sete** - *nf*	thirst
1662	**seta** - *nf*	silk
1663	**scimmia** - *nf*	ape, monkey
1664	**voto** - *nm*	vote, grade
1665	**barba** - *nf*	beard
1667	**fegato** - *nm*	liver
1668	**dichiarazione** - *nf*	declaration
1669	**consegna** - *nf*	delivery
1670	**cassa** - *nf*	cash, case
1671	**giudizio** - *nm*	judgment
1672	**esistenza** - *nf*	existence

1673	**diamante** - *nm*	diamond
1674	**miele** - *nm*	honey
1675	**femmina** - *nf*	female
1676	**ministero** - *nm*	ministry
1677	**divorzio** - *nm*	divorce
1678	**brillante** - *adj; nm*	brilliant, bright; diamond
1679	**furto** - *nm*	theft
1682	**vendita** - *nf*	sale, selling
1684	**chiacchiera** - *nf*	gossip
1686	**blocco** - *nm*	block
1687	**discussione** - *nf*	discussion
1690	**rivoluzione** - *nf*	revolution
1692	**bastone** - *nm*	stick
1693	**azienda** - *nf*	company, business
1694	**bagaglio** - *nm*	luggage
1696	**pesca** - *nf*	fishing, catch, peach
1699	**pagano** - *nm*	pagan, heathen
1702	**pancia** - *nf*	belly
1703	**vicenda** - *nf*	event
1705	**volante** - *nm; adj*	steering wheel; flying
1706	**leggenda** - *nf*	legend
1709	**tecnologia** - *nf*	technology
1710	**mistero** - *nm*	mystery
1712	**palco** - *nm*	stage
1720	**atmosfera** - *nf*	atmosphere
1721	**cameriere** - *nm&f*	waiter, butler / waitress, maid
1722	**impegno** - *nm*	commitment
1724	**robot** - *nm*	robot
1725	**imperatore** - *nm*	Emperor
1731	**sincero** - *nm*	sincere
1733	**parcheggio** - *nm*	parking, park
1734	**rifugio** - *nm*	refuge
1735	**sposo** - *nm*	groom
1736	**telecamera** - *nf*	camera
1737	**equipaggio** - *nm*	crew
1740	**penna** - *nf*	pen
1741	**nozze** - *nfpl*	wedding
1742	**biblioteca** - *nf*	library
1744	**frase** - *nf*	phrase, sentence
1748	**leone** - *nm*	lion
1749	**istruzione** - *nf*	instruction, education
1750	**cambiamento** - *nm*	change
1751	**cimitero** - *nm*	cemetery
1752	**reazione** - *nf*	reaction
1754	**cioccolato** - *nm*	chocolate
1755	**orgoglio** - *nm*	pride
1757	**giocatore** - *nm*	player, gambler
1758	**cretino** - *adj; nm*	stupid; cretin
1760	**golf** - *nm*	golf, sweater, jersey
1761	**ara** - *nf*	macaw, altar
1762	**capacità** - *nf*	capacity
1765	**bandiera** - *nf*	flag
1768	**contea** - *nf*	county
1769	**umanità** - *nf*	humanity
1770	**professionista** - *adj; nm&f; nm*	professional; professional; expert
1771	**calore** - *nm*	heat
1773	**disposizione** - *nf*	arrangement
1775	**delitto** - *nm*	crime
1777	**umore** - *nm*	mood, humor
1778	**superficie** - *nf*	surface
1779	**divano** - *nm*	sofa
1780	**cabina** - *nf*	cabin
1781	**saluto** - *nm*	greeting
1782	**raggio** - *nm*	radius, spoke, beam, range, ray
1783	**fiato** - *nm*	breath
1786	**ritmo** - *nm*	rhythm
1787	**costo** - *nm*	cost
1789	**pubblicità** - *nf*	advertising
1790	**sport** - *nm*	sport, sports

1791	**eccitante** - *adj; nm*	exciting; stimulate, upper
1792	**zuppa** - *nf*	soup
1793	**diario** - *nm*	diary
1794	**cavo** - *nm; adj*	cable, wire; hollow
1796	**collina** - *nf*	hill
1799	**struttura** - *nf*	structure
1801	**riserva** - *nf*	reserve, reservation
1802	**analisi** - *nf*	analysis
1804	**cintura** - *nf*	belt
1806	**patata** - *nf*	potato, pussy (coll)
1807	**sforzo** - *nm*	effort
1808	**scrittore** - *nm*	writer
1809	**reputazione** - *nf; nm*	reputation; credit, standing
1810	**spiegazione** - *nf*	explanation
1812	**religione** - *nf*	religion
1814	**rinforzo** - *nm*	reinforcement
1815	**conseguenza** - *nf*	result, consequence
1817	**evento** - *nm*	event
1818	**traditore** - *adj; nm*	treacherousl.; traitor
1819	**proiettile** - *nm*	bullet, projectile
1820	**costume** - *nm*	costume, custom, suit
1824	**vasca** - *nm*	tub
1825	**giuria** - *nf*	jury
1826	**sfida** - *nf*	challenge
1827	**catena** - *nf*	chain
1828	**schiavo** - *nm*	slave
1830	**beva(anda)** - *nf*	drink
1831	**febbre** - *nf*	temperature, fever
1833	**tragedia** - *nf*	tragedy
1834	**monte** - *nm*	mountain, mount
1836	**olio** - *nm*	oil
1837	**barone** - *nm*	baron
1838	**pizza** - *nf*	pizza
1842	**capo** - *nm*	boss
1844	**carattere** - *nm*	character
1846	**fila** - *nf*	row, line
1847	**pene** - *nm*	penis
1850	**petrolio** - *nm*	oil, petroleum
1851	**schermo** - *nm*	screen, monitor
1854	**gentiluomo** - *nm*	gentleman
1855	**argento** - *nm*	silver
1856	**orso** - *nm*	bear
1857	**fico** - *nm*	fig
1859	**ripresa** - *nf*	recovery
1860	**circo** - *nm*	circus
1861	**organizzazione** - *nf*	organization
1862	**tassa** - *nf*	fee, tax
1863	**arabo** - *adj; nm/f*	Arabic; Arab
1864	**indiano** - *adj; nm/f*	Indian; Indian
1865	**tappeto** - *nm*	carpet
1866	**massa** - *nf*	mass
1869	**file** - *nm*	file (set of records)
1870	**terapia** - *nf*	therapy
1872	**soggetto** - *nm*	subject
1874	**punizione** - *nf*	punishment
1876	**immaginazione** - *nf*	imagination
1878	**botto** - *nf; nm*	blow, hit; explosion
1879	**difficoltà** - *nf*	difficulties, difficulty, trouble
1882	**luglio** - *nm*	July
1883	**gioiello** - *nm*	jewel
1885	**cultura** - *nf*	culture
1886	**botte** - *nf*	barrel, cask
1889	**gomma** - *nf*	rubber, gum, tire
1891	**impresa** - *nf*	firm, enterprise
1896	**sorveglianza** - *nf*	surveillance
1898	**scambio** - *nm*	exchange
1900	**indovino** - *nm*	fortune-teller
1901	**coincidenza** - *nf*	coincidence
1902	**gabbia** - *nf*	cage
1903	**duca** - *nm*	duke
1905	**comitato** - *nm*	committee

1906 **magazzino** - *nm* warehouse, magazine
1907 **misura** - *nf* measure
1908 **disegno** - *nm* drawing
1911 **fisico** - *adj; nm* physical (fisica= physics)
1912 **episodio** - *nm* episode
1916 **sapore** - *nm* flavor, taste
1917 **confusione** - *nf* confusion
1919 **drago** - *nm* dragon
1920 **valle** - *nf* Valley
1922 **gesto** - *nm* gesture
1923 **bimbo** - *nm* baby, child
1925 **circostanza** - *nf* circumstance
1927 **villa** - *nf* villa
1928 **centesimo** - *adj; nm* hundredth; cent
1929 **percorso** - *nm* route
1931 **terrore** - *nm* terror
1932 **affetto** - *nm; adj* affection, love; affected
1934 **tocco** - *nm* touch
1935 **deposito** - *nm* deposit
1936 **coniglio** - *nm* rabbit
1938 **preparato** - *adj; nm* prepared; specimen, compound
1940 **pasto** - *nm* meal
1941 **garage** - *nm; nf* garage (box); garage (autoparking)
1943 **visita** - *nf* visit
1944 **mezzogiorno** - *nm* noon, midday
1945 **caos** - *nm* chaos
1947 **cappotto** - *nm* coat
1948 **succo** - *nm* juice
1951 **marco** - *nm* mark
1952 **armadio** - *nm* wardrobe, closet
1953 **ideale** - *adj; nm* ideal; ideal
1955 **espressione** - *nf* expression
1956 **piazza** - *nf* square, plaza
1960 **vice** - *nm* vice, deputy
1962 **tatto** - *nm* (sense) touch, tact
1963 **rovina** - *nf* ruin, ruination
1966 **passeggero** - *nm* passenger
1969 **cognome** - *nm* last name
1970 **licenza** - *nf* license
1971 **suono** - *nm* sound
1975 **cantina** - *nf* cellar, basement, winery
1976 **identità** - *nf* identity
1977 **coro** - *nm* choir
1978 **busta** - *nf* envelope
1979 **ottobre** - *nm* October
1980 **temperatura** - *nf* temperature
1981 **bambola** - *nf* doll
1986 **istituto** - *nm* institute
1988 **partner** - *nm* partner
1989 **acciaio** - *nm* steel
1990 **passaporto** - *nm* passport
1991 **unione** - *nf* union
1993 **DNA** - *abbr* DNA
1994 **tigre** - *nf* tiger
1997 **arto** - *nm* limb
2003 **intervista** - *nf* interview
2004 **cortesia** - *nf* courtesy
2005 **linguaggio** - *nm* language, speech
2006 **squalo** - *nm* shark
2011 **internet** - *nm* Internet
2012 **conferenza** - *nf* conference
2013 **romanzo** - *nm* novel, romance
2016 **chitarra** - *nf* guitar
2018 **congresso** - *nm* congress
2019 **pazzia** - *nf* madness
2020 **brindisi** - *nm* toast (social drinking), pledge
2021 **appetito** - *nm* appetite, hunger
2022 **fango** - *nm* mud, dirt

2027	**fantasia** - *nf*	fantasy
2029	**roccia** - *nf*	rock
2030	**lancia** - *nf*	spear
2035	**frutta** - *nf*	fruit
2036	**clacson** - *nm*	horn (automotive)
2038	**emozione** - *nf*	emotion
2043	**munizione** - *nf*	munition
2047	**corretto** - *nm*	correct
2049	**chiappa** - *nf*	(colll) butt cheek, bottom, backside
2050	**maresciallo** - *nm*	marshal
2052	**abitante** - *nm*	inhabitant
2053	**addestramento** - *nm*	training
2054	**brusio** - *nm*	buzz
2055	**distretto** - *nm*	district
2056	**nervo** - *nm*	nerve
2057	**flotta** - *nf*	fleet
2058	**branco** - *nm*	herd, pack, flock
2059	**tecnico** - *adj; nm*	technical; technician
2060	**merce** - *nf*	goods, wares, merchandise
2061	**sconosciuto** - *adj; nm*	unknown; stranger, unkown
2062	**stivale** - *nm*	boot
2063	**campanello** - *nm*	bell
2065	**veicolo** - *nm*	vehicle
2066	**preghiera** - *nf*	prayer
2067	**biscotto** - *nm*	cookie, biscuit
2068	**ammiraglio** - *nm*	admiral
2070	**ambasciatore** - *nm*	ambassador
2072	**alcol** - *nm*	alcohol
2073	**trasmissione** - *nf*	transmission
2074	**verme** - *nm*	worm, maggot
2076	**tono** - *nm*	tone
2078	**straniero** - *adj; nm/f*	foreign, alien; foreigner
2079	**divisione** - *nf*	division
2080	**acquisto** - *nm*	buy, purchase
2081	**produttore** - *nm*	producer
2083	**bionda** - *nf/m; adj*	blonde
2085	**batteria** - *nf*	battery, drums
2087	**cravatta** - *nf*	necktie
2089	**giugno** - *nm*	June
2091	**procedura** - *nf*	procedure
2093	**infanzia** - *nf*	childhood
2094	**aumento** - *nm*	increase
2095	**stretto** - *adj; nm*	strict, strait; narrow
2098	**distruzione** - *nf*	destruction
2099	**vedovo** - *nm/f*	widower, widow
2101	**tramite** - *nm; prep*	means, medium; through
2102	**fermata** - *nf*	stop
2104	**registrazione** - *nf*	registration
2106	**terrorista** - *nf*	terrorist
2108	**servo** - *nm*	servant
2110	**tema** - *nf*	theme, topic
2112	**carburante** - *nm*	fuel
2113	**sfortuna** - *nf*	bad luck
2115	**accento** - *nm*	accent
2116	**materia** - *nf*	matter
2119	**demonio** - *nm*	devil, demon
2121	**simbolo** - *nm*	symbol
2122	**orario** - *nm; adj*	time, hours, timetable; hourly
2124	**ossigeno** - *nm*	oxygen
2125	**giovedì** - *nm*	Thursday
2127	**bacio** - *nm*	kiss
2128	**pallottola** - *nf*	bullet
2131	**maglietta** - *nf*	t-shirt
2133	**segretario** - *nm/f*	secretary
2134	**banco** - *nm*	bench, counter, bank, desk
2135	**fatica** - *nf*	fatigue
2136	**elemento** - *nm*	element
2137	**ostaggio** - *nm*	hostage

2139	**pastore** - *nm*	shepherd, pastor
2140	**salvatore** - *nm*	savior
2142	**confronto** - *nm*	comparison
2143	**palestra** - *nf*	gym
2144	**origine** - *nf*	origin, source
2147	**istinto** - *nm*	instinct
2148	**burro** - *nm*	butter
2149	**grilletto** - *nm*	trigger
2150	**abitudine** - *nf*	habit
2151	**imbarazzo** - *nm*	embarrassment
2153	**maggio** - *nm*	May
2154	**marte** - *nm*	Mars
2156	**sofferenza** - *nf*	suffering
2157	**giurato** - *adj; nm*	swon; juror
2158	**eroina** - *nf*	heroin, heroine
2161	**agio** - *nm*	ease
2162	**custodia** - *nf*	custody
2164	**droga** - *nf*	drug
2166	**temporale** - *adj; nm*	temporal; (thunder) storm
2168	**ione** - *nm*	ion
2171	**economia** - *nf*	economy, economics
2172	**intervento** - *nm*	intervention
2173	**miniera** - *nf*	mine
2177	**legame** - *nm*	bond, tie, link, connection
2178	**insetto** - *nm*	insect, bug
2181	**metodo** - *nm*	method
2184	**tensione** - *nf*	tension, voltage
2185	**trono** - *nm*	throne
2186	**giungla** - *nf*	jungle
2189	**caporale** - *nm*	corporal
2190	**tradimento** - *nm*	betrayal, treason, treachery
2193	**pozzo** - *nm*	well
2194	**possesso** - *nm*	possession
2195	**demone** - *nm*	demon
2198	**mobile** - *adj; nm*	mobile; furniture
2199	**medaglia** - *nf*	medal
2201	**atteggiamento** - *nm*	attitude
2204	**sentiero** - *nm*	pathway, trail
2205	**rifiuto** - *nm*	refusal, rejection, waste
2208	**salsa** - *nf*	sauce
2210	**monaco** - *nm&f*	monk
2213	**fune** - *nm; nf*	cable, wire; rope, linen
2214	**inviato** - *nm*	envoy, correspondent
2216	**stipendio** - *nm*	salary
2217	**comunità** - *nf*	community
2218	**inizio** - *nm*	beginning
2219	**varo** - *nm*	launch, launching
2222	**ritrovato** - *nm*	finding, discovery
2223	**manuale** - *adj; nm*	manual
2224	**sacrificio** - *nm*	sacrifice
2229	**franco** - *adj; nm*	frank, free; franc
2232	**lira** - *nf*	lira
2233	**pelo** - *nm*	hair, fur, coat
2235	**trasporto** - *nm*	transport
2236	**cassaforte** - *nf*	safe, strongbox
2237	**capitolo** - *nm*	chapter
2239	**tara** - *nf*	tare, defect, faint
2242	**tubo** - *nm*	tube, pipe
2244	**codardo** - *adj; nm/f*	cowardly; coward
2245	**riparo** - *nm*	shelter
2246	**tradizione** - *nf*	tradition
2247	**martedì** - *nm*	Tuesday
2249	**gonna** - *nf*	skirt
2250	**mucca** - *nf*	cow
2252	**educazione** - *nf*	education
2260	**mail** - *nf*	email
2262	**condotto** - *adj; nm*	conducted; duct, conduit, canal
2264	**strumento** - *nm*	tool

2265	**bentornato** - *int; nm*	Welcome back!; welcome
2270	**popolazione** - *nf*	population
2273	**manager** - *nm*	manager
2275	**quota** - *nf*	quota, share, quote
2276	**porno** - *adj; nm*	porn
2277	**euro** - *nm*	Euro
2278	**pacchetto** - *nm*	package
2279	**polso** - *nm*	wrist, pulse
2280	**fratellino** - *nm*	(younger) brother (coll)
2284	**intelligenza** - *nf*	intelligence
2285	**confessione** - *nf*	confession
2288	**scommessa** - *nf*	bet
2290	**denuncia** - *nf*	complaint
2293	**seno** - *nf*	breast
2295	**pacco** - *nm*	pack, parcel
2296	**comunista** - *adj; nm*	communist
2298	**mela** - *nf*	apple
2299	**carrozza** - *nf*	carriage
2301	**scienziato** - *nm*	scientist
2304	**novembre** - *nm*	November
2306	**apertura** - *nf*	opening
2307	**amministrazione** - *nf*	administration
2310	**anniversario** - *nm*	anniversary
2311	**cacciatore** - *nm*	hunter
2312	**complesso** - *adj; nm*	complex, whole; complex
2313	**ipotesi** - *nf*	hypothesis, speculation, assumption
2314	**hall** - *nf*	hall, lobby
2315	**agosto** - *nm*	August
2317	**estero** - *nm*	abroad
2318	**asilo** - *nm*	asylum, kindergarten, nursery (school)
2320	**supporto** - *nm*	support
2321	**generazione** - *nf*	generation
2322	**nebbia** - *nf*	fog, mist
2323	**salita** - *nf*	climb
2325	**volume** - *nm*	volume
2328	**comunicazione** - *nf*	communication
2329	**egoista** - *adj; nm*	selfish; egoist
2333	**patatina** - *nf*	french fry, potato chip, plump little girl (coll), pussy (coll)
2337	**copione** - *nm*	script
2338	**coma** - *nm*	coma
2340	**lama** - *nf; nm*	blade; llama
2341	**statua** - *nf*	statue
2343	**record** - *nm*	record
2344	**astronave** - *nf*	spaceship
2345	**operaio** - *nm; adj*	worker; working, labouring
2346	**concetto** - *nm*	concept
2349	**bara** - *nf*	coffin
2351	**autore** - *nm*	author
2355	**psichiatra** - *nm*	psychiatrist
2358	**autunno** - *nm*	autumn, fall
2359	**ambasciata** - *nf*	embassy
2360	**quantità** - *nf*	amount
2364	**collezione** - *nf*	collection
2367	**infarto** - *nm*	infarct
2371	**vampiro** - *nm*	vampire
2373	**cortile** - *nm*	courtyard, yard
2374	**allenatore** - *nm*	coach
2376	**scudo** - *nm*	shield
2377	**sviluppo** - *nm*	development
2378	**autostrada** - *nf*	motorway, highway
2380	**elenco** - *nm*	list, directory
2381	**matematico** - *adj; nm*	mathematical; mathemactician
2382	**collegamento** - *nm*	connection, link

2384	**autorizzazione** - *nf*	authorization
2385	**aprile** - *nm*	April
2387	**insalata** - *nf*	salad
2389	**sceneggiatura** - *nf*	screenplay
2394	**cartello** - *nm*	cartel, sign
2396	**vacca** - *nf*	cow
2397	**ansia** - *nf*	anxiety
2398	**preside** - *nm*	dean, principal
2399	**equilibrio** - *nm*	equilibrium
2401	**unghia** - *nf*	nail
2402	**fica (figa)** - *nf*	fanny, pussy (both used: fanny,pussy, fig)
2403	**lusso** - *nm*	luxury
2405	**metallo** - *nm*	metal
2406	**personalità** - *nf*	personality
2407	**portafoglio** - *nm*	portfolio, wallet
2408	**canna** - *nf*	cane, barrel, rod
2410	**lavoratore** - *nm; adj*	worker; hard-working
2412	**orrore** - *nm*	dread, terror
2413	**reato** - *nm*	crime
2419	**testamento** - *nm*	will
2420	**satana** - *nm*	Satan
2421	**galleria** - *nf*	gallery
2424	**riuscita** - *nf*	success
2425	**esecuzione** - *nf*	execution
2426	**bicicletta (bici)** - *nf*	bicycle, (bike)
2428	**colloquio** - *nm*	(job) interview, talk, meeting
2429	**elezione** - *nf*	election
2430	**umorismo** - *nm*	humor, sense of humor
2431	**percento** - *nm*	per cent
2432	**assistenza** - *nf*	assistance
2434	**muso** - *nm*	muzzle, nose, face
2437	**fallimento** - *nm*	failure, bankruptcy
2438	**martello** - *nm*	hammer
2440	**assassinio** - *nm*	murder, assasination
2442	**industria** - *nf*	industry
2443	**indizio** - *nm*	clue, indication
2444	**sorellina** - *nf*	litte sister, younger sister, baby sister
2446	**preda** - *nf*	prey
2447	**guadagno** - *nm*	gain
2449	**disagio** - *nm*	discomfort
2450	**prostituta** - *nf*	prostitute
2451	**asso** - *nm*	ace
2452	**stadio** - *nm*	stadium, stage
2453	**chiusa** - *nf*	close, lock, sluice
2455	**serpente** - *nm*	snake, serpent
2456	**giunto** - *nm; adj*	joint, coupling; joined
2457	**perla** - *nf*	pearl
2459	**mammina** - *nf*	mummy
2460	**microfono** - *nm*	microphone
2463	**meta** - *nf*	goal, destination
2465	**trasferimento** - *nm*	transfer
2466	**stress** - *nm*	stress
2469	**scopata** - *nf*	sweep, fuck, shag
2471	**singolo** - *adj; nm*	single
2472	**carità** - *nf*	charity
2473	**consigliere** - *nm*	advisor, councilor
2474	**spasso** - *nm*	fun
2475	**promessa** - *nf*	promise
2476	**cioccolata** - *nf*	chocolate
2478	**applauso** - *nm*	applause
2480	**dicembre** - *nm*	December
2482	**civiltà** - *nf*	civilization
2483	**funzione** - *nf*	function
2485	**valigetta** - *nf*	briefcase
2487	**sostegno** - *nm*	support
2488	**protetta** - *nf*	protection
2490	**ingegnere** - *nm*	engineer
2492	**targa** - *nf*	plate, nameplate
2494	**considerazione** - *nf*	consideration

2495 **repubblica** - *nf* republic

2496 **esperimento** - *nm* experiment

2498 **cucciolo** - *nm* puppy

2499 **muscolo** - *nm* muscolo

2500 **udienza** - *nf* hearing, audience

F. Numerals

Rank	**Italian** - *Part of Speech*	English
64	**primo** - *num; adj*	first
66	**due** - *adj; num*	two
139	**tre** - *adj; num*	three
278	**quattro** - *adj; num*	four
280	**cinque** - *adj; num*	five
399	**dieci** - *adj; num*	ten
417	**milione** - *adj; num*	million
508	**sette** - *adj; num*	seven
544	**otto** - *adj; num*	eight
745	**nove** - *adj; num*	nine
1019	**cento** - *adj; num*	hundred
1078	**migliaio** - *adj; num*	thousand
1105	**zero** - *adj; num*	zero
1124	**sei** - *adj; num*	six
1139	**quarto** - *adj; num; nm*	fourth; quarter
1186	**venti** - *adj; num*	twenty
1356	**centinaio** - *adj; num*	to displeasure, dislike, be sorry
1518	**miliardo** - *adj; num*	billion
1602	**dodici** - *adj; num*	twelve
2075	**quindici** - *adj; num*	fifteen
2234	**sesto** - *adj; num*	sixth
2254	**undici** - *adj; num*	eleven
2274	**quinto** - *adj; num*	fifth

G. Prepositions

Rank	Italian - *Part of Speech*	English
6	**a** **al, allo, all', alla, ai, agli, alla - prep*	to, in, at
8	**per** - *prep*	for, to, by, in
9	**in** **nel, nello, nell', nella, nei, negli, nelle - prep*	in, into
17	**con** - *prep*	with, by
19	**da** **dal, dallo, dall', dalla, dai, dagli, dalle*	from
28	**di** *del, dello, dell', della, dei, degli, delle -prep*	of, to; than, and
72	**su** **sul, sullo, sulll', sulla, sui, sugli, sulle - adv; prep*	on,up; on, about
93	**via** - *prep; adv; nf*	via, by; away; street, way
106	**dopo** - *prep; adv*	after
130	**tra** – *prep*	between, among
152	**dentro** – *prep*	in, inside
175	**sotto** - *adv; prep*	under, below; under
201	**fino** - *prep; adv; adj*	till; even; fine, subtle
213	**secondo** - *prep; nm; adv; adj*	according to; second
219	**meno** - *adv; adj; prep; conj*	less; less; unless; no so (much as)
229	**salvo** - *prep; adj*	save, but; safe
237	**contro** - *adv; prep*	to displeasure, dislike, be sorry
267	**dietro** - *prep; nm; adj; adv*	behind; back, rear; after; after
275	**verso** - *prep; nm*	to, towards; direction, way
317	**sopra** - *adv; prep*	above, on
334	**davanti** - *adj; adv; prep*	front; in front
354	**fra** - *prep*	between, among
376	**lungo** - *prep; adj; nm*	long; along; length
427	**durante** - *prep; adv*	during, in, over; while
456	**oltre** - *adv; prep*	over; over, more than, beyond
458	**circa** - *adv; prep*	about
614	**attraverso** - *adv; prep*	through, across
643	**entro** - *prep*	within, by
929	**tranne** - *prep*	except
1162	**nonostante** - *prep; conj; adv*	despite; altough; even though, nevertheless
1379	**attorno** - *adv; prep*	about; around
2046	**quassù** - *prep*	up here
2100	**eccetto** - *prep*	except
2101	**tramite** - *nm; prep*	means, medium; through
2259	**presso** - *prep; adv; adj*	at,in; near; close

H. Pronouns

Rank	Italian - *Part of Speech*	English
2	**che** - *conj; pron; adj*	that; which, who; what
5	**un, uno, una** - *art; pron*	a, an; one
11	**mi** – *pron*	me
13	**si** – *pron*	one-, its-, thems-, him-, her-, yourself
15	**ti** – *pron*	you
16	**cosa** - *pron; nf*	what; thing
21	**come** – *pron*	as, how
22	**io** – *pron*	I
23	**ci** – *pron*	ourselves, us
24	**questo** - *adj; pron*	this; such, this one
27	**tu** – *pron*	you
29	**me (stesso)** - *pron*	me (myself)
30	**mio** – *pron*	my
33	**te** – *pron*	you
35	**lei** – *pron*	she, her
36	**ne** - *adj; pron*	any; of it, of them
46	**chi** – *pron*	to displeasure, dislike, be sorry
49	**quello** – *pron*	one
53	**lui** – *pron*	him, he
55	**niente** - *pron; nm*	nothing, anything, none
63	**noi** – *pron*	we
65	**suo (- a)** - *pron*	his (her)
75	**loro** – *pron*	their
76	**vi** - *pron; adv*	you; there
82	**voi** – *pron*	you
87	**li** – *pron*	them
91	**altro** - *adj; pron*	other, another, more
95	**proprio** - *adj; nm; pron; adv*	one's own; own; its; just, exactly
104	**nessuno** - *adj; pron*	no; nobody, no one, none, anyone
110	**qualcuno (- a)** - *pron*	someone
115	**cui** - *pron*	which
121	**ce** - *pron*	us
124	**qualche** - *adj; pron*	some, few, any; a few
147	**nostro** - *pron*	our
187	**stesso** - *adj; pron*	same; itself
202	**nulla** - *nf; pron*	nothing; nothing, anything
214	**ciò** - *pron*	that, it
222	**quale** - *adj; pron; conj*	what, which; which; as
223	**vostro** - *pron*	your (pl)
298	**qual** - *adv; pron*	everytime, whenever; what, which
406	**alcuni** - *pron; adj*	some, several; few, any
470	**chiunque** - *pron*	anyone
489	**ve** - *pron*	you
566	**alcune** - *pron*	several, some
698	**qualcun** - *pron*	meter; tape measure
727	**tale** - *adv; pron; art*	such; such; a, an
876	**ognuno** - *pron*	each
999	**egli** - *pron*	he
1108	**sé** - *pron*	himself, herself
1657	**essi** - *pron*	they, them
1688	**ella** - *pron*	she
1701	**glielo (di glie e lo)** - *pron*	it to him

1784 **colui** - *pron* he

1853 **onde** - *adv; conj; pron* hence, whence; so that, so as; of which, whose

1918 **essa** - *pron* it

1964 **esso** - *pron* it, he

2209 **altrettanto** - *adv; adj; pron* as; as much; just as many

2319 **ciascuno** - *adj; pron* each, all, every; everyone, everybody

I. Verbs

Rank	Italian - *Part of Speech*	English
7	**essere** - *verb*	to be
12	**avere** - *verb*	to have
37	**fare** - *verb*	to do
41	**sapere** - *verb*	to know
44	**andare** - *verb*	to go, move, proceed, run
47	**dire** - *verb*	to say
54	**volere** - *verb*	to want
60	**stare** - *verb*	to stay
61	**potere** - *verb; nm*	to be able; power
78	**dovere** - *verb; nm*	to have to, muste, should; duty, obligation
94	**vedere** - *verb*	to see
108	**porre** - *verb*	to put, place
118	**venire** - *verb*	to come
131	**guardare** - *verb*	to look, watch
134	**sembrare** - *verb*	to seem, look, appear, sound
136	**parlare** - *verb*	to speak, talk
137	**dispiacere** - *verb*	to displeasure, dislike, be sorry
142	**aspettare** - *verb*	to wait
146	**piacere** - *verb*	to pleasure; like
154	**pensare** - *verb*	to think
164	**bastare** - *verb*	to suffice
168	**portare** - *verb*	to bring
172	**sentire** - *verb*	to feel, hear
176	**prendere** - *verb*	to take
185	**ideare** - *verb*	to design
186	**capire** - *verb*	to understand
192	**succedere** - *verb*	to happen, occur, succeed
193	**volgere** - *verb*	to turn
203	**trovare** - *verb*	to find
204	**dare** - *verb*	to give
206	**servire** - *verb*	to serve
210	**leggere** - *verb*	to read
211	**scusare** - *verb*	to excuse
220	**morire** - *verb*	to die
230	**credere** - *verb*	to believe
235	**uccidere** - *verb*	to kill
238	**tornare** - *verb*	to return
244	**cercare** - *verb*	to search
247	**chiamare** - *verb*	to call
263	**perdere** - *verb*	to lose
264	**uscire** - *verb*	to go out, leave
266	**importare** - *verb*	to import
269	**lasciare** - *verb*	to leave
272	**sperare** - *verb*	to hope
273	**chiedere** - *verb*	to ask (for), enquire
286	**entrare** - *verb*	to enter
294	**passare** - *verb*	to pass, spend, switch
296	**capitare** - *verb*	to happen, occur
300	**vivere** - *verb*	to live
301	**riuscire** - *verb*	to succeed, able
305	**ascoltare** - *verb*	to listen
307	**conoscere** - *verb*	to know
308	**significare** - *verb*	to mean
315	**visitare** - *verb*	to visit, see
318	**mangiare** - *verb*	to eat
319	**provare** - *verb*	to try
338	**parere** - *verb; nm*	to think, seem; opinion
340	**tenere** - *verb*	to hold, keep
344	**finire** - *verb*	to end, finish
350	**lavorare** - *verb*	to work
364	**spiacere** - *verb*	to be sorry

367	**agire** - *verb*	to act
368	**smettere** - *verb*	to stop
369	**dormire** - *verb*	to sleep
380	**cenare** - *verb*	to have dinner
382	**arrivare** - *verb*	to arrive
400	**restare** - *verb*	to stay, remain, maintain
410	**mettere** - *verb*	to put
418	**diventare** - *verb*	to become
425	**continuare** - *verb*	to continue
428	**ricevere** - *verb*	to receive
433	**iniziare** - *verb*	to start
434	**giocare** - *verb*	to play
435	**permettere** - *verb*	to allow
443	**preoccupare** - *verb*	to worry
453	**mandare** - *verb*	to send
472	**usare** - *verb*	to use
474	**cambiare** - *verb*	to change
475	**funzionare** - *verb*	to function
492	**peccare** - *verb*	to sin
502	**addossare** - *verb*	to lean
505	**pagare** - *verb*	to pay
511	**cariare** - *verb*	to rot
521	**dimenticare** - *verb*	to forget
535	**silenziare** - *verb*	to mute
540	**ricordare** - *verb*	to remember
547	**interessare** - *verb*	to affect
551	**aiutare** - *verb*	to help
567	**vestire** - *verb*	to dress
568	**rispondere** - *verb*	to answer
569	**sedere** - *verb*	to sit down
576	**partire** - *verb*	to leave
583	**valere** - *verb*	to be worth
586	**ordinare** - *verb*	to order
591	**vincere** - *verb*	to win
598	**immaginare** - *verb*	to imagine
606	**esistere** - *verb*	to exist
610	**unire** - *verb*	to unite
613	**scappare** - *verb*	to escape
617	**chiudere** - *verb*	to close
625	**rimanere** - *verb*	to stay
626	**cacciare** - *verb*	to hunt, throw out
630	**controllare** - *verb*	to check
633	**scrivere** - *verb*	to write
635	**volare** - *verb*	to fly
636	**promettere** - *verb*	to promise
649	**fermare** - *verb*	to stop
650	**calmare** - *verb*	to calm
665	**colpire** - *verb*	to hit
672	**correre** - *verb*	to run
681	**scherzare** - *verb*	to joke
689	**intendere** - *verb*	to hear, mean, intend
693	**toccare** - *verb*	to touch
694	**muovere** - *verb*	to move
696	**salare** - *verb*	to salt
697	**comprare** - *verb*	to buy
700	**scegliere** - *verb*	to choose
702	**sbrigare** - *verb*	to hurry up
703	**adorare** - *verb*	to worship, adore, love
707	**scommettere** - *verb*	to bet
718	**fottere** - *verb*	to fuck
719	**combattere** - *verb*	to fight
723	**sposare** - *verb*	to marry
725	**amare** - *verb*	to love
726	**rompere** - *verb*	to break
731	**armare** - *verb*	to arm
737	**piangere** - *verb*	to cry
739	**ballare** - *verb*	to dance
741	**nascere** - *verb*	to be born
742	**alzare** - *verb*	to raise
746	**salvare** - *verb*	to save
755	**saltare** - *verb*	to skip, jump
758	**ridere** - *verb*	to laugh
764	**fregare** - *verb*	to rub, care
765	**sparare** - *verb*	to shoot

768	**incontrare** - *verb*	to meet
773	**temere** - *verb*	to fear, be afraid
778	**drogare** - *verb*	to drug
783	**imparare** - *verb*	to learn
785	**cominciare** - *verb*	to begin
787	**riguardare** - *verb*	to concern
790	**seguire** - *verb*	to follow
791	**aprire** - *verb*	to open
797	**tornire** - *verb*	to throw
800	**rendere** - *verb*	to make
829	**presentire** - *verb*	to foresee
831	**scoprire** - *verb*	to discover
833	**ferire** - *verb*	to hurt
839	**ringraziare** - *verb*	to thank
844	**suonare** - *verb*	to play (music or instrument), sound, ring
860	**difendere** - *verb*	to defend
862	**supporre** - *verb*	to suppose
866	**attentare** - *verb*	to attempt
868	**scendere** - *verb*	to get off
871	**baciare** - *verb*	to kiss
887	**tirare** - *verb*	to pull
890	**filare** - *verb*	to spin
892	**svegliare** - *verb*	to wake
900	**nascondere** - *verb*	to hide
901	**rischiare** - *verb*	to risk
908	**divergere** - *verb*	to diverge
909	**camminare** - *verb*	to walk
915	**dipendere** - *verb*	to depend
916	**gridare** - *verb*	to shout
919	**ottenere** - *verb*	to get, obtain
920	**rodere** - *verb*	to gnaw, fret, prey on
921	**salire** - *verb*	to go up, climb, rise
944	**rilassare** - *verb*	to relax
950	**preferire** - *verb*	to prefer
962	**indirizzare** - *verb*	to address
965	**fingere** - *verb*	to pretend
970	**notare** - *verb*	to note
985	**guidare** - *verb*	to lead
986	**decidere** - *verb*	to decide
991	**vendere** - *verb*	to sell
992	**cadere** - *verb*	to fall
1003	**girare** - *verb*	to turn
1005	**insegnare** - *verb*	to teach
1007	**porgere** - *verb*	to extend
1009	**contare** - *verb*	to count
1010	**cantare** - *verb*	to sing
1012	**creare** - *verb*	to create
1042	**evitare** - *verb*	to avoid
1043	**accettare** - *verb*	to accept
1046	**mantenere** - *verb*	to keep, maintain
1048	**lottare** - *verb*	to fight
1049	**distruggere** - *verb*	to destroy
1057	**arrabbiare** - *verb*	to get angry, get mad
1061	**arrestare** - *verb*	to stop
1079	**occupare** - *verb*	to occupy
1098	**presentare** - *verb*	to present, submit
1103	**spiegare** - *verb*	to explain
1111	**accadere** - *verb*	to happen
1113	**sbagliare** - *verb*	to make a mistake
1120	**attendere** - *verb*	to wait for
1128	**ammazzare** - *verb*	to kill
1135	**proteggere** - *verb*	to protect
1149	**affrontare** - *verb*	to face
1158	**desiderare** - *verb*	to wish
1164	**dannare** - *verb*	to damn
1169	**risolvere** - *verb*	to solve
1172	**pilotare** - *verb*	to pilot, fly
1174	**raggiungere** - *verb*	to reach
1183	**discutere** - *verb*	to discuss
1195	**spaventare** - *verb*	to scare, frighten
1197	**preparare** - *verb*	to prepare
1214	**rubare** - *verb*	to steal
1228	**studiare** - *verb*	to study

1229	**praticare** - *verb*	to practice
1230	**togliere** - *verb*	to remove, take off
1233	**tentare** - *verb*	to attempt, try, tempt
1236	**costruire** - *verb*	to build
1239	**fugare** - *verb*	to dispel
1242	**sorridere** - *verb*	to smile
1251	**sopravvivere** - *verb*	to survive
1256	**piantare** - *verb*	to plant
1259	**mancare** - *verb*	to miss
1261	**collegare** - *verb*	to connect, link
1266	**raccontare** - *verb*	to tell
1271	**fidare** - *verb*	to trust
1275	**mostrare** - *verb*	to show
1282	**appartenere** - *verb*	to belong
1283	**rovinare** - *verb*	to ruin
1301	**impazzire** - *verb*	to go crazy
1309	**commettere** - *verb*	to commit
1313	**crescere** - *verb*	to grow
1314	**perdonare** - *verb*	to forgive
1315	**battere** - *verb*	to beat
1316	**invitare** - *verb*	to invite
1318	**fumare** - *verb*	to smoke
1319	**respirare** - *verb*	to breathe
1322	**dirigere** - *verb*	to direct
1326	**colorare** - *verb*	to to color
1340	**abbandonare** - *verb*	to abandon sth, leave sth.
1350	**fuggire** - *verb*	to flee
1358	**scomparire** - *verb*	to disappear
1367	**ripetere** - *verb*	to repeat
1375	**scalare** - *verb*	to climb
1376	**maledire** - *verb*	to curse
1381	**assicurare** - *verb*	to ensure, insure
1384	**levare** - *verb*	to upbeat
1387	**trafficare** - *verb*	to trade, deal, traffic
1389	**riposare** - *verb*	to rest
1401	**stregare** - *verb*	to bewitch
1406	**risultare** - *verb*	to to result
1410	**affascinare** - *verb*	to fascinate
1415	**sistemare** - *verb*	to fix
1421	**specchiare** - *verb*	to mirror
1422	**proporre** - *verb*	to propose, put forward
1431	**mentire** - *verb*	to lie
1437	**firmare** - *verb*	to sign
1455	**offrire** - *verb*	to offer
1463	**coinvolgere** - *verb*	to involve
1469	**marciare** - *verb*	to march
1473	**licenziare** - *verb*	to dismiss
1477	**bloccare** - *verb*	to block
1479	**incendiare** - *verb*	to fire
1498	**tracciare** - *verb*	to draw
1506	**passeggiare** - *verb*	to stroll, walk
1512	**tempestare** - *verb*	to batter, besiege, annoy
1521	**costringere** - *verb*	to force
1525	**sopportare** - *verb*	to bear
1531	**meritare** - *verb*	to deserve
1537	**affittare** - *verb*	to rent
1540	**buttare** - *verb*	to throw
1545	**gelare** - *verb*	to freeze
1548	**sognare** - *verb*	to dream
1550	**trattare** - *verb*	to treat
1553	**sparire** - *verb*	to disappear
1556	**resistere** - *verb*	to resist
1557	**prevedere** - *verb*	to foresee
1563	**tradire** - *verb*	to betray
1564	**votare** - *verb*	to vote
1565	**attaccare** - *verb*	to attack
1568	**dubitare** - *verb*	to doubt
1569	**sorprendere** - *verb*	to surprise
1586	**tagliare** - *verb*	to cut
1596	**assassinare** - *verb*	to assassinate
1597	**dimostrare** - *verb*	to show
1599	**odiare** - *verb*	to hate

1610	**raccomandare** - *verb*	to recommend
1611	**confondere** - *verb*	to confound
1614	**inventare** - *verb*	to invent
1617	**esplodere** - *verb*	to explode
1618	**abitare** - *verb*	to live
1619	**divertire** - *verb*	to entertain
1621	**mordere** - *verb*	to bite
1627	**convenire** - *verb*	to agree
1629	**apprezzare** - *verb*	to appreciate
1649	**beccare** - *verb*	to peck, catch
1650	**alare** - *verb*	to andiron
1655	**urlare** - *verb*	to scream
1666	**soffrire** - *verb*	to suffer
1685	**scopare** - *verb*	to sweep, fuck
1691	**complicare** - *verb*	to complicate
1700	**augurare** - *verb*	to wish
1704	**rivedere** - *verb*	to review, revise
1707	**guadagnare** - *verb*	to earn, gain
1711	**accomodare** - *verb*	to accommodate
1713	**stringere** - *verb*	to tighten
1715	**ritornare** - *verb*	to return
1717	**superare** - *verb*	to exceed
1718	**nuotare** - *verb*	to swim
1726	**festeggiare** - *verb*	to celebrate
1727	**danzare** - *verb*	to dance
1728	**benedire** - *verb*	to bless
1732	**gestire** - *verb*	to handle, manage
1738	**organizzare** - *verb*	to organize, arrange
1743	**pregare** - *verb*	to pray
1745	**ricominciare** - *verb*	to recommence
1746	**pulire** - *verb*	to clean
1747	**bruciare** - *verb*	to burn
1756	**combinare** - *verb*	to combine
1759	**disporre** - *verb*	to have
1763	**spostare** - *verb*	to move
1766	**saggiare** - *verb*	to test
1767	**indossare** - *verb*	to wear, put on
1776	**impegnare** - *verb*	to commit
1795	**salutare** - *adj; verb*	healthy; to greet, say goodbye to
1797	**attraversare** - *verb*	to cross
1798	**coprire** - *verb*	to cover
1805	**condannare** - *verb*	to convict
1821	**torcere** - *verb*	to twist
1822	**accompagnare** - *verb*	to accompany
1839	**legare** - *verb*	to tie
1840	**accusare** - *verb*	to accuse
1845	**ricompensare** - *verb*	to reward
1849	**raccogliere** - *verb*	to gather
1867	**viaggiare** - *verb*	to travel
1868	**indovinare** - *verb*	to guess
1871	**catturare** - *verb*	to capture
1873	**assumere** - *verb*	to take, assume
1875	**considerare** - *verb*	to consider
1880	**spegnere** - *verb*	to switch off, turn off
1895	**completare** - *verb*	to complete
1909	**tacere** - *verb*	to be silent
1910	**riprendere** - *verb*	to resume
1930	**sperimentare** - *verb*	to experiment, experience
1937	**sanare** - *verb*	to heal
1942	**coronare** - *verb*	to crown
1946	**causare** - *verb*	to cause
1954	**occorrere** - *verb*	to take
1957	**annunciare** - *verb*	to announce
1958	**telefonare** - *verb*	to call, telephone
1959	**principiare** - *verb*	to principiare
1961	**ammettere** - *verb*	to admit
1967	**riconoscere** - *verb*	to recognize
1968	**deludere** - *verb*	to disappoint
1972	**abbassare** - *verb*	to lower
1973	**patire** - *verb*	to suffer
1982	**ruotare** - *verb*	to rotate

1985	**cucinare** - *verb*	to cook
1987	**trasferire** - *verb*	to transfer
1996	**accendere** - *verb*	to switch, turn on
1998	**spingere** - *verb*	to push
1999	**partecipare** - *verb*	to take part
2002	**avvertire** - *verb*	to warn
2007	**offendere** - *verb*	to offend
2008	**premiare** - *verb*	to reward
2009	**convincere** - *verb*	to convince
2014	**avventurarsi** - *verb*	to venture
2015	**litigare** - *verb*	to quarrel
2025	**tendere** - *verb*	to stretch
2031	**recuperare** - *verb*	to recover, retrieve
2034	**badare** - *verb*	to look after
2037	**influenzare** - *verb*	to influence
2041	**lanciare** - *verb*	to launch
2042	**ridurre** - *verb*	to reduce
2064	**confermare** - *verb*	to confirm
2069	**moneta** - *verb*	
2077	**incastrare** - *verb*	to fit
2086	**picchiare** - *verb*	to beat
2088	**cessare** - *verb*	to cease
2090	**risorgere** - *verb*	to rise again
2092	**osare** - *verb*	to dare
2096	**avvicinare** - *verb*	to approach
2103	**rifiutare** - *verb*	to refuse
2109	**rinunciare** - *verb*	to give up
2114	**mollare** - *verb*	to give
2117	**registrare** - *verb*	to record
2120	**recitare** - *verb*	to recite
2123	**peggiorare** - *verb*	to worsen
2126	**sospirare** - *verb*	to sigh
2129	**spesare** - *verb*	to pay the expenses
2130	**richiedere** - *verb*	to request
2132	**procedere** - *verb*	to continue
2141	**rappresentare** - *verb*	to represent
2145	**empero** - *verb*	empire
2146	**spettare** - *verb*	to belong
2160	**possedere** - *verb*	to own
2167	**comportare** - *verb*	to involve
2169	**tramontare** - *verb*	to set
2170	**aggiungere** - *verb*	to add
2175	**campionare** - *verb*	to sample
2176	**scortare** - *verb*	to escort
2183	**rispettare** - *verb*	to respect
2187	**consegnare** - *verb*	to deliver
2188	**soddisfare** - *verb*	to satisfy
2197	**vomitare** - *verb*	to throw up, puke
2202	**rientrare** - *verb*	to re-enter
2206	**imputare** - *verb*	to attribute sth to
2212	**dichiarare** - *verb*	to declare, claim
2225	**divenire** - *verb*	to become
2226	**popolare** - *adj; verb*	populair; to populate
2227	**investire** - *verb*	to invest
2238	**cifrare** - *verb*	to encipher
2258	**rapire** - *verb*	to kidnap
2261	**dipingere** - *verb*	to paint
2266	**cremare** - *verb*	to cremate
2268	**impattare** - *verb*	to impact
2269	**proibire** - *verb*	to prohibit
2271	**liberare** - *verb*	to release
2272	**giudicare** - *verb*	to judge
2281	**produrre** - *verb*	to produce
2282	**rigare** - *verb*	to scratch
2283	**sospettare** - *verb*	to suspect
2286	**abituare** - *verb*	to accustom
2287	**spendere** - *verb*	to spend
2291	**bucare** - *verb*	to puncture
2292	**assomigliare** - *verb*	to look like, resemble
2294	**gemere** - *verb*	to moan
2308	**riportare** - *verb*	to report, take back
2339	**giungere** - *verb*	to reach
2347	**precedere** - *verb*	to precede

2348	**regalare** - *verb*	to give
2350	**esagerare** - *verb*	to exaggerate
2352	**macchiare** - *verb*	to sully
2353	**condividere** - *verb*	to share
2354	**concedere** - *verb*	to grant
2366	**detestare** - *verb*	to loathe
2368	**rallentare** - *verb*	to decelerate
2372	**murare** - *verb*	to wall
2375	**eliminare** - *verb*	to eliminate
2379	**gettare** - *verb*	to throw
2383	**fucilare** - *verb*	to shoot
2395	**scordare** - *verb*	to forget
2400	**contenere** - *verb*	to contain
2404	**panare** - *verb*	to bread, dip in breadcrumbs
2409	**pisciare** - *verb*	to piss
2414	**riparare** - *verb*	to repair
2415	**comunicare** - *verb*	to communicate
2416	**pattugliare** - *verb*	to patrol
2418	**curare** - *verb*	to treat
2423	**migliorare** - *verb*	to improve
2427	**scavare** - *verb*	to dig
2435	**comprendere** - *verb*	to understand
2436	**spedire** - *verb*	to send
2439	**falsare** - *verb*	to distort
2445	**appellare** - *verb*	to appeal
2458	**comandare** - *verb*	to command
2461	**poetare** - *verb*	to poetize
2464	**piovere** - *verb*	to rain
2479	**ritrattare** - *verb*	to retract, recant
2481	**identificare** - *verb*	to identify
2486	**movimentare** - *verb*	to ship, move, handle
2491	**autorizzare** - *verb*	to permit, authorize
2497	**lavare** - *verb*	to wash
2501	**riflettere** - *verb*	to reflect

5. Italian-English Dictionary Alphabetical Order

Rank	Italian - *Part of Speech*	English
	A	
6	**a** **al, allo, all', alla, ai, agli, alla - prep*	to, in, at
1340	**abbandonare** - *verb*	to abandon sth, leave sth.
1972	**abbassare** - *verb*	to lower
241	**abbastanza** - *adv*	enough
2052	**abitante** - *nm*	inhabitant
1618	**abitare** - *verb*	to live
1317	**abito** - *nm*	dress, suit, attire
2286	**abituare** - *verb*	to accustom
2150	**abitudine** - *nf*	habit
1111	**accadere** - *verb*	to happen
815	**accanto** - *adv*	next
1996	**accendere** - *verb*	to switch, turn on
2115	**accento** - *nm*	accent
1200	**accesso** - *nm*	access
1043	**accettare** - *verb*	to accept
1829	**accetto** - *adj*	acceptable
1989	**acciaio** - *nm*	steel
555	**accidente** - *nf*	accident, fit, incident, damn
1711	**accomodare** - *verb*	to accommodate
1822	**accompagnare** - *verb*	to accompany
155	**accordo** - *nm*	agreement, deal
1914	**accorto** - *adj*	shrewd
1255	**accusa** - *nf*	accusation, charge, prosecution
1840	**accusare** - *verb*	to accuse
239	**acqua** - *nf*	water
2080	**acquisto** - *nm*	buy, purchase
1660	**adatto** - *adj*	suitable
2053	**addestramento** - *nm*	training
450	**addio** - *nm*	goodbye, farewell
2155	**addirittura** - *adv*	even
502	**addossare** - *verb*	to lean
85	**adesso** - *adv*	now
1884	**adorabile** - *adj*	adorable
703	**adorare** - *verb*	to worship, adore, love
2138	**adulto** - *adj*	adult
481	**aereo** - *adj; nm*	air, aerial; plane, airplane
1134	**aeroporto** - *nm*	airport
361	**affare** - *nm*	deal, bargain, business, affair
1410	**affascinare** - *verb*	to fascinate
695	**affatto** - *adv*	at all, quite
1932	**affetto** - *nm; adj*	affection, love; affected
2477	**affinché** - *conj*	so that, in order to
1537	**affittare** - *verb*	to rent
1149	**affrontare** - *verb*	to face
974	**agente** - *nm*	agent
1571	**agenzia** - *nf*	agency
2170	**aggiungere** - *verb*	to add
2161	**agio** - *nm*	ease
367	**agire** - *verb*	to act
2315	**agosto** - *nm*	August
150	**ah** - *int*	ha
1648	**ahi** - *int*	ouch
551	**aiutare** - *verb*	to help
215	**aiuto** - *nm*	help
1292	**ala** - *nf*	wing
1650	**alare** - *verb*	to andiron
1392	**alba** - *nf*	sunrise, dawn
930	**albergo** - *nm*	hotel

878	**albero** - *nm*	tree
2072	**alcol** - *nm*	alcohol
792	**alcun** - *adj*	any
566	**alcune** - *pron*	several, some
406	**alcuni** - *pron; adj*	some, several; few, any
2417	**alieno** - *adj*	alien
1062	**allarme** - *nm*	alarm
2374	**allenatore** - *nm*	coach
59	**allora** - *adv*	then
281	**almeno** - *adv*	at least
2467	**alt** - *int*	halt
984	**altezza** - *nf*	height
442	**alto** - *adj*	high, tall
2209	**altrettanto** - *adv; adj; pron*	as; as much; just as many
594	**altrimenti** - *adv; conj*	otherwise
91	**altro** - *adj; pron*	other, another, more
2230	**altrove** - *adv*	elsewhere
742	**alzare** - *verb*	to raise
1196	**amante** - *nm&f; adj*	lover; fond
725	**amare** - *verb*	to love
1330	**amaro** - *adj; nm*	bitter; bitter, tonic liqour
1096	**amato** - *adj*	beloved
2359	**ambasciata** - *nf*	embassy
2070	**ambasciatore** - *nm*	ambassador
1480	**ambiente** - *nm*	environmnent, room, ambience
1407	**ambulanza** - *nf*	ambulance
1234	**amen** - *int*	amen
776	**americano** - *adj; nm/f*	American; American
1354	**amicizia** - *nf*	friendship
107	**amico** - *nm/f*	friend
1128	**ammazzare** - *verb*	to kill
1961	**ammettere** - *verb*	to admit

2307	**amministrazione** - *nf*	administration
2068	**ammiraglio** - *nm*	admiral
293	**amo** - *nm*	hook, bait
189	**amore** - *nm*	(my) love
1802	**analisi** - *nf*	analysis
51	**anche** - *adv; nf*	also, even; anchor
67	**ancora** - *adv; conj*	yet, still, more; more
44	**andare** - *verb*	to go, move, proceed, run
299	**andata** - *nf*	going
352	**andato** - *adj*	gone
956	**anello** - *nm*	ring
1011	**angelo** - *nm*	angel
937	**angolo** - *nm*	angle, corner
563	**anima** - *nf*	soul
766	**animale** - *nm; adj*	animal
2310	**anniversario** - *nm*	anniversary
89	**anno** - *nm*	year
1957	**annunciare** - *verb*	to announce
2397	**ansia** - *nf*	anxiety
1449	**anticipo** - *nm*	advance, anticipation
1841	**antico** - *adj*	ancient
964	**anzi** - *adv*	rather
743	**aperto** - *adj*	open
2306	**apertura** - *nf*	opening
715	**appartamento** - *nm*	flat, apartment
1282	**appartenere** - *verb*	to belong
2445	**appellare** - *verb*	to appeal
174	**appena** - *adv*	just, (as) soon (as)
2021	**appetito** - *nm*	appetite, hunger
2478	**applauso** - *nm*	applause
1635	**apposta** - *adj*	on purpose
1629	**apprezzare** - *verb*	to appreciate
644	**appuntamento** - *nm*	appointment
1729	**appunto** - *adv*	just

2385	**aprile** - *nm*	April
791	**aprire** - *verb*	to open
1761	**ara** - *nf*	macaw, altar
1863	**arabo** - *adj; nm/f*	Arabic; Arab
1552	**area** - *nf*	area
1855	**argento** - *nm*	silver
1448	**argomento** - *nm*	topic, subject, argument
402	**aria** - *nf*	air
436	**arma** - *nf*	weapon
1952	**armadio** - *nm*	wardrobe, closet
731	**armare** - *verb*	to arm
1811	**armato** - *adj*	armed
1057	**arrabbiare** - *verb*	to get angry, get mad
1061	**arrestare** - *verb*	to stop
382	**arrivare** - *verb*	to arrive
512	**arrivederci** - *int*	goodbye
414	**arrivo** - *nm*	arrival
945	**arte** - *nf*	art
1279	**articolo** - *nm*	article
1397	**artista** - *nm*	artist
1997	**arto** - *nm*	limb
1503	**ascensore** - *nm*	lift, elevator
305	**ascoltare** - *verb*	to listen
838	**ascolto** - *nm*	listening
2318	**asilo** - *nm*	asylum, kindergarten, nursery (school)
142	**aspettare** - *verb*	to wait
411	**aspetto** - *nm*	appearance, look, aspect
1596	**assassinare** - *verb*	to assassinate
2440	**assassinio** - *nm*	murder, assasination
622	**assassino** - *nm/f*	killer, murderer
1447	**assegno** - *nm*	check
1381	**assicurare** - *verb*	to ensure, insure
2221	**assicurato** - *adj*	secured, assured, insured
1603	**assicurazione** - *nf*	insurance
1344	**assieme [a]** - *adv*	together [with]
1141	**assistente** - *adj; nm&f*	assistant; assistant
2432	**assistenza** - *nf*	assistance
2451	**asso** - *nm*	ace
484	**assolutamente** - *adv*	absolutely
2256	**assoluto** - *adj*	absolute
2292	**assomigliare** - *verb*	to look like, resemble
1873	**assumere** - *verb*	to take, assume
1290	**assurdo** - *adj*	absurd
2344	**astronave** - *nf*	spaceship
1720	**atmosfera** - *nf*	atmosphere
1565	**attaccare** - *verb*	to attack
692	**attacco** - *nm*	attack
2201	**atteggiamento** - *nm*	attitude
1120	**attendere** - *verb*	to wait for
1933	**attentamente** - *adv*	carefully
866	**attentare** - *verb*	to attempt
387	**attento** - *adj*	careful
353	**attenzione** - *nm*	caution
348	**attimo** - *nm*	moment, instant
1399	**attività** - *nf*	activity
1132	**atto** - *nm*	act
1252	**attore** - *nm*	actor
1379	**attorno** - *adv; prep*	about; around
1800	**attraente** - *adj*	attractive
1797	**attraversare** - *verb*	to cross
614	**attraverso** - *adv; prep*	through, across
1636	**attrice** - *nf*	actress
2297	**attuale** - *adj*	current
1700	**augurare** - *verb*	to wish
1187	**augurio** - *nm*	wish, greeting, omen

2094	**aumento** - *nm*	increase
1527	**autista** - *nf*	driver, chauffeur
343	**auto** - *nm*	car
981	**autobus** - *nm*	bus
2351	**autore** - *nm*	author
1338	**autorità** - *nf*	authority
2491	**autorizzare** - *verb*	to permit, authorize
2384	**autorizzazione** - *nf*	authorization
2378	**autostrada** - *nf*	motorway, highway
2358	**autunno** - *nm*	autumn, fall
160	**avanti** - *adv*	forward, ahead, on
12	**avere** - *verb*	to have
2014	**avventurarsi** - *verb*	to venture
2002	**avvertire** - *verb*	to warn
2096	**avvicinare** - *verb*	to approach
487	**avvocato** - *nm*	lawyer
1693	**azienda** - *nf*	company, business
880	**azione** - *nf*	action

B

1523	**babbo** - *nm*	dad, father
1015	**baby** - *nmf*	baby
871	**baciare** - *verb*	to kiss
2127	**bacio** - *nm*	kiss
2034	**badare** - *verb*	to look after
1694	**bagaglio** - *nm*	luggage
426	**bagno** - *nm*	bathroom
739	**ballare** - *verb*	to dance
232	**bambino** - *nm/f*	child, baby, boy/girl
1981	**bambola** - *nf*	doll
684	**banca** - *nf*	bank
2134	**banco** - *nm*	bench, counter, bank, desk
1245	**banda** - *nf*	band, gang
1765	**bandiera** - *nf*	flag
677	**bar** - *nm*	bar, caffé
2349	**bara** - *nf*	coffin
1665	**barba** - *nf*	beard
654	**barca** - *nf*	boat
1837	**barone** - *nm*	baron
581	**base** - *nf*	basis
933	**basso** - *adj; nm*	low, bottom, lower; bass
437	**bastardo** - *nm*	bastard
164	**bastare** - *verb*	to suffice
1692	**bastone** - *nm*	stick
834	**battaglia** - *nf*	battle
1315	**battere** - *verb*	to beat
2085	**batteria** - *nf*	battery, drums
1649	**beccare** - *verb*	to peck, catch
1395	**becco** - *nm*	beak
98	**beh, be** - *int*	well!
884	**bellezza** - *nf*	beauty
166	**bello (bel)** - *adj; nm/f*	nice,beautiful; handsome, hunk/ beautiful woman
26	**bene** - *adj; adv; nm*	very; well, good; good, asset
1728	**benedire** - *verb*	to bless
416	**benissimo** - *adv*	very well, fine
2265	**bentornato** - *int; nm*	Welcome back!; welcome
683	**benvenuto** - *adj; int; nm*	welcome
1429	**benzina** - *nf*	petrol, gasoline
359	**bere** - *nm*	drinking
1417	**bersaglio** - *nm*	target
1298	**bestia** - *nf*	beast
1830	**beva(anda)** - *nf*	drink
646	**bianco** - *adj*	white
1608	**bibbia** - *nf*	Bible
1742	**biblioteca** - *nf*	library
1052	**bicchiere** - *nm*	(drinking) glass
2426	**bicicletta (bici)** - *nf*	bicycle, (bike)
803	**biglietto** - *nm*	ticket
1923	**bimbo** - *nm*	baby, child
2083	**bionda** - *nf/m; adj*	blonde

620	**birra** - *nf*	beer
2067	**biscotto** - *nm*	cookie, biscuit
116	**bisogno** - *nm*	need
1477	**bloccare** - *verb*	to block
1686	**blocco** - *nm*	block
808	**blu** - *adj*	blue
422	**bocca** - *nf*	mouth
1515	**bomba** - *nf*	bomb
821	**bordo** - *nm*	edge
733	**borsa** - *nf*	bag
1577	**bosco** - *nm*	wood
1886	**botte** - *nf*	barrel, cask
1037	**bottiglia** - *nf*	bottle
1878	**botto** - *nf; nm*	blow, hit; explosion
658	**braccio** - *nm*	arm
2058	**branco** - *nm*	herd, pack, flock
253	**bravo** - *adj; nm*	good, fine, clever; bravo
1030	**breve** - *adj*	short
1678	**brillante** - *adj; nm*	brilliant, bright; diamond
2020	**brindisi** - *nm*	toast (social drinking), pledge
1747	**bruciare** - *verb*	to burn
2289	**bruno** - *adj*	brown, dark
2054	**brusio** - *nm*	buzz
471	**brutto** - *adj; nm*	ugly, bad, nasty; bad, ugliness
2291	**bucare** - *verb*	to puncture
952	**buco** - *nm*	hole
1426	**bugia** - *nf*	lie, falsehood
1262	**bugiardo** - *adj*	liar
854	**buio** - *adj; nm*	dark; dark
482	**buonanotte** - *int*	good night
691	**buonasera** - *int*	good evening
306	**buongiorno** - *int*	good morning
182	**buono** - *adj; nm*	good; voucher, coupon
2148	**burro** - *nm*	butter
1978	**busta** - *nf*	envelope
1540	**buttare** - *verb*	to throw

C

1780	**cabina** - *nf*	cabin
626	**cacciare** - *verb*	to hunt, throw out
2311	**cacciatore** - *nm*	hunter
1091	**cadavere** - *nm*	dead body
992	**cadere** - *verb*	to fall
532	**caffè** - *nm*	coffee, café
1305	**calcio** - *nm*	football, soccer
596	**caldo** - *adj; nm*	hot; heat
506	**calma** - *nf*	calm
650	**calmare** - *verb*	to calm
911	**calmo** - *adj*	calm
1771	**calore** - *nm*	heat
1750	**cambiamento** - *nm*	change
474	**cambiare** - *verb*	to change
810	**cambio** - *nm*	change
415	**camera** - *nf*	room
1721	**cameriere** - *nm&f*	waiter, butler / waitress, maid
1224	**camicia** - *nf*	shirt
896	**camion** - *nm*	truck
909	**camminare** - *verb*	to walk
1644	**cammino** - *nm*	path
989	**campagna** - *nf*	countryside, country
2063	**campanello** - *nm*	bell
2175	**campionare** - *verb*	to sample
973	**campione** - *nm; adj*	sample, champion; champion
412	**campo** - *nm*	field
1634	**canale** - *nm*	channel
1561	**cancello** - *nm*	gate
1442	**cancro** - *nm*	cancer
347	**cane** - *nm*	dog
2408	**canna** - *nf*	cane, barrel, rod

1010	**cantare** - *verb*	to sing
1975	**cantina** - *nf*	cellar, basement, winery
1544	**canto** - *nm*	singing, song
662	**canzone** - *nf*	song
1945	**caos** - *nm*	chaos
910	**capace** - *adj*	capable, able
1762	**capacità** - *nf*	capacity
448	**capello** - *nm*	hair
186	**capire** - *verb*	to understand
2174	**capitale** - *adj*	capital
296	**capitare** - *verb*	to happen, occur
2237	**capitolo** - *nm*	chapter
1842	**capo** - *nm*	boss
2189	**caporale** - *nm*	corporal
938	**cappello** - *nm*	hat
1947	**cappotto** - *nm*	coat
1844	**carattere** - *nm*	character
2112	**carburante** - *nm*	fuel
1414	**carcere** - *nm*	prison
511	**cariare** - *verb*	to rot
1189	**carico** - *adj*	load, freight
675	**carino** - *adj*	cute, nice, pretty
2472	**carità** - *nf*	charity
640	**carne** - *nf*	meat
366	**caro** - *adj; nm*	dear, expensive; dear
955	**carriera** - *nf*	career
1457	**carro** - *nm*	wagon
2299	**carrozza** - *nf*	carriage
629	**carta** - *nf*	paper, card, map
2394	**cartello** - *nm*	cartel, sign
68	**casa** - *nf*	house, home
796	**casino (casinò)** - *nm*	mess (casino)
196	**caso** - *nm*	case
1695	**caspita** - *int*	good heavens
1670	**cassa** - *nf*	cash, case
2236	**cassaforte** - *nf*	safe, strongbox
1471	**cassetta** - *nf*	cassette

1215	**castello** - *nm*	castle
1827	**catena** - *nf*	chain
1066	**cattivo** - *adj; nm/f*	bad; baddie, bad person
1871	**catturare** - *verb*	to capture
432	**causa** - *nf*	cause
1946	**causare** - *verb*	to cause
1465	**cavaliere** - *nm*	knight
523	**cavallo** - *nm*	horse
1794	**cavo** - *nm; adj*	cable, wire; hollow
580	**cavolo** - *nm*	cabbage, kale
1312	**cazzata** - *nf*	crap
114	**cazzo** - *nm; int*	dick; fuck
121	**ce** - *pron*	us
1352	**cella** - *nf*	cell
858	**cellulare** - *adj*	cell phone
380	**cenare** - *verb*	to have dinner
1928	**centesimo** - *adj; nm*	hundredth; cent
1356	**centinaio** - *adj; num*	hundred
1019	**cento** - *adj; num*	hundred
953	**centrale** - *adj; nf*	central; main office, (nuclear) power station
520	**centro** - *nm*	center
386	**cerca** - *nf*	search
244	**cercare** - *verb*	to search
857	**cerchio** - *nm*	circle; rim
1625	**cerimonia** - *nf*	ceremony
660	**certamente** - *adv*	of course
81	**certo** - *adj; adv*	certain; of course;
546	**cervello** - *nm*	brain
2088	**cessare** - *verb*	to cease
2	**che** - *conj; pron; adj*	that; which, who; what
46	**chi** - *pron*	who
1684	**chiacchiera** - *nf*	gossip
247	**chiamare** - *verb*	to call
585	**chiamata** - *nf*	(telephone) call

2049	**chiappa** - *nf*	(colll) butt cheek, bottom, backside
1364	**chiaramente** - *adv*	clearly
391	**chiaro** - *adj*	clear; light
525	**chiave** - *nf*	key
273	**chiedere** - *verb*	to ask (for), enquire
638	**chiesa** - *nf*	church
1452	**chilo** - *nm*	kilo
1355	**chilometro** - *nm*	kilometer
894	**chissà** - *int; adv*	who knows!; perhaps
2016	**chitarra** - *nf*	guitar
617	**chiudere** - *verb*	to close
470	**chiunque** - *pron*	anyone
2453	**chiusa** - *nf*	close, lock, sluice
578	**chiuso** - *adj*	closed
23	**ci** - *pron*	ourselves, us
100	**ciao** - *int*	hello, bye
2319	**ciascuno** - *adj; pron*	each, all, every; everyone, everybody
464	**cibo** - *nm*	food
1306	**cieco** - *adj*	blind
362	**cielo** - *nm*	sky
2238	**cifrare** - *verb*	to encipher
1288	**cima** - *nf*	top
1751	**cimitero** - *nm*	cemetery
817	**cinema** - *nm*	cinema, movie theater
1067	**cinese** - *adj; nmf*	Chinese
280	**cinque** - *adj; num*	five
1804	**cintura** - *nf*	belt
214	**ciò** - *pron*	that, it
2476	**cioccolata** - *nf*	chocolate
1754	**cioccolato** - *nm*	chocolate
657	**cioè** - *adv*	i.e., that is, namely
458	**circa** - *adv; prep*	about
1860	**circo** - *nm*	circus
1925	**circostanza** - *nf*	circumstance
265	**città** - *nf*	city
1640	**cittadino** - *nm*	citizen
1598	**civile** - *adj; nm*	civil; civilian
2482	**civiltà** - *nf*	civilization
2036	**clacson** - *nm*	horn (automotive)
679	**classe** - *nf*	class, classroom
2391	**classico** - *adj*	classic
799	**cliente** - *nm*	customer
1843	**clinico** - *adj*	clinical
824	**club** - *nm*	club
1490	**coda** - *nf*	queue, tail
2244	**codardo** - *adj; nm/f*	cowardly; coward
759	**codice** - *nm*	code, codex
1123	**coglione** - *nm*	balls, nuts, asshole
1969	**cognome** - *nm*	last name
1901	**coincidenza** - *nf*	coincidence
1463	**coinvolgere** - *verb*	to involve
1739	**cola** - *adv*	there (form)
888	**colazione** - *nf*	breakfast, lunch
2382	**collegamento** - *nm*	connection, link
1261	**collegare** - *verb*	to connect, link
1223	**college** - *nm*	college
2364	**collezione** - *nf*	collection
1796	**collina** - *nf*	hill
2428	**colloquio** - *nm*	(job) interview, talk, meeting
575	**colonnello** - *nm*	colonel
1326	**colorare** - *verb*	to to color
855	**colore** - *nm*	color
288	**colpa** - *nf*	fault, guilt; blame
976	**colpevole** - *adj*	guilty
665	**colpire** - *verb*	to hit
430	**colpo** - *nm*	hit
946	**coltello** - *nm*	knife
1784	**colui** - *pron*	he
2338	**coma** - *nm*	coma
621	**comandante** - *nm*	commander
2458	**comandare** - *verb*	to command
704	**comando** - *nm*	command

719	**combattere** - *verb*	to fight
1505	**combattimento** - *nm*	combat
1949	**combattuto** - *adj*	hard-fought
1756	**combinare** - *verb*	to combine
21	**come** - *pron*	as, how
785	**cominciare** - *verb*	to begin
1905	**comitato** - *nm*	committee
2240	**commerciale** - *adj*	commercial, trade
1309	**commettere** - *verb*	to commit
1382	**commissione** - *nf*	commission, committee
1311	**comodo** - *adj*	comfortable
488	**compagnia** - *nf*	company
934	**compagno** - *nm/f*	companion, mate
960	**compito** - *nm*	task
652	**compleanno** - *nm*	birthday
2312	**complesso** - *adj; nm*	complex, whole; complex
530	**completamente** - *adv*	completely
1895	**completare** - *verb*	to complete
1260	**completo** - *adj; nm*	complete, full; suit
1691	**complicare** - *verb*	to complicate
1280	**complimento** - *nm*	compliment
1458	**comportamento** - *nm*	behavior
2167	**comportare** - *verb*	to involve
697	**comprare** - *verb*	to buy
2435	**comprendere** - *verb*	to understand
777	**computer** - *nm*	computer
846	**comune** - *adj; nm*	common; community, town
2415	**comunicare** - *verb*	to communicate
2328	**comunicazione** - *nf*	communication
2296	**comunista** - *adj; nm*	communist
2217	**comunità** - *nf*	community
256	**comunque** - *adv; conj*	anyway; though
17	**con** - *prep*	with, by
2354	**concedere** - *verb*	to grant
2179	**concentrato** - *adj*	concentrated
1516	**concerto** - *nm*	concert
2346	**concetto** - *nm*	concept
1805	**condannare** - *verb*	to convict
2353	**condividere** - *verb*	to share
1065	**condizione** - *nf*	condition
2262	**condotto** - *adj; nm*	conducted; duct, conduit, canal
2012	**conferenza** - *nf*	conference
2064	**confermare** - *verb*	to confirm
2285	**confessione** - *nf*	confession
1529	**confine** - *nm*	border, boundery
1611	**confondere** - *verb*	to confound
2142	**confronto** - *nm*	comparison
1917	**confusione** - *nf*	confusion
886	**congratulazione** - *nf*	congratulation
2018	**congresso** - *nm*	congress
1936	**coniglio** - *nm*	rabbit
1126	**conoscenza** - *nf*	knowledge
307	**conoscere** - *verb*	to know
1669	**consegna** - *nf*	delivery
2187	**consegnare** - *verb*	to deliver
1815	**conseguenza** - *nf*	result, consequence
1875	**considerare** - *verb*	to consider
2494	**considerazione** - *nf*	consideration
2473	**consigliere** - *nm*	advisor, councilor
558	**consiglio** - *nm*	advice, council, board
2334	**contadino** - *adj*	farmer
1532	**contante** - *adj; nm*	cash
1009	**contare** - *verb*	to count
712	**contatto** - *nm*	contact
1210	**conte** - *nm*	count
1768	**contea** - *nf*	county
2400	**contenere** - *verb*	to contain
634	**contento** - *adj*	happy

1995	**continuamente** - *adv*	continuously, continually
425	**continuare** - *verb*	to continue
1573	**continuato** - *adj*	continued
947	**continuo** - *adj*	continuous
310	**conto** - *nm*	bill
891	**contrario** - *nm*	contrary
959	**contratto** - *nm*	contract
237	**contro** - *adv; prep*	against, counter; against, versus
630	**controllare** - *verb*	to check
2324	**controllato** - *adj*	checked
374	**controllo** - *nm*	control
1627	**convenire** - *verb*	to agree
1400	**conversazione** - *nf*	conversation
2009	**convincere** - *verb*	to convince
1025	**convinto** - *adj*	convinced
2045	**coperto** - *adj*	covered
1579	**copertura** - *nf*	coverage
1377	**copia** - *nf*	copy
2337	**copione** - *nm*	script
1060	**coppia** - *nf*	couple
1798	**coprire** - *verb*	to cover
363	**coraggio** - *nm*	courage
1626	**coraggioso** - *adj*	courageous
1331	**corda** - *nf*	rope
1977	**coro** - *nm*	choir
1942	**coronare** - *verb*	to crown
311	**corpo** - *nm*	body
672	**correre** - *verb*	to run
2047	**corretto** - *nm*	correct
1504	**corridoio** - *nm*	aisle, hallway
813	**corso** - *nm*	course
2004	**cortesia** - *nf*	courtesy
2373	**cortile** - *nm*	courtyard, yard
861	**corto** - *adj*	short
16	**cosa** - *pron; nf*	what; thing
1368	**coscienza** - *nf*	consciousness, conscience, awareness
48	**così** - *adv; conj*	so, thus; that
1413	**coso** - *nm*	thing
1787	**costo** - *nm*	cost
1521	**costringere** - *verb*	to force
1236	**costruire** - *verb*	to build
1820	**costume** - *nm*	costume, custom, suit
2087	**cravatta** - *nf*	necktie
1012	**creare** - *verb*	to create
1327	**creatura** - *nf*	creature
230	**credere** - *verb*	to believe
1408	**credito** - *nm*	credit
99	**credo** - *nm*	creed, credo
2266	**cremare** - *verb*	to cremate
1313	**crescere** - *verb*	to grow
1758	**cretino** - *adj; nm*	stupid; cretin
1321	**criminale** - *adj nm&f*	criminal; criminal
936	**crimine** - *nm*	crime
1374	**crisi** - *nf*	crisis
385	**cristo** - *nm*	Christ
1500	**croce** - *nf*	cross
1589	**crudele** - *adj*	cruel
2498	**cucciolo** - *nm*	puppy
717	**cucina** - *nf*	kitchen
1985	**cucinare** - *verb*	to cook
1190	**cugino** - *nm/f*	cousin
115	**cui** - *pron*	which
312	**culo** - *nm*	ass
1885	**cultura** - *nf*	culture
250	**cuore** - *nm*	heart, core
390	**cura** - *nf*	care
2418	**curare** - *verb*	to treat
1832	**curioso** - *adj*	curious
2162	**custodia** - *nf*	custody

D

19	**da** **dal, dallo, dall', dalla, dai, dagli, dalle*	from
1164	**dannare** - *verb*	to damn
706	**dannazione** - *nf*	damn
795	**danno** - *nm*	damage
1727	**danzare** - *verb*	to dance
923	**dappertutto** - *adv*	everywhere
204	**dare** - *verb*	to give
850	**data** - *nf*	date
982	**dato** - *adj; nm*	given; fact, datum
334	**davanti** - *adj; adv; prep*	front; in front
88	**davvero** - *adv*	really
1347	**debito** - *nm*	straight line, tuition, debt
1059	**debole** - *adj*	weak
986	**decidere** - *verb*	to decide
1520	**decisamente** - *adv*	definitely, decidedly
820	**decisione** - *nf*	decision
447	**deciso** - *adj*	decided
1775	**delitto** - *nm*	crime
2071	**delizioso** - *adj*	delicious
1968	**deludere** - *verb*	to disappoint
2195	**demone** - *nm*	demon
2119	**demonio** - *nm*	devil, demon
441	**denaro** - *nm*	money
847	**dente** - *nm*	tooth
152	**dentro** - *prep*	in, inside
2290	**denuncia** - *nf*	complaint
1935	**deposito** - *nm*	deposit
1219	**deserto** - *adj; nm*	desert (food); desert
1158	**desiderare** - *verb*	to wish
941	**desiderio** - *nm*	desire
735	**destino** - *nm*	destiny
550	**destro** - *adj*	right
779	**detective** - *nmf*	detective
2366	**detestare** - *verb*	to loathe
1163	**dettaglio** - *nm*	detail
28	**di** *del, dello, dell', della, dei, degli, delle -prep*	of, to; than, and
1673	**diamante** - *nm*	diamond
2196	**diamine** - *int*	heck
1793	**diario** - *nm*	diary
218	**diavolo** - *nm*	Devil
2480	**dicembre** - *nm*	December
2212	**dichiarare** - *verb*	to declare, claim
1668	**dichiarazione** - *nf*	declaration
399	**dieci** - *adj; num*	ten
267	**dietro** - *prep; nm; adj; adv*	behind; back, rear; after; after
860	**difendere** - *verb*	to defend
754	**differenza** - *nf*	difference
316	**difficile** - *adj*	difficult
1879	**difficoltà** - *nf*	difficulties, difficulty, trouble
521	**dimenticare** - *verb*	to forget
1719	**dimentico** - *adj*	oblivious
1597	**dimostrare** - *verb*	to show
92	**dio** - *nm*	God
1087	**dipartimento** - *nm*	department
915	**dipendere** - *verb*	to depend
2261	**dipingere** - *verb*	to paint
47	**dire** - *verb*	to say
1168	**direttamente** - *adv*	directly
1170	**diretto** - *adj*	direct
661	**direttore** - *nm*	director, (senior) manager
1076	**direzione** - *nf*	direction, management
1322	**dirigere** - *verb*	to direct

554	**diritto** - *nm; adj; adv*	right, law; straight; straight
2449	**disagio** - *nm*	discomfort
1323	**disastro** - *nm*	disaster
1554	**disco** - *nm*	disc
1041	**discorso** - *nm*	speech
1687	**discussione** - *nf*	discussion
1183	**discutere** - *verb*	to discuss
1908	**disegno** - *nm*	drawing
1716	**disgustoso** - *adj*	disgusting
2331	**disperato** - *adj*	desperate
137	**dispiacere** - *verb*	to displeasure,dislike, be sorry
2363	**dispiaciuto** - *adj*	sorry
2026	**disponibile** - *adj*	available
1759	**disporre** - *verb*	to have
1773	**disposizione** - *nf*	arrangement
1159	**distanza** - *nf*	distance
2422	**distintivo** - *adj*	distinctive
2055	**distretto** - *nm*	district
1049	**distruggere** - *verb*	to destroy
2098	**distruzione** - *nf*	destruction
1201	**disturbo** - *nm*	disorder
1069	**dito** - *nm*	finger
1779	**divano** - *nm*	sofa
2225	**divenire** - *verb*	to become
418	**diventare** - *verb*	to become
908	**divergere** - *verb*	to diverge
2448	**diversamente** - *adv*	otherwise
560	**diverso** - *adj*	different
372	**divertente** - *adj*	funny, humorous
1555	**divertimento** - *nm*	fun, entertainment
1619	**divertire** - *verb*	to entertain
2079	**divisione** - *nf*	division
2390	**diviso** - *adj*	divided
1677	**divorzio** - *nm*	divorce
1993	**DNA** - *abbr*	DNA
845	**documento** - *nm*	document
1602	**dodici** - *adj; num*	twelve
601	**dolce** - *adj; nm*	sweet, fresh; sweet, dessert
1513	**dolcezza** - *nf*	sweetness, gentleness
561	**dolore** - *nm*	ache, pain
337	**domanda** - *nf*	demand, question
194	**domani** - *adv; nm*	tomorrow
963	**domattina** - *adv*	tomorrow morning
1017	**domenica** - *nf*	Sunday
671	**don** - *nm*	Don (title of respect/religious title)
157	**donna** - *nf*	woman
1325	**dono** - *nm*	gift
106	**dopo** - *prep; adv*	after
1965	**dopotutto** - *adv*	after all
1122	**doppio** - *adj*	double
369	**dormire** - *verb*	to sleep
1468	**dosso** - *nm*	back
289	**dottore** - *nm*	doctor, Dr.
57	**dove** - *adv*	where
78	**dovere** - *verb; nm*	to have to, muste, should; duty, obligation
2048	**dovunque** - *adv*	anywhere
1919	**drago** - *nm*	dragon
1073	**dritto** - *adj; adv*	straight, upright; right
2164	**droga** - *nf*	drug
778	**drogare** - *verb*	to drug
895	**dubbio** - *adj; nm*	doubtful; doubt
1568	**dubitare** - *verb*	to doubt
1903	**duca** - *nm*	duke
66	**due** - *adj; num*	two
676	**dunque** - *adv*	therefore
427	**durante** - *prep; adv*	during, in, over; while
584	**duro** - *adj*	hard

E

3	**e, ed** - *conj*	and
1816	**ebbene** - *conj*	so, well
1299	**ebreo** - *adj; nm*	Jewish, Jew
1464	**eccellente** - *adj*	excellent
1616	**eccellenza** - *nf*	excellence
2100	**eccetto** - *prep*	except
1813	**eccezionale** - *adj*	exceptional, outstanding
1791	**eccitante** - *adj; nm*	exciting; stimulate, upper
119	**ecco** - *adv*	here
1714	**eccoli** - *int*	here they are (eccolo/i (m), eccola/e (f)
2191	**eccome** - *int*	all right!, I´ll say!
1501	**eccoti** - *int*	here you are
2171	**economia** - *nf*	economy, economics
904	**edificio** - *nm*	building
2252	**educazione** - *nf*	education
809	**effetto** - *nm*	effect
999	**egli** - *pron*	he
2329	**egoista** - *adj; nm*	selfish; egoist
161	**eh** - *int*	huh
77	**ehi** - *int*	Hey
722	**ehm** - *int*	hum
2023	**elegante** - *adj*	elegant
2136	**elemento** - *nm*	element
2380	**elenco** - *nm*	list, directory
2082	**elettrico** - *adj*	electric, electrical
2429	**elezione** - *nf*	election
1460	**elicottero** - *nm*	helicopter
2375	**eliminare** - *verb*	to eliminate
1688	**ella** - *pron*	she
1032	**emergenza** - *nf*	emergency
2038	**emozione** - *nf*	emotion
2145	**empero** - *verb*	empire
827	**energia** - *nf*	energy
873	**enorme** - *adj*	huge
499	**entrambi** - *adj*	both, either
286	**entrare** - *verb*	to enter
1094	**entrata** - *nf*	entrance
643	**entro** - *prep*	within, by
1912	**episodio** - *nm*	episode
1507	**epoca** - *nf*	era
1106	**eppure** - *conj*	and yet
2399	**equilibrio** - *nm*	equilibrium
1737	**equipaggio** - *nm*	crew
1495	**erba** - *nf*	grass, pot, herb
843	**eroe** - *nm*	hero
2158	**eroina** - *nf*	heroin, heroine
612	**errore** - *nm*	error
2350	**esagerare** - *verb*	to exaggerate
1339	**esame** - *nm*	exam, test
389	**esattamente** - *adv*	exactly
378	**esatto** - *adj*	exact
2425	**esecuzione** - *nf*	execution
607	**esempio** - *nm*	example
515	**esercito** - *nm*	army
1672	**esistenza** - *nf*	existence
606	**esistere** - *verb*	to exist
870	**esperienza** - *nf*	experience
2496	**esperimento** - *nm*	experiment
1451	**esperto** - *adj*	expert
1617	**esplodere** - *verb*	to explode
1238	**esplosione** - *nf*	explosion
1955	**espressione** - *nf*	expression
1918	**essa** - *pron*	it
7	**essere** - *verb*	to be
1657	**essi** - *pron*	they, them
1964	**esso** - *pron*	it, he
1063	**est** - *nm*	East
940	**estate** - *nf*	summer

1497	**esterno** - *adj; nm*	external, outside, out; outside, exterior
2317	**estero** - *nm*	abroad
1926	**estremamente** - *adv*	extremely
907	**età** - *nf*	age
2107	**eterno** - *adj*	eternal
2277	**euro** - *nm*	Euro
1817	**evento** - *nm*	event
2215	**evidente** - *adj*	evident
1042	**evitare** - *verb*	to avoid
2365	**evviva** - *int*	cheers, hoorah
874	**ex** - *adj; nmf*	former; ex
2300	**extra** - *adj*	extra

F

69	**fa** - *adv*	ago
1296	**fabbrica** - *nf*	factory
969	**faccenda** - *nf*	affair
171	**faccia** - *nf*	face
370	**facile** - *adj*	easy
1411	**facilmente** - *adv*	easily
1510	**falla** - *nf*	leak
2437	**fallimento** - *nm*	failure, bankruptcy
1403	**fallito** - *adj*	failed
526	**fallo** - *nm*	foul
2439	**falsare** - *verb*	to distort
1349	**falso** - *adj*	false
465	**fame** - *nm*	hunger
207	**famiglia** - *nf*	family
1852	**familiare** - *adj*	familiar
1109	**famoso** - *adj*	famous
1530	**fan** - *nm*	fan
1034	**fanculo** - *int*	fuck
2022	**fango** - *nm*	mud, dirt
2027	**fantasia** - *nf*	fantasy
1102	**fantasma** - *nf*	ghost
360	**fantastico** - *adj*	fantastic
37	**fare** - *verb*	to do
1115	**faro** - *nm*	lighthouse, beacon, headlight
1578	**fase** - *nf*	phase
1180	**fastidio** - *nm*	bother, annoyance, nuisance
287	**fata** - *nf*	fairy, femme fatale
2135	**fatica** - *nf*	fatigue
39	**fatto** - *nm; adj*	fact, event; made, done
1475	**fattoria** - *nf*	farm
132	**favore** - *nm*	favor
1831	**febbre** - *nf*	temperature, fever
869	**fede** - *nf*	faith, wedding ring
1887	**fedele** - *adj*	faithful
1680	**federale** - *adj*	federal
1667	**fegato** - *nm*	liver
261	**felice** - *adj*	happy
1444	**felicità** - *nf*	happiness
1675	**femmina** - *nf*	female
2033	**femminile** - *adj*	female
833	**ferire** - *verb*	to hurt
1074	**ferito** - *adj*	injured
649	**fermare** - *verb*	to stop
2102	**fermata** - *nf*	stop
407	**fermo** - *adj; nm*	still, firm; stop, arrest
1446	**ferro** - *nm*	iron
356	**festa** - *nf*	party
1726	**festeggiare** - *verb*	to celebrate
1622	**fiamma** - *nf*	flame
1093	**fianco** - *nm*	side
1783	**fiato** - *nm*	breath
2402	**fica (figa)** - *nf*	fanny, pussy (both used: fanny,pussy, fig)
1857	**fico** - *nm*	fig
1232	**fidanzato** - *nm*	boyfriend

1271	**fidare** - *verb*	to trust
875	**fiducia** - *nf*	confidence
1600	**fiero** - *adj*	proud
271	**figlia** - *nf*	daughter
151	**figlio** - *nm*	son
678	**figliolo** - *nm*	son, boy (affectuos or patronizing)
1653	**figura** - *nf*	figure, frame
1652	**figurato** - *adj*	figurative
1846	**fila** - *nf*	row, line
890	**filare** - *verb*	to spin
1869	**file** - *nm*	file (set of records)
234	**film** - *nm*	movie
1445	**filo** - *nm*	wire
1027	**finale** - *adj; nm/f*	final; final, ending, finish/final (sports)
483	**finalmente** - *adv*	finally
409	**finché** - *conj*	until, till
212	**fine** - *nm; nf; adj*	purpose; end; fine
752	**finestra** - *nf*	window
965	**fingere** - *verb*	to pretend
344	**finire** - *verb*	to end, finish
243	**finito** - *adj*	finished, over
201	**fino** - *prep; adv; adj*	till; even; fine, subtle
1265	**finora** - *adv*	so far
793	**fiore** - *nm*	flower
1437	**firmare** - *verb*	to sign
1911	**fisico** - *adj; nm*	physical (fisica= physics)
728	**fiume** - *nm*	river
1803	**florido** - *adj*	florid
2057	**flotta** - *nf*	fleet
1474	**folle** - *adj*	crazy
1466	**follia** - *nf*	madness
451	**fondo** - *nm; adj*	background, bottom, fund; deep
1509	**fonte** - *nf*	source, spring
1281	**foresta** - *nf*	forest
651	**forma** - *nf*	form
1612	**formaggio** - *nf*	cheese
84	**forse** - *adv*	perhaps
252	**forte** - *adj; nm; adv*	strong; forte; loudly
328	**fortuna** - *nf*	luck
812	**fortunato** - *adj*	lucky
148	**forza** - *nf*	power
156	**fossa** - *nf*	pit, dich, gravel
336	**foto** - *nm*	photo
1641	**fotografia** - *nf*	photography, photo
718	**fottere** - *verb*	to fuck
354	**fra** - *prep*	between, among
2386	**francamente** - *adv*	frankly
772	**francese** - *adj*	French
2229	**franco** - *adj; nm*	frank, free; franc
1744	**frase** - *nf*	phrase, sentence
2280	**fratellino** - *nm*	(younger) brother (coll)
209	**fratello** - *nm*	brother
1647	**frattempo** - *nm*	meanwhile, meantime
516	**freddo** - *adj*	cold
764	**fregare** - *verb*	to rub, care
1730	**fresco** - *adj*	fresh, cool
431	**fretta** - *nf*	hurry
543	**fronte** - *nf*	front, forehead
2035	**frutta** - *nf*	fruit
2383	**fucilare** - *verb*	to shoot
978	**fucile** - *nm*	rifle, gun
1239	**fugare** - *verb*	to dispel
1350	**fuggire** - *verb*	to flee
1318	**fumare** - *verb*	to smoke
1016	**fumo** - *nm*	smoke
2213	**fune** - *nm; nf*	cable, wire; rope, linen
1287	**funerale** - *nm*	funeral
475	**funzionare** - *verb*	to function
2483	**funzione** - *nf*	function
322	**fuoco** - *nm*	fire

86	**fuori** - *adv*	out, outside
1514	**furbo** - *adj*	sly, cunning
1095	**furgone** - *nm*	van
1679	**furto** - *nm*	theft
460	**futuro** - *adj*	future

G

1902	**gabbia** - *nf*	cage
1191	**galera** - *nf*	jail
2421	**galleria** - *nf*	gallery
618	**gamba** - *nf*	leg
1231	**gara** - *nf*	race, competition
1941	**garage** - *nm; nf*	garage (box); garage (autoparking)
1086	**gas** - *nm*	gas
927	**gatto** - *nm*	cat
1545	**gelare** - *verb*	to freeze
1877	**geloso** - *adj*	jealous
2294	**gemere** - *verb*	to moan
373	**generale** - *adj; nm*	general
2321	**generazione** - *nf*	generation
321	**genere** - *nm*	gender, kind, genre
2356	**generoso** - *adj*	generous
1893	**geniale** - *adj*	ingenious
1058	**genio** - *nm*	genius
439	**genitore** - *nm*	parent
138	**gente** - *nm*	people
491	**gentile** - *adj*	kind, gentle
1854	**gentiluomo** - *nm*	gentleman
1732	**gestire** - *verb*	to handle, manage
1922	**gesto** - *nm*	gesture
2379	**gettare** - *verb*	to throw
977	**ghiaccio** - *nm*	ice
111	**già** - *adv*	already
1112	**giacca** - *nf*	jacket
1921	**giallo** - *adj*	yellow
1359	**giapponese** - *adj*	Japanese
1047	**giardino** - *nm*	garden
1984	**gigante** - *adj*	giant
1365	**ginocchio** - *nm*	knee
434	**giocare** - *verb*	to play
1757	**giocatore** - *nm*	player, gambler
330	**gioco** - *nm*	game
1055	**gioia** - *nf*	joy
1883	**gioiello** - *nm*	jewel
925	**giornale** - *nm*	newspaper, journal
1492	**giornalista** - *nm*	journalist
446	**giornata** - *nf*	day
113	**giorno** - *nm*	day
371	**giovane** - *adj*	young
1432	**giovanotto** - *nm*	young man
2125	**giovedì** - *nm*	Thursday
1003	**girare** - *verb*	to turn
1785	**girato** - *adj*	endorsed, turned (moved around axis), shot (movie)
227	**giro** - *nm*	tour
254	**giù** - *adv*	down
2272	**giudicare** - *verb*	to judge
814	**giudice** - *nm*	judge
1671	**giudizio** - *nm*	judgment
2089	**giugno** - *nm*	June
2339	**giungere** - *verb*	to reach
2186	**giungla** - *nf*	jungle
2456	**giunto** - *nm; adj*	joint, coupling; joined
2157	**giurato** - *adj; nm*	swon; juror
1825	**giuria** - *nf*	jury
928	**giustizia** - *nf*	justice
158	**giusto** - *adj; adv*	right, just, fair; correctly
1701	**glielo (di glie e lo)** - *pron*	it to him
1118	**gloria** - *nf*	glory
1181	**gola** - *nf*	throat

1760	**golf** - *nm*	golf, sweater, jersey
1889	**gomma** - *nf*	rubber, gum, tire
2249	**gonna** - *nf*	skirt
1273	**governatore** - *nm*	governor
570	**governo** - *nm; adj*	government; governmental
524	**grado** - *nm*	degree
377	**gran** - *adj*	great
129	**grande** - *adj*	great, great
1131	**grandioso** - *adj*	great
1583	**grasso** - *adj*	fat
1284	**gratis** - *adv*	free
1899	**grato** - *adj*	grateful
841	**grave** - *adj*	serious, severe
1334	**grazia** - *nf*	grace, pardon
56	**grazie** - *int*	thank you
916	**gridare** - *verb*	to shout
2149	**grilletto** - *nm*	trigger
514	**grosso** - *adj*	big, thick
438	**gruppo** - *nm*	group, band
1707	**guadagnare** - *verb*	to earn, gain
2447	**guadagno** - *nm*	gain
467	**guaio** - *nm*	trouble
131	**guardare** - *verb*	to look, watch
577	**guardia** - *nf*	guard
248	**guerra** - *nf*	war
2032	**guerriero** - *adj*	warrior
802	**guida** - *nf*	guide, driving
985	**guidare** - *verb*	to lead
1405	**gusto** - *nm*	taste

H

2314	**hall** - *nf*	hall, lobby
781	**hotel** - *nm*	hotel

I

1953	**ideale** - *adj; nm*	ideal; ideal
185	**ideare** - *verb*	to design
2481	**identificare** - *verb*	to identify
1976	**identità** - *nf*	identity
429	**idiota** - *adj; nmf*	idiotic, stupid; idiot
320	**ieri** - *adv; nm*	yesterday
4	**il, lo, l', la, i, gli, le*** - *art*	the
1913	**illegale** - *adj*	illegal
1788	**imbarazzante** - *adj*	embarrassing
2151	**imbarazzo** - *nm*	embarrassment
1541	**imbecille** - *nm; adj*	imbecile
598	**immaginare** - *verb*	to imagine
1876	**immaginazione** - *nf*	imagination
1044	**immagine** - *nf*	image
801	**immediatamente** - *adv*	immediately
783	**imparare** - *verb*	to learn
2268	**impattare** - *verb*	to impact
1301	**impazzire** - *verb*	to go crazy
1776	**impegnare** - *verb*	to commit
1722	**impegno** - *nm*	commitment
1725	**imperatore** - *nm*	Emperor
2361	**impiegato** - *adj*	office worker, employee
270	**importante** - *adj*	important
1014	**importanza** - *nf*	importance
266	**importare** - *verb*	to import
562	**impossibile** - *adj*	impossible
1891	**impresa** - *nf*	firm, enterprise
1345	**impressione** - *nf*	impression
1366	**impronta** - *nf*	footstep, imprint, impression, mark
1697	**improvvisamente** - *adv*	suddenly
1033	**improvviso** - *adj*	sudden
2206	**imputare** - *verb*	to attribute sth to

9	**in** **nel, nello, nell', nella, nei, negli, nelle - prep*	in, into
1593	**incarico** - *nm*	appointment
2077	**incastrare** - *verb*	to fit
1479	**incendiare** - *verb*	to fire
479	**incidente** - *nm; adj*	accident, incident; incident
943	**incinta** - *adj*	pregnant
768	**incontrare** - *verb*	to meet
590	**incontro** - *nm*	meeting, encounter
495	**incredibile** - *adj*	unbelievable
2484	**incredibilmente** - *adv*	incredibilmente
1456	**incubo** - *nm*	nightmare
1658	**indagine** - *nf*	investigation, survery, inquiry
1864	**indiano** - *adj; nm/f*	Indian; Indian
236	**indietro** - *adv*	back
962	**indirizzare** - *verb*	to address
2443	**indizio** - *nm*	clue, indication
1767	**indossare** - *verb*	to wear, put on
1868	**indovinare** - *verb*	to guess
1900	**indovino** - *nm*	fortune-teller
2442	**industria** - *nf*	industry
2093	**infanzia** - *nf*	childhood
2367	**infarto** - *nm*	infarct
842	**infatti** - *adv*	indeed
2084	**infelice** - *adj*	unhappy
1297	**infermiera** - *nf*	nurse
599	**inferno** - *nm*	hell
2231	**infine** - *adv*	finally, at last
2342	**infinito** - *adj*	Infinity
2037	**influenzare** - *verb*	to influence
2001	**informato** - *adj*	informed
659	**informazione** - *nf*	information
2490	**ingegnere** - *nm*	engineer
611	**inglese** - *adj; nmf*	English; English(wo)man
1481	**ingresso** - *nm*	entrance
433	**iniziare** - *verb*	to start
2218	**inizio** - *nm*	beginning
1029	**innamorato** - *adj; nm*	in love; lover
1026	**innocente** - *nm; adj*	innocent
972	**inoltre** - *adv*	sample, champion; champion
2387	**insalata** - *nf*	salad
1005	**insegnare** - *verb*	to teach
2178	**insetto** - *nm*	insect, bug
190	**insieme** - *adv; nm*	together; set, whole
637	**insomma** - *adv*	in short
1575	**intanto** - *adv*	in the meantime
807	**intelligente** - *adj*	intelligent, clever, smart
2284	**intelligenza** - *nf*	intelligence
689	**intendere** - *verb*	to hear, mean, intend
537	**intenzione** - *nf*	intention
592	**interessante** - *adj*	interesting
547	**interessare** - *verb*	to affect
1144	**interesse** - *nm*	interest
2097	**internazionale** - *adj*	international
2011	**internet** - *nm*	Internet
826	**interno** - *adj; nm*	internal; interior, inside
749	**intero** - *adj; nm*	entire, full, whole; whole
2172	**intervento** - *nm*	intervention
2003	**intervista** - *nf*	interview
501	**intorno** - *adv*	around, round
794	**inutile** - *adj*	useless, unnecessary
268	**invece** - *adv*	instead
1614	**inventare** - *verb*	to invent

1459 **inverno** - *nm* winter
2227 **investire** - *verb* to invest
2214 **inviato** - *nm* envoy, correspondent
2369 **invisibile** - *adj* invisible
1316 **invitare** - *verb* to invite
22 **io** - *pron* I
2168 **ione** - *nm* ion
2313 **ipotesi** - *nf* hypothesis, speculation, assumption
889 **isola** - *nf* island
980 **ispettore** - *nm* inspector
1336 **istante** - *nm* instant
2147 **istinto** - *nm* instinct
1986 **istituto** - *nm* institute
1749 **istruzione** - *nf* instruction, education
1543 **italiano** - *adj; nm* Italian

J

1708 **junior** - *adj* junior

L

224 **là** - *adv* there
1420 **labbro** - *nm* lip
1070 **laboratorio** - *nm* laboratory
1453 **lacrima** - *nf* tear
1099 **ladro** - *adj* thief
538 **laggiù** - *adv* over there, down there
1156 **lago** - *nm* lake
2340 **lama** - *nf; nm* blade; llama
2030 **lancia** - *nf* spear
2041 **lanciare** - *verb* to launch
1220 **lancio** - *nm* launch, throw, launching
1278 **largo** - *adj* wide, large, loose
269 **lasciare** - *verb* to leave
954 **lassù** - *adv* up there, above, yonder
780 **lato** - *nm* side
883 **latte** - *nm* milk
2497 **lavare** - *verb* to wash
350 **lavorare** - *verb* to work
2410 **lavoratore** - *nm; adj* worker; hard-working
109 **lavoro** - *nm* work, job
1151 **legale** - *adj; nm* legal; lawyer
2177 **legame** - *nm* bond, tie, link, connection
1839 **legare** - *verb* to tie
893 **legge** - *nf* law
1706 **leggenda** - *nf* legend
210 **leggere** - *verb* to read
656 **leggero** - *adj* light
1607 **legno** - *nm* wood
35 **lei** - *pron* she, her
1237 **lentamente** - *adv* slowly
2303 **lento** - *adv* slow
1748 **leone** - *nm* lion
522 **lettera** - *nf* letter
1384 **levare** - *verb* to upbeat
819 **lezione** - *nf* lesson
167 **lì** - *adv* there
87 **li** - *pron* them
2271 **liberare** - *verb* to release
519 **libero** - *adj* free
767 **libertà** - *nf* freedom
381 **libro** - *nm* book
1970 **licenza** - *nf* license
1473 **licenziare** - *verb* to dismiss
1632 **liceo** - *nm* high school
1370 **lieto** - *adj* happy
1549 **limite** - *nf* limit
1601 **lindo** - *adj* clean, neat

571	**linea** - *nf*	line, figure
732	**lingua** - *nf*	tongue, language
2005	**linguaggio** - *nm*	language, speech
2232	**lira** - *nf*	lira
748	**lista** - *nf*	list
2015	**litigare** - *verb*	to quarrel
774	**livello** - *nm*	level
882	**locale** - *adj; nm*	local; club
392	**lontano** - *adj*	far
75	**loro** - *pron*	their
1048	**lottare** - *verb*	to fight
1882	**luglio** - *nm*	July
53	**lui** - *pron*	him, he
603	**lunare** - *adj*	lunar, moon
1646	**lunedì** - *nm*	Monday
376	**lungo** - *prep; adj; nm*	long; along; length
588	**luogo** - *nm*	place
1188	**lupo** - *nm*	wolf
2403	**lusso** - *nm*	luxury

M

14	**ma** - *conj*	but
2352	**macchiare** - *verb*	to sully
949	**macchina** - *nf*	machine
140	**madre** - *nf*	mother
1008	**maestà** - *nf*	majesty
541	**maestro** - *nm*	master, teacher, meastro
327	**magari** - *adv*	maybe, perhaps, even
1906	**magazzino** - *nm*	warehouse, magazine
2153	**maggio** - *nm*	May
1221	**magia** - *nf*	magic
2163	**magico** - *adj*	magical
2131	**maglietta** - *nf*	t-shirt
995	**magnifico** - *adj*	magnificent
1645	**mago** - *nm*	magician
45	**mai** - *adv*	never
1125	**maiale** - *nm*	pig, pork
2260	**mail** - *nf*	email
2309	**malapena** - *adv*	barely
899	**malato** - *adj*	ill, sick
1068	**malattia** - *nf*	disease, illness
122	**male** - *adv; nm*	bad, evil
863	**maledetto** - *nm*	accursed, damn
1376	**maledire** - *verb*	to curse
663	**maledizione** - *nf; int*	curse; damn
2462	**malvagio** - *adj*	evil, wicked
125	**mamma** - *nf*	mom
2459	**mammina** - *nf*	mummy
2273	**manager** - *nm*	manager
1591	**mancanza** - *nf*	lack
1259	**mancare** - *verb*	to miss
1213	**mancato** - *adj*	failed, unsuccessful
579	**manco** - *adv*	even, not even (with negative verb form)
453	**mandare** - *verb*	to send
318	**mangiare** - *verb*	to eat
1337	**maniera** - *nf*	way, manner
205	**mano** - *nm*	hand
1046	**mantenere** - *verb*	to keep, maintain
2223	**manuale** - *adj; nm*	manual
1402	**mappa** - *nf*	map
1469	**marciare** - *verb*	to march
1951	**marco** - *nm*	mark
527	**mare** - *nm*	sea, seaside
2050	**maresciallo** - *nm*	marshal
1353	**marino** - *adj; nf*	marine, sea; marina, marine, navy
276	**marito** - *nm*	husband
2154	**marte** - *nm*	Mars
2247	**martedì** - *nm*	Tuesday

2438	**martello** - *nm*	hammer
1562	**maschera** - *nf*	mask
1424	**maschio** - *adj; nm*	male
1866	**massa** - *nf*	mass
852	**massimo** - *adj; nm*	maximum
2381	**matematico** - *adj; nm*	mathematical; mathemactician
2116	**materia** - *nf*	matter
1412	**materiale** - *adj; nm*	material
457	**matrimonio** - *nm*	marriage, wedding
468	**mattina** - *nf*	morning
1081	**mattino, mattina** - *nm*	morning
856	**matto** - *adj; nm*	crazy; madman
29	**me (stesso)** - *pron*	me (myself)
2199	**medaglia** - *nf*	medal
295	**media** - *nf*	media, average
1193	**medicina** - *nf*	medicine
605	**medico** - *adj*	(medical) doctor
1130	**medio** - *adj*	average, medium, middle
112	**meglio** - *adv*	better, best
2298	**mela** - *nf*	apple
1419	**membro** - *nm*	member
849	**memoria** - *nf*	storage
219	**meno** - *adv; adj; prep; conj*	less; less; unless; no so (much as)
2118	**mentale** - *adj*	mental
341	**mente** - *nm*	mind
1431	**mentire** - *verb*	to lie
998	**mentito** - *adj*	false, deceptive
231	**mentre** - *conj*	while, as, whereas
1570	**meraviglia** - *nf*	wonder
835	**meraviglioso** - *adj*	wonderful
942	**mercato** - *nm*	market
2060	**merce** - *nf*	goods, wares, merchandise
177	**merda** - *nf*	shit
1531	**meritare** - *verb*	to deserve
1268	**merito** - *nm*	merit
329	**mese** - *nm*	month
478	**messaggio** - *nm*	message
1560	**mestiere** - *nm*	craft, skill, trade
2463	**meta** - *nf*	goal, destination
709	**metà** - *nf*	half
2405	**metallo** - *nm*	metal
2181	**metodo** - *nm*	method
699	**metro(politana)** - *nm; (nf)*	meter; tape measure; (underground, metro)
410	**mettere** - *verb*	to put
1324	**mezzanotte** - *nf*	midnight
314	**mezzo** - *nm; adj*	half, middle, means; half, middle
1944	**mezzogiorno** - *nm*	noon, midday
11	**mi** - *pron*	me
2460	**microfono** - *nm*	microphone
1674	**miele** - *nm*	honey
1078	**migliaio** - *adj; num*	thousand
1088	**miglio** - *nm*	mile
853	**miglior** - *adj*	best
2423	**migliorare** - *verb*	to improve
277	**migliore** - *adj*	best
1518	**miliardo** - *adj; num*	billion
417	**milione** - *adj; num*	million
1023	**militare** - *adj; nm*	military; soldier
553	**mille** - *adj*	one thousand
1249	**minaccia** - *nf*	threat
2173	**miniera** - *nf*	mine
1333	**minimo** - *adj*	minimum
1676	**ministero** - *nm*	ministry
1045	**ministro** - *nm*	minister
2335	**minore** - *adj*	less, minor, lower, lesser, smaller
242	**minuto** - *adj; nm*	minute
30	**mio** - *pron*	my
1212	**miracolo** - *nm*	miracle

1462	**miseria** - *nf*	misery
2207	**missile** - *adj*	missile
647	**missione** - *nf*	mission
1710	**mistero** - *nm*	mystery
1907	**misura** - *nf*	measure
2198	**mobile** - *adj; nm*	mobile; furniture
1476	**moda** - *nf*	fashion, style
1428	**modello** - *adj*	model
128	**modo** - *nm*	way, manner
184	**moglie** - *nf*	wife
2114	**mollare** - *verb*	to give
2267	**mollo** - *adj*	soaked, flabby
52	**molto** - *adv; adj*	very, much
141	**momento** - *nm*	moment
2210	**monaco** - *nm&f*	monk
1303	**mondiale** - *adj*	world
145	**mondo** - *nm*	world
2069	**moneta** - *verb*	
1036	**montagna** - *nf*	mountain
1834	**monte** - *nm*	mountain, mount
1394	**morale** - *adj*	moral
1621	**mordere** - *verb*	to bite
220	**morire** - *verb*	to die
2051	**mortale** - *adj; adv*	mortal; deadly, fatal; deathly
179	**morto** - *adj*	dead, died
1341	**mosca** - *nf*	fly, Moscow
948	**mosso** - *adj*	blurred, rough, wavy, moved
1198	**mostra** - *nf*	show
1275	**mostrare** - *verb*	to show
688	**mostro** - *nm*	monster
1881	**motel** - *nc*	motel
404	**motivo** - *nm*	reason
1165	**moto** - *nm*	motion, motorbike
1097	**motore** - *adj; nm*	motor; enginge, motor
2255	**motorio** - *adj*	motor
2486	**movimentare** - *verb*	to ship, move, handle
2489	**movimentato** - *adj*	lively, busy
1137	**movimento** - *nm*	movement
2250	**mucca** - *nf*	cow
1286	**mucchio** - *nm*	pile
2043	**munizione** - *nf*	munition
694	**muovere** - *verb*	to move
2372	**murare** - *verb*	to wall
825	**muro** - *nm*	wall
2499	**muscolo** - *nm*	muscolo
1639	**museo** - *nm*	museum
309	**musica** - *nf*	music
2434	**muso** - *nm*	muzzle, nose, face

N

741	**nascere** - *verb*	to be born
1654	**nascita** - *nf*	birth
900	**nascondere** - *verb*	to hide
2228	**nascosto** - *adj*	hidden
788	**naso** - *nm*	nose
1488	**nastro** - *nm*	tape
477	**natale** - *nf*	Christmas
798	**natura** - *nf*	nature
1013	**naturale** - *adj*	natural
632	**naturalmente** - *adv*	naturally
490	**nave** - *nm*	ship
1133	**nazionale** - *adj*	national
1217	**nazione** - *nf*	nation, country
36	**ne** - *adj; pron*	any; of it, of them
423	**né** - *conj*	neither, nor
221	**neanche** - *adv; conj*	not even, neither; not even
2322	**nebbia** - *nf*	fog, mist
667	**necessario** - *adj*	necessary
1774	**negativo** - *adj*	negative
685	**negozio** - *nm*	shop, store

1450	**negro** - *adj; nm*	black, negro; negro, nigger
729	**nemico** - *adj; nm*	enemy
251	**nemmeno** - *adv; conj*	not even, neither
1136	**neppure** - *adv; conj*	not even, neither
552	**nero** - *adj*	black
2056	**nervo** - *nm*	nerve
1153	**nervoso** - *adj*	nervous
240	**nessun** - *adj*	no
104	**nessuno** - *adj; pron*	no; nobody, no one, none, anyone
1150	**neve** - *nf*	snow
55	**niente** - *pron; nm*	nothing, anything, none
1021	**nipote** - *nm*	grandson, granddaughter, nephew, niece
18	**no** - *adv*	no, not
1623	**nobile** - *adj*	noble
63	**noi** - *pron*	we
1992	**noioso** - *adj*	boring
159	**nome** - *nm*	name
1	**non** - *adv*	not, non
600	**nonna** - *nf*	grandmother
597	**nonno** - *nm*	grandfather
1162	**nonostante** - *prep; conj; adv*	despite; altough; even though, nevertheless
655	**nord** - *nm*	north
572	**normale** - *adj*	normal, regular
2370	**normalmente** - *adv*	normally
147	**nostro** - *pron*	our
1310	**nota** - *nf*	note
970	**notare** - *verb*	to note
602	**notizia** - *nf*	news
2010	**noto** - *adj*	known
165	**notte** - *nm*	night
745	**nove** - *adj; num*	nine
2304	**novembre** - *nm*	November
1594	**novità** - *nf*	news
1741	**nozze** - *nfpl*	wedding
1974	**nucleare** - *adj*	nuclear
1823	**nudo** - *adj*	naked
202	**nulla** - *nf; pron*	nothing; nothing, anything
257	**numero** - *nm*	number
1718	**nuotare** - *verb*	to swim
143	**nuovo** - *adj*	new
2243	**nuvoloso** - *adj*	overcast, cloudy

O

43	**o** - *conj*	or
1092	**obiettivo** - *nm*	target, objective
708	**occasione** - *nf*	opportunity
1362	**occhiali** - *nmpl*	glasses
226	**occhio** - *nm*	eye
1954	**occorrere** - *verb*	to take
1079	**occupare** - *verb*	to occupy
2180	**occupato** - *adj*	busy
1434	**oceano** - *nm*	ocean
1599	**odiare** - *verb*	to hate
463	**odio** - *nm*	hatred
881	**odore** - *nm*	smell
2007	**offendere** - *verb*	to offend
1455	**offrire** - *verb*	to offer
1440	**oggetto** - *nm*	object
149	**oggi** - *adv; nm*	today
117	**ogni** - *adj*	every
876	**ognuno** - *pron*	each
50	**oh** - *int*	oh
97	**ok** - *int*	ok
199	**okay** - *int*	okay
1836	**olio** - *nm*	oil
456	**oltre** - *adv; prep*	over; over, more than, beyond
1269	**ombra** - *nf*	shadow

565	**omicidio** - *nm*	murder
1439	**onda** - *nf*	wave
1853	**onde** - *adv; conj; pron*	hence, whence; so that, so as; of which, whose
2200	**onestamente** - *adv*	honestly
1396	**onesto** - *adj*	honest
444	**onore** - *nm*	honor
2000	**ooh** - *int*	ooh
864	**opera** - *nf*	opera
2345	**operaio** - *nm; adj*	worker; working, labouring
939	**operazione** - *nf*	operation
1208	**opinione** - *nf*	opinion
1346	**opportunità** - *nf*	opportunity
639	**oppure** - *conj*	or, or else
42	**ora** - *adv; conj; nf*	now; now; now, time, hour
2122	**orario** - *nm; adj*	time, hours, timetable; hourly
586	**ordinare** - *verb*	to order
396	**ordine** - *nm*	order
1145	**orecchio** - *nm*	ear
1738	**organizzare** - *verb*	to organize, arrange
1861	**organizzazione** - *nf*	organization
1755	**orgoglio** - *nm*	pride
1772	**orgoglioso** - *adj*	proud
1494	**originale** - *adj; nm*	original
2144	**origine** - *nf*	origin, source
454	**ormai** - *adv*	by now, almost, by then
1004	**orologio** - *nm*	clock, watch
903	**orribile** - *adj*	horrible
2412	**orrore** - *nm*	dread, terror
1856	**orso** - *nm*	bear
2092	**osare** - *verb*	to dare
2182	**oscuro** - *adj*	dark, obscure
419	**ospedale** - *nm*	hospital
1167	**ospite** - *nm*	guest, host
2124	**ossigeno** - *nm*	oxygen
1226	**osso** - *nm*	bone
2137	**ostaggio** - *nm*	hostage
919	**ottenere** - *verb*	to get, obtain
485	**ottimo** - *adj*	excellent
544	**otto** - *adj; num*	eight
1979	**ottobre** - *nm*	October
1119	**ovest** - *nm*	West
724	**ovunque** - *adv*	everywhere, whereever
730	**ovviamente** - *adv*	obviously
1293	**ovvio** - *adj*	obvious

P

2278	**pacchetto** - *nm*	package
2295	**pacco** - *nm*	pack, parcel
339	**pace** - *nm*	peace
105	**padre** - *nm*	father
789	**padrone** - *nm/f*	boss, master, owner, host/mistress, hostess
324	**paese** - *nm*	country, village
1699	**pagano** - *nm*	pagan, heathen
505	**pagare** - *verb*	to pay
1302	**pagina** - *nf*	page
836	**pago** - *adj*	content, statisfied
346	**paio** - *nm*	pair
1024	**palazzo** - *nm*	palace
1712	**palco** - *nm*	stage
2143	**palestra** - *nf*	gym
653	**palla** - *nf*	ball
2128	**pallottola** - *nf*	bullet
2404	**panare** - *verb*	to bread, dip in breadcrumbs
1702	**pancia** - *nf*	belly
1038	**pane** - *nm*	bread
1430	**panico** - *nm*	panic

1053	**pantalone** - *nm*	trousers
413	**papa** - *nm*	Pope
191	**papà** - *nm*	dad, daddy
961	**paradiso** - *nm*	paradise
1733	**parcheggio** - *nm*	parking, park
1211	**parco** - *nm;*	park, parklan; frugal, sober
1342	**parecchio** - *adv; adj*	a lot of, several; some
1656	**parente** - *nm*	relative
338	**parere** - *verb; nm*	to think, seem; opinion
1357	**pari** - *adv*	equal
136	**parlare** - *verb*	to speak, talk
1661	**parlato** - *adj*	spoken
326	**parola** - *nf*	word
96	**parte** - *nf*	part
1999	**partecipare** - *verb*	to take part
1483	**partenza** - *nf*	departure
971	**particolare** - *adj*	particular
2493	**particolarmente** - *adv*	particolarmente
576	**partire** - *verb*	to leave
865	**partito** - *nm*	party
1988	**partner** - *nm*	partner
503	**parto** - *nm*	birth, childbirth
751	**passaggio** - *nm*	passage
1990	**passaporto** - *nm*	passport
294	**passare** - *verb*	to pass, spend, switch
1147	**passato** - *adj*	past
1966	**passeggero** - *nm*	passenger
1506	**passeggiare** - *verb*	to stroll, walk
1385	**passione** - *nf*	passion
403	**passo** - *nm*	passage, step, pace, stride
1940	**pasto** - *nm*	meal
2139	**pastore** - *nm*	shepherd, pastor
1806	**patata** - *nf*	potato, pussy (coll)
2333	**patatina** - *nf*	french fry, potato chip, plump little girl (coll), pussy (coll)
2433	**patetico** - *adj*	pathetic
1973	**patire** - *verb*	to suffer
1897	**patrio** - *adj*	patrio
1546	**patto** - *nm*	pact
2416	**pattugliare** - *verb*	to patrol
180	**paura** - *nf*	fear
1179	**pausa** - *nf*	break
1472	**pavimento** - *nm*	floor
1056	**paziente** - *adj; nm&f*	patient
1222	**pazienza** - *nf*	patience
1894	**pazzesco** - *adj*	crazy
2019	**pazzia** - *nf*	madness
394	**pazzo** - *adj*	crazy
492	**peccare** - *verb*	to sin
556	**peggio** - *adj*	worse
2123	**peggiorare** - *verb*	to worsen
716	**pelle** - *nf*	skin
2233	**pelo** - *nm*	hair, fur, coat
645	**pena** - *nf*	penalty
1847	**pene** - *nm*	penis
1740	**penna** - *nf*	pen
154	**pensare** - *verb*	to think
848	**pensata** - *nf*	thought
922	**pensiero** - *nm*	thought
1332	**pensione** - *nf*	board, pension, retirement
8	**per** - *prep*	for, to, by, in
2431	**percento** - *nm*	per cent
40	**perché** - *conj; adv*	because, why; why
616	**perciò** - *conj; adv*	therefore; accordingly
1929	**percorso** - *nm*	route
263	**perdere** - *verb*	to lose
1244	**perdita** - *nf*	loss, leak, waste

1314	**perdonare** - *verb*	to forgive
1184	**perdono** - *nm*	pardon, forgiveness
1764	**perduto** - *adj*	lost
1209	**perfettamente** - *adv*	perfectly
397	**perfetto** - *adj*	perfect
1270	**perfino** - *adv*	even
705	**pericoloso** - *adj*	dangerous
877	**periodo** - *nm*	period
2457	**perla** - *nf*	pearl
435	**permettere** - *verb*	to allow
283	**però** - *conj; adv*	but, yet; however
867	**persino** - *adv*	even
1892	**perso** - *adj*	lost
173	**persona** - *nf*	person
1372	**personaggio** - *nm*	character
589	**personale** - *adj*	staff
2406	**personalità** - *nf*	personality
1454	**personalmente** - *adv*	personally
1138	**pesante** - *adj*	heavy
1696	**pesca** - *nf*	fishing, catch, peach
769	**pesce** - *nm*	fish
994	**peso** - *nm*	weight
2392	**pessimo** - *adj*	very bad, terrible
1850	**petrolio** - *nm*	oil, petroleum
1491	**petto** - *nm*	chest
449	**pezzo** - *nm*	piece
146	**piacere** - *verb*	to pleasure; like
1538	**piacevole** - *adj*	pleasant
721	**pianeta** - *nf*	planet
737	**piangere** - *verb*	to cry
217	**piano** - *nm; adj*	plan, floor, piano; plane, flat
1256	**piantare** - *verb*	to plant
1300	**piatto** - *nm*	dish, plate
1956	**piazza** - *nf*	square, plaza
2086	**picchiare** - *verb*	to beat
249	**piccolo** - *adj*	little, small
291	**piede** - *nm*	foot
510	**pieno** - *adj*	full
1343	**pietà** - *nf*	pity
1177	**pietra** - *nf*	stone
1637	**pillola** - *nf*	pill
1172	**pilotare** - *verb*	to pilot, fly
1104	**pioggia** - *nf*	rain
2464	**piovere** - *verb*	to rain
2409	**pisciare** - *verb*	to piss
1482	**piscina** - *nf*	pool
1160	**pista** - *nf*	track
355	**pistola** - *nf*	gun
34	**più** - *adj; adv*	more, most
455	**piuttosto** - *adv*	rather, quite, pretty
1838	**pizza** - *nf*	pizza
1050	**po' (pò)** - *adv*	bit
1835	**pochino** - *adv*	a little
274	**poco** - *adj; adv; nm*	little; a litte, not much; bit
1535	**poesia** - *nf*	poetry
2461	**poetare** - *verb*	to poetize
90	**poi** - *adv*	then
1888	**poiché** - *conj*	as, because, for
975	**politico** - *adj; nm*	political; politician
216	**polizia** - *nf*	police
627	**poliziotto** - *nm*	policeman
1117	**pollo** - *nm*	chicken
2279	**polso** - *nm*	wrist, pulse
1114	**polvere** - *nf*	dust
720	**pomeriggio** - *nm*	afternoon
823	**ponte** - *nm*	bridge
2226	**popolare** - *adj; verb*	populair; to populate
2270	**popolazione** - *nf*	population
750	**popolo** - *nm*	people
837	**porco** - *nm*	pig
1007	**porgere** - *verb*	to extend
2276	**porno** - *adj; nm*	porn

108	**porre** - *verb*	to put, place
2407	**portafoglio** - *nm*	portfolio, wallet
168	**portare** - *verb*	to bring
906	**portato** - *adj*	brought
1950	**positivo** - *adj*	positive
595	**posizione** - *nf*	position
2160	**possedere** - *verb*	to own
2194	**possesso** - *nm*	possession
290	**possibile** - *adj*	possible
624	**possibilità** - *nf*	possibility
762	**posto** - *nm*	place, spot, location
1107	**potente** - *adj*	powerful
1631	**potenza** - *nf*	power
61	**potere** - *verb; nm*	to be able; power
714	**povero** - *adj; nm*	poor; the poor
2193	**pozzo** - *nm*	well
641	**pranzo** - *nm*	lunch
1258	**praticamente** - *adv*	practically
1229	**praticare** - *verb*	to practice
1551	**precedente** - *adj; nm*	previous, preceding; precedent
2347	**precedere** - *verb*	to precede
1620	**preciso** - *adj*	precise
2446	**preda** - *nf*	prey
950	**preferire** - *verb*	to prefer
1071	**preferito** - *adj*	favorite
1743	**pregare** - *verb*	to pray
2066	**preghiera** - *nf*	prayer
127	**prego** - *int*	please, you're welcome
2008	**premiare** - *verb*	to reward
1176	**premio** - *nm*	prize
176	**prendere** - *verb*	to take
443	**preoccupare** - *verb*	to worry
1039	**preoccupato** - *adj*	worried
1197	**preparare** - *verb*	to prepare

1938	**preparato** - *adj; nm*	prepared; specimen, compound
1098	**presentare** - *verb*	to present, submit
1484	**presente** - *adj; nm*	this, present; present
829	**presentire** - *verb*	to foresee
1173	**presenza** - *nf*	presence
2398	**preside** - *nm*	dean, principal
357	**presidente** - *nm*	president
1155	**preso** - *adj*	took
902	**pressione** - *nf*	pressure
2259	**presso** - *prep; adv; adj*	at,in; near; close
1393	**prestito** - *nm*	loan
183	**presto** - *adv*	soon, early
1166	**prete** - *nm*	priest
1557	**prevedere** - *verb*	to foresee
2257	**prezioso** - *adj*	precious
840	**prezzo** - *nm*	price
466	**prigione** - *nm*	prison
1502	**prigioniero** - *nm*	prisoner
62	**prima** - *adv; art*	first, before; before
1478	**primavera** - *nf*	spring
64	**primo** - *num; adj*	first
1001	**principale** - *adj*	main
747	**principe** - *nm*	prince
912	**principessa** - *nf*	princess
1959	**principiare** - *verb*	to principiare
1240	**privato** - *adj; nm*	private; personal life, privacy
1848	**probabile** - *adj*	likely
379	**probabilmente** - *adv*	probably
188	**problema** - *nf*	problem
2132	**procedere** - *verb*	to continue
2091	**procedura** - *nf*	procedure
830	**processo** - *nm*	process
1539	**procuratore** - *nm*	attorney

1638	**prodotto** - *nm*	product
2281	**produrre** - *verb*	to produce
2081	**produttore** - *nm*	producer
1582	**produzione** - *nf*	production, output
2263	**professionale** - *adj*	professional
1770	**professionista** - *adj; nm&f; nm*	professional; professional; expert
701	**professore** - *nm*	teacher, professor
2024	**profondamente** - *adv*	deeply
1206	**profondo** - *adj*	deep
1493	**profumo** - *nm*	perfume
905	**progetto** - *nm*	project
615	**programma** - *nf*	program
2269	**proibire** - *verb*	to prohibit
1819	**proiettile** - *nm*	bullet, projectile
2475	**promessa** - *nf*	promise
636	**promettere** - *verb*	to promise
181	**pronto** - *adj; adv*	ready
1422	**proporre** - *verb*	to propose, put forward
609	**proposito** - *nm*	purpose, intention
1371	**proprietà** - *nf*	property
1427	**proprietario** - *nm*	owner, landlord
95	**proprio** - *adj; nm; pron; adv*	one's own; own; its; just, exactly
405	**prossimo** - *adj*	next
2450	**prostituta** - *nf*	prostitute
1135	**proteggere** - *verb*	to protect
2488	**protetta** - *nf*	protection
1409	**protezione** - *nf*	protection
564	**prova** - *nf*	test
319	**provare** - *verb*	to try
504	**provato** - *adj*	tried
2355	**psichiatra** - *nm*	psychiatrist
1789	**pubblicità** - *nf*	advertising
545	**pubblico** - *adj*	public
1247	**pugno** - *nm*	fist
1746	**pulire** - *verb*	to clean
1178	**pulito** - *adj*	clean, clean
1874	**punizione** - *nf*	punishment
1360	**punta** - *nf*	tip, point
258	**punto** - *nm*	point
1216	**pur** - *adv*	while
302	**pure** - *adv*	also
1605	**puro** - *adj*	pure
1028	**purtroppo** - *adv*	unfortunately
279	**puttana** - *nf*	whore
1143	**puzza** - *nf*	stink

Q

200	**qua** - *adv*	here
1485	**quadro** - *nm*	painting, picture, panel, square
2039	**quaggiù** - *adv*	hither
298	**qual** - *adv; pron*	everytime, whenever; what, which
124	**qualche** - *adj; pron*	some, few, any; a few
70	**qualcosa** - *nf*	something, anything
698	**qualcun** - *pron*	meter; tape measure
110	**qualcuno (- a)** - *pron*	someone
222	**quale** - *adj; pron; conj*	what, which; which; as
1588	**qualità** - *nf*	quality
331	**qualsiasi** - *adv*	any
459	**qualunque** - *adj*	any
38	**quando** - *adv; conj*	when
2360	**quantità** - *nf*	amount
102	**quanto** - *adv; conj*	as, how much; than
1185	**quartiere** - *nm*	district, neighbourhood, quarter

1139	**quarto** - *adj; num; nm*	fourth; quarter
228	**quasi** - *adv*	almost, nearly
2046	**quassù** - *prep*	up here
278	**quattro** - *adj; num*	four
49	**quello** - *pron*	one
628	**questione** - *nf*	question
24	**questo** - *adj; pron*	this; such, this one
25	**qui** - *adv; conj*	here; where
133	**quindi** - *adv*	then
2075	**quindici** - *adj; num*	fifteen
2274	**quinto** - *adj; num*	fifth
2275	**quota** - *nf*	quota, share, quote

R

1398	**rabbia** - *nf*	anger
1849	**raccogliere** - *verb*	to gather
1610	**raccomandare** - *verb*	to recommend
1266	**raccontare** - *verb*	to tell
1567	**racconto** - *nm*	(short) story
2470	**radar** - *adj*	radar
480	**radio** - *adj; nm*	radio
1192	**ragazzina** - *nf*	little girl
996	**ragazzino** - *nm*	little boy, sonny (condenscending)
153	**ragazzo** - *nm/f*	boy, boyfriend / girl. girlfriend
1782	**raggio** - *nm*	radius, spoke, beam, range, ray
1174	**raggiungere** - *verb*	to reach
197	**ragione** - *nm*	reason
2111	**ragionevole** - *adj*	reasonable
2368	**rallentare** - *verb*	to decelerate
2305	**rapidamente** - *adv*	quickly
1486	**rapina** - *nf*	robbery
2258	**rapire** - *verb*	to kidnap
539	**rapporto** - *nm*	relationship
2141	**rappresentare** - *verb*	to represent
805	**razza** - *nf*	race, breed, stingray
335	**re** - *nm*	king
738	**reale** - *adj*	real, actual
1753	**realmente** - *adv*	really
557	**realtà** - *nf*	reality
2413	**reato** - *nm*	crime
1752	**reazione** - *nf*	reaction
1642	**recente** - *adj*	recent
2120	**recitare** - *verb*	to recite
2343	**record** - *nm*	record
2031	**recuperare** - *verb*	to recover, retrieve
2348	**regalare** - *verb*	to give
1723	**regale** - *adj*	kingly
673	**regalo** - *nm*	gift, present
784	**regina** - *nf*	queen
1604	**regista** - *nm*	director
2117	**registrare** - *verb*	to record
2104	**registrazione** - *nf*	registration
1146	**regno** - *nm*	kingdom
711	**regola** - *nf*	rule
932	**relazione** - *nf*	report
1812	**religione** - *nf*	religion
800	**rendere** - *verb*	to make
1435	**reparto** - *nm*	department, ward
2495	**repubblica** - *nf*	republic
1809	**reputazione** - *nf; nm*	reputation; credit, standing
1576	**resistenza** - *nf*	resistance
1556	**resistere** - *verb*	to resist
1319	**respirare** - *verb*	to breathe
1295	**respiro** - *nm*	breath
872	**responsabile** - *adj; nm*	responsible; person in charge
1204	**responsabilità** - *nf*	responsibility
400	**restare** - *verb*	to stay, remain, maintain

332	**resto** - *nm*	rest
1391	**rete** - *nf*	network, net
1051	**retro** - *nm*	back, rear
1348	**retta** - *nf*	straight line; tuition
1890	**reverendo** - *adj*	reverend
1291	**revisione** - *nf*	review, revision
2454	**ribelle** - *adj*	rebel
1040	**ricco** - *adj*	rich
753	**ricerca** - *nf*	search, research
428	**ricevere** - *verb*	to receive
1624	**richiamo** - *nm*	recall
2130	**richiedere** - *verb*	to request
1154	**richiesta** - *nf*	request
1745	**ricominciare** - *verb*	to recommence
1845	**ricompensare** - *verb*	to reward
1967	**riconoscere** - *verb*	to recognize
540	**ricordare** - *verb*	to remember
282	**ricordo** - *nm*	memory
758	**ridere** - *verb*	to laugh
983	**ridicolo** - *adj*	ridiculous
2042	**ridurre** - *verb*	to reduce
2202	**rientrare** - *verb*	to re-enter
2103	**rifiutare** - *verb*	to refuse
2205	**rifiuto** - *nm*	refusal, rejection, waste
2501	**riflettere** - *verb*	to reflect
1734	**rifugio** - *nm*	refuge
2282	**rigare** - *verb*	to scratch
787	**riguardare** - *verb*	to concern
587	**riguardo** - *nm*	regard, respect
944	**rilassare** - *verb*	to relax
625	**rimanere** - *verb*	to stay
1814	**rinforzo** - *nm*	reinforcement
839	**ringraziare** - *verb*	to thank
2109	**rinunciare** - *verb*	to give up
2414	**riparare** - *verb*	to repair
2245	**riparo** - *nm*	shelter
1367	**ripetere** - *verb*	to repeat
2308	**riportare** - *verb*	to report, take back
1389	**riposare** - *verb*	to rest
1285	**riposo** - *nm*	rest, rest period
1910	**riprendere** - *verb*	to resume
1859	**ripresa** - *nf*	recovery
1496	**risata** - *nf*	laugh
901	**rischiare** - *verb*	to risk
1526	**rischio** - *nm*	risk
1801	**riserva** - *nf*	reserve, reservation
1308	**riso** - *nm*	rice
1169	**risolvere** - *verb*	to solve
2090	**risorgere** - *verb*	to rise again
2183	**rispettare** - *verb*	to respect
549	**rispetto** - *nm*	respect
568	**rispondere** - *verb*	to answer
1533	**risposta** - *nf*	answer
924	**ristorante** - *nm*	restaurant
1406	**risultare** - *verb*	to to result
1351	**risultato** - *nm*	result
513	**ritardo** - *nm*	delay, retardation
1786	**ritmo** - *nm*	rhythm
1715	**ritornare** - *verb*	to return
744	**ritorno** - *nm*	return
2479	**ritrattare** - *verb*	to retract, recant
2222	**ritrovato** - *nm*	finding, discovery
966	**riunione** - *nf*	meeting, reunion, assembly
301	**riuscire** - *verb*	to succeed, able
2424	**riuscita** - *nf*	success
1704	**rivedere** - *verb*	to review, revise
1690	**rivoluzione** - *nf*	revolution
259	**roba** - *nf*	stuff, things
1724	**robot** - *nm*	robot
2029	**roccia** - *nf*	rock
920	**rodere** - *verb*	to gnaw, fret, prey on
1858	**romantico** - *adj*	romantic
2013	**romanzo** - *nm*	novel, romance
726	**rompere** - *verb*	to break

669	**rosso** - *adj*	red
1020	**rotta** - *nf*	route
1963	**rovina** - *nf*	ruin, ruination
1283	**rovinare** - *verb*	to ruin
1214	**rubare** - *verb*	to steal
674	**rubato** - *adj*	stolen
533	**rumore** - *nm*	noise
1253	**ruolo** - *nm*	role
1982	**ruotare** - *verb*	to rotate
1254	**russo** - *adj; nm/f*	Russian; Russian

S

1080	**sabato** - *nm*	Saturday
1574	**sabbia** - *nf*	sand
342	**sacco** - *nm; adv*	bag, sack; a lot
2224	**sacrificio** - *nm*	sacrifice
1924	**sacro** - *adj*	sacred
1766	**saggiare** - *verb*	to test
73	**saio** - *nm*	habit
696	**salare** - *verb*	to salt
913	**sale** - *nm*	salt
921	**salire** - *verb*	to go up, climb, rise
2323	**salita** - *nf*	climb
2208	**salsa** - *nf*	sauce
755	**saltare** - *verb*	to skip, jump
1418	**salto** - *nm*	leap, jump
1795	**salutare** - *adj; verb*	healthy; to greet, say goodbye to
619	**salute** - *nf; int*	health; cheers, bless you
1781	**saluto** - *nm*	greeting
746	**salvare** - *verb*	to save
2140	**salvatore** - *nm*	savior
229	**salvo** - *prep; adj*	save, but; safe
582	**san** - *adj*	St., saint
1937	**sanare** - *verb*	to heal
284	**sangue** - *nm*	blood
518	**santo** - *adj; nm/f*	holy; saint
41	**sapere** - *verb*	to know
1916	**sapore** - *nm*	flavor, taste
2420	**satana** - *nm*	Satan
1113	**sbagliare** - *verb*	to make a mistake
398	**sbagliato** - *adj*	mistaken, incorrect, wrong
1006	**sbaglio** - *nm*	mistake
1536	**sbirro** - *nm*	cop
702	**sbrigare** - *verb*	to hurry up
1294	**scala** - *nf*	ladder, scale, stairs
1375	**scalare** - *verb*	to climb
1898	**scambio** - *nm*	exchange
613	**scappare** - *verb*	to escape
664	**scarpa** - *nf*	shoe
993	**scatola** - *nf*	box
2427	**scavare** - *verb*	to dig
700	**scegliere** - *verb*	to choose
462	**scelta** - *nf*	choice
2468	**scelto** - *adj*	chosen
1142	**scemo** - *adj*	fool
494	**scena** - *nf*	scene
868	**scendere** - *verb*	to get off
2389	**sceneggiatura** - *nf*	screenplay
1851	**schermo** - *nm*	screen, monitor
681	**scherzare** - *verb*	to joke
1416	**scherzo** - *nm*	joke
1828	**schiavo** - *nm*	slave
1002	**schiena** - *nf*	back
666	**schifo** - *nm*	disgust
1939	**schifoso** - *adj*	lousy (fa schifo= it sucks)
1388	**scienza** - *nf*	science
2301	**scienziato** - *nm*	scientist
1663	**scimmia** - *nf*	ape, monkey
1404	**sciocchezza** - *nf*	foolishness
1441	**sciocco** - *adj*	silly
2288	**scommessa** - *nf*	bet
707	**scommettere** - *verb*	to bet
1358	**scomparire** - *verb*	to disappear

2061	**sconosciuto** - *adj; nm*	unknown; stranger, unkown
1685	**scopare** - *verb*	to sweep, fuck
2469	**scopata** - *nf*	sweep, fuck, shag
531	**scoperto** - *adj; nm*	uncovered, open, bare; overdraft
914	**scopo** - *nm*	purpose
831	**scoprire** - *verb*	to discover
2395	**scordare** - *verb*	to forget
786	**scorso** - *adj*	last
2176	**scortare** - *verb*	to escort
384	**scritto** - *adj*	written
1808	**scrittore** - *nm*	writer
1547	**scrivania** - *nf*	desk
633	**scrivere** - *verb*	to write
2376	**scudo** - *nm*	shield
260	**scuola** - *nf*	school
1241	**scusa** - *nf*	sorry, excuse
211	**scusare** - *verb*	to excuse
20	**se** - *conj*	if
1108	**sé** - *pron*	himself, herself
1904	**sebbene** - *conj; adv*	although, though; even though
2028	**secco** - *adj*	dry
1248	**secolo** - *nm*	century
213	**secondo** - *prep; nm; adv; adj*	according to; second
569	**sedere** - *verb*	to sit down
1090	**sedia** - *nf*	chair
832	**segnale** - *nm*	signal, sign
822	**segno** - *nm*	sign
2133	**segretario** - *nm/f*	secretary
509	**segreto** - *nm*	secret
790	**seguire** - *verb*	to follow
1124	**sei** - *adj; num*	six
2441	**selvaggio** - *adj*	wild
134	**sembrare** - *verb*	to seem, look, appear, sound
469	**semplice** - *adj*	simple
604	**semplicemente** - *adv*	simply
74	**sempre** - *adv*	always
1423	**senatore** - *nm*	senator
2293	**seno** - *nf*	breast
1000	**sensazione** - *nf*	sensation
2336	**sensibile** - *adj*	sensible
349	**senso** - *nm*	direction, sense, meaning
2204	**sentiero** - *nm*	pathway, trail
1082	**sentimento** - *nm*	feeling
172	**sentire** - *verb*	to feel, hear
120	**senza** - *conj*	without
2388	**sepolto** - *adj*	buried
233	**sera** - *nf*	evening
770	**serata** - *nf*	evening
593	**sergente** - *nm*	sergeant
1383	**seriamente** - *adv*	seriously
313	**serio** - *adj*	serious
1528	**serpe** - *nf*	snake
2455	**serpente** - *nm*	snake, serpent
206	**servire** - *verb*	to serve
493	**servizio** - *nm*	service, report
2108	**servo** - *nm*	servant
534	**sesso** - *nm*	sex
1585	**sessuale** - *adj*	sexual
2234	**sesto** - *adj; num*	sixth
1662	**seta** - *nf*	silk
1659	**sete** - *nf*	thirst
508	**sette** - *adj; num*	seven
1584	**settembre** - *nm*	September
285	**settimana** - *nf*	week
1499	**settore** - *nm*	sector
782	**sezione** - *nf*	section, department
1826	**sfida** - *nf*	challenge
2113	**sfortuna** - *nf*	bad luck
1915	**sfortunatamente** - *adv*	unfortunately

1807	**sforzo** - *nm*	effort
1101	**sguardo** - *nm*	look
2044	**shock (choc)** - *adj*	shock
10	**sì** - *int*	yes, yeah
13	**si** - *pron*	one-, its-, thems-, him-, her-, yourself
2251	**siccome** - *conj*	since
736	**sicuramente** - *adv*	certainly
461	**sicurezza** - *nf*	safety, security
169	**sicuro** - *adj*	sure, safe, secure
1171	**sigaretta** - *nf*	cigarette
308	**significare** - *verb*	to mean
163	**signora** - *nf*	lady, Mrs.
79	**signore** - *nm/f*	Mr. / Mrs.
325	**signorina** - *nf*	young lady
535	**silenziare** - *verb*	to mute
2121	**simbolo** - *nm*	symbol
623	**simile** - *adj*	similar, alike
1524	**simpatico** - *adj*	nice, sympathetic
2017	**sin** - *conj*	since
2105	**sinceramente** - *adv*	sincerely
1731	**sincero** - *nm*	sincere
1203	**sindaco** - *nm*	mayor
2471	**singolo** - *adj; nm*	single
529	**sinistro** - *adj*	left
897	**sissignore** - *int*	Yes sir
476	**sistema** - *nf*	system
1415	**sistemare** - *verb*	to fix
2203	**sito** - *adj*	place, website
440	**situazione** - *nm*	situation
1089	**smesso** - *adj*	stopped
368	**smettere** - *verb*	to stop
1559	**soccorso** - *nm*	rescue
1542	**sociale** - *adj*	social
771	**società** - *nf*	society
1438	**socio** - *nm*	partner
2188	**soddisfare** - *verb*	to satisfy
2241	**sodo** - *adj*	hard
2156	**sofferenza** - *nf*	suffering
2248	**sofferto** - *adj*	suffered
1666	**soffrire** - *verb*	to suffer
1872	**soggetto** - *nm*	subject
1548	**sognare** - *verb*	to dream
445	**sogno** - *nm*	dream
1161	**solamente** - *adv*	only
670	**soldato** - *nm*	soldier
135	**soldo** - *nm*	money
486	**solito** - *adj; nm*	usual
31	**solo** - *adj*	only
421	**soltanto** - *adv*	only, solely
1100	**soluzione** - *nf*	solution
2192	**sommo** - *adj*	highest
1263	**sonno** - *nm*	sleep
1525	**sopportare** - *verb*	to bear
317	**sopra** - *adv; prep*	above, on
859	**soprattutto** - *adv*	mostly
1251	**sopravvivere** - *verb*	to survive
2159	**sordo** - *adj*	deaf
333	**sorella** - *nf*	sister
2444	**sorellina** - *nf*	litte sister, younger sister, baby sister
1681	**sorgere** - *adj*	to arise, rise
1569	**sorprendere** - *verb*	to surprise
574	**sorpreso** - *adj*	surprised
1242	**sorridere** - *verb*	to smile
1896	**sorveglianza** - *nf*	surveillance
2253	**sospeso** - *adj*	suspended
2283	**sospettare** - *verb*	to suspect
1243	**sospetto** - *adj; nm*	suspected, suspicious; suspicion
2126	**sospirare** - *verb*	to sigh
2487	**sostegno** - *nm*	support
175	**sotto** - *adv; prep*	under, below; under
987	**sottofondo** - *nm*	background
2302	**sottovoce** - *adv*	whisper
828	**spada** - *nf*	sword

1487	**spagnolo** - *adj; nm/f*	Spanish; Spaniard
687	**spalla** - *nf*	shoulder
765	**sparare** - *verb*	to shoot
1553	**sparire** - *verb*	to disappear
2474	**spasso** - *nm*	fun
1195	**spaventare** - *verb*	to scare, frighten
2327	**spaventoso** - *adj*	frightening, scary
710	**spazio** - *nm*	space
1592	**spazzatura** - *nf*	trash
1421	**specchiare** - *verb*	to mirror
473	**speciale** - *adj*	special
1363	**specialmente** - *adv*	specially, particulary, especially
497	**specie** - *nf*	species, kind
2436	**spedire** - *verb*	to send
1880	**spegnere** - *verb*	to switch off, turn off
2287	**spendere** - *verb*	to spend
2393	**spento** - *adj*	off, turned off
761	**speranza** - *nf*	hope
272	**sperare** - *verb*	to hope
1930	**sperimentare** - *verb*	to experiment, experience
1329	**spesa** - *nf*	expense
2129	**spesare** - *verb*	to pay the expenses
498	**spesso** - *adv; adj*	often; thick
631	**spettacolo** - *nm*	show, spectacle, performance
2146	**spettare** - *verb*	to belong
1289	**spia** - *nf*	light, spy, indication
364	**spiacere** - *verb*	to be sorry
1084	**spiaggia** - *nf*	beach
1103	**spiegare** - *verb*	to explain
1810	**spiegazione** - *nf*	explanation
1998	**spingere** - *verb*	to push
2411	**spinto** - *adj*	pushed
713	**spirito** - *nm*	spirit
2332	**spiritoso** - *adj*	humorous
1522	**splendido** - *adj*	wonderful
1257	**sporco** - *adj*	dirty, soiled
1790	**sport** - *nm*	sport, sports
723	**sposare** - *verb*	to marry
1077	**sposato** - *adj*	married
1735	**sposo** - *nm*	groom
1763	**spostare** - *verb*	to move
383	**squadra** - *nf*	team
2006	**squalo** - *nm*	shark
2452	**stadio** - *nm*	stadium, stage
1373	**stagione** - *nf*	season
806	**stamattina** - *nf*	this morning
917	**stampa** - *nf*	press, printing
818	**stanco** - *adj*	tired
2362	**standard** - *adj*	standard
559	**stanotte** - *adv*	tonight
303	**stanza** - *nf*	room
60	**stare** - *verb*	to stay
255	**stasera** - *nf*	tonight, this evening
2341	**statua** - *nf*	statue
935	**stavolta** - *adv*	this time
775	**stazione** - *nf*	station
898	**stella** - *nf*	star
187	**stesso** - *adj; pron*	same; itself
958	**stile** - *nm*	style
2216	**stipendio** - *nm*	salary
2062	**stivale** - *nm*	boot
1250	**stomaco** - *nm*	stomach
1380	**stop** - *nm; int*	stop
198	**storia** - *nf*	history, story
2165	**storto** - *adv*	awry
225	**strada** - *nf*	(large) street, road
2078	**straniero** - *adj; nm/f*	foreign, alien; foreigner
323	**strano** - *adj*	strange
1517	**straordinario** - *adj*	extraordinary; overtime

1401	**stregare** - *verb*	to bewitch
2466	**stress** - *nm*	stress
2095	**stretto** - *adj; nm*	strict, strait; narrow
1713	**stringere** - *verb*	to tighten
680	**stronzata** - *nf*	bullshit
395	**stronzo** - *nm*	shit, asshole
2264	**strumento** - *nm*	tool
1799	**struttura** - *nf*	structure
1320	**studente** - *nm*	student
1228	**studiare** - *verb*	to study
1590	**studiato** - *adj*	studied
642	**studio** - *nm*	office, study
1983	**stufo** - *adj*	fed up, sick and tired
1572	**stupendo** - *adj*	wonderful
401	**stupido** - *adj*	stupid
72	**su** **sul, sullo, sulll', sulla, sui, sugli, sulle - adv; prep*	on,up; on, about
162	**subito** - *adv*	immediately, at once
192	**succedere** - *verb*	to happen, occur, succeed
144	**successo** - *nm*	success
1948	**succo** - *nm*	juice
686	**sud** - *nm*	south
1470	**sufficiente** - *adj*	enough, sufficient
1433	**suicidio** - *nm*	suicide
65	**suo (- a)** - *pron*	his (her)
844	**suonare** - *verb*	to play (music or instrument), sound, ring
1971	**suono** - *nm*	sound
1581	**super** - *adj*	super
1717	**superare** - *verb*	to exceed
1778	**superficie** - *nf*	surface
1199	**superiore** - *adj*	higher, superior
862	**supporre** - *verb*	to suppose
2320	**supporto** - *nm*	support
892	**svegliare** - *verb*	to wake
1152	**sveglio** - *adj*	awake
1580	**svelto** - *adj*	quick, brisk, fast
2377	**sviluppo** - *nm*	development
1909	**tacere** - *verb*	to be silent
1267	**taglia** - *nf*	size
1586	**tagliare** - *verb*	to cut
1390	**tagliato** - *adj*	cut
1140	**taglio** - *nm*	cut, cutting
727	**tale** - *adv; pron; art*	such; such; a, an
1615	**talmente** - *adv*	so
126	**tanto** - *adv*	much, so
1865	**tappeto** - *nm*	carpet
2239	**tara** - *nf*	tare, defect, faint
245	**tardi** - *adv*	late
2492	**targa** - *nf*	plate, nameplate
1304	**tasca** - *nf*	pocket
1862	**tassa** - *nf*	fee, tax
1962	**tatto** - *nm*	(sense) touch, tact
1182	**tavola** - *nf*	table
757	**tavolo** - *nm*	table
811	**taxi** - *nm*	taxi
1443	**tazza** - *nf*	cup
990	**tè** - *nm*	tea
33	**te** - *pron*	you
1022	**teatro** - *nm*	theater
2059	**tecnico** - *adj; nm*	technical; technician
1709	**tecnologia** - *nf*	technology
1121	**tedesco** - *adj, nm/f*	German; German
1736	**telecamera** - *nf*	camera
1958	**telefonare** - *verb*	to call, telephone
1127	**telefonata** - *nf*	phone call
304	**telefono** - *nm*	phone, telephone
1207	**televisione (TV)** - *nf*	television
2110	**tema** - *nf*	theme, topic
773	**temere** - *verb*	to fear, be afraid
1980	**temperatura** - *nf*	temperature

1512	**tempestare** - *verb*	to batter, besiege, annoy
1558	**tempio** - *nm*	temple
80	**tempo** - *nm*	time, weather
2166	**temporale** - *adj; nm*	temporal; (thunder) storm
2025	**tendere** - *verb*	to stretch
573	**tenente** - *nm*	lieutenant
340	**tenere** - *verb*	to hold, keep
2184	**tensione** - *nf*	tension, voltage
1233	**tentare** - *verb*	to attempt, try, tempt
1519	**tentativo** - *nm*	attempt
1157	**teoria** - *nf*	theory
1870	**terapia** - *nf*	therapy
1264	**termine** - *nm*	term
208	**terra** - *nf*	land, earth
1425	**terreno** - *nm; adj*	ground, soil; earthly
542	**terribile** - *adj*	terrible
1613	**territorio** - *nm*	territory
1931	**terrore** - *nm*	terror
2106	**terrorista** - *nf*	terrorist
851	**terzo** - *adj; nm*	third
195	**tesoro** - *nm*	treasure
926	**test** - *nm*	test
170	**testa** - *nf*	head
2419	**testamento** - *nm*	will
1386	**teste** - *nm*	witness
1085	**testimone** - *nm*	witness
1276	**tetta** - *nf*	tit
1035	**tetto** - *nm*	roof
15	**ti** - *pron*	you
1994	**tigre** - *nf*	tiger
2326	**tipico** - *adj*	typical
178	**tipo** - *nm*	type, kind
887	**tirare** - *verb*	to pull
931	**tiro** - *nm*	shot, shooting, throw
1378	**titolo** - *nm*	title

507	**tizio** - *nm*	someone, person, guy, chap
693	**toccare** - *verb*	to touch
1467	**toccato** - *adj*	touched
1934	**tocco** - *nm*	touch
1230	**togliere** - *verb*	to remove, take off
1235	**tomba** - *nf*	tomb
2076	**tono** - *nm*	tone
1630	**topo** - *nm*	mouse
1821	**torcere** - *verb*	to twist
238	**tornare** - *verb*	to return
756	**tornio** - *nm*	lathe
797	**tornire** - *verb*	to throw
1307	**torre** - *nf*	tower
967	**torto** - *adj*	injustice
1277	**totale** - *adj; nm*	total
1633	**totalmente** - *adv*	totally
130	**tra** - *prep*	between, among
1328	**traccia** - *nf*	track
1498	**tracciare** - *verb*	to draw
2190	**tradimento** - *nm*	betrayal, treason, treachery
1563	**tradire** - *verb*	to betray
1818	**traditore** - *adj; nm*	treacherousl.; traitor
2246	**tradizione** - *nf*	tradition
452	**traduzione** - *nm*	translation
1387	**trafficare** - *verb*	to trade, deal, traffic
1833	**tragedia** - *nf*	tragedy
2101	**tramite** - *nm; prep*	means, medium; through
2169	**tramontare** - *verb*	to set
929	**tranne** - *prep*	except
548	**tranquillo** - *adj*	quiet
1175	**trappola** - *nf*	trap
2465	**trasferimento** - *nm*	transfer
1987	**trasferire** - *verb*	to transfer
2073	**trasmissione** - *nf*	transmission

2235	**trasporto** - *nm*	transport
393	**tratta** - *nf*	section, trade, bill, draft
1550	**trattare** - *verb*	to treat
1511	**tratto** - *nm*	stretch
139	**tre** - *adj; num*	three
528	**treno** - *nm*	train
2152	**trenta** - *adj*	thirty
1054	**tribunale** - *nm*	court
690	**triste** - *adj*	sad
968	**troia** - *nf*	slut
2185	**trono** - *nm*	throne
123	**troppo** - *adv*	too much
203	**trovare** - *verb*	to find
1202	**trucco** - *nm*	makeup, trick
1436	**truppa** - *nf*	troop
27	**tu** - *pron*	you
2242	**tubo** - *nm*	tube, pipe
1628	**tunnel** - *nm*	tunnel
58	**tuo** - *adj*	your
1031	**turno** - *nm*	round, shift
1272	**tuttavia** - *adv; conj*	however, nevertheless; but, yet
32	**tutto** - *adv; nm*	all
496	**tv** - *nm*	TV

U

997	**ubriaco** - *adj*	drunk
1110	**uccello** - *nm*	bird
235	**uccidere** - *verb*	to kill
1018	**ucciso** - *nm/f*	victim, killed person
2500	**udienza** - *nf*	hearing, audience
763	**ufficiale** - *adj; nm*	official
2330	**ufficialmente** - *adv*	officially
365	**ufficio** - *nm*	office
1369	**uguale** - *adv*	equal
536	**uh** - *int*	uh
1225	**ultimamente** - *adv*	lately
297	**ultimo** - *adj*	last, latest
1769	**umanità** - *nf*	humanity
668	**umano** - *adj*	human
1777	**umore** - *nm*	mood, humor
2430	**umorismo** - *nm*	humor, sense of humor
5	**un, uno, una** - *art; pron*	a, an; one
2254	**undici** - *adj; num*	eleven
2401	**unghia** - *nf*	nail
358	**unico** - *adj*	alone, single, unique
1683	**uniforme** - *adj*	uniform
1991	**unione** - *nf*	union
610	**unire** - *verb*	to unite
1075	**unità** - *nf*	unit
1116	**università** - *nf*	university
1227	**universo** - *nm*	universe
103	**uomo** - *nm*	man
1148	**uovo** - *nm*	egg
1698	**urgente** - *adj*	urgent
1655	**urlare** - *verb*	to scream
740	**urlo** - *nm*	yell, cry, shout
472	**usare** - *verb*	to use
264	**uscire** - *verb*	to go out, leave
1205	**uscita** - *nf*	exit
648	**uso** - *nf*	use, usage
979	**utile** - *adj; nm*	helpful, useful; profit

V

1129	**vacanza** - *nf*	holiday, vacation
2396	**vacca** - *nf*	cow
682	**vaffanculo** - *int*	fuck off
583	**valere** - *verb*	to be worth
2485	**valigetta** - *nf*	briefcase

1508	**valigia** - *nf*	suitcase
1920	**valle** - *nf*	Valley
988	**valore** - *nm*	value
2371	**vampiro** - *nm*	vampire
1643	**vantaggio** - *nm*	advantage
2211	**vario** - *adj*	various, varied
2219	**varo** - *nm*	launch, launching
1824	**vasca** - *nm*	tub
489	**ve** - *pron*	you
262	**vecchio** - *adj; nm/f*	old; old (wo)man
94	**vedere** - *verb*	to see
2099	**vedovo** - *nm/f*	widower, widow
2065	**veicolo** - *nm*	vehicle
1609	**veleno** - *nm*	poison
500	**veloce** - *adj*	fast, quick
1335	**velocemente** - *adv*	quickly
1246	**velocità** - *nf*	speed
991	**vendere** - *verb*	to sell
1218	**vendetta** - *nf*	vengeance
1682	**vendita** - *nf*	sale, selling
1489	**venerdì** - *nm*	Friday
118	**venire** - *verb*	to come
1186	**venti** - *adj; num*	twenty
760	**vento** - *nm*	wind
246	**veramente** - *adv*	really
879	**verde** - *adj*	green
1566	**vergine** - *adj; nf*	virgin
1274	**vergogna** - *nf*	shame
345	**verità** - *nf*	truth
2074	**verme** - *nm*	worm, maggot
71	**vero** - *nm*	true
1606	**versione** - *nf*	version
275	**verso** - *prep; nm*	to, towards; direction, way
567	**vestire** - *verb*	to dress
517	**vestito** - *nm*	dress, dressed
1595	**vetro** - *nm*	glass
76	**vi** - *pron; adv*	you; there
93	**via** - *prep; adv; nf*	via, by; away; street, way
1867	**viaggiare** - *verb*	to travel
408	**viaggio** - *nm*	travel, trip, journey
1960	**vice** - *nm*	vice, deputy
1703	**vicenda** - *nf*	event
292	**vicino** - *adj; adv*	close, near
957	**video** - *adj*	video
2357	**vietato** - *adj*	forbidden
2220	**vigliacco** - *adj*	coward
1927	**villa** - *nf*	villa
816	**villaggio** - *nm*	village
591	**vincere** - *verb*	to win
2040	**vincitore** - *adj*	winner
734	**vino** - *nm*	wine
2316	**violento** - *adj*	violent
1194	**violenza** - *nf*	violence
1461	**virus** - *nm*	virus
1651	**visione** - *nf*	vision
1943	**visita** - *nf*	visit
315	**visitare** - *verb*	to visit, see
918	**viso** - *nm*	face
1064	**vissuto** - *adj*	lived
83	**vita** - *nf*	life, waist
951	**vite** - *nf*	screw, grapevine, vine
885	**vittima** - *nf*	victim
1072	**vittoria** - *nf*	victory
300	**vivere** - *verb*	to live
351	**vivo** - *adj*	alive, live
375	**voce** - *nm*	entry, voice, item
388	**voglia** - *nf*	desire
82	**voi** - *pron*	you
1705	**volante** - *nm; adj*	steering wheel; flying
635	**volare** - *verb*	to fly
1689	**volentieri** - *adv*	willingly
54	**volere** - *verb*	to want
193	**volgere** - *verb*	to turn

1361	**volontà** - *nf*	will
101	**volta** - *nf*	time, turn, vault
2325	**volume** - *nm*	volume
2197	**vomitare** - *verb*	to throw up, puke
223	**vostro** - *pron*	your (pl)
1564	**votare** - *verb*	to vote
1664	**voto** - *nm*	vote, grade
1083	**vuoto** - *adj*	empty

W

1534	**weekend** - *nm*	weekend

Z

1105	**zero** - *adj; num*	zero
804	**zia** - *nf*	aunt
420	**zio** - *nm*	uncle
424	**zitto** - *adj*	silent, quiet
608	**zona** - *nf*	area
1587	**zucchero** - *nm*	sugar
1792	**zuppa** - *nf*	soup

6. Further Reading & Resources

For more tools, tips & tricks visit our site www.mostusedwords.com.

Bilingual books

In the beginning of the book I already spoke about the importance of reading when you're trying to acquire a new language.

We're creating a selection of multi-language texts, and our selection is ever expanding.

Current bilingual texts available are English, Spanish, German, Italian, Dutch and French.

For more information, check www.mostusedwords.com/parallel-texts

Language learning methods

You'll find reviews of other 3rd party language learning applications, software, audio courses and apps on our website. There are so many available, and some are (much) better than others. We help you sort the good from the bad, and help you find a language learning method that is **good, efficient and right for you**.

Check out our reviews at www.mostusedwords.com/reviews

Contact:

If you have any questions, you can contact me through e-mail info@mostusedwords.com.

21592796R00227

Printed in Great Britain
by Amazon